To Ed & Ann
May God bless
you

THE FACE OF AFRICA
Looking Beyond The Shadows

Stan Chu Ilo

Bloomington, IN Milton Keynes, UK

authorHOUSE

AuthorHouse™
1663 Liberty Drive, Suite 200
Bloomington, IN 47403
www.authorhouse.com
Phone: 1-800-839-8640

AuthorHouse™ UK Ltd.
500 Avebury Boulevard
Central Milton Keynes, MK9 2BE
www.authorhouse.co.uk
Phone: 08001974150

First published by AuthorHouse 4/18/2006

ISBN: 1-4208-9705-5 (sc)
ISBN: 1-4208-9706-3 (dj)

Library of Congress Control Number: 2005910250

Printed in the United States of America
Bloomington, Indiana

This book is printed on acid-free paper.

Advance praise for
The Face Of Africa: Looking Beyond The Shadows

"A very technical insight to Africa's development. This book shows that one cannot push aside a people's life to improve it. It clearly argues that people must be the means and end of their development. It addresses the condition of Africa from the point of view of Afro-Christian theology. Indeed, if adopted in national development strategies, it could set off a new paradigm in the region's development with Africans at its centre. Stan Chu Ilo has done a great job and offered Africa a new text that should be read for the future of this great continent."

Dr Hilary Nwokeabia, Senior Economist, United Nations Conference for Trade and Development, Geneva and Senior Fellow, Economic Commission for Africa, Addis Ababa.

"This is a compelling work for our times. It creates hope, challenges despair, re-establishes authentic human and original African values, and invites the reader to consider civilizations and cultures as the product of hard working men and women who dare the tide and make history. The book is good news, namely, there is still goodness in the world. The author, Stan Chu Ilo, Nigerian born has made an invaluable contribution to the theme of globalization, placing African self-determination, qualitative leadership, responsibility, integrity, self respect, and optimism in the centre of discourse. The distorted face of Africa is only a facade. Africa is beauty and life, beyond the shadows."

Prof. Obiora F. Ike, Director of the Catholic Institute for Development Justice and Peace, Nigeria. Author, *Globalization and African Self Determination: What is Our Future?*

"In the process of globalization today Black Africa is completely forgotten by the international community. Furthermore, Africa is a despised continent, which is only known by its misery: economic recession, AIDS, wars of all kinds… However, Africa alone is not responsible for this catastrophic situation. The international community and capitalism are deeply involved in encouraging wars, dictatorship etc. in the name of a false democracy. In this perspective, the book of Stan Chu Ilo is a very precious contribution, which is showing clearly the pervasive mechanism hidden behind the so called African misery. Anyone who wishes to have helpful information about the socio-economic and political situation of the Black Continent should inescapably read the work of this young African researcher."

Prof. Dr. Bénézet Bujo, Director and Chair, Centre for Moral Theology and Social Ethics, University of Fribourg, Switzerland. Author, *Foundations of an African Ethic, Beyond the Universal Claims of Western Morality*.

"Stan Chu Ilo, has opened the sore that is Africa.... Brilliant, well researched but controversial attempt to open up discussion on a complex, multi-dimensional issue. It is a must read for everyone that, genuinely cares about this continent. It is an open indictment to a majority of African leaders, whose actions and inactions have pushed promising Africans to desperation leading to this panicky, but massive exodus from Africa. This book should be a revolutionary battle cry, for young African scholars who are committed to taking the driver's seat, in the search for an answer to this riddle and ridicule of generational poverty in the midst of plenty. "

- Willy Mamah, British Chevening Scholar, Cardiff University, Wales, United Kingdom.

"From the opening statement of the preface to the very last word of the conclusion of *The Face of Africa: Looking Beyond the Shadows*, Ilo imprints on his readers a robust faith, an undying hope and a buoyant optimism for the African project, defined in terms of building truly integrated societies, workable political structures, realistic national constitutions and a solid foundation for economic development. The central argument of this book is that the world as it is presently constituted may be unjust and unfair to Africa and the face of Africa today may be ugly, yet these are mere shadows of the real Africa. The real Africa still has all it takes to be a rich and prosperous continent, a land of opportunities for the young and the old. This is a bold attempt at contextual theology. "

- Joseph Oládèjo Fáníran, Ph. D., Director of the Centre for the Study of African Culture and Communication, Catholic Institute of West Africa, Port Harcourt, Rivers State, Nigeria.

"Stan Chu Ilo has written a manifesto of hope for Africa and for the world, calling on Africans to look inward to build a true home for themselves in the world, and calling on all people to express love through action."

- **Prof. Rachel Wortis**, Ph. D., Trent University, Peterborough, Ontario, Canada.

"At last here comes a volume, which has the TRUE story of Africa. The author writing out of love for his suffering continent, slams the victim theory. 'Africa must throw away the toga of victimhood and take her destiny by hand.' Central issues to the present African problem like the 'exploitation of ordinary Africans by their political and religious elites, the corruption in African governments and the high rate of ethnic tension and religious conflicts' are firmly and courageously addressed here. The author presents to the continent noble sons and daughters of Mother Africa like Steve Biko, Nelson Mandela, Winnie Mandela, Wangari Maathai, Desmond Tutu, Walter Sisulu, Julius Nyerere, Samora Machel, Nobert Zongo, Dele Giwa, etc, as models for better Africa. This work is a compendium."

- **Ebere Bosco Amakwe**, Ph. D., HFSN, Centre for Communication Studies, Gregorian University, Rome.

"You are blessed with a great compound. But in all great compounds there must be people of all minds—some good, some bad, and some fearless and some cowardly; those who bring wealth and those who scatter it, those who give advice and those who only speak the words of palm wine. That is why we say that whatever tunes you play in the compound of a great man there is always someone to dance to it.
I salute you!"

Advice to the chief priest, Ezeulu, to be patient and supportive of his underperforming son, in Chinua Achebe's *Arrow of God*.

ooooo ooooo ooooo ooooo

"Only God's love is able to make brothers and sisters of people of all races and cultures, can heal the painful divisions, ideological conflicts, economic imbalance and violence which oppress humanity today."

Pope John Paul II

DEDICATION

To Mum and Dad, **Ozo na Adaozo VinRose Iloelunachukwu:**

Community leaders, committed educationists, courageous optimists working for a better future for Africa at the grassroots. They embody the highest values of both our Igbo tribe and the Christian faith and work hard to impart these into all members of our family and to thousands of others.

To my late sister, **Bibiana Chinenyego (1968-1998),** a truly liberated African woman and educator who died doing what she loved doing best.

TABLE OF CONTENTS

FOREWORD

"Lord, our night is too long and our day too dark."
- An African at prayer

This book is a stirring manifesto for social reconstruction and interior transformation in Africa. It is a passionate and compelling cry of love from the heart of the young Nigerian scholar, Stan Chu Ilo. Afflicted with an identity crisis, with a stockpile of accumulated hate and wounded memories, Africa—a continent in search of a future—is a permanent, and too-often neglected, sore on the conscience of the world today. In our world of superabundance, Africa is stark evidence that compassion is in exile.

Ilo makes the compelling argument that the only hope for Africa is not flight from, but engagement in and with Africa. In contrast to reactionary, episodic, and crisis-related approaches, Ilo proposes a "total picture approach model" emphasizing systemic, gradual, and proactive change. His diagnosis that Africa is not at peace today because of structural, social sins is as compelling as it is well-researched. African countries need to prioritize food production, provision of water and health care, eradication of poverty, education, and the strengthening of core institutions. Particularly distressing is the situation of women and children. Hope and redemptive change demand new understanding and respect for women and children in African society.

When all is said and done, what is needed, concludes the author, following Nelson Mandela, is the "reconstruction of the soul of Africa." The only alternative to the current culture of death is the cultivation of a "civilization of love" (Pope John Paul II). Only the power of love— love is the heart of the world and the heart of God— with its religion of friendship and culture of forgiveness and mercy offers genuine hope.

The author has written this volume as a personal reflection on the African experience. Containing elements of philosophy, social analysis, and Afro-Christian perspective, this book is the fruit of over 10 years of personal research and reflection. As a high school student, he was shocked by what Africans had to endure in the eras of slavery, colonialism and apartheid. He was disturbed by the gap between the poor African countries especially his country Nigeria and the Western world. Having been born just after the 30 months war in his country, he personally has seen the face of suffering, social dislocation and poverty and knows that it is a monster. In his undergraduate days, he began to write and publish articles in national dailies and magazines reflecting on the African experience. Overtime he discovered that some of the things he wrote found resonance with other young Africans concerned about their future in Africa. He, therefore, set out building convergences with other Africans who are thinking and acting to steer the future of the continent. It is these young people who are daily being led into new forms of slavery outside Africa as prostitutes, drug couriers, and petty workers. It is these young people who seek refugee status in Western countries to escape the suffocating existence in a continent that has much hope but greater misery. These are the restless and listless ones who in their romantic idealism tend to do the impossible and the ignoble in order to leave Africa and survive in the industrialized countries.

In this work, the author makes a case for a culture of hope in Africa from the perspective of love. He calls for respect for Africans by non-Africans. He sketches in a "total picture approach model" to help Africans recover a truly authentic African identity and understand their place in the world.

This work is addressed to Africans both in Africa and particularly those who live abroad. He also addresses this work to non-Africans especially policy makers for Western governments, donor agencies, religious and political groups who are looking for an alternative vision for Africa and who are developing donor-apathy over Africa because of the failed policies of democracy and development in the continent.

Throughout, the author emphasizes that love is the only viable road to our human destiny. This emphasis on love is for me of fundamental and crucial importance. For love is not, first of all, something we do. Love is who we are, as gift and call, to be lived out. It is in loving (or not loving) that we are (or are not) human. Instead of "I think, therefore, I am," the deepest truth is that "I was loved, therefore, I am," and "I love, therefore, I am." In a world broken by suffering and evil, the passion of love is a suffering love: compassion. Thus the author's urgent call to all men and women of goodwill, all over the world, to practice a spirituality of compassion receives my full blessing and support. We can do nothing else but reach out to Africa in love, not with handouts of sympathy, but with the deeds and incarnations of love.

It is my hope and prayer that many Africans and non-Africans will, not only read this urgent call to a ministry of compassion and solidarity, but will heed its call. Africa is waiting!

James H. Olthuis
Professor of Philosophical Theology
Institute for Christian Studies, Toronto,
and Psychotherapist in private practice.

Easter, 2005

PREFACE

Nigeria is a Promised Land
Africa is a Great Continent
We are marching on
To take our place
Among all the Nations of the World.

This was the song we sang in the late 1970s and early 1980s during our early morning assembly as elementary school pupils. This marching song, which incidentally was taught by my father, who was the principal of my school, has never left my consciousness. It captures clearly the hopes and dreams, the pride and ambition of the pioneers of the nation-states of Africa. This song, unfortunately, is no longer being sung in elementary schools in Nigeria. Whatever reasons may have informed the dropping of this song from elementary schools in Nigeria, the truth is that this song's sentiments no longer resonate with many ordinary Africans. Many Africans are losing hope in Africa. The African nationalists who composed songs like this, to infuse hope and pride in young Africans, did not live to see the rebirth of Africa, because it never took place under their watch.

The nationalists often confused dream with reality and hope with achievement. The nationalists in Africa, who took over the reins of their respective African countries, gloried in the establishment of independent political entities, but failed to see the shifting sands on which their respective countries were built. As a result, they failed to set Africans to task in working concretely and realistically for a new Africa and laying the building blocks for a truly liberated and prosperous Africa. Within a decade of gaining independence, most African countries rumbled through nights of violence, political instability, and civil war, because, using the famous expression of Africa's foremost novelist, Chinua Achebe, 'the center could no longer hold' and things fell apart in Africa. Today, the living condition of Africans is worse than it was when most of their countries gained independence in the early 1960s. The Special Envoy to the United Nations Secretary General on HIV/AIDS in Africa, Stephen Lewis agrees with this position when he writes, "It must be understood, without any hint of heady romanticism, that Africa in the 1950s and 1960s…was a continent of vitality, growth, and boundless expectation….There was something about the environment of such hope, anticipation, affection, energy, indomitability. The Africa I knew was poor, but it wasn't staggering under the weight of oppression, disease, and despair; it was absolutely certain that it could triumph over every exigency. There were countless health emergencies—polio, measles, malaria, malnutrition—but it never felt like Armageddon. In fact, life expectancy began to rise in the late 1960s, until the reversal induced by the Structural Adjustment Programs on the one hand, and AIDS on the other." (Stephen Lewis, 2005, 44-45). Many Africans do not see their countries in their present condition as 'promised lands', otherwise they would love to live and work in Africa, instead of escaping to the West, nor are most Africans convinced that Africa is a great continent.

However, in spite of this perplexing scenario in Africa, I do have a deep conviction that Nigeria and other African countries can still become a promised land; a land of hope; a land of beauty and a land where men and women, young and old can find fulfillment and pursue their ordered end in peace and love. I have never ceased to dream about better days that shall come to Africans. The frustrating and unacceptable situation in Africa appears to be giving birth to a new spring of hope welling up in the hearts of many young Africans like myself, who were born more than one decade after the decolonization process in Africa. Most of us have never known the good old days in Africa. Many young Africans are filled with righteous rage against their leaders and their Western collaborators, who have made life unbearable for them in their native land. They are the ones who are beginning to join the new movement in Africa for the articulation of a new vision for a new Africa. These young Africans have seen the misty myth of Independence evaporate in the clouds of uncertainty, unemployment, civil unrest, poverty, pain and diseases which they experience in Mother Africa.

My unshakeable hope in a better future for Africa inspired me to write this book. The imposing mountains of economic and social ruin; the rising moans and groans of numberless Africans, can sometimes conceal the inner energy and ardent hopes of millions of Africans. These Africans are struggling against the untested assumption, that the inhibiting conditions and the suffocating strain, of the cracking social, political, and economic foundations of present day Africa, are incapable of supporting the structures of a new Africa. Africans are not searching for univocal paradigms for a better future constructed along different ethnic axes. Nor is Africa in need of paternalistic recommendations and unrealistic mercenary total development packages from Western ideologues, politicians and philanthropists, forced down the throats of Africans as pre-condition for aid and technical support and assistance. Just as there is no single answer to the African condition, so also is there no single answer to the question many children in Africa are asking: 'Why do many of us go to bed hungry? Why is the world so silent about our fate? What is God's plan for us?'

I am convinced that the present African condition is not part of God's plan for Africa. God's dream for Africa is the dream he has for the world and for every child that is born to earth. His dream is that the world should be a peaceful and safe place for everyone; that no human person on planet earth should go to bed hungry and unsure of tomorrow; that people should have a place they can call home and have access to the basic necessities of life and mutually benefit from the fruits of human civilizations; and that all should be happy and healthy and sing their own special song to the world. It is only when people shine through with human fulfillment and human security that they can give glory to God, because God is glorified in a person fully alive (Irenaeus). Unfortunately, we men and women are individually and collectively destroying the world through greed, selfishness, unbridled passion for power and domination, unjust and unfair acts and wars. This explains the African condition.

The African condition is the clearest evidence today of the presence of injustice in the world. The African condition is not inevitable nor is the future of Africa bleak. The sad situation of the continent has a history, because Africa was not originally poor otherwise Western explorers and businessmen would not have come to Africa; nor will Western national economic ventures and businesses be flourishing in Africa today if Africa was a poor continent. Africa's poverty has a beginning and will definitely have an end through the sacrifice and hard work of Africans. Resurrecting the fading hopes and dreams of past heroes and heroines and present generation of Africans, should be the goal and ongoing quest and task of every African. We should always remember Africa. We Africans should carry the fate and fortune of Mother Africa as an existential breastplate.

What Africans need is a firm belief in their innate abilities; an openness to the positive signs in their group history; and an appreciation and appropriation of the riches of their environment and natural resources. This should give rise to a determined commitment to the truth about African history and clear-sighted visioning on steps to be taken toward the emergence of a new Africa. This vision should be jointly generated through national dialogues across the board and reified in the cultural traditions of respective African groups.

Time has come for Africans and non-Africans, who have been involved with Africa within the last four decades, to admit the simple truth that all development programs, democratic processes, and donor initiatives in the continent since independence, have largely been unsuccessful in bettering the condition of life of Africans. Many Westerners above 50 years will remember clearly, that the cry of Africa has been constant, since the end of the Second World War. It has become louder and more painful in our day, in spite of the launching of the UN Millennium Development Goals. Every day in the Western media, the story of Africa that is presented is one of wars, diseases, misery, poverty and shame; of people constantly in need of food, water, shelter, stable democracy, healthcare, and clothing. When will all these end? When will Africa stand on her feet? When will Africans cease from being recipients of charitable donations for human survival and emergency relief for those who are apparently condemned by the international community to die? When will Africans become the subjects of their own development and not objects of pity and charity? Many people will agree that past and present development paradigms in Africa have not helped in laying the foundation for sustainable development. On the contrary, they have sustained a structure that has spread poverty with greater intensity among Africans. There is the need for a new thinking on how to move Africa away from the poverty trap. This is another reason that inspired this book.

The reasons for the failure of development and donor initiatives in Africa are multiple and embody various factors and components (African and non-African), which we shall try to present in this book. Steps towards sustainable development and genuine home-grown democracy have not begun in Africa. What we have today in most countries of Africa is only a patchwork; wrought as in an emergency room, carried on without rhythm and rhyme which will ultimately produce the same sad reality for Africans. Valued time and resources have been wasted in Africa trying to patch up the cracks that are breaching the walls of Africa in all spheres of life. What we have today, as nation-states in Africa should be revisited because as presently constituted, they embody real dangers and threats for the future growth and progress of the continent. Africans, as the African Nobel laureate, Wole Soyinka argued during the Nigerian Civil War, should put aside the mentality that present political entities in Africa are absolute indissoluble creations of God. He envisioned one day "when the black nations will themselves sit down together, and, by agreement, set compass and square rule to paper to reformulate the life-expending, stultifying, constrictive imposition of this divine authority (colonialists)."

Africans have to admit the truth that their continent needs to go back to the basics. Africans need to ask themselves fundamental questions about the orientation and direction of their societies and address the reasons why Africa is not realizing her potentials. Why is a substantial percentage of Africans sweltering in the heat of grinding extreme poverty, inexcusable suffering and generalized discontentment? Something is fundamentally wrong with the structuring of African societies and nationalities today; but there is nothing wrong with the African personality or African culture and civilization. I use the socio—ethical concept of structures of sin to interpret the most pressing challenges facing Africa and how they could be addressed. Ours is a religio-cultural and social analysis of Africa.

Many people have written of the African condition and the reasons for her present situation. Sometimes blames are often heaped on Westerners for their past and ongoing injustice towards Africans. However, using the time-worn platitudes that Africans are victims, who are suffering because of the West, is only an easy escape route that will prevent Africans from asking the basic existential questions: Why is this happening to us? What should we do as a people by and for ourselves to change our lot? Many other writers blame the African condition on Africans alone, especially African leaders who have squandered their national wealth, leaving their respective countries with democratic, social, cultural, and economic deficits. My conclusion is that both Africans and non-Africans are to blame for the present African situation, but that Africans should take responsibility for their continent and redefine her future. Many writers have proffered different development paradigms in Africa and proposed new visions for a renascent Africa.

I have tried in this work to integrate as much as I could different aspects of the discourse on the Africa condition, within the last four decades. I have particularly identified the stochastic constraints to growth and innovation in Africa in terms of the low stocks in the human-capital and cultural development. This is amplified by the cultural crisis that have spread misery and ethical confusion in the land of Africa and inaugurated a season of anomie among the young and the elderly. I have captured the African condition as *homelessness, pointing out that cultural and human development is the irreducible decimal in any proposal for the transformation of the continent.* I have offered a deeper religio-anthropological reflection, framed within a wider political and economic discourse on poverty, cultural alienation, unjust structures, racism and lack of an educational framework, which passes knowledge with regard to skills and technology from one generation to the next, supplemented by the educational heritage from outside Africa. We shall try in this book to initiate a discourse on the basis for *the homelessness of Africans* in the past and present history of Africa within the prevailing climate of economic globalization. Our goal is to tell the story of Africa in an objective manner. This is why we have titled this work, *The Face of Africa*, reflecting the contrasting situation in Africa: happiness in the midst of grinding poverty; hope in the midst of depressing circumstances; want in the midst of untapped wealth; peace in the midst of sporadic unrests; life in the midst of unnecessary deaths; and faith in the midst of a shaking moral platform and laughter in the midst of constant grief. This presents a complex picture that demands a multipronged approach. That is why we propose *a total picture approach model* for both interpreting the African reality as well as in responding to it in a more fundamental and comprehensive manner.

We have used tools of Christian anthropology and theology as well as analytical data generated both from extensive research ranging over mountains of works by many social scientists, economists, journalists, social workers, religious writers, and commentators on the African reality. Our data were generated through quantitative and qualitative approaches comparatively weighted against and sometimes complemented by the findings of many national and international bodies both within and outside Africa. Our ultimate goal in this book is to provide a new paradigm for a holistic understanding and better engagement with Africa. We attempt a presentation of the face of Africa that is truthful and objective. It is however a picture, which induces hope, challenges despair and asserts dignity and respect for Africans. We also seek to expose the baseless foundation of some stereotypes on Africa, which have made it impossible for non-Africans to engage with Africans in an open, meaningful, respectful, and equal manner. This work offers a helpful guide for non-Africans and Africans living abroad, who wish to be involved in development initiatives in Africa, on the cultural, ethnic, historical, and religious dynamics of respective African regions.

Understanding the possibilities in Africa and the uniqueness of Africans is a first step in any engagement with the continent. I do believe that Africa is a gift and blessing to the world and I try in this book to show the unlimited gifts of Africans and Africa to the world and how to tap into them. There is the need to build African societies from bottom to top; grassroots village-based initiatives tend to produce more results and impact on the lives of people, over bogus national approaches, which are often utopian and textured by political and ethnic considerations that make them unworkable.

Given my own personal limitations, I do not wish to claim expertise on an issue as complicated and diverse as the history and condition of one of the most complex and vibrant races on earth. I wish, therefore, to make a preliminary admission: this work is not a port of arrival; it is only an invitation to collaborative search on how to change the fortune of our beloved continent and how Africans and Africa can realize their historic destiny. It is an invitation to all men and women of goodwill outside Africa to spare a thought for a continent which gave birth to humanity and which might provide a countervailing and counterbalancing pressure to stem the movement of history towards the clash of civilizations characterized by terrorist acts, economic protectionism, military rivalries and generalized anxiety about the future and the loss of the sense of the sacred. The deep religious sentiments of Africans, especially with regard to the Christian faith, offer evidence that religion and faith make sense for understanding our world and for interpreting and effecting the movement of history. This is why many Africans are praying everyday for a better Africa and a better world freed from injustice, hatred, poverty, natural disasters, diseases, suffering, and pain. Like Pliny the Elder who once said of Africa, "out of Africa always something new" (*ex Africa semper aliquid novi*), my prayer is that more new visions for Africa should emerge and that a new kind of committed leadership, a new kind of committed Africans, and a new impetus of hope should emerge in Africa to change the face of this continent. It is my prayer that Africans will once more begin to take pride in being Africans and seek to be connected with the finest heritage of Africa as well as accept the sad aspects of African history. This book is a call for a new kind of civilization in Africa and the rest of the world—the civilization of love. If this book contributes in any way in bringing this about, it would have served its purpose.

This work is the fruit of over a decade of research, personal reflection, dialogues and writings. My debt of gratitude is immense to many people. I am grateful to the United Nations Department of Public Information, New York, for providing me with many resources on the history of development initiatives in Africa since the 1970s. I gathered a lot of information and data on Africa's struggle to stand on her feet from numerous editions of *Africa Renewal* (formerly *Africa Recovery*) magazines published by this office. UNAID and UNICEF provided me with numerous materials on HIV/AIDS and malaria and the challenges facing African children today. My special thanks to the following news magazines and papers for permission to use previously published works of mine: *Catholic Register* (Toronto), *National Catholic Reporter* (Kansas City), and *Encounter* Journal of African Philosophy and Life (Rome). The first section of Chapter Four is the development of a public lecture I gave, "The African Condition: From Misery to Hope," under the auspices of the Kiwanis International (Peterborough, Ontario) in June, 2003; while the second section of Chapter One is a modified version of a public lecture I gave at Life Theological Seminary, Ikorodu, Lagos-Nigeria, titled "Religious Tolerance in a Pluralistic Society: The Religion We Need." The theme of civilization of love, which is constant in this book, draws from a number of my published essays on this theme, which is my understanding of what the world needs to enthrone a new order of justice and peace on earth. Some of these essays appeared as 'The Meaning and Significance of Jubilee 2000" (Bigard Theological Studies, December, 2000), and "Jubilee 2000 and the Task of Building a Civilization of Love" (Wisdom Satellite Magazine, June, 2000).

I am grateful to Hilary Nwokeabia, Senior Economist at the United Nations Conference on Trade and Development (UNCTAD) with whom I spent some time in Geneva going through this work. His experience and expertise on economic and political developments in Africa was a rich mine house from which I drew. He read and reviewed this work. I am grateful to the following academics who read and reviewed my work: Professor Uche-Lynn Ugwueze, Professor Jim Olthuis (my lecturer on Philosophical Anthropology at Institute for Christian Studies, Toronto, and who also wrote a beautiful foreword to this work), Professor Bénézet Bujo, Professor Obiora Ike, Professor Rachael Wortis, Dr. Joseph Faniran, and Dr. Ebere Bosco Amakwe. I have also drawn immensely from lectures and personal conversations and dialogue with my professor at St. Michael's University, Toronto, Lee Cormie and my Professor at Regis College, David Demson. My friend and colleague Rev. Joseph Ogbonnaya accompanied me with his profound insights and fraternal encouragements through out the course of this work. The African civil right activist, Jerry Willy Mamah, my childhood friend and fellow traveler on this path of seeking for a better face for Africa, read through this work and offered helpful suggestions for revision of some of the ideas. Words are not enough to thank John O'Brien, the Editor of the Peterborough Diocesan Newspaper, *The Herald,* who read the first draft of this book and who spent many weeks helping me to give shape to this work. Rev. Dr. Iheanyi Enwerem, Dr. Don Graham, Marilyn Adair, Bob and Colleen Hartlen and Nancy Graham all read different chapters of the second draft. I thank especially Brian and Bev O'Toole who edited the third draft of this work. Carolyn Brioux, who edited the fourth and final draft of this work and went beyond the work of editing to make suggestions about formatting and the general shape of this work deserves special commendation for her numerous sacrifice for the success of this work. My thanks to her flow in profusion for her friendship, patience, faith and commitment to excellence.

I have been enriched in the course of my work by the friendship and fraternity of Revs Joachim Nnanna, Cyprian Ihedoro, Leo Ilechukwu, Ifunanya Aneke, Michael Chime, Chinedu Anieke, Innocent Inienwe, Ogbogu Ubaka, Ado Oyoyo Chukwuka, Ikenna Okafor, Anthony

Ibegbunam, Cosmas Ajawara, Alex Ojacor, Basil Okeke, Remmy Onyelu, Emefiena Ezeanni, Bedemoore Udechukwu, Vic Valles, Clair Hickson and Brian McColl; Miss Nicole Pauley, Christopher Cook; Dom and Catherine Adesanya, Dr Dan Okoro, and a host of African clerics, intellectuals and students in Peterborough and Toronto, Canada as well as in Atlanta, London, Rome, Vienna and Frankfurt. My thanks go also to Professor Richard Onwuanibe, my lecturer in the Faculty of Philosophy in Seat of Wisdom Seminary Owerri, Nigeria under whom I began to study the African condition inspired by his studies and publications on writings of African revolutionaries especially Frantz Fanon. I have also drawn immense inspiration from my mentors and friends Rev. Dr. Matthew Kukah, Archbishop Anthony Obinna of Owerri, Nigeria, and Cardinal Anthony Olubunmi Okogie of Lagos, and Rev. Dr. George Ehusani, all of whom are leading clerics in Africa, promoting the social mission of the Church in the much needed effort to bring peace, progress, and prosperity to African nations and peoples.

I have enjoyed the friendship and support of Rev. Joseph Moran, Rev. Norbert Glasmacher, Rev. Christopher Reynolds, Deacon and Mrs. Gerald McMurray, Chris Dunn, Teresa Hickey, Heribert and Susan Michel and Lee Lawson all of whom make up my loving home away from home. I wish to thank all the Board members of our charitable organization, Canadian Samaritans for Africa for teaching me that it is possible for Africans and Westerners to work together through ordinary means for ordinary Africans. The parishioners of St. Peter-in-Chains in Peterborough, Ontario have taught me the meaning of love by creating an atmosphere of friendship and solidarity, which mirrors the vision of the world that Jesus Christ taught us through the civilization of love. I specially thank my special friend Ellen MacAdam for lending her support to this work and for being supportive of my academic and pastoral commitments. I wish to thank the following Canadian family friends of mine whose love and encouragement have been immense: Phil and Eli Jessup, Dr Paul and Mary Morrocco, Loretto Lane, Louise Houston, Paul and Darlene Shaughnessy, Terry and Margaret Shaughnessy, Vince and Gloria Crowley, Mary and Charlie Porter, Catherine and Peter Offierski, Vince O'Donoghue and family, Mike and Barbara Sheehan, Brigitte Kurowski-Wilson, Marie Moser, Dr. Karen Logan, MaryAnn Greco, Donna Barrett, Vince and Anne Beresford, Paul and Dorothy O'Reilly and Ann Sheridan. Irene Andayo (Uganda), Hazel Zindonga (Zimbabwe), Anna Boateng and Nana Akua Konadu (Ghana), Nadesh Compoare (Burkina Faso), Girma Bekele (Ethiopia) all students in various universities in

Ontario, Canada helped me to generate the data on the African reality from their diverse experience of growing up in Africa.

I owe the freedom to engage in literary and academic ventures of this kind to the permission and blessing of my superiors Bishops Nicola De Angelis, Anthony Gbuji, and John Okoye. I wish to thank them all. My greatest inspiration comes from my family especially my parents whose love, intellectual formation, motivation, and influence have continued to guide my life. I wish to also thank my siblings (VinMartin, Cajetan, Onyinye and Udo), sisters-in-law (Ijeoma and Onyinye) and my brother-in-law, Martin, nieces and nephews for being such a wonderful family. There is no greater way of thanking my parents for their love for me and their work for grassroots development in our community, than by dedicating this work to them. Our family is a closely-knit family and when we lost my immediate elder sister, Bibiana, who incidentally was born on the same date but different year as me, it was and remains a heavy blow to the family. I also dedicate this work to the memory of my sister, Bibiana with whom I shared a lot including her passion for education and the liberation of African women. Her expertise in African history and literature was informally passed on to me through our debates, disputes, and dialogues. When she died in 1998, I inherited her library, which equipped me with materials on African history and literature. My final appreciation goes to my publisher, Author House, who kept my dream alive. To God, who is the author and meaning of everything; the source of all that I have and will ever be, be thanksgiving and praise for all that is and all that will ever be.

Stan Chu Ilo
October 1, 2005, the 45th Independence Anniversary of Nigeria.

By Way Of Introduction

I have the audacity to believe that people everywhere can have three meals a day for their bodies, education and culture for their minds and dignity, equality and freedom for their spirits. I believe that what self-centered persons have torn down, other-centered people can build up. I still believe that one day humanity will bow before the altars of God, and be crowned triumphant over war and bloodshed, and non-violent, redemptive goodwill will proclaim the rule of the land. And the lion and the lamb lie down together and every person shall sit under his/her own vine and fig tree and none shall be afraid. I still believe that we shall overcome. - Martin Luther King, Jr., Nobel Peace Prize Speech, April 3, 1968.

Africans hold the key to the future of the African continent. The world, as presently constituted, will not have a substantial hand in the transformation of Africa, unless there are radical changes in the present global social, economic, political, and cultural power relations. Africans, who are looking outside the continent for the path to a better Africa, are not correctly interpreting the historical process. The international community, especially the West, may make some incidental efforts to partner with Africa for Africa's good, but such contributions will consistently be marginal, half-hearted and conditioned by considerations outside Africa. The events in Somalia, Rwanda, Liberia, Northern Uganda, the two Congos, Darfur in the Sudan and the intermittent misery brought about by drought and desert locust invasion in the northern parts of the Sahel (especially Niger, Mauritania, Senegal, and Mali); have shown that the Western world does not often wish to pay the price for the good of Africa, unless there are high economic and political benefits for the Western nation in question. This has become the logic of life in our times. I cannot say with certainty that Africa would have acted in a contrary way if her situation were reversed with that of the West.

There is a great wealth of goodwill towards Africa and deep-felt compassion among ordinary Westerners for the African condition, however, at the political and corporate levels, there is no clear and consistent

1

pro-active policy for African development. This could be because there is some thinking that the future of Western societies is not tied to the future of Africa. Africa, as presently perceived among many non-Africans, has little to offer non-African societies. With the vastly expanding horizons of conflicts in Africa and the ever-revolving chain of poverty and suffering; with the exodus of the best and finest minds of Africa to the developed world; and with the increasing numbers of asylum seekers from Africa flooding into Western societies, any ordinary Westerner would naturally think that Africans are constantly in need of help and in dire existential straits. Africa, in the eyes of many people outside Africa, has little to offer except perhaps the groans and moans of a massive sea of a helpless, hopeless, and hapless people.

The invasion of Western societies by Africans is already intimidating most Westerners and rightly so, because no society has an infinite capacity for tolerance nor are Westerners unaware of the fact that given a fair playing ground, most Africans could compete favorably with their brothers and sisters from all over the world. The immigration restrictions imposed on Africans who wish to travel to Western countries, and the rejection of the refugee claims of many Africans who *escape* to Western countries, are indications that Westerners would rather have Africans stay in Africa. The presence of Africans in London, Toronto, New York, Rome, Berlin, Paris, or Amsterdam, is often perceived by some Westerners as an invasion rather than a blessing. No matter how comfortable most Africans may be abroad, they never escape these questions: *When will you go home? Will you ever return home? When last did you see your people at home?* Westerners may pose these questions to Africans with the best of intentions; however, they are loaded with meanings for Africans, as well as for the Western questioners, which sometimes are not easily discerned.

The truth is that Africans are not at home with themselves and their continent. The 'homelessness' of Africans has a deeper philosophical meaning other than physical homelessness. Ordinarily, homelessness refers to a state of not having a place someone can call a home. That person might be a street person or rejected person. Homelessness, in this regard, has a physical significance of destitution; a wanderer having no property other than perhaps a rag-tag collection of sundry materials for sleeping and resting in the heat or cold of the day and night. We see many of these hungry and marginal persons all over the dark alleys of our streets in developing countries as well in the most industrialized nations of the world. They are hungry and disillusioned; they are abandoned and left behind in the broken lower rungs of social progress. These are people caught by the dreary hand of poverty in societies, whose lack of love has created situations in which the weak live without love and hope, and die in desperation.

Homelessness can also have a deeper layer of meaning for a person, as well as for a group. This, in a certain sense, was well-reflected by the German philosopher Martin Heidegger, when he talked about the devastation that World War II brought to many people in Germany. His argument is that even though many people were left without houses, the real meaning of homelessness should not be seen only in their losing their building. "However hard and bitter, however, hampering and threatening that lack of houses remains, *the proper plight of dwelling* does not lie merely in a lack of houses…The proper dwelling plight lies in this, that mortals ever search anew *for the essence of dwelling that they must ever learn to dwell.* What if man's homelessness consisted in this, that man still does not even think of the proper plight of dwelling as *the plight?* Yet as soon as man gives thought to his homelessness, it is a misery no longer. Rightly considered and kept well in mind, it is the sole summons that *calls* mortals into their dwelling" (Heidegger, 1993, 363).

This is well represented by Wendell Berry in *The Hidden Wound* (Berry, 1989, 137), where he argues that the dislocation of modern society stems from a fundamental dualism, which excerpts the Creator from creation and the individual from community. In this kind of condition, a genuine realism that grapples firmly with life and society in its fundamental aspects of being and loving, co-existing and solidarity is destroyed because the values on which it stands have been undermined by certain lack of objectivity. Homelessness conceived in this light, is not the unfortunate condition of people living on the streets, but the malaise of modern life that relates to modes of thinking and acting. This produces human beings stripped of any sense of purpose other than their self-defined aims; whose mode of valuation is restricted to self and group referents, who only strive for things that please them without due regard to social responsibility and the call to respond to God and our neighbor in love that mirrors God in whose image and likeness we have been made. Homelessness in its most fundamental meaning is rootlessness whether at the personal or group level. It bespeaks of a basic lack of proper orientation that affects the destiny of a person or a group. We often hear people say that they are at peace or at home with themselves even in very trying circumstances. On the other hand, people have a terrible sense of anxiety and frustration when they are not at home with themselves. To be at home means to be one with oneself, to be in touch with one's inner self, and to be flexible enough to admit one's vulnerability and not deny it or run away from it.

Any person who is homeless at this deeper level lives as she or he is not meant to live. To be homeless in this sense is to live a lie. To live a lie is a very painful experience. Such a person does not find inner connection nor does he or she find any existential compass. Life can only be purposeful and creative if one finds a certain balance in the midst of daily challenges, at the deepest level where our human fragility meets with divine transcendence. The strength to live is also to be identified by the weakness of not wanting to live. One who is frightened by the presence of imminent danger sometimes finds uncanny courage to confront the danger head-on. We need to be homeless to appreciate our homes. The human person needs to experience a certain amount of personal self-exile to appreciate the value of having a true home. This is the root of human anxiety and transcendence: the capacity of each person to go beyond himself or herself when faced with the danger of self-extinction. This also entails the determination to take life as a gift that must be received with openness to the possibilities of joy and suffering, which come from attempting to appreciate the world around us and penetrate and transform it. This also demands that we are vulnerable and open enough to accept that *we do not have the last word.*

People are often torn apart because they have not reconciled the war within themselves, and have not come to terms with who they are. The pain of the strife within is heightened by the reality that we are constantly battling with living and dying. At each point, one is called forth by life to define one's existence in the context of one's origin and ultimate destiny. When people are homeless and don't realize it, they wander in a desert of confusion and despair adapting unreflectively to conflicting and bewildering tendencies. When people are homeless and realize it, they ask fundamental questions about their present life and engage their future in such a way that they seek to find their way to their home. Life is the constant movement between homelessness and homeliness, between self-exile and a return to home and between being far from home in a temporal sense and being home with the ultimate Source of Being, in Whom we all find a home.

Africans as a people are homeless. The unfortunate thing is that most Africans do not realize it. In the first half of the 20th Century, Pan-Africanists like W. E. B. Dubois, George Padmore, Marcus Garvey, Mamadou Dia, Modibo Keita, Sekou Toure, Leopold Senghor, Kwame Nkrumah, and Nnamdi Azikiwe all advocated the return of Africans to their African motherland, the political emancipation of colonial Africa and the restoration of the dignity of Africans (then called Negroes) in the United States of America and other parts of the world where they were

4

suffering racism and all forms of human rights abuses. (As a movement, Pan-Africanism had different concerns. There were obviously different trajectories of Pan-Africanism expressed in different slogans by different advocates, for instance the Back to Africa Movement wanted a return to the African homeland by all ex-slaves so that they could build a great nation. The Universal Negro Movement Associations and African Communities Imperial League had the slogan, 'Africa for Africans at home and abroad,' Marcus Garvey framed this desire in the slogan 'Africa for Africans,' while for Kwame Nkrumah Africans should seek first the political kingdom. All these pointed however to the desire of Africans in Diaspora to return to their motherland, Africa. A return, which was framed into different ideological presuppositions of a conquest of freedom that has political, economic, spiritual and cultural content, and the emergence in Africa of an idyllic state of life obviously buoyed by Black consciousness represented in concepts like Négritude.)

This return would include native Spanish-speaking Africans of Cuba, the Portuguese speakers in the slums of Brazil and Portugal, the Dutch speakers in Holland, the French-speaking Blacks scattered from Haiti to Martinique and from France to Belgium, Arab-speakers in the Middle East, Afro-Saxons in the Americas, citizens of Trinidad and Tobago, Grenada, Dominican Republic, Britain, and Canada. However, the Pan-Africanists failed to appreciate the fact that the concept, *African*, is complex because being an African does not necessarily mean being a Black person. The Pan-Africanists had in mind the concept of *Africanness* as *Blackness*. The reason, however, for the complexity of the concept of Africa or African is based on the fact that Africa is a continent with a rich tapestry of racial and sociological diversity. Africa is made up of over a thousand different tribes, languages, cultural, and religious traditions.

According to Aylward Shorter, "In Africa, relatively isolated human groups created their own societies and traditions within particular physical environments. They represent multiple adaptations to different and similar environments. Historically, they were not usually created by large-scale migrations and far-reaching conflicts, as happened in Europe and Asia. They were the creatures of filtering dynastic groups... These 'tribes' or 'ethnic groups' were categories of interaction, representing clusters of groups and sub-groups, languages and dialects, shading into one another. Traditionally, these ethnic groups shared ideas and practices over wide areas. 19th century trade and slavery 'ethnicized' such groups. Colonialism politicized them further by formalizing customary law, creating federation and paramountcies, and delimiting native reserves" (Shorter, 1998, 19).

Besides the ethnic diversity of Africa, the continent is also made up of European and Asian races numbering several millions who have settled and intermarried with African native tribes. The population of the African countries of South Africa, Zimbabwe, Namibia, Angola, Mozambique, Madagascar, and Ethiopia is a rich mix of African, Caucasian, Asian and Indian races. There is also a significant Arab and Arab-African population in the Magrib region of Africa as well as in Madagascar, Sudan, and Somalia, and parts of Chad and Nigeria. The racial and cultural diversity of Africa is more elaborate than that in Europe and Asia. This is because as Jared Diamond writes, "even before the arrival of the White colonialists, Africa already harbored not just blacks but five of the world's six major divisions of humanity, and three of them are confined as natives to Africa. One quarter of the world's languages are spoken in Africa....Africa's diverse peoples resulted from diverse geography and its long prehistory. Africa is the only continent to extend from the northern to the southern temperate zone, while also encompassing some of the world's driest deserts, largest tropical rain forests, and highest equatorial mountains. Humans have lived in Africa far longer than anywhere else" (Jared Diamond, 1999, 377). Thus, the Pan-Africanists' idea was a good one in the attempt to restore the dignity of Africans, but it was, according to Frantz Fanon, 'a vague formula' in its call for all Africans to return to their homeland. This was a physical or geographical attempt to conquer the homelessness of Africans.

Many thinkers and writers on the African reality have tended to lump Africa together as one entity. This has proven to be very destructive of the cultural identities of the peoples and empires of Africa. My own approach in this book is to interpret Africa in the evolution of her history. This focuses on those areas of African history that have roped the people who live in the African continent in similar complexities, difficulties and challenges. In that sense, Africa is *one* because most countries in Africa face similar economic, political, cultural, and social problems. There is also the identity crisis about what it means to be called an African. I have made use of the experiences of four Africans from Ghana, Burkina Faso, Uganda, and Zimbabwe in trying to establish a certain comparative outlook of the cultural and historical diversity of Africa. This is because in this book, I am writing about the historical and existential complexities of present-day *Africans understood as the people who owe their origin and allegiance to the African continent of today.*

Culturally, one can discern a certain commonality among Africans, but this sameness is more visible along the various geographical regions of Africa who have a long history of cultural exchanges, namely, the Magrib, the Nile Valley and Ethiopia, the East and Central Africa, Southern Africa, the Congo Basin, the Sudan, and the forest areas where the ancient empires of Songhai, Mali, and Ghana once existed. There is also some commonality in terms of the Hamitic and Bantu languages, which have given rise to various language groups in Africa. However, in Africa one can see people who speak the same language but come from different races. The concept 'African' cannot be limited to racial, linguistic, or cultural factors even though it entails all these. In this work, I intend to apply *the term 'Africa' or 'Africans' in a historical and interpretative sense to the people who live within the African continent, who face similar challenges and those who live outside the continent who have some affinity to Africa as part of their origin, identity, and history.*

The name 'Africa,' according to Ali Mazrui (Mazrui, 1986, 25), has been traced to a Berber origin. Many others have traced the name 'Africa' to Greco-Roman ancestry. Contact between the Roman Empire and Africa had been long. Emperor Constantine was said to have sent a monk to the Sudan as an emissary to explore the possibilities of acquiring some raw materials from the Sudanese kings and forcing them to accept Roman rule. The ancient Romans referred to their colonial province in present day Tunisia as 'Africa,' possibly because the name came from the Latin or Greek word for that region or its people or perhaps because the word came from one of the local languages, either of Berber or Phoenician. Perhaps the Romans named it after the Latin word *'aprica'* (sunny) or they were using the Greek word *'aphrike'* (without cold or winter). The word could as well have come from the Semitic language referring to Africa as *'tunisia,'* which means ears of corn. The Arab merchants subsequently called the place *'africa' 'ifriqiya.'* Whatever be the case, the question of the origin of the word is not as important as the question of the survival of the people who today identify themselves as Africans or of people of African descent.

The Jews have shown that in as much as a physical return to one's homeland is possible and desirable; the more fundamental return is ontological. The return I envision here is one that relates to the recovery of one's true identity, the identification of the threats to the survival of one's race or nation, the open and sincere acceptance of the facts about a people's history and the consistent commitment to return home at a deeper, spiritual and cultural level. Even though most Jews would like to do the *aliya* (the physical return to Israel), there is a certain commitment to the Jewish cause, which is higher, and beyond their physical presence in the State of Israel. Viewed in this light, overcoming the homelessness of Africans goes beyond physical return to Africa; it entails an ongoing awareness by Africans of the fact of their homelessness and putting in constant focus the need for its overcoming. What do we mean when we speak of the homelessness of Africans?

The homelessness of Africans does not merely refer to the fact that there are millions of Africans who are far from their physical home, nor does it mean the pervasive effects of the brain drain on African economy and social life. *The homelessness of Africans refers to the abandonment of the African continent by Africans physically, but more fundamentally, an emotional and cultural abandonment of Africa by Africans. It means the alienation of Africans from their cultural and spiritual roots, which affects their sense of identity and negatively hampers the evolution of their societies whether in the African continent or outside it. It is the existential exile into which the historical conditioning and cultural asphyxiation of Africans have placed them, making it impossible for the full blossoming of the African personality and the emergence of truly liberated, self-regenerating and organic African societies and ethnic nationalities in various African countries. It is also the root cause of the seeming failure of Africans to work together locally and internationally to evolve robust frameworks for a new era in which the light of African existence extinguished in the night of historical injustice can be relit through a cultural rebirth.* Homelessness leads to a lack of faith in the future of the continent, and the failure of Africans to tap into the positive energy of the continent to re-invent its soul. I am referring above all to the failure of African countries to take a critical look at their condition, and find from within the heart of Mother Africa the road they should take. *The homelessness of Africans also refers to the loss of identity of millions of Africans and the unending search by Africans for who they are and their place in today's world.*

There is today, a sense of frustration among most Africans who think that the African project is a colossal failure. I think, however, that the African project has yet to take off. The task of building truly integrated societies, workable political structures and realistic national constitutions, and the laying of the foundation for economic development in Africa has not started. It would be logically inconsistent to think that the African project is a failure when it has not yet begun. Africa has not yet begun her journey to authentic democracy and development, nor has she started to recover her sense of selfhood. There are many complexities in the continent which have not been properly addressed by Africans. I agree with Claude Ake, that the bane of African development is the lack of the necessary structures for democracy and growth. "The problems of emancipation of the poor in Africa are compounded by the fact that the very processes by which they participate reinforces their disempowerment. The peasant is not politically mobilized in the market-place of formally equal legal subjects who are negotiating their interests and finding common ground, but through patron-client chains, leveraging parochial identities, bribery and intimidation. In these circumstances, voting becomes a metaphor for powerlessness and exploitation." (Claude Ake, 1996, 10).

Africans who wish to claim *perpetual victimhood* are not responding adequately to the African condition. The argument among some Africans is that Africa is poor because the West is rich and in order for Africa to be rich, she must be helped by the West 'to be like the *Whites*.' This is a wrong conclusion based on a chimerical interpretation of history and a false assumption on the meaning and content of development and progress. There are many other variables which many Africans should address as central to their condition. These include the question of the exploitation of ordinary Africans by their political and religious elites, the corruption in African governments, and the high rate of ethnic tension and religious conflicts. The causes of these problems may be historical, but the solution is not beyond the ability of Africans. We must however admit that there was historical injustice committed against Africa by the West. There is also an ongoing exploitation and destruction of Africa by the contagion of globalization, but that does not make Africa a victim whose past and future fate has been pre-ordained by the actions and inactions of the Western and industrialized world. The *victims' theory* tends to make Africans placid in reinventing their future and to look up to Westerners for help. Africans do not have to wait for her so-called victimizers to repair what they destroyed, nor do Africans need to continue mouthing the timeworn mantra that external influences conspire to stymie the progress of the African continent.

I agree that the world as presently constituted is unjust and unfair to Africa. Indeed, "ensuring social, environmental, and individual reparation of damage relates not only to Africa's distant past but also to the negative environmental, health and human rights impacts that trans-national corporations continue to have in many parts of Africa" (South African Council of Churches & Southern African Catholic Bishops' Conference, 2002, 5.12). However, the decisive factor here is the Africans and what they are doing or failing to do in the historical process. The global world order, even though it externally advances the principles of justice, does not in practice work on just principles, but on exaggerated national and group interests. Indeed, the African condition cannot be interpreted appropriately, without taking into consideration the present unjust global structures. These are sustained by the absolute triumph of capital and the free market and the unlimited power of the Western financial institutions like the International Monetary Fund (IMF) and the World Bank to progressively destroy African economies through death-dealing, people–unfriendly economic theories. The world is also actively working against Africa's authentic development in the area of knowledge; where there is a deliberate attempt to reshape the dynamics of learning and rationality in Africa along the educational aims narrowly defined as Western worldview.

The sense of justice in a world ablaze with the flames of neo-liberal capitalism is much more nuanced. However, Africans must predicate the response to the present situation in the continent on what they can do for themselves and not on what the North will do for her. Africans may have been hit by the negative exploitative currents of the industrialized world, but they must reject any kind of mentality that makes them victims of the past and of the future. The victim who always relies on the victimizer for reprieve would never be let off the crushing chain that the victimizer has cast on him.

The *victims' theory*, which holds that Africa is suffering as a result of her past encounter with the Western world is a strong argument but not a helpful one in the present circumstances. The numerous conference and position papers published and projected, to make a case for reparation to the Africans and African-Americans, for the evils of slave trade and the denial of civil rights to the African-Americans, have not won over many sympathizers to the Africans many years since the Black Consciousness Movement. The history of the exploitation of one people by another is an old one. No imperial or quasi-imperial nation renounces power, or ceases to exploit another voluntarily, unless such exploitation no longer serves any useful purpose. As Rubem A. Alves argues, "The event of liberation, therefore, implies the interruption of the normal course of history. History is negated, is resisted, and is denied the right to follow the course it has determined for itself. But history is negated only to the extent to which the power that negates it is free from it. If it were not free from history it would be a child of history, a new embodiment of its will to power, a reflex of its structures of domination. Only what is free from history is able to oppose and transgress it. There is no liberation in history, no creation of the new, if there is no freedom and transcendence over the given subjective and objective conditions intrinsic to history. On the other side, however, there is no liberation if freedom from history does not determine itself as freedom for history" (Alves, 1972, 122).

This position is validated in the course of human history. There is no possibility of overcoming an unacceptable situation, without the determined will of the people who suffer the consequences of unjust structures to change the course of history in the direction of their common good. It is we Africans who have to win our freedom. Our ancestors did it in the past against the agents of darkness who enslaved them and took away their freedom; our nationalists did it against the colonialists who defied their land and exploited the peoples and resources of Africa; our brothers and sisters in South Africa stood against the monstrous apartheid regime that held them in thralldom for many decades. Today, Africans are challenged to stand together, to think together and work together to change their lot. The agents of the imperialists and the neo-capitalists will not remove the chain around the neck of Africans, because it helps to sustain the economies and political hegemony of many Western countries, especially those who once colonized and enslaved Africans. Like the Yorubas say, "The rabbit that eats yams and enjoys them will return for more."

Let me state clearly that I believe that the evils of slavery, colonialism, apartheid, and racism, which the African peoples suffered, remains a strong argument in calling for pro-active and non-reactive acts of solidarity to Africa. However, this is only a dream, which will never be realized, unless global power relations change in the direction of greater justice and solidarity. It is easy for Africans to blame their poverty on slavery and colonialism; it is easy for Africans to blame their bad leaders as the agents of the West and to cry for the lost age of Africa's innocence and renascence; it will, however, take real sacrifice and struggle for the Africans to win over their continent once more.

However, the *victims' theory* can never win the victims any reprieve. Africans must throw away the toga of *victimhood* and take their destiny by the hand. To cry for justice is just not enough; to work for justice is better. *I do believe that Africa as constituted today has all it takes to be a rich and prosperous continent; a land of opportunities for the young and old; a piece of the world where men and women can still be humans, because they are at home with themselves and in touch with the natural and transcendental spiritual worlds. Africa can still become a land, where human sensitivity has not been blotted by individualism, materialism, secularism, or scientific determinism of a bio-technological kind.* This is because, despite the attractions of westernization and liberalism, most Africans still advert to core values with regard to family, life, community, and human relations. I do believe that Africa has within her womb the seeds for greatness and the potential to be the next phase in an integrated progressive movement of human history; however, the journey has to begin with the Africans accepting that they alone hold the key to their future. From the heart of Africa comes the proverb that *'God provides food for every bird, but he does not bring it to the bird's nest.'*

The erection of structures of justice in the world, would undercut the foundation of a system, that has created the gap between the rich and the poor nations. African peoples must come to terms with the historical challenges they face in the complex world of today, which is systemic in its exclusion of the developing countries. The identification of some commonalities among peoples and religions, the seeming convergence of the interests of peoples and nations, and greater knowledge of the various histories and cultures of races and nations have not helped the world to create a clear and consistent agenda for global peace and development. On the contrary, the fear of one another and the struggle for survival and dominance have become more aggressive and violent. Group assertion has become bold and totalizing between the South and the North, and especially between radical Islamic fundamentalists and Western powers. The glories of a new world presaged by the fall of communism, have become mere dust in the wind, and the proponents of the end of history have become afraid of the new paths of history.

Africa's sense of homelessness is at the root of the present African condition. Africa has always been very marginal in world history. George Hegel had no place for Africa in his cartography of world's history and civilization. The journey of the human spirit at the level of consciousness, in his interpretation of history does not pass through Africa, because Africans' consciousness has not attained to the level of any substantial objective existence. According to Hegel, "Africa is the land of gold, closed upon itself, the land of children, it is the gold-land confused within itself—the land of childhood, which lying beyond the day of self-conscious history, is enveloped in the dark mantle of night" (Hegel, 1990, 91). This negative reading of history has been refuted by the great African Egyptologist, Diop Cheikh Anta, who has a different reading of human history. Based on primary evidence, Diop established that Egypt belongs to Africa and is the heart of human civilization (See Diop Cheikh Anta, *The African Origin of Civilization* edited and translated by Mercer Cook, Chicago, Illinois: Lawrence Hill Books, 1974. See also Chancellor Williams, *The Destruction of Black Civilization*, Chicago, Illinois: Third World Press, 1987). Martin Bernal's work, *The Afro-Asiatic Roots of Greek Civilization*, relying on secondary sources makes the same argument. Another work, *Introduction to African Civilization*, establishes that the human race originated from Egypt and Ethiopia. UNESCO's *General History of Africa* also integrates these insights on Africa in its admission that Africa is the birthplace of the human race. The authors of the document, *The New Partnership for Africa's Development* (NEPAD) conclusively admit in no 14, "Modern science recognizes Africa as the cradle of humankind. As part of the process of reconstructing the identity and self-confidence of the peoples of Africa, it is necessary that this contribution to human existence be understood and valued by the Africans themselves. Africa's status as the birthplace of humanity should be cherished by the whole world as the origin of all its peoples.

Accordingly, the New Partnership for Africa's Development must preserve this common heritage and use it to build a universal understanding of the historic need to end the underdevelopment and marginalization of the continent" (Maloka, 2004, 467). The task of setting right the biased history of Africa told by non-Africans is very urgent. All around the world, the picture of Africa is one of despair, violence, diseases, suffering among other evils. Even the Africans themselves are buying into this image and are gradually losing faith in the possibility of a better future for themselves in Africa. Chinua Achebe, arguably the most celebrated African novelist, has said that the bane of the African continent is that Africa does not have many Africans telling the story of Africa. In an articulate reaction to Joseph Conrad's *Heart of Darkness*, which painted a gory picture of Africa, Chinua Achebe bemoans the distortion of the face of Africa by most Western writers who have preposterous and bizarre concepts about Africa.

According to Frederick Buell, there is a vicious and covertly bigoted stereotype about the developing countries. Particularly with regard to Africa, this bifurcated account represents a post-Modern version of the colonial-racist imagination. The line is familiar and simple: everything bad and evil resides in Africa, everything good and worthy of imitation resides in the West. Africa needs to become Western in order to modernize. Some Africans have bought into this logic and think their future can only be guaranteed if Africa became Western or if Africans migrated to the West. A reading of works like *The coming Anarchy* (Robert Kaplan), *The End of History and the Last Man* (Francis Fukuyama), and *The Clash of Civilization and the Remaking of World Order* (Samuel Huntington) to mention but a few, reveals this bigoted and narrow reading of history with regard to the interpretation of the African reality. Perhaps many Africans do not know how rich the story of Africa is or how important this story is to both Africa and the rest of the world. *The world needs a unique Africa and not an assimilated or disappearing Africa.*

Many clans and tribes in Africa are forgetting their own stories and strengths and submerging their memories in a heap of shame. Africans must recognize that they are homeless, when they suffer collective amnesia, or allow the selective accounts of non-Africans, to falsify the African story or to present that story only as the encounter of Africans with the West. Africans need to return home. They need to take up their history once more and read; they need to listen to the musings of their children and the historical moorings of her peoples; they need to recover their religious tradition and its high ethical content and weave it into the received religions of Christianity and Islam; they need to open their eyes and see themselves for who they are: a people who are about to begin a real journey to a future.

The mistake that most African nations have made is to build on the false assumptions that things would get better in Africa over time; that God somehow in his infinite majesty and goodness would turn things around in Africa. That is a mere illusion. I do believe that religion has a vital and irreplaceable role to play in the transformation of the African continent—this is why I became a priest. Africans take religion seriously; religion is central to their understanding of life and the movement of history. I do, however, believe that the religious institutions in Africa, like their political counterparts, are in need of a radical renewal and reorientation if they are to play any significant role in reshaping the future of Africa. Many Africans might not be condemned if they think that there is too much religion in Africa, without a concomitant percolation of the values of true religion in the structures of African society. God works in history, but history is made by godly men and women who attempt to understand reality, enter into reality, and make reality to conform to God's plan. This is why there is the need for a critical theological and philosophical anatomy of the bases for the upsurge of religious sentiments in Africa: the content of these sentiments, the message of the religious leaders, and the general direction of the religious groups in Africa. I attempt an identification of what I consider to be structural sins within religious and political institutions; and chart a way forward for religious groups in Africa so that they can become real agents for social change, transformation, and spirituality for the people of Africa.

There are many countries in Africa who need to begin a real journey to nation building. This might mean the structural break-up of their countries or a radical mutation of the power relation among the ethnic groups. Nigeria, for instance, has spent over 45 years of her post-Independence trying to fix the problems of ethnicity and religious differences, without much success. Many politicians in Nigeria, who are exploiting the present dysfunctional political situation in that country, do not believe that the question of the unity of the country should be put on the table. These are people who are swimming in an ocean of wealth, surrounded by a vast desert of poverty, and whose hold on power is built into the inchoate economic, political, and social structures in the country. Thus, they do not want a negotiation of the bases of the country and the evolution of a new form of power-relations that would address the structural injustice that is ruining the lives and future of millions of Nigerians.

The question that is important for us here is: Why should Nigerians continue to patch up the structure that is Nigeria, instead of pulling down the structure and erecting a better one on a firm foundation? Many pan-Nigerians, think that dismembering the country is not a good idea, but they fail to bring up new ideas for addressing the many questions in the country about the exclusion and ongoing injustice against some ethnic groups in the country (the exploitation of the minority oil-producing ethnic groups of the country, who in spite of the presence of Nigeria's oil wealth in their land are the least developed part of the country). There is still the unanswered question of the religious freedom of Nigerian Christians in the core Muslim states of Northern Nigeria, where strict *Sharia* Islamic law has been introduced without regard to the rights of the Christians.

The poverty of Africa questions the basis of the claim to a common humanity. It mocks any global pretension to a more just and humane world; it also undercuts any bold assertion of the power and impact of globalization. The growing number of people in Africa, who die of preventable and curable diseases, makes a mockery of a more prosperous world, which has bridged the gap between the virtual and the real in science and technology. Many might be deceived into thinking that globalization is bringing the world together through new forms of information techniques, the cable networks, economic integration, and multiculturalism among others. However, the intentions of the leading nations in a globalizing world is not the establishment of a new world order of justice and equality, but a hegemonic Western ideal, which would keep most people in the developing world constantly on their knees without any clear sense of civilizational direction. There is a gradual hardening of economic protectionism and cultural identities of various nations, races, and religions, which would produce an evolving world order that would only recognize those nations, races, and religions that clearly and concretely articulate their vision and direction. This articulation must translate into some form of economic prosperity and a measure of self-autonomy.

The American war against terrorism has already indicated at the beginning of the millennium, that fundamental changes will be witnessed in the way nations relate with one another. The world has been changed fundamentally because 9/11 took place in the United States of America. With the rise in terrorist activities all over the Western world and Russia, we cannot pretend that the world will be much interested in African concerns. There is a reinterpretation of what is right and wrong in international politics in light of the interests of the leading nations of the world. The bipolar vision of the world as one constituted by those who are for 'us' (America) and those who are against 'us,' pioneered by George W. Bush is a paradigm shift from the post-Cold War global understanding of the world order. It even tends to elevate the United States to the level of God's preferred ambience, from where freedom and prosperity will spread to the rest of the world according to how each part of the world identifies with the so-called 'American war on terror.' In this kind of world, the meaning of democracy, freedom, war, terrorism, and other frequently used terms are becoming increasingly relativized according to the intentions and interests of those nations that have made them constant refrains in international politics.

In a world like this, we are dealing with cultural and ideological hubris of grand proportions and the dismantling of universal norms that govern human relations and international interests. In the process, we have lost the sense of right and wrong in place of expedience. The present 'war' against terrorism has diverted the whole priority of the international community and thrown the world into an unending fray of convoluted crises, collective schizophrenia, intermittent massive fear-mongering that make nations prepare for imaginary wars in unspecified territories. The real battle to be fought should have been a war against poverty in the world. A commitment to the ideals of justice and love, equality and fairness among all peoples and races, among all religions, and between the North and the South is the key to global peace and happiness.

Most of the developed countries that are presently haunted by the fear of terrorism had a hand in creating the monster of poverty, hatred, and insecurity the world over, by the kind of policies they have adopted since the end of the Second World War in most developing countries of Africa and the Middle East. The truth, however, is that if the developed countries had fought the war against poverty and injustice in the world with the same zeal with which they are fighting against terrorism today, they would not be fighting this present war with invisible enemies who have no clear boundaries and no battle lines.

Terrorism is a war without borders unleashed upon peoples and nations, especially innocent people, by some faceless cowards whose main goal is to inflict maximum destruction and pain on those they hate or those who they think hate them. America's military intervention in Iraq attempted unsuccessfully to redefine the Christian just war principle. The concept of asymmetrical warfare was developed by international terrorists' organizations that depend on secret assistance from some governments to whom they owe no allegiance. This makes it impossible for them to be tracked down economically, politically, and militarily. In the face of this emerging scenario, there was the need to build a global network of solidarity against terrorists, whose complex network is very fluid and widespread. The conquest of terrorism cannot be achieved through any isolationist policy on the part of the United States, which is developing the inner architecture for building a new global empire. *No single person's destiny or worldview is higher than the collective good of his or her nation, just as no single nation's interest should transcend that of the global community.*

Indeed, wrong policies and actions by governments in their relationship either with their own citizens or other nations are the reasons for terrorism in the world. *Terrorism is the consequence of injustice and poverty in the world. It is the cry from the hearts of the weak to the strong; it is only the external expression of inward frustration by a thin top layer of the massive sea of a frustrated portion of our restive world.* **However, terrorism can never be justified for any reason.** The victory over the perpetrators of terror in any part of the world can never be realized through the kind of experiment that the American government undertook in Iraq. The liberation of one people by another is only another language for imperialism, whether it is cultural, political, or economic. It is a cultural arrogance that deprecates the values dear to another people. It does violence to our collective humanity, because it diminishes the mosaic of diverging civilizations and traditions that give beauty to the world. As Hegel and the Christian paleontologist Teilhard de Chardin had postulated, every civilization grows from within, through the liberation of the inner spirit of the people. According to Hegel, the state is a "self-originating, self-developing, self-knowing and self-actualizing mind," which defines itself in the historical process in her constitution and in the mode of living of her people. Thus, every state must pass through phases of decay, dictatorship, and even war before it arrives at a synthesis of her collective good built from her past history and mistakes.

Africa will have her day. This present state of affairs in Africa will not last forever. However, Africans must realize that they are facing a new world, which wishes to ignore them as the war on terrorism tends to topple the millennium goals that seek to pull down the walls of poverty, which is the greatest global terrorism. Failed states are always fertile grounds for terrorism. Thus, the world community must stand by Africa so that her states do not implode. Unfortunately, African countries cannot hope that the developed countries like the United States, Britain, France, Germany, Canada, Norway, and others would prioritize the development of Africa as much as they would focus on their national securities in the face of global terrorism. This is why I think Africans hold the key to Africa's future and should not hope for a better and more sensitive world that would listen to and respond courageously to the crises in the continent.

The West and all men and women of goodwill do have a stake in

Africa. In the concluding part of chapter one, I propose a new model of relation between African countries and the rest of the world, especially the Western world. This is what I call *the total picture approach model*, which is both, germane for the Africans and the non-Africans interested in Africa. This theory advances an integral approach to the African condition. It argues that the African condition is multi-pronged and as such demands a multi-faceted approach. It proposes that African countries should formulate policies that strengthen their capacities for long-term sustainable development initiatives. That means that Africans should own their continent and take positive steps to formulate a strategic vision for their respective countries. This vision sees Africa's crises as secondary to the goals of authentic development. This does not mean that poverty-reduction initiatives should be abandoned in the short run, because they should be the necessary first step in many African countries. However, they should not be seen as ends in themselves, but as the first step in a wider economic canvass that looks beyond the crisis. There is the urgent need to provide social services, to give jobs to many jobless Africans; to stem the human hemorrhage that has been caused by unending civil strife in many African countries and to meet the immediate need of disease prevention and control, especially with regard to malaria and the HIV/AIDS pandemic. Again these responses should aim at setting the ground for the 'long haul' in terms of building the relevant lasting structures whose absence resulted in the crises in the first place.

The *crisis reaction approach* in Africa, should not shape the nature of future policies for the development of the continent, because crises are accidentals, but policies relate more to the substantial and constant challenges of living. The problems that face African nations should never be treated in isolation of each other, because all of them reveal basic structural and foundational cracks in African countries. This proposal seeks to reverse the trend whereby Africa's most important aspirations (education, food production, cultural and economic development, and institutional building) are often abandoned in the quest to address the intermittent crises in the continent. These crises (civil strife, war, diseases like AIDS/HIV, natural disasters, refugees, gender equality, etc.) have come to define the face of Africa. This vision is one that advances a macro-policy, which sees the broader picture, but builds on the micro-level in terms of its implementation, and the framing of the steps for its realization. Thus, small scale workers, village cooperatives, professional support groups, and the civil society at large, should be given all the necessary encouragement to blossom so that they can help to give leg to the macro-level vision at the grassroots where the validity of policies of all kinds should be tested.

What has happened is that the international community and African governments continue to 'react' to crises in Africa without much success. The failure to permanently solve these problems is mainly because they are symptoms of a disease. The symptoms are often treated while the disease remains. These crises can only be averted by addressing the factors that lead to them in the first place, that is, by prioritizing human development while not forgetting present crises. The history of Africa is unique, but it is part of the history of humanity. The mistake many advanced civilizations have made in the course of world history is to think that their advancement can only be achieved by distancing themselves from other cultures. Such preservations have a very short life span. Africans, however, must explore the rich human and material resources of their continent; they must learn to deepen their love for their culture and history; they must be open and flexible enough to adapt to new realities globally with a discernment that longs for the best for her children.

In these pages, I write of my experience and the experiences of many young Africans like myself who are disturbed by the present condition of Africa. I write about the challenges facing most Africans who are growing up in the African continent without any hope of quality education, without any guarantee of adequate food, water, housing, and clothing; without any hope of getting a job, and without any prospect of living in peace with their neighbors. I write also about the millions of young Africans who are dying of malaria and HIV/AIDS, and the African women whose fate and fortune have been shackled by a male-dominated society. I write of the failed states of Africa who are caught up in a cycle of violence and disorder and who are not asking the right questions about their future. This stems from the fact that the people in leadership positions have become the greatest enemies of their people through corruption, excessive authoritarianism, a stubborn hold on power, and lack of openness to consensus-building. I also write about the pain of knowing that some of these problems of Africa were caused by many Western nations like the United States, Britain, France, Germany, Belgium, Portugal, Spain, and Italy, who today have turned their backs on most African countries. Many Africans have become exhausted in the battle for national survival and for a living space to pursue their ordered ends. However, I propose that they should stand up once more and work for a better tomorrow, which is possible, and within their reach. How this becomes possible is part of the ongoing dialogue, which I propose in this book.

The face of Africa is not just about pain and sorrow as has always been presented by most Western news agencies and publications; it is also the face of hope. I take up this theme in various parts of this book. I base my reflection on what I understand as the Christian vision of hope, which is not opposed to the Islamic vision or the African traditional religious belief of a better tomorrow. I try to reconstruct and resurrect a sense of hope from the realities that many can observe in the African continent. This vision is incarnated in an African philosophy of history. In doing this, I look at the perspectives and experiences of young Africans like myself, who were born after the decolonizing process in most parts of Africa and the 'millennials' who make up the vanguard for the erection of more humane and just structures in the social, economic, political, and cultural life of Africa.

I am thinking of these young Africans who have never known the good old days; they are the ones who wish to compete equally with the rest of the world in many areas of intellectual, cultural, economic, and political life. Many of these people do not have any possibility of going to school. Those of them who study in the universities, for instance, have no good libraries, no seats in lecture halls, no good laboratories, and no social services; however, they still graduate as specialists who can literally squeeze water out of a stone.

These are people who are disillusioned by their failed leaders and who do not see any reason why most governments in Africa should continue to exist. They long for a good life worthy of the dignity of the human person. They also want to give back to their parents some fruits of their labors, since the elderly in most African countries do not have any retirement package from their governments, and can only survive based on what members of their families provide for them. These young people have watched their siblings die of preventable diseases; they have seen their cousins suffer from man-made social evils; they have seen their friends killed in violence and they can no longer put up with a society that has to change or cease to exist.

In these pages, I share my own personal stories of life in Africa and my personal reading and interpretation of the present situation of Africa. My proposal is that the face of Africa today is ugly, but behind the ugly face is the beauty that has been distorted by historical and cultural factors. However, the future of Africa is bright, because her present condition is only the sign of the urgent need for the peoples of Africa to begin the journey to reclaim their future. I have also outlined how non-Africans who are interested in the African condition can be involved with the peoples of Africa. A proper understanding of the African continent and her peoples, her history and cultural evolution is a necessary first step for those who wish to be engaged with the Africans.

Central to this understanding is the structure of the African societies. No meaningful engagement with Africans can take place if non-Africans use their own categories to interpret the life and societies of Africans. Most governments in Africa are not sufficiently accountable to the people or responsive to the needs of their citizens; there is a need to re-conceptualize the ways donations are made to African governments. Most groups working in Africa must be 'embedded' within the governmental structures, but understanding the dynamics of governments in Africa would help Africans and non-Africans to work directly with the ordinary people without necessarily using the agencies of governments. I do believe that a strong and vibrant civil society in African countries is a necessary condition for bringing about long and lasting changes in Africa in all sectors. It would also promote a sense of duty and accountability on the part of the government and energize the grassroots base, where the struggle for the soul of Africa would be won or lost in the years to come. "At the heart of democracy lies the practice of self-government, by which citizens through their own associations attain their own ends without always turning to the state to take care of all things. Thus, civil society is another form of 'government of the people, by the people, for the people,' especially in spheres beyond the competence of politics and government officials. For by civil society is meant the active associational life of free citizens pursuing together both the common good and their own particular ends within it. Democracy depends so much on the free activities of civil society, both within and outside of politics, as almost to be a synonym for it" (Novak, 2004, 169).

My proposal is that international organizations and Western humanitarian agencies should engage African peoples at the grassroots level and work with civil societies and movements in Africa; while at the same time prioritizing capacity building over hand-outs and donations, which only help to perpetuate a dependency syndrome among African nations. Any development or donor initiatives that do not impact the people in African villages will not make any difference in the lives of African people. Any program for the transformation of Africa, which is not village-centered, will have little impact on African societies. Unfortunately, many Western donors and non-governmental organizations continue to engage African people using local (national) administrative structures, which though private-based still parallel the elitist, superficial, and unaccountable governmental structures in Africa. These programs have little trickle down effect and cannot set the pace for sustainable development.

However, it must be emphasized that Africans ought to take their future in their hands and not look up to receiving annual grants and importing everything from Western and Asian countries. This is the principle that led to the New Partnership for Africa's Development (NEPAD). This initiative seeks a greater partnership between Africa and Western nations on the grounds that African nations take the initiatives by setting the agenda, establishing good governance, protecting human rights, and promoting public accountability. This would help stem the dependency syndrome among African nations.

Africans, however, should not be overly enthusiastic about NEPAD, because it is not the first policy initiative taken for Africa's development and may not be the last. Some of these past policies like the Structural Adjustment Program, the Heavily Indebted Poor Countries initiatives, and the Poverty Reduction Strategy Paper have all left most Africans in poverty. As a result of these top-down mercenary policies, millions of Africans are today victims of macroeconomic management regimes and a competitive free market that aims at capitalization without people empowerment and places profit, efficiency, and profligacy for a few over poverty, suffering, and powerlessness for many. The failure of successive strategies to change the face of Africa is not because of the African environment, but because these policies fail to address the unjust economic structures in the world and they tend not to address the needs of the ordinary people. NEPAD was not a bottom-top policy; it was an elitist formulation by an elitist club of African leadership. This new initiative was undertaken with little input from the ordinary people for whom it was meant.

NEPAD is more discussed among Western industrialized countries than by the ordinary Africans in the villages and streets of Africa. By seeking to integrate Africa into the global market, NEPAD might perpetuate the systematic and subtle destruction of the African economy that began in its aggressive forms in the early 1970s. Africa's economy is 46.5% integrated into the global economy, but that integration has brought so much misery and frustration that more integration would wreck more havoc. NEPAD has no consistent agenda on debt cancellation, or on putting an end to the privatization of basic services (water, electricity, communication, agriculture, etc.) in African countries. Most of the basic services are increasingly becoming exclusive rights of the few rich people, while a greater majority of Africans that are poor and marginalized swelter in the heat of want. NEPAD has no plan for a more favorable trade relation between Africans and the G8 which has not yet mobilized the $64 billion required to finance NEPAD's five areas of concern (peace and security, good governance, water, knowledge and health, trade and investment).

NEPAD is thus an offer, which should be critically examined and studied before its ideology of privatization and ownership is accepted. With NEPAD, it is not yet *uhuru* for Africans. However, something positive could come out of NEPAD at the end of the day, depending on how the interests of the ordinary people are taken into consideration by involving them in the general direction of this new initiative. However, Africans must reject any development model that "fails to offer any alternative to the dominant market fundamentalist development model that places unquestioning faith in uncontrolled, private sector led, rapid economic growth as the answer to the problem of rampart poverty, increases unemployment, and widens inequality in the short and medium term, while making national economies extremely vulnerable to speculative capital and market sentiment." Africa needs to work with the international community with a view to avoiding a greater dependency that perpetuates her suffering and threatens the future of young Africans.

This dependency ramifies to all sectors of African life. This is true even in religious institutions in Africa. Most churches in Africa, for instance, are still considered mission churches that need foreign help from the Western 'mother churches' to survive. In this kind of situation, the churches in Africa cannot develop the autonomy (for example, in contextualizing theology and in developing theological formation that is 'African friendly'), which it needs to incarnate the Gospel values in their countries, without playing out the scripts of some other institutions outside Africa. This is also the case with the Islamic religion: most of the Islamic groups and brotherhoods in Africa draw their financial strength from countries in the Arab world and as the saying goes, 'he who pays the piper dictates the tune.' Radical Islamism is growing in places like Nigeria, Sudan, Algeria, Libya, and Egypt, because the Islamic brotherhoods in these countries receive a lot of financial and ideological support from radical Islamic groups in the Middle East. At the end of the day, unless Africa develops a capacity for self-sustenance in all spheres of life, she will remain a beggarly continent without initiative and creativity, especially at the cultural and economic fronts, which is defining the world of emergent possibilities.

This work also argues that Africa is a gift to the world in terms of her cultural and religious (especially Christian) traditions, the dynamism of her people, her numerous natural resources and the undying commitment of most Africans, especially the African women for a better future for their children and in the deep sense of family life and community in Africa. Tracing the bases for this assertion will form the concluding part of this book. The vision that I present is one of hope built on love. I use Christian and African philosophical and theological categories to interpret the most pressing challenge facing African countries—the dismantling of the structures of sin that make it impossible for the African genius to emerge. I trace these structures in the two most important institutions in Africa: the religious and the political. African societies have always been centers of love and community and places where everyone can be at home with life. Love is the basis for the existence of traditional African societies—this love translates into life. This life refers to the life of the individual, the lives of others in the community, and the life of the community as a whole. This life is reflected also in the natural and spiritual world around and above the human world. The vital force, which defines life and reality in Africa, is centered on love.

Can we say that most African societies and countries are loving and compassionate? I find it hard to answer this question in the affirmative. For instance, a Nigerian musician, Bright Chimezie, captures the flight of love in Nigeria when he sang, "Where is love when children are dying everyday? Where is love when people are killing each other? Where is love when people are dying of hunger? Where is love when people are fighting each other?" Love is the answer to the problem of existence, but love is not simply a concept but an act; it is not words, but deeds. How much love do we have in the world today? Are our political and economic institutions animated by love and compassion? Do we have a sense of compassion in the world today when many people are dying of hunger, war, disease, and frustration? How connected are human beings with one another and with the higher levels of being. The human need for intimacy, love, and transcendence is as real as life. At the same time, our capacity to love is also infinite. It is when one observes the solitary condition of humanity today and the pain and suffering of many in the world that we can appreciate the fact that a loveless world is a meaningless and directionless world.

Many years ago, the Christian paleontologist, Teilhard de Chardin, (Chardin, 1969, 327) whose reading of history has had much influence on many people the world over, wrote of the convergence of humanity around the circle of love whose center is Jesus Christ. He holds that the world can only be sufficiently progressive if human beings can lay hold of the world, embrace its goods, and encounter the riches of cultures and peoples in an open encounter that is incomplete but capable of indefinite perfection, where faith and hope meet their fulfillment in love. History for him is not static and essentialist, it is evolving in the direction of a qualitatively new way of being a human person, to achieve a more total and better living situation and a qualitatively new society.

Gustavo Guttierez argues, "To conceive history as a process of the liberation of man is to consider freedom as a historical conquest; it is to understand that the step from an abstract to a real freedom is not taken without a struggle against all the forces that oppress man, a struggle full of pitfalls, detours, and temptations to run away. The goal is not only better living conditions, a radical change of structures, a social revolution; it is much more: the continuous creation, never ending, of a new way to be a man, a permanent cultural revolution"(Guttierez, 1973, 32-33). This conception is at the center of life and reality in Africa. African society is self-liberating; African cultural life has a liberative openness to the preservation of life and the removal of anything that destroys life and human fulfillment. Love is the vital principle that holds African societies together; the sense of community, the sense of interconnectedness, the sense of family and hospitality, the sense of hope and of a concrete future that is protected by God and into whose womb humanity can enter is central to African *vitalogy and self and group liberative motif.*

These are values, which at the institutional levels in Africa are being threatened but which still blossom in African villages and streets among the ordinary people. In a sense, it is the educated and enlightened Africans who invariably play leadership roles in Africa that should be blamed for the present situation in Africa wherein the most cherished values of the people are not reflected in the structures of the countries of Africa. There is an emergent sub-culture, evidently rising from the leadership in African religious and political institutions, which have institutionalized certain negative values, which are antithetical to authentic African values found among the ordinary people and consequential to the African sense of generosity, hard work, community, respect for life, and a sense of responsibility and purpose.

The authentic movement of history should be a movement towards *love and hope.* Hegel had presented history as a succession of events on one hand and an interpretative process on the other. World history for Hegel is the actuality of mind in its whole compass of internality and externality (Frederick G. Weiss, 1974, 306). History moves towards the absolute mind, which many Hegelians, after the interpretative tradition of Alexandre Kojeve, define as the emergence of the universal and homogenous state—liberal democracy—in which the human search for recognition is found. However, history is not to be interpreted only in Hegelian terms.

Most Asian/Sinic civilizations interpret history as a cyclic movement, a journey of eternal return. But Africans have an idea of concrete history, which is a movement, which horizontally connects us to cultures, persons, and nature, and vertically connects us to the transcendent Being, God.

25

For the Africans, history is concrete when it is referring to the past and the present. The future is not an experience but a possibility which one cannot define because it is in the hand of God. However, the past and the present make sense for the individual and the community because they make up the quantum pre-given that defines life and reality. However, progress within history in African thinking is built on the conviction that there is a better tomorrow for individuals and groups as long as they are at right with God. Thus the future has a positive possibility because it is in the hand of a benevolent God, who gives to one and all the opportunity to be as long as they upheld the moral and spiritual order. African sense of history is an integrated acceptance of the connection between the past and present, the divine and human in the evolution and determination of the future. It embodies hope as integrative principle that gives the courage to be for individuals and groups as they search for answers to the problems and challenges of existence in the light of their perception of the presence and power of the divine in the human world and their connection to it.

The Western linear sense of history as progress towards prosperity and better living conditions appears univocal or one-dimensional in its aggressive rejection of God as the hidden hand that directs history; the elevation of the ingenuity of human creativity and absolutization of individual moral choices. The philosopher Martin Heidegger has pointed out the difficulty of interpreting time and history, because the question to be asked is about the person *(Dasein)* who is the maker of history by his or her involvement with life. He tends to emphasize that we raise the fundamental question of who we are and our place in history. Is history a pre-given or should it be interpreted in the light of the acting person?

The Christian conception of time and history provides a rich insight. In Christianity, time is not a question of mere historical conception,[1] but

---

[1] This Christian conception of time is based on my re-reading of John Paul II's, **Redemptor Hominis** and the Second Vatican Council's Pastoral Constitution on the Role of the Church in the Modern World, **Gaudium Et Spes**, 22 in which Christ is presented as the center of history. The document states that in Christ the human person is revealed and the fullness of a person's being and the term of his or her existence is interpreted in the light of Christ. This conception is a good ground for inter-religious dialogue for this is a bold claim made by Christians, which bears re-reading by non-Christians to find how they can anchor the movement of history on some positive values in their religions. It is important that religious institutions begin a deeper search for the real face of their religions and join in the task of visioning that is needed for a better world. See also, **Jesus Christ Word of the Father**, The theological-Historical Commission for the Great Jubilee of the Year 2000, (New York: the Cross Road Publishing Company, 1997) 26-27. Ali Mazrui, **The African A Triple Heritage** (Boston: Little Brown and Company, 1986).

of a theological and revelational one: the coming of Christ is the center of history because it gives history its meaning and its saving efficacy, by incarnating the saving principle of love and hope in the human world. All historical events, whether before or after Christ, are to be interpreted in the light of Christ and evaluated in the light of his work and person. In Christ, we can find an interpretative and evaluative compass for the movement of history. Time is thus the condition for the possibility of liberation and salvation of the human person and human societies both in the political and economic, as well as in the cultural and spiritual spheres. The time for liberation is NOW. Time is also cosmic embracing all creation. In the light of the Incarnation, world history is no longer to be viewed in a purely ideological and profane manner, but in the light of its salvation in the happiness, truth, and love which God gives us in Christ.

The world is in the process of becoming, and the act of creation is continuously moving in the direction of its liberation when our limited perception of truth, our fractious institutions and our imperfect expressions of love at the personal, group, and corporate levels will be realized because of the saving presence of God's Spirit in history. The historical-chronological background of the New Testament goes back to the initial process of creation, but it rises beyond a merely temporal conception to a redemptive ever-present reality, that is love-centered because it is Christ-centered. We find ourselves then in a realm of complexities and possibilities.

The Christian vision provides this understanding that we are made for one another and for God; that life has meaning only when it is given up for something higher than life and that people are not enemies and rivals to be conquered and defeated, but persons to be encountered in the mutual act of love and understanding. This world seen in the light of Christ is not a vale of tears or a war front where we feed on hatred, vengeance, and selfishness. Human suffering and pain and the increasing incidents of acts of terrorism and hatred do not constitute part of the purpose of creation. Poverty, exploitation, and injustice are the signs of a world in need of liberation from man-made negative forces. The human person is made to love and this is incarnated in the heart of each person and in the heart of all human civilizations.

However, this Christian vision is not absolute; it resonates in various religions and can be enriched from insights from other religions. The parliament of world religions, in its Chicago declaration of September 4, 1993 (Hans Kung, 1996, 12-17), calls on the various religions to articulate a joint vision to promote human development and reduce the increasing cases of violence and wars carried out in the name of religion. It also calls on world religions to build a culture of peace, solidarity, and tolerance among them. As in the thoughts of Socrates: wisdom demands that we do not claim any kind of certainty since everything we say and all social realities are liable to some form of revision in the light of newer truth. One should be careful, before drinking to the dregs, any political or religious theories, especially a totalizing one that is being projected by tunnel-vision thinkers. I do, therefore, think that the Christian vision, which I present as a response to the African condition, is one in the many other possibilities that can be offered to the African continent.

The vision that is needed for a better world is one that embodies the whole picture of the human person, because the human person is over and above social institutions. We need to appreciate once more in the world the imponderable value of the human person, his or her dignity and nobility, and the summons from God that each person should live fully in the world. This dignity is well captured by Shakespeare when he writes, "What a piece of work is a man! How noble in reason! How infinite in faculties! In form and moving, how express and admirable! In action, how like an angel! In apprehension, how like a god! The beauty of the world! The paragon of animals!"

This vision is germane for Africa, a continent in which the dignity of the human person is often insulted by sub-human living conditions, violence, and disease. Africa, in addition, is a continent in search of a future, which it can only find by embodying the sense of love and community in her social, political, economic, and cultural life. The love of life demands a culture of hard work and hope. This conception is deeply embedded in the religious traditions of Africa where love, hard work, commitment to life and reality, solidarity and community are central to authentic religion. The only logic that can convince African people to take up the task of living again in spite of many present difficulties is the power of love, which radicalizes everything. The Africans need to know that they can find justice and love in the political and social process and that they would find justice, love, solidarity, and equity in the world.

Unless we are able to make real and concrete the love of God in our society we cannot lay claim to authentic humanity. Love is the heart of the world and the heart of God. I, therefore, make a case that Africa should be loved by both Africans and non-Africans. This appeal is also made on behalf of the voiceless sea of people who are marginalized all over the world. These are people who are suffering, because we live in a world that has a superabundance of wealth but a scarcity of love.

CHAPTER ONE

THE SHADOWS OF AFRICA

The disintegration caused by external influences in African society reveals a dilemma for Africans. They are becoming more and more hybridized. The rapidity with which the traditional is being lost or severely modified, and with which the new is being apparently adopted, leave very little time for the Africans to fully understand the new forms of European customs and institutions they are adopting. They do not have the time, or do not take the trouble, to make a judicious selection of what is best in the European for a grafting upon what is best in old Africa.
- E. A. Ayandele

1.1 A Crisis of Identity

What does it mean to be an African in the world today? What do the Africans think of themselves? What does the outside world think of Africa? These are questions of vital importance in appreciating the present condition of the African continent and her future.

There is a crisis of identity among Africans, which stems from their lack of self-definition and their confusion about their place in the world. This is at the root of the homelessness of the Africans. This crisis affects every aspect of life in Africa: cultural, intellectual, economic, political, religious, and social. A people who are not self-conscious and who cannot define where they stand culturally, from a human point of view cannot really and concretely take control of their fate and fortune in the historical process. A people who do not believe in themselves and take firm control of their destiny cannot define their future. A people who neglect their history and cultural identity may not have the foundational impetus to appropriate their inner riches and strengths.

An essential component of survival is an innate belief in oneself. Believing in oneself demands an admission of the fact of one's history, the acceptance of the truth of one's present reality and a courageous confrontation with the challenges of the moment with an eye on charting a new path for the future. The question of African identity is one that has occupied the minds of most perceptive Africans, since the end of the era of slavery, the beginning of colonialism and the emergence of Pan-Africanism, Négritude and nationalist movements in Africa. The question is about what it means to be an African. The cultural traditions of Africa, the history of Africa, African civilization, African values, African religion and spirituality, and her stock of knowledge and rationality along with what she has gained or lost in her contact with cultures and civilizations outside Africa, all constitute African identity. As Rowan Williams has argued in his influential work, *Lost Icons: Reflections on Cultural Bereavement*,[1] a loss of identity creates cultural bereavement, leaving a people with fragmented systems, a vague sense of right or wrong, a lack of direction and imprisonment in immediacy and selfishness. It also weakens the people's ability to work together to build a better society. Many Africans do believe that the recovery of African identity will involve *an African memory*: a retelling of the African story in an objective way and a healing of memories. This narrative imagination will create the space for conversation, for group reflection and group action to recover what was golden in the past, to capture what is valid for the present and to project into the future by a synthesis of the total reality of the experience of Mother Africa. As an Igbo tribal saying renders it: *ncheta ka* ('it pays to remember' or 'memory offers more'). Remembering the past offers a 'surplus value' for it makes the past to come alive not as concrete past, but a reconfigured reality that offers meaning to the present and hope for the future. Every African must remember Africa; every African must remember also the inter-connection between civilizations and cultures and the sad and glorious phases of our human history. It is in reaching deep into these African and global realities that Africans can collectively say: *never again*. Never again will Africans allow themselves to become slaves to non-Africans or internal slaves within Africa to fellow Africans. Never again will they allow bad governments and dictators to squander the wealth and future of their children. Never again will they allow ethnic division to destroy the works and dreams of the past heroes and heroines of Africa. Never again shall the future of African children be sacrificed for the sake of greed and power mongering. Never again shall Africans allow diseases that are preventable and curable to decimate the continent. However, to recover this sense of African identity will take a long journey that will demand a collective consciousness and a collective effort. It demands sacrifice.

The need for a true African identity has assumed greater resonance in the present global situation, where Africans are facing seemingly insuperable difficulties, different subtle forms of discrimination and economic blockages from non-African peoples, nations and financial institutions.

This is also made more urgent because of the internal national problems that have kept millions of Africans on the margins of the good things of life. Africans struggle with the question of their self-understanding, both in terms of their personality and their living condition. This has relevance in determining the place of Africans in the world and their destiny in a globalizing world.

The question should be asked whether Africans believe in themselves and in their continent. In today's world, according to Samuel P. Huntington, "Peoples and nations are attempting to answer the most basic question humans face: Who are we?, and they are answering that question in the traditional way human beings have answered it, by reference to the things that mean most to them. People define themselves in terms of ancestry, religion, language, history, values, customs, and institutions. They identify with cultural groups: tribes, ethnic groups, religious communities, nations, and at the broadest level, civilizations. People use politics not just to advance their interests but also to define their identity. We know who we are only when we know who we are not and often when we know who we are against."[2]

The absence of a true African identity is tied to the absence of authentic African cultural values in present day African societies. It is true that people are, "unable to live in peace until furnished with a social identity, an outward garb which, by representing them to others, gives them confidence in themselves. This search for 'identity' pervades modern life...The cultivation of 'identity' is a mode of being-for-others, to use the existentialist jargon, a way of claiming space in a public world."[3] It is quite true that the African continent has many cultural traditions, but there is a convergence of values in the continent based on shared historical experience. However, these values are sometimes not reflected in the way Africans live and work in families, businesses and in political life. It is important in the inter-civilizational conflicts of the contemporary world, for Africans to define who they are and who they want to be. Oscillating between Western models of economics, government and cultural patterns and their African variants is only a step towards worsening the existential crisis of Africans.

This is also the situation with the two major religions that have taken root in Africa: Christianity and Islam. The reason for the apparent failure of both religions to reshape the African world is because of the failure of adherents of the two religions to adapt the main creedal and ethical contents of these two religions to African cultural life. Added to this, is the negative dynamics that have accompanied African Tradition Religions because of its misinterpretation by the early Christian and Islamic missionaries. Unless Christianity becomes culture in Africa, Africans cannot lay claim to its vibrant presence in the continent. Christianity is dying in the Western world because it is no longer the way of life of Westerners, who are vigorously fighting, albeit unsuccessfully, to separate religion from their culture. Given the present state of the Christian faith in the West, it is no longer possible for Westerners to dictate or define the future direction of global Christianity.

Islam appears to adopt a universalism, which yokes all Muslims in a brotherhood, which is clothed in an Arabic cultural garment. However, the political and economic conditions in Islamic countries like Indonesia and Turkey do show that Islam, like all other religions, is not hostile to cultural and political pluralisms "Just the same, any religion that promises reward or punishment after death for actions performed during life, as Islam does, embodies a theory of liberty, even if that theory is tacit and undeveloped. Historically, Islamic theologians have scarcely lingered on this premise, the workings of human liberty. But those who bet that the hunger for liberty burns as much in the bosom of Muslims as it does among Christians and Jews are not likely to be wrong."[4] Muslims in Africa must be the agents for the modernization and Africanization of Islam based on the particular context of each African country. The challenge facing many Muslims in sub-Saharan Africa is to make Islam adapt to the cultural situation in those countries, which also have a significant Christian presence. Both Muslims and Christians in Africa must be open enough to accept that their respective religions are only one of the many possible religious practices in Africa.

Many African Traditional Religionists are becoming increasingly vocal in their opposition to Christianity and Islam. In the case of Christianity, many see no reason why they should convert to Christianity, when Western societies that brought the Christian faith to Africa are rejecting Christianity and some of her teachings. In the case of Islam, the African traditional worshipers are not easily drawn to Islam because African Muslims have not proselytized as extensively as their forebears. In addition, there is a conflict in Africa, among Muslims which is not easily discernable over what kind of Islam will hold sway among Africans. This conflict is often seen in the random doctrinal clashes between the radical Islamic brotherhoods and the more liberal groups and between the Islamic adherents in North Africa and their brothers and sisters in sub-Saharan Africa.

Christianity today faces a crisis of identity especially in the West that has been historically Christian. Many people in Western countries are convinced that religion must be separated from politics. Politicians and policy-makers have accepted the secularity of their countries and draw a fine line between their private religious practices and their public life. However, I do not think that having a secular state should mean the adoption of secularism, which denies the place of religion in public life. Religion and faith must become culture, just as faith and life ought to be intimately united in the daily existence of the adherents of any form of religious belief. This means that religion can be real if it embraces every aspect of life whether for the individual or a people or a nation. The separation of religion and politics in many Western societies often implies the rejection of religion.

The secular state is to be perceived, in my perspective, as a country in which the politics and the government are not an extension of the governance of an institutional religion. It means the autonomy of the secular realm free of any religious creed and any leaning to any particular faith. It means also that government should not be controlled by religious organizations. However, this should not be construed to mean that politicians should not publicly profess their faith and apply their moral convictions in their involvement in government; nor does it mean the rejection of religious signs and symbols or, more deeply, the place of religious values in the state and public square. "The Church made Europe into a community of nations. Often divided among themselves, often enemies, they nonetheless remained conscious of their original fraternity. Through what is now happening, and through a change of spirit in their consciences, Christians now stand by, watching the destruction of one of history's most precious concepts."[5]

Thomas E. Woods has shown how Western civilization was established on the foundation of the Christian faith.[6] He continues the argument of many Christian writers like Christopher Dawson that it was Christianity that truly established the basis of true liberalism, which today has been widely misinterpreted as unfettered freedom from traditional social control, traditional beliefs, institutions, morality and the foundations of human nature and human destiny. Dawson argues that Christianity gave birth to liberalism, because "at the root of the development of Western freedom and Western democracy there lies the medieval idea that men possess rights even against the state and that society is not a totalitarian political unit but a community made up of a complex variety of social organisms each possessing an autonomous life and its own free institutions."[7]

This position is well presented by Benedict XVI, when he writes of the cultural crisis in Europe, "The act of setting aside Europe's Christian roots is not, after all, the expression of a superior tolerance that respects all cultures equally, and refrains from privileging any of them, but rather the absolutization of a way of thinking and living that stands in radical contrast, among other things, to the other historical cultures of humanity...As a religion of the persecuted, as a universal religion that reached beyond states and peoples, Christianity denied the state the right to regard religion as a part of its own order, and so claimed freedom for faith."[8] When Western civilization, which defines itself historically as Christian, institutionally denies the place of Christianity in any aspect of the public square, it loses the inner dynamics of her life and places herself in the bumps and bends of ethical relativism, and an amorphous multiculturalism that has no real content.

The continent of Africa that received the Christian faith through Western civilization suffers from this crisis of civilization in the West. The only way African Christians can escape from this crisis is for Africans to evolve a uniquely African variant of the Christian faith. Many African theologians are increasingly calling attention to the danger of regarding Western Christianity as the single model of Christian faith. Western Christianity is only one way among many ways of responding to Christ. According to Lamin Sanneh,[9] there is resurgence in worldwide Christianity, which is proving that religious convictions transcend ethnic, national and cultural barriers and so cannot be restricted to the personal domain as many Western politicians and policy makers are trying to establish. Religion is entangled with our roots that we cannot deny its hold on us and its intimate connection to our history. Western secularism lacks a universalizing power, because it does not resonate in other cultures with the same rhythm of association. Secularity is not at odds with Christianity but proponents of secularism forget that secularity, a principle with its germs in Christianity, was meant to protect the state and individual rights and not to suppress religion by any means. It is important that the rest of global Christianity should see the emerging churches in Africa as part of the budding forth of African identity. Indeed, other Christian ways and paths that are emerging in Africa can no longer be considered marginal, but are an essential part of the Christian identity and a unique contribution of Africans to the multiple richness and diverse expressions of the Christian experience.

The consequence of the neglect of the unique religio-cultural experience of the Africans by the early Christian missionaries, is the oscillation among African Christians between the African Traditional Religions and their various acquired faiths. This has led to shallow religious practices that have been wrongly perceived as evidence of Christian religious revival in Africa. Any discerning student of religion in Africa would easily notice this conflict present in the syncretism of a substantial percentage of adherents to Christianity. Sometimes the wars of religion and the conflicts between adherents of Islam and Christianity in places like Nigeria, Uganda, Kenya, Tanzania and Egypt reveal a total departure from the real values of these religions in the hearts of the people. It also shows that religion has become both a means of political control and economic progress in some African countries. Thus, religion is made a means and not an end, while religious and political leaders easily mingle and mutually sustain each other's claim to power and hegemony. In cases where religious leaders have risen to defend the interest of good governance and the plight of the ordinary people, they have been faced with persecution. However, in places like the Democratic Republic of Congo, Liberia, Benin, Mozambique and Nigeria, at the end of the day they helped reshape economic and social policies and changed the course of the political process.

An authentic religion in Africa is one that is shorn of pragmatic suasions, psychosocial elixir and effete consolatory religious platitudes for the afflicted of Africa. It must be activist, engaging squarely with the forces of injustice in the continent, while giving the people a reason to hope and a reason to suffer in the present for a better future. It ought also to promote a culture of love and life built on the ongoing dynamics of personal and group conversion and transformation.

True religion has three basic components: conversion, transformation and transcendence. Conversion is the recognition of who we are. It is to see ourselves in a mirror and to take off our masks. In this discovery, we come to appreciate our origin (God) and our destiny (a better future that moves beyond shadows even unto the light of eternity) which we share with others. This also makes us realize our vulnerability and our need for love and connections with God, our fellow human beings and nature. Conversion leads to transformation which leads the human person to long for change in one's life and in the lives of others and the community. It means taking a step up the scale of being in the direction of a deeper appreciation of who we are and the meaning of life, community, death, happiness, peace, justice and other higher realities. As we step higher and higher, we transcend the particularities and concreteness of selfishness and wickedness and expand in a wholesome manner as a liberated and loving people, who can live for others and not only for ourselves and who now live for a tomorrow not just for today. In transcendence we see the presence and power of love which is the summit of our journey on earth. The measure of the true value of any religion is to what extent it promotes the peace and happiness of humankind and projects the ideal of love. The religion we need in the world of today is not the one that tends to totalize and swallow everyone in the blaze of dogmatism or violence, but one that creates conditions for love and peace and readily concretizes in the hearts of adherents genuine concern for others, especially the weaker members of society. Any religion that preaches ultimate peace with God but promotes war, terrorism and division is one that has lost its soul.

Every true religion must make people be at home with who they are, and see themselves in a spiritual and temporal chain that connects one to all. This kind of religion is possible in Africa, and the whole world, if only religious adherents would be open to conversion, transformation and transcendence. This is particularly realistic for Africa because Africans are incurably religious. What is urgently needed is religious leadership to steer Africans to the highest heights of the worship of the true God and service to their fellow men and women. There is a deep religious sentiment in Africa where everything is seen through the eyes of faith. This cultural life is easily amenable to the three main religions in Africa. The question then that should be asked is how Africans in their religious profession and vibrant religious expression define their religious identity: who do Africans say God is and why do Africans flock to churches, mosques, temples and shrines in large numbers? Are Africans at home with the Christian and Islamic faiths because they have become ways of life which answer the Africans' hunger for deep religious experience that permeates all life? Are Africans religious because religion conduces to the present African condition or are they religious because they love God and wish to establish his kingdom here on earth?

Do Africans believe in themselves and in their respective countries? Do they see their fate and fortune intimately tied with the future of their countries? After the horrors of Hiroshima and Nagasaki, Japan within five decades put herself on the prosperous map of the world and by the late 1990's was enjoying a higher balance sheet in her trade with Western countries like United States and Britain. This is a paradigm of what national survival means: a commitment to hard work, a high priority placed on education, especially science and technology, an agrarian revolution, strong patriotic sentiment, attachment to national progress and development, and authentic religious sentiments and practices. There is an urgent need for African countries to look inward and search for African solutions to African problems. There should emerge a culture of excellence amplified by a deep sense of national purpose for the reinvention of the African soul. This cannot come about unless there is an invasion, as it were, of new ideas. This is not a sprint but a marathon, and Africa needs to put on the shoes of the long-distance runner. What is needed is a culture of patience smelted in the furnace of hope, which gives the rare strength for delayed gratification. The problems of Africa will not go away overnight and Africans must be prepared to go through the mills and pay the price of development and democracy in the right coin. It might take some time for the continent to begin a real journey to national integration and development; however, taking the first positive step is essential in beginning the journey. It would be disastrous if Africans abandon themselves into the inexorable hand of the historical process evidently controlled by Western capitalist hawks, who worship the gods of the New York stock exchange and understand only the language of competition and profit.

The African continent cannot survive by depending on Western grants. There are not enough grounds to justify Africa's beggarly status in the world. The leadership of African countries should not blame the African condition only on Western exploitation. Any exploiter will always have local turncoats among the exploited in order to carry out any act of injustice. There is no reason why the present trend in the continent cannot be reversed by Africans. This is because there is no difficulty that nations face which they cannot overcome with committed visionary leadership and patriotic citizens. The African continent cannot survive if her greatest and brightest stars have an antipathy for their countries and cannot apply their talents to the development of their respective countries. There is a sense of angst among Africans and most people of African origin think that their bread is buttered in Western countries, where everything seems to work better than in Africa. Leaving Africa is often seen as answers to prayers and those who live abroad are considered the most privileged. Why is it that most African intellectuals, writers, artists, musicians, athletes and religious leaders prefer to live abroad and/or to spend their vacations in Europe and North America? Many Africans want to leave the continent to look for greener pastures because they do not think that there is any future for their respective countries. In a certain sense, this might be true when we look at the growing insecurity in the continent, the collapsed social structures of society, the growing inefficiency of public corporations and the failure of governments. Most public corporations in Africa are citadels of corruption and triumphs of sprawling inefficiency. But unless Africans *think home* and act decisively and courageously, this continent will continue to be one whose future remains in a dreamland. Keeping this concern in perspective is necessary and determinative for the continent and her peoples. What does the future hold for our children and what does the future hold for our culture and our civilization?

1.2 Africa in the Eyes of Non-Africans

What does the outside world think of Africa? This is a question which may take us down memory lane. In the first place, I wish to assert clearly that I do not think there is anything wrong with the land and clime of Africa. There is nothing poisonous about the air the people who live in Africa breathe. There is nothing strange about the character of Africans as those who have encountered authentic Africans can testify. There is nothing wrong with the African mind nor are Africans prone to violence. Africans enjoy the kinds of things every other person in any part of the world enjoys: love, fun, sports, religion, nature, good food and drink, friendship, education, and society in general. Sometimes in my encounter with non-Africans in North America and Europe, I am asked some funny questions like: Do you have dogs in Africa (some do not even know that Africa is a continent of 53 different countries)? Do you eat meat in Africa? Do you have McDonalds in Africa? The story is told of an African who visited Europe for the first time and was taken to a lunch by his Italian host. While he was enjoying the meat and bones served, the following dialogue ensued between them:

"Waoh, you seem to be enjoying this meat, my dear African friend."

"Yes, I like beef," replied the African.

"Really, I didn't know you ate beef in Africa; I thought you ate only antelope and other wild animals."

"No," replied the African, "wild animals are kept in the zoo and actually it is the lions and tigers that eat beef."

Then watching as the African chopped away the meat from the bone, the European wondered, "Why then do you enjoy beef and particularly the bones...?"

"Well," replied the African, "it is because you offered me no carrot." The European, I suppose, would also be wondering whether Africans ate carrots too.

I was once asked by an Italian friend what I liked doing for sports and when I told him I liked swimming, he was very much surprised. According to him, swimming doesn't take much physical strength and he thought Africans were more interested in hunting wild animals and in mountain climbing. There is a clear lack of adequate knowledge about Africa among non-Africans. The information people have about the continent of Africa is greatly distorted. I was once told by a Canadian who heard of the crisis in Darfur that I must be absolutely lucky to be out of that mess. He asked me if my family was safe. I laughed away reminding him that I am a Nigerian and not a Sudanese, but thanked him though for his concern. I was, however, shocked at how little he knew about Africa given his education and exposure. This is unfortunate in the world of today where there is a lot of information on literally anything around the globe. A deeper understanding of the various cultures and civilizations of the world would help to promote dialogue, collaboration and community in the world. The situation in some parts of Africa might sometimes give a wrong impression about this beautiful continent.

The present situation in Africa has nothing to do with the African person as such; it has everything to do with the process of history in Africa. An interpretative historical analysis of Africa within the last two hundred years is necessary in proffering any kind of prognosis into the future of Africa. It would also offer some analytical keys in both appreciating the difficulties and challenges facing this continent and how best to respond to the emerging situations in this continent of emergent probability. There are both external and internal factors that conspire in placing most Africans at the very margins of the good things of life. The external factors shall be explored in this chapter as they relate to what non-Africans, and especially what the West brought to Africa through acts of commission, omission and distancing. We shall also expose how Africans cooperate with Westerners to contour the face of Africa. The internal factors relate to what we Africans have brought upon our continent by our collective failure to build a community of love, justice, peace and solidarity. This is the main task that we take in the second and third chapters.

Many people thought that the rise of pro-democratic movements in Africa with the end of the Cold War in the 1990's would mark the rebirth of the African continent. Unfortunately, successive events have shown that transplanting Western democracy to Africa has only perpetuated Africa's identity crisis. The pro-democratic movements in Africa were only a leftover of the battle for freedom which left the Eastern Bloc in an age-encrusted wall of dictatorship and autocracy. The factors that led to the collapse of the Berlin Wall were not particularly related to Africa, just as the factors that led to the erection of that wall had nothing to do with the African continent.

It was not strange that African countries imploded after the end of the Cold War, because some of the wars in Africa and the tension and rebellions in countries like Angola, NguemaMozambique, South Africa, Namibia, and the two Congos were sustained by Western countries. These Western countries supported one group against the other based on their allegiance to Western or Eastern Bloc. This stance was well-captured by the former American Secretary of State, Henry Kissinger, when he wrote with regard to the ideological battle in Africa, especially in Angola and Mozambique: "While ideologically strongly opposed to militant Marxism, the Ford Administration had never sought to prevent Marxist or quasi-Marxist governments from coming to power in Africa so long as their roots were indigenous. We maintained working contacts with left-wing African countries such as Algeria and Tanzania, and, as noted, we recognized successor Marxist regimes in other Portuguese colonies. Our red line was intervention from outside the continent and domination from Moscow."[10]

Particularly significant in this ideological war between the West and the East was the case of South Africa. It was not surprising that Nelson Mandela's release on February 11, 1990 and the movement towards majority rule and the abrogation of the apartheid policy took place only at the end of the Cold War. Nelson Mandela was regarded by the repressive apartheid government and its Western backers as a dangerous communist terrorist. Since the fear of communism was the beginning of Western wisdom it was safer to put Mandela away for 27 years. In this way, he was effectively prevented from spreading his so-called communist agenda to the rest of Africa. Today's terrorist in the eyes of some Western governments might become tomorrow's heroes depending on whose interests are being served. Those countries in Southern Africa like Mozambique and Angola that espoused Marxist agenda were hounded and harassed on all fronts by the United States, South Africa and Britain. The rebel groups, Mozambican National Resistance (*Resistencia Nacional Mocambicana*, RENAMO) and the National Union for the Total Independence of Angola (UNITA) that fought against these African governments had the backing of some Western governments. Nobody has yet explained the mysterious plane crash that killed the dynamic and well-loved former President of Mozambique, Samora Machel. President Machel and 33 of his top officials perished on the fateful Sunday evening of October 19, 1986. Machel was a good friend of Nelson Mandela and offered military and financial support to the African National Congress fighting the apartheid regime in South Africa. The crash that took his life occurred in South Africa's air space in the Eastern Transvaal region. Even though the International Commission of Inquiry cleared the South African government of any complicity in the crash, many Southern Africans are convinced that there was foul play.

The divisions in African countries, caused by the divide between the West and the East were not resolved by the Western powers that created them. This was because they had no real interest in the future of the continent beyond raw materials and other mineral resources. They were more concerned with dealing with the consequences of the end of the Cold War, and the conflicts it brought to most countries of Eastern Europe.

The emergence of democracies in Africa after the Cold War only revealed the inner contradictions in African countries. It also highlighted the need for a different system of government, based on a paradigm shift that builds on a true understanding and interpretation of the process of social integration in African societies. Democracy is not the total answer to social inequalities and stratification nor should it be a mask over social disintegration; it is also not the answer to political instability in many African countries. Democracy does not mean the setting up of political parties, national elections, and the establishment of national parliaments or even the inauguration of a president. African countries undertook all these 'democratic processes' after their Independence, but all of them failed. Democracy emerges with the presence of a political culture and political socialization. These precede democracy rather than being the result of democracy. This is particularly true given the fact that the citizens of most African countries do not understand and respect the law and inner workings of Western democracy; but they appreciate and respect their long-held traditional social networks of interest protection, local administration and social and political organizations with its chain of command.

Democracy in its Western variant is not the single model for organizing human societies all over the world and should not be imposed on Africans without regard to the African context. The specific virtues of Western democracy or lack of it are not connatural to all cultures nor are they applicable to all cultures. All cultures respect and cherish freedom and abhor tyranny through their vision of human dignity, human nature and the proper ordering of society. This might not be consciously articulated, but it is buried in the heart of all human civilization. "As Tocqueville pointed out, democracy takes on different forms in different cultures— its development would be different in France, he predicted, from its development in America."[11] Building a vibrant civil society in Africa is a basic step towards an enduring participatory and inclusive democracy. "A weak state is alchemy for disaster and a poor platform for erecting the structure of democracy or civil society...A weak state reflects the weakness of the constitutive elements of its society. When a weak state becomes incapacitated and loses legitimacy, other alternative power contenders come to the fore."[12] Most African countries are weak states, because the basic components of statehood are non-existent and the civil society lacks the vibrancy that offers an alternate response to governance. When there is no proper articulation of the shared sentiments of the people, especially the uncaptured and silent majority, there can be no genuine democracy.

Many social scientists like Francis Fukuyama, have developed the theory that history is moving towards liberal democracy, and the future of nations is to be interpreted through the prism of their advance towards it. Freedom will always reign over repression and inner conviction will most certainly triumph over compulsion and domination; however, the evolution of a constitutional democracy in Africa is a journey that demands the building of the relevant structures. The fundamental question for Africans in this regard is: What kind of democracy is being proposed and what form of government is being proposed for African countries? I agree with the English poet, Alexander Pope, that the form of government is not as important as the quality of the leadership and I would add, the quality of the citizenry. As he wrote in *The Contestation of Fools:* "For forms of government let fools contest; whatever is best administered is best." Building a strong and enlightened populace is the first step to an African woven liberal democracy.

This is not peculiar to Africa, as Robert D. Kaplan has argued.[13] According to Kaplan, democracy carried in the vessels of Westernization, to countries that are not sufficiently prepared for it, would mean disaster. This was the case in the Sudan of 1985, which after electing a democratic government descended into anarchy and brutal tyranny, which led to the Arabization of Africans and the persecution of non-Muslims and women. It was in this Sudan that Osama bin Laden found shelter as Khartoum replaced Beirut, albeit temporarily as the terrorism capital of the Arab world. Elections in Sudan have largely been sectarian. According to Gabriel Warburg, since 1989 when Sudan became a militant Sunni-Islamist state under the guidance of Hasan al-Turabi, the question whether the Islamic political tradition as expressed in its Islamic constitution is compatible with democracy has remained unanswered. Sudan offers a case where democracy has produced an autocratic Islamic government that actively works against the interest of a greater portion of the population including Black Muslims and Christians. It could be true, as Francis Deng has argued that in Africa, referring specifically to Sudan, democracy has become a dictatorship of numbers build atop ethnic, racial and religious identities.[14]

Tunisia for instance was not a democracy in 1992 but was more peaceful than Algeria or Nigeria which went into national crises after elections were cancelled by military governments in 1992 and 1993 respectively. The democratic Zimbabwe of today is more chaotic than Gaddafi's non-democratic Libya. In Nigeria, Sierra Leone, Cote d'Ivoire, Congo-Brazzaville, and Mali, elections have variously led to civil wars, killings, riots and chaos. The worst ethnic genocide in African history in Rwanda happened under the aegis of a multiparty democracy, when ethnic bigots hid under the banner of multipartyism to unleash the horrors of hatred on fellow Africans. The conclusion must be made that democracy is the capstone of other social and economic achievements. Democracy cannot be imposed as most colonial Lords in Africa did prior to Independence. All these democracies failed because they had no foundation. Democracy in the Western world evolved. Basing on the thought of Alexis Tocqueville who studied democracy in America, Kaplan argues that democracy evolved in the West not through the kind of moral fiat which the West is trying to impose throughout the world, but as an organic outgrowth of development. European society had reached a level of complexity and sophistication at which the aristocracy, so as not to overburden itself, had to confer a measure of equality upon other citizens and allocate some responsibility to them: a structured division of the population into peacefully competing interest groups was necessary if both tyranny and anarchy were to be averted.[15] However, even with the emergence of democracy in the Western world, the world witnessed the horrors of the Holocaust perpetrated by a 'democratic' Germany.

The history of Africa within the last five decades has been a history of failed democratic experiments. However, the reasons for the failure of democracies in Africa and her arrested development are to be found in the convoluted history of the continent. The experience of slavery, colonial exploitation, racism, apartheid, debt burden, the demon of globalization, and the present isolationistic tendency of the world towards Africa has frozen the continent in the cold valley of despair. It is this situation worsened by the failed leadership in Africa and the pervasive corruption in the continent that is accountable for the present condition of Africa and has given Africa a negative image in the international community. There are three ways in which Africa has been seen in the eyes of the outside world, especially in the Western Hemisphere: Africa as a 'dark' continent, Africa as a continent to be exploited, and Africa as a continent to be encountered as part of a common humanity.

Africa as a dark continent bereft of any genuine good for humanity: This is the kind of mentality that regards Africa as a land of darkness and death or as one early explorer described it "a universal den of desolation, misery, and crime." Olufemi Taiwo has demonstrated in a well-researched paper that at the ideological level, this perception of Africa can be traced to G. W. F. Hegel.[16] According to Taiwo, for Hegel, Africa proper is shut up from the rest of the world by its geography as well as by the strange character of her peoples. Africans lack the category of universality. "This arises from the fact that they are one with their existence; they are arrested in immediacy. This means that they have not separated themselves from nature. 'The Negroes,' wrote Hegel 'exhibits the natural man in his completely wild and untamed state.' As such, the African is shorn of the idea of the self that is separate from his needs and, simultaneously, has no knowledge of 'an absolute Being,' an Other and a Higher than his individual selfs."[17] Hegel, who wrote that Africa is 'enveloped in the dark mantle of the night' disparages Africa this way, "At this point we leave Africa, not to mention it again. For it is no historical part of the world; it has no movement or development to exhibit. Historical movements in it--that is its northern part—belong to the Asiatic or European world. Carthage displayed there an important transitionary phase of civilization; but, as a Phoenician colony, it belongs to Asia. Egypt will be considered in reference to the passage from the human mind from its Eastern to its Western phase, but it does not belong to the African Spirit. *What we properly understand by Africa, is the Unhistorical, Undeveloped Spirit, still involved in the conditions of mere nature, (my emphasis)* and which had to be presented here only as on the threshold of the World's History."[18]

There are many non-Africans today who still think like Hegel. This kind of thinking is based on a lack of adequate information about the African continent. It is also based on prejudice and untested assumptions and stereotypes of Africa and Africans built and sustained by Western media and partisan Western commentators. There is an obvious paternalistic mindset among non-Africans with regard to Africa. What many Westerners have not understood is that Africa is not all about naked children rummaging for food in refuse dumps or dying men and women with wasted flesh hanging on mere skeletons; Africa is not a land of violence and turmoil. There is much to Africa than what is presented in Western media; there is another face of Africa which is not easily seen in Western media. These negative images of Africa even though sometimes stemming from pure motives, rob Africans of their dignity and give false impressions on the possibility of a better future for Africa.

As the G8 deliberated in Gleneagles, Scotland in June 2005 over the fate of the world, especially the African condition, many Western leaders were pontificating about Africa albeit with a considerable bias fed by misinformation and settled stereotypes. They ignore the significant progress being made in African countries like Nigeria, South Africa, Ghana and Senegal in the fight against corruption and dictatorship. Some of the G8 leaders display a paternalistic attitude toward Africa. They think Africa is a child that should be given benchmarks of good behavior and rewarded accordingly as she has followed these conditions. Those Western leaders and agencies who see Africa and Africans as backward and lacking in proper rationality, with regard to the ordering of their society, will always impose on Africa their own way of life, and interpret the African world with Western biases and categories—a category which unfortunately has been built over centuries of regarding Africa as a land 'enveloped in the dark mantle of the night.'

When the first Western (Portuguese) explorers arrived in Africa in 1440, many of them died as a result of diseases, especially malaria, which were not known to the Western world at that time. Many outsiders have not overcome this initial image of Africa and would rather have nothing to do with Africans. This kind of thinking also contributed to the slave trade, to racism and discrimination which many Africans suffer even to this day at the hands of some non-Africans who are not liberated from the mental bondage of racial exclusivity.

The mantra that Africans are suffering because of Africa's over population is actively supported by people who do not think that African population is a key factor in Africa's development. They argue that there is no rationale in bringing more people into the world in Africa when those who are living do not have the basic necessities of life. Millions of dollars were spent actively promoting all forms of birth control including abortion in Africa, while the real causes of poverty in Africa were being ignored. Jacqueline Kasun has exposed the fallacy of the overpopulation myth as it affects Africa and other developing countries vis-à-vis the developed world in her great work, *The War Against Population*.[19] Her exposition of the intricate web of deception that has characterized the anti-population movement and its distortion of reality is breath-taking. She argues that since 1950, in the effort to promote one agenda or another, whether it is sterilization, abortion, infanticide, assisted suicide or euthanasia, the messengers of doom and their spin-doctors have gone to work. They frighten humanity with one portending calamity or another, whether it is in connection with population, resource exhaustion or climate change. When one of those loses credibility they come up with another purveyed through the schools, media, and governmental agencies and non-governmental organizations as well as the United Nations.[20] The unexamined, uncritical and diversionary over-population dogma, which is perceived as the cause of the collapsing social and economic structures in Africa is, to say the least, one that is founded on misleading logic and a distortion of facts. Its proponents do not understand the African world nor do they mean well for the continent and her peoples. Some of these aggressive campaigns for the reduction of African population have fizzled out because HIV/AIDS appears to be helping their cause.

There are many governments and organizations today that will not have anything to do with the African continent, because they believe that nothing good will come out of this continent. The negative publicity given to the events in Africa whether it is war, the HIV/AIDS epidemic, economic hardship or political instability tends to justify this position. Many people, who think this way, feel that Africa has nothing to offer the world other than an unending tale of suffering and human misery. What kind of investment would people who think this way make in Africa? What kind of engagement would they enter into with African governments and agencies? They would rather treat Africa with the proverbial long spoon. It is this mentality in the modern era that led to the Rwandan genocide. The international community looked the other way, when Africans killed each other, in a war which otherwise could have been avoided. Reflecting on the Rwandan tragedy, the former commander of the UN Assistance Mission for Rwanda (UNAMIR), General Romeo Dellaire bemoans, "It's a story of betrayal, failure, naïveté, indifference, hatred, genocide, war, inhumanity and evil. ...overshadowed by one of the fastest, most efficient, most evident genocides in recent history. In just one hundred days over 800,000 innocent Rwandan men, women and children were brutally murdered while the developed world, impassive and apparently unperturbed, sat back and watched the unfolding apocalypse or simply changed channels."[21] The lingering wars and refugee crisis in the Great Lakes region, the carnage that has been happening in Southern and Western Sudan and the human atrocities committed in Liberia and Sierra Leone would have been averted if the international community regarded the African continent as one that has some good. The crime being committed by Western pharmaceutical agencies in refusing to make available low priced antiretroviral (ARV) medication for HIV/AIDS to millions of Africans, would have been stopped by a resolution of the United Nations, if the lives of Africans were regarded as worth any value by the international community. It is worth highlighting the fact that the way Africa and Africans are treated by the world is more a result of the way they are perceived by non-Africans.

Africa as a land to be exploited for the good of the Western world without any good for the Africans. In 1964, the United Nations Survey of Economic Conditions had this to say of the African continent: "Africa is well-endowed with mineral and primary energy resources. With an estimated 9 percent of the world population, the region accounts for approximately 28 percent of the total value of world mineral production and 6 percent of its crude petroleum output. In recent years, its share of the latter is increasing. Of sixteen important metallic and non-metallic minerals the share of Africa in 10 varies from 22 to 95 percent of the world production."[22]

As Walter Rodney notes, in order to understand the root of the poverty and underdevelopment of Africa, it is necessary to ask why Africa is not realizing her potentials and why much of her wealth and foreign reserve go to non-Africans, who reside for the most part outside the African continent. The problem is that we live in a capitalistic world wherein the weaker nations and economies are being squeezed to death for the well-being of the richer nations. Those non-Africans who see Africa as a land to be exploited use every means at their disposal to pauperize the land. According to one of the foremost Pan-Africanists, W. E. B. Dubois, the West always sees Africa "...as a means and not as an end; as a hired tool and welter of raw materials and not as a land of human beings."[23] This explains the reason for colonialism and slavery, and the evils of neo-colonialism and globalization. The debt burden, which has been imposed on most African countries, by the Bretton Woods institutions of the IMF and the World Bank, the G8 and the Paris Club, is a continuation of the exploitation of the African continent. Chinweizu and Walter Rodney[24] have documented the exploitation of the continent by Western powers. Their works are well-researched and contain useful information on the extent and degree of this exploitation. While I am sentimentally moved by the facts they present, I do find their conclusions one-sided. There are many things that Africa has gained in her contact with the Western world and the whole contact has not been one that served Africans any good. It was a mixed bag of "...friendship and hostility, good and evil, profit and loss; and the fortunes of Africa and Europe, through all these years were caught and woven over more tightly."[25]

Africa as part of the world that needs the world as the world needs her. I have met many wonderful people in the Western world since I left my home country, Nigeria, some four years ago. I have experienced incredible friendship from people in North America and Europe. Some of the nicest people I have met are sons and daughters of men and women who paid the ultimate price in their attempts to bring Christianity to Africa. Assunta Tagliaferri has documented a long list of many Westerners who died working for a better life for Africans.[26] There are many hospitals and schools in Africa which bear the names of some extraordinary missionaries and colonial officials, who sacrificed a lot to bring the riches of education and health to Africa. When the Ebola disease broke out in Kitwit, Zaire, Western nuns were the first victims of the disease as they tried to save the lives of Africans. My father told me that had it not been for the donations of food given to some families during the Civil War in Nigeria by Western charities; millions would have died of hunger and starvation. I was surprised during a visit to a small Italian village of Ravaledo, a few kilometers away from the shores of the famous Lake Como in North-Western Italy, to see peasant farmers who spent their days on the hills with their sheep, raising money to help those suffering from HIV/AIDS in Africa. I have been touched by the great acts of kindness of people from the Western world for Africa. My Alma Mater in Nigeria was single-handedly built by the German Catholic diocese of Munich. A friend of mine from Northern Uganda who helped me research this work told me that, but for the Western missionaries, the world would not have heard of the atrocities being committed against ordinary citizens both by the ruling government of Museveni and the LORD's resistance army. She also told me that most people in Uganda owe their education to mission schools. I cannot forget so easily that wonderful Canadian woman who adopted a Kenyan boy who escaped from his country out of poverty and was helped to start a new life. I have met two great Canadians, Craig Kielburger (founder of Free the Children) and Ryan Hreljac (founder of Ryan's Well Foundation), who have devoted their lives to saving the lives of their fellow children dying in Africa and other parts of the world. I have seen and heard enough evidence from those who have lived in the Western world, that convinces me that Africa is loved by the ordinary Westerner.

Many non-Africans have died in Africa working or assisting in peace-keeping operations. Some others have died in the health care sector. There are many Africans who study abroad who are being sustained and supported by many Western families and foundations. Some of us could never have had Western education abroad but for the grants from universities and individuals in many Western countries. Most of today's African intellectuals were trained through scholarships given by Western governments and Christian churches. There have been incredible acts of kindness from many Western governments for Africa whether in period of crisis or distress. How can anyone ever forget the Live Aid led by Bob Geldof in 1985 for the drought-ravaged people of Ethiopia and the Live 8 concerts organized by *Make Poverty History* Campaign before the G8 summit in June 2005? There are many people who think these efforts merely scratch the surface of the issues of poverty and injustice in the world, because there is a structural connection between the poverty of Africa and the wealth of the West—a situation whose reversal demands more than the advocacy that revolves around few musical stars and celebrities. However, these movements point to the fact that there are many Westerners who are uncomfortable with the African condition and who are convinced that something radical has to be done to stop the bleeding of Africa by Africans and their Western collaborators (government, companies and organizations).

Indeed Western generosity has been so great and so readily available in some African countries, that many Africans are taking it for granted or are abusing and misusing these acts of kindness. Many Western donor agencies are the primary sources of financial support to many non-governmental organizations (NGOs) working in various aspects of life in Africa. Whether these grants are being properly used is still in doubt as some African NGOs are gradually becoming like the governments in Africa: a conduit pipe for wasting hard-earned money being sent by ordinary Westerners for Africa. Some of these NGOs dish out bounties to themselves and their reference group, while their leaders live above the ordinary citizens. NGOs are fast becoming a source of livelihood instead of a means for capacity-building for the people of Africa and for building up the structures, which governmental inefficiency have either destroyed or failed to rebuild.

The exploitation of Africa is an institutional reality actively executed by some Western business conglomerates and governments. However, many Westerners are coming to the conclusion long held by men and women of goodwill that if poverty assaults the human dignity of Africans, then the dignity of all people is assaulted in every part of the world. They believe that humanity cannot continue to live in peace if a greater section of the world continues to live in inexcusable poverty. There are many people in the developed world who are worried about Africa and really want to be involved in her progress. They are looking for genuine partnerships in Africa. They also need to know that their sacrifices will not be in vain. The belief in a common humanity is one that is founded on the collective experience of humanity as one seamless garment with many colors. Our fate and fortune are intimately tied and no nation on earth can prosper alone without opening herself to threats from outside. An essential component of any civilization worthy of its name is how much respect and attention it gives to the weakest members of that society, and how she preserves and promotes the dignity of all her members and the common good.

In the world today, a great deal of money is being spent piling weapons of mass destruction in defense of the developed world, but little is spent on creating a level playing field for the whole of humanity. The amount of money spent on homeland security in places like the United States, Britain, Russia and France is enormous, yet it appears not to guarantee total safety. As at August 2005, it is estimated that the annual military budget for the occupation of Iraq by the United States is a little over $200 billion (USD), which means that the Bush administration spends $5.6 billion every month that it stays in Iraq averaging $183 million a day. However, despite all these heavy expenses, peace is far from being restored in that troubled land, while there are more terrorist acts in Iraq by 2005 than it was during the regime of Saddam Hussein. An unjust world will always produce more terrorists; a world that promotes unfair business practices between the North and the South will always produce more terrorists. The answer to terrorism is the creation of a common humanity with regard to access to wealth, education and availability of means. This will help stem the gathering storm of religious fundamentalism especially promoted by radical Islamists. Those who are easily exploited by religious charlatans are the poor of the land who have nothing to lose by dying in violence, suicide bombings and other terrorist activities. We see these powerless young people being wasted as suicide bombers in the Middle East and Chechnya and as child soldiers in many countries of Africa and Asia. Their anger is as real as their hunger and deprivation; their capacity for evil is highlighted in the context of the contrary virtues which their lives would have been blessed with but for their sense of existential nudity. These are the vulnerable and exploited poor of the world.

Poverty is the greatest threat to world peace and the war against terrorism will never be won by more defenses and more border policing and monitoring, nor even by immigration control, but by building a world where justice would be the song on the lips of all men and women. This is true of the Palestinians as well as the Jews, of the Afghans as well as the Iraqis, and of the Africans as well as the Eastern Europeans. That kind of world would respect the dignity, right and value of every person. The life of an African is no less important than the life of a French person, nor is the life of an American more important than the life of a Chechen, or the life of a Russian more important than the life of an Iraqi or a Burmese. Many Westerners appear to understand that the common wealth of humanity should not remain in the hands of a few, hence their concern and active involvement in fighting the many problems that face the continent of Africa.

1.3 The Slave Trade

Each day traders are kidnapping our people-children of this country, sons of our nobles and vassals, even people of our family....Corruption and depravity are so widespread that our land is entirely depopulated....We need in this kingdom only priests and school teachers, and no merchandise, unless it is wine and flour for Mass...It is our wish that this kingdom not be a place for the trade or transport of slaves.

These goods exert such a great attraction over the simple and ignorant people that they believe in them and forget their belief in God....My Lord, a monstrous greed pushes our subjects, even Christians, to seize members of their own families, and of ours, to do business by selling them as captives. [27]

This diplomatic dispatch, which was sent in 1526 from King Jòao III of Congo to King Affonso of Portugal, represented the greatest and oldest evidence of the basic attitude of the Africans to the slave trade. It was also evidence of the deceit that was involved in this evil trade. The Portuguese had given the king the impression that they were in his kingdom to bring Christianity to the people and to trade with them on an equal basis, however, with time, the real motives of these Portuguese became clear in the nature of the trade they adopted and in the way they treated the Africans. This change, which led to the forceful kidnapping of the Congolese for shipping abroad, led the King to protest in this letter to the Portuguese monarchy. If Africans knew what their children suffered in the hands of the 'White men' in the New World, would they have cooperated in this evil? Africans were not innocent in the enslavement of their own and should be blamed for cooperating with outsiders to wreck incalculable havoc on their land. However, many Africans of that time were deceived into believing that their loved ones were going to a better place and that they would be well-cared for and would eventually return home. Before they knew the truth, they were already caught up in a revolving chain of evil which enslaved both the victims and the perpetrators and African society at large. Some of the missionaries in the era of slavery even rationalized this evil away and led Africans into believing that slavery was a good thing for them from God. Count Zinzendorf, a Moravian spiritual leader, argued this way, *"God punished the first Negroes by making them slaves, and your conversion will make you free, not from control of your masters, but simply from your wicked habits and thoughts, and all that make you dissatisfied with your lot."*[28]

The African theologian Bénézet Bujo,[29] argues that slave trade found some justification among Westerners of this time in a passage of scripture (Genesis 9:18-27) which narrates Noah's cursing of Ham. The text was understood in Christian tradition to apply to Black people, who were cursed because of the sin of their father Ham. In 1873 the Congregation of

51

Indulgences published even a prayer for the conversion of Ham's offspring in Central Africa, approved with a 300 days indulgence by Pope Pius IX. Part of the prayer read: 'Let us pray for the most miserable Ethiopian peoples in Central Africa, who form a tenth of humanity, so that God Almighty may take away from their hearts the curse of Ham and give them the blessings of Jesus Christ, our God and Lord.' Christian mentality of this kind helped to legitimize slavery.

Many Africans were led to believe, as Bryan Edwards has argued, that they were being taken to a situation infinitely more desirable than their African condition. This kind of thinking as I would argue has re-emerged in contemporary Africa, where many Africans think that the situation in the developed world is better than the situation in Africa and would rather be 'slaves' living in Europe or North America than remain in Africa. However, the Africans then, like those of today who flock to the Western world, did not know that they were giving away the future of their continent and mortgaging their political, economic and social life. Even though there was some form of slavery in the traditional African society, it was of a different kind from the inhuman magnitude of the Trans-Atlantic or Trans-Saharan slave trades.[30]

Slavery is one of those evils that has gripped humanity since the beginning of time. As the collective conscience of humanity continues to grow, men and women are beginning to realize that certain acts like slavery are not only injurious to the victims but sear the souls of the perpetrators. Slavery is an ancient social institution known and practiced among peoples and races of the world. It had existed among the Assyrians, Egyptians, Phoenicians, Hebrews, Persians, Indians and Chinese. The Greek colonies in the Mediterranean were founded by Greek pirates who descended on the towns and sold the population into slavery. The Greek leisure class found slavery convenient. At one time, over 90% of the Greek population was made up of slaves. The Roman Empire at some point in her early history was comprised of more slaves than freemen. The slaves, who were drawn mainly from Britain, Asia, and Africa, were the tillers of the soil, masons, court jesters, cooks, hairdressers, musicians, and gladiators. Many European groups not only enslaved their weaker neighbors but also their own lower classes as well. If slavery were not already a social institution in Europe, the Europeans would not have enslaved the other races outside Europe.

Social evils always start as a subjective social construct from a small social arc before it diffuses through the social veins spreading its dangerous tentacles to vast regions. The Greek philosopher Aristotle saw slavery as just and expedient, for some are naturally free and some are naturally slaves, "Any piece of property can be regarded as a tool enabling a man to live; and as his property is an assemblage of such tools including his slaves; and a slave being a living creature like any other servant, is a tool worth many tools."[31] Plato before him also argued in his **Republic**, that Greeks as a superior race should not be taken as slaves in war: "There will then be no Greek slaves in our state and it will advise other Greek states to follow suit....That would encourage them to let each other alone and turn against the barbarians."[32] A logical conclusion from this would be that in Plato's Greek states there were slaves who were not Greeks. The monuments of Greek and Roman civilizations were built on the sweat, blood and shoulders of slaves.

There were also slaves in African society. Egyptian hieroglyphs reveal that pygmy slaves of African origin were instrumental in the constructions undertaken in ancient Egypt, such as the building of pyramids. Except for the Masai of East Africa, who were interested in capturing cattle and the cattle owners who opposed them, most African traditional societies had slaves. One could become a slave in traditional African society if one was a criminal, a captive of war, as well as pawns for debts. There were cases where one voluntarily gave himself into slavery to a master whom he would serve and who would guarantee him protection. The conditions of slaves were generally humane; there were exceptions in some cultures where slaves were used for sacrifices. There were instances when pawns married their creditors or of bondswomen being married to their masters. Slaves also rose to positions of prominence especially in the coastal region of West Africa. Under the 'house system' of family organization, Jaja of Opobo, one of the most prominent African chiefs in that region who resisted the Western slavery of Africans and the colonial scourge was a former slave in the 'house system.'

The first Africans to be sold into slavery may have been the Nubians who lived south of Egypt and who were sold into Europe and the Middle East. During the Carthaginian period, vast numbers of African slaves were sold from Sudan to North Africa. This was a tragic development which led to the slave trade between North African Berbers, Arabs and Africans across the Sahara desert. Over time, however, the most important source of slaves for the Islamic world, until the 15th Century, was East Africa. The majority of the slaves from there found their way to Asia. In Turkey, Arabia and Persia they became an important section of the population. There is recorded evidence of African slave revolts in Baghdad and Basra in the 10th Century.[33] Subsequently, this trade spread to present-day West Africa as Muslim caravans crossed the hazardous Sahara desert in search of slaves whom they took by force of arm. The only way that people escaped slavery at the hands of Muslim slave dealers was by converting to Islam, since Muslims did not enslave fellow Muslims. The capital of the dying ancient Ghana Empire, Kumbi, became a noted slave market for the Arabs. Thus, when the Almoravids conquered the empire, many of its inhabitants were carried off and sold as slaves in North Africa. The ancient Mali Empire was also flourishing ground for slave trade between the Arabs and the West Africans. The Islamic historian Ibn Battuta recorded that the aristocracy in Mali was actively involved in these iniquitous transactions on slaves. On his pilgrimage to Mecca in 1324, King Mansa Musa of Mali Empire crossed the Sahara with a convoy of over five hundred slaves. The rulers of the Hausa states of West Africa were extensive dealers of slaves with the Arab Muslims. The expansion of the Kanem Bornu Empire to the Southeast towards Lake Chad was driven by the ambition to gain new territories and subsequently new slaves for export to the Arab world. Giles Milton's new book, **White Gold**, chronicles the extraordinary story of Thomas Pellow and North Africa's one million European slaves in the early 18th century.[34]

However, the merchandizing of African slaves across the Atlantic was by far the most extensive form of slavery. The Portuguese were the first to come to the coast of Africa in search of gold. However, when they could not find gold and sent a cargo of slaves to Lisbon, who were sold at great profit, they soon realized that trade in African slaves would be a very good business. In 1475, Portuguese ships crossed the Equator and gradually Portuguese explorers like Bartolomew Diaz (who rounded the Cape of Good Hope), Captain Diogo Cao (who came to the Congo River), and Vasco da Gama (who went beyond the Coast, from East Africa across the Indian Ocean into India as far as Calcutta) were opening up the African hinterland. The Portuguese by the end of the 15th Century had many trading posts in Africa (Elmina Castle, Gwato, Cape Verde Island) which served as conduits for slave trade between Guinea and Congo and the New World. The discovery of the New World and the building of plantations for the large-scale production of sugar, cotton and tobacco necessitated cheap and abundant labor which the physiology of the Indians could not endure. It is significant that it was a Christian missionary, Bishop Bartolomez de Las Casas, who petitioned the Holy Roman Empire to allow the importation of Negro slaves to the New World. Las Casas (who is seen as a hero for liberation theologians in South America), who appealed to the Spanish monarchy, asked them to intervene to obtain justice for the Indians, who were dying from their toils in the fields. Since the Blacks did not die like the Indians it was believed that God had made them natural laborers to serve the interests of the Whites. The African political thinker, Ali Mazrui had argued that the reason the Europeans did not enslave the Indians further nor consider Arab or Asian slaves was, aside from the geographical proximity of Africa to Europe, because, "Africans as black emphasized the extremities of the spectrum of pigmentation, the polar opposites of color and race. It was easier for the Europeans, therefore, to dehumanize those that were furthest from them in culture and complexion, and proceed to enslave them."[35]

It was argued that the Africans by their nature could stand the rigors of hard work and suffering more than the Indians. Herein lies the root of Europe's enslavement of Africans. Africans were regarded as subhuman, beasts of burden and the descendents of the devil whose only lot was suffering and banality. A German slave merchant, Soemmering, arrogantly asserted, "The people are more insensible than others towards pain and natural evils, as well as towards injuries and unjust treatment. In short, there is none so well adapted to be slaves of others."[36] Thus, before the middle of the 16th Century, governments, corporations and pirates from Britain, France, Denmark, Germany, Sweden, Portugal, Spain and Holland were all barrel and stock in the trade on slaves—all had countless slave ports (factories) in Africa, the largest of which was the Portuguese port in Luanda, which supplied millions of slaves to Portuguese plantations in Brazil.

The Atlantic slave trade was the most iniquitous transaction of human beings ever known in history; it was the forced migration of the highest number of human beings ever known in history. The nature of the trade was as inhuman as it was degrading. A Liverpool pamphlet justifying slavery said this of the African slaves: "Many a man, woman or child who might otherwise have been killed for a mere caprice or for the love of seeing blood flow or as a toothsome ingredient of a banquet was sold to a slave trader..."[37] This erroneous or misguided ontology of the African person governed the trade for the four centuries that it lasted. The Africans "... were regarded as mere instruments to serve the ends of the White men... who acquired the Africans as slaves...uncivilized, heathen and inferior beings. Here was the beginning of deep-rooted contemptuous prejudices which are likely to die-hard. Apparently, slavery is the proper condition of the black race. Who can say that this assumption has been completely eradicated from the European and the Asian consciousness?"[38]

In the interpretation of the African condition, one cannot but place in context the historical distortion of the African personality in the consciousness of most Africans. Many African-Americans still suffer this ontological construct which defines them in the light of their past history as descendants of slaves. However, it is the struggle for recognition as a basis for inter-subjective relation between the Black man and the White man which is at stake in this consideration. Unless people are recognized for who they are irrespective of color, race, sex or creed, their lives cannot carry an equal value in the thinking of today's racists just like their slave merchant forebears.

In the Trans-Atlantic slave trade, Africans were humiliated and dehumanized. The sugar plantations in the Caribbean islands, the vast tobacco fields of North America, the rice plantations of Carolina and the cotton plantations of the South needed cheap slave laborers. The ports of Liverpool, Bristol, London, Seville and Bordeaux among many other cities were seething with slaves. Reflecting on the condition of the slaves and the many years of this exploitation, Offiong laments, "This process of rapine and carnage went on for over four hundred years; for ferocity, it has no parallel in the diabolical annals of human oppression."[39]

Slaves were obtained by banditry, warfare, trickery, kidnapping, alliance, and peaceful partnership. In no time, the African states of Asante, Benin, Dahomey, Kongo, Ndongo, and Oyo were turned into cities of bloody ravages of war to capture slaves for Western governments and companies. These wars were made more intensive and bloodier because of the importation of guns which the African chiefs bartered for slaves. There was social disorder and insecurity, economic paralysis and political turmoil in the whole of the continent of Africa. During the years of the slave trade Africa was in the throes of death in all aspects of her collective life. The Trans-Atlantic slave trade typified the worst form of abuse of human dignity. Ottobah Cuguano, an ex-slave reflects sadly on his experience at the hands of his European captors and masters, "*They do not take away a man's property like other robbers, but they take away a man himself, and subject him to their service and bondage which is a greater robbery and crime.*"[40]

The slave trade created an ever-widening circle of cruelty and destruction that at length wrecked African civilization everywhere (Norman Laye). This must be kept in perspective in understanding the unbroken cycle of violence in Africa and among African-Americans. Slave trade created a racial (African) underclass in the world who were left in the broken lower levels of the global ladder of progress, seemingly powerless to change their condition and powerless to make people of other races appreciate them for who they are. The Japanese and the Chinese were able to win their dignity and self-respect through industrialization and some measure of military and economic power. The conquest of freedom is perhaps the most basic challenge facing all civilizations, especially those civilizations in the developing countries whose main elements are suffering and existential homelessness as a result of the poverty of their respective countries.

The slave trade also led to a certain aggressive instinct in the Africans of that time as they strove and thirsted for self-preservation. Erich Fromm has argued very convincingly that there is a certain aggressive instinct that comes as a spontaneous reaction to intense and unjustified suffering inflicted on a person or the members of a group to which one is identified. This aggression often occurs after the damage has been done (in this case after slavery and racism) and is not a defense against a threatening danger and it often occurs with greater intensity in violent behaviors. "As a condition for the unstunted development of the human organism, freedom is a vital biological interest of man, and threats to his freedom arouse defensive aggression as all other threats to his vital interests. Is it surprising then that aggression and violence continue to be generated in a world in which the majority are deprived of freedom, especially the people of the so-called underdeveloped countries?....those in the power, i.e., the Whites were accustomed to considering the yellows, the Browns and the Blacks as non persons who are not expected to react humanly."[41]

We might not fully understand the reason for the increasing violence in many African American neighborhoods in Chicago or New York, but there is some kind of struggle going on in the soul of every African American or African for some form of recognition, which traces its origin to slavery and is worsened by poverty and increasing powerlessness. The root of the racism directed against Africans must be traced back to the slave trade. The beginning of the 'homelessness' of Africans and Blacks all over the world today goes back to the slave trade. Many African-Americans are still searching for their roots both ancestrally and culturally. For over 400 years, Europeans viewed Africans as naturally corrupt, as descendants of the apes, and lacking in any culture and civilization. This feeling has not been totally transformed even in the face of higher and newer insights that have dawned on humanity.[42]

In the slave trade, Africans were devalued and quantified in monetary terms; a prime slave man could be exchanged for 4 dame guns and a few other meretricious items like copper, cotton cloth, powders and creams. One could buy 300 slaves for an assortment of sundry goods amounting to £1400, just a little over $5 per slave. The slaves once acquired were chained together and marched to the coast where they were locked-up in wooden cages to await the arrival of the European merchant. They were usually tied together and hoarded into baracoons and hulks anchored on estuaries and creeks, while awaiting the triangular journey to the Americas. Before auctioning the slaves, prospective buyers inspected their wares (i.e. slaves)

"...they prodded the slaves' stomachs, looked at their teeth, peered into their eyes, pinched their muscles and gauged the working capacity of each slave."[43] When the goods had been bartered with cheap guns from Europe and other items, the new owners of the slaves marked their initials on the slaves' faces with a brazen iron.

The most unfortunate side of the Trans-Atlantic slave trade was the five to six weeks' transportation across the 'Middle Passage' or the Great Triangle to the plantations. The slave ships were constructed in such a way as to make it possible to accommodate the largest number of slaves in the minimum deck-space; slaves were enclosed under grated hatchways between decks and were as comfortable as a person would be in his coffin. "The space was so low that they sat between each other's legs, and stowed so close together that there was no possibility of lying down or at all changing their position night and day."[44] These slaves lived in the worst of conditions and thousands died from diseases, hunger, exhaustion, suffocation, suicide, and frustration. Others were thrown into the sea as a result of insubordination or at the fear of shipwreck as a result of overloading.

The sugar and coffee plantations of Brazil, the sugar plantations of the Caribbean Islands and the tobacco, rice and cotton farms of North America were seething with millions of African slaves who provided cheap labor for the economies of Europe and North America. The hardship and brutality that these Africans received from their overseers was unimaginable given "the extent of human suffering involved, and the callous disregard for human life and the indignity displayed by those who dealt in slaves."[45] There was unending misery for the slaves who were worked to the bones; those who died from exhaustion were promptly replaced and their graves remain unmarked in many instances, since most of them had no names and no identity. As for welfare, the slaves were not entitled to salaries, health care, housing, etc. They looked hungry, angry, dejected, and emaciated. They looked like mere skeletons with repulsive and shocking appearances.

The years of slavery were years of paralysis and isolation for Africa with unmitigated human suffering and degradation. Writing on this, the late Nigerian statesman, Obafemi Awolowo bemoans, "The subjective phase of the Black African's mind which was under-developed at the time of intercourse with the White race, became depressed, darkened and worse under-developed."[46] African slaves were filled with a sense of shame, guilt, and inferiority which haunts many Africans to this day. There was also the depopulation of the land especially of the most productive labor force. Those who were taken as slaves were usually the young men and women between the ages of 21 and 35. The estimate of the number of Africans taken into slavery is open to anybody's guess as there was no record of the slaves taken from Africa, those who died in the long voyage across the Atlantic, and those who landed safely in the New World. Between 1532, when the first slaves were transported across the Atlantic, and the 1880s when the noxious trade wound down, over 20 million Africans were estimated to have been taken into slavery and over 2 million died on the way to the New World.

The Trans-Atlantic slave trade paved the way for the poverty of the African continent. In the first place, it disrupted Africa's political, economic and social life for over three hundred years. It effectively put an end to any meaningful integration of the diverse African ethnic groups. The wars that were fought in order to capture slaves set the pyre for the final cremation of the last vestiges of the various peoples and empires of Africa. These wars created ethnic animosities, which have continued to hamper the unity of the ethnic groups. Within some ethnic groups, there still exists a class system built around slaves, outcasts and freeborn. In my Igbo tribe of Eastern Nigeria, there are people of Aro clan, the main slave merchants in Igboland, who are scattered in various parts of the tribe and who have not been properly integrated into their local communities. In the second place, it drove Africans away from the coast as people ran to escape capture from slave merchants. It is no wonder that over 70% of the African continent is landlocked today and transporting merchandise to and from the coasts and across national borders, takes a substantial percentage of Africa's exports and imports.

The slave trade took place at a period when Europe was swimming in the warm waters of various intellectual and political renewals. The intellectual life of humanity was also in ferment in many other parts of the world. The slave trade cut Africa off from the changing dynamics brought about by the Enlightenment and the revolutions in the United States and Europe and robbed her of the opportunity of integrating her civilization, rationality and scientific heritage into the world wide movement for their mutual enrichment and refinement. The flowering of science and technology, which presaged the Industrial Revolution that mechanized agriculture and industries and made the use of massive slave labor meaningless, was not open to the African world because of the slave trade. It was obviously the Industrial Revolution that made the abolition of the slave trade expedient. It did not, however, change the way Africans were seen and treated by the wider world at that point in time. The Trans-Atlantic slave trade was one of the pillars of the emerging Western economies of the later half of the 19th Century. The evil of that trade alone is a strong enough argument for the present campaign for the cancellation of African debts as reparation to Africans. "While African slaves were part of the technology of production in the West, Western slavers were part of the technology of destruction within Africa. The slave trade coincided with the gun trade. African slaves arriving in the Americas helped the West to be more productive; Western guns arriving in Africa helped Africans to be more destructive."[47] As Walter Rodney writes, "When one tries to measure the effect of slave trading on the African continent, it is very essential to realize that one is measuring the effect of social violence rather than trade in the normal sense of the word."[48]

The slave trade in Africa is also seen as the cause of the landlocked situation of most African countries today. Slavery represents the face of an inhuman world; it is the sign of the lost paradise of humanity where wickedness and selfishness reign supreme. It stems from the lack of a true sense of God and when it is elevated to the institutional levels in forms of state-sponsored slave trade or corporate slave business, it reveals the dark crevices that eat away the authentic soul of men and women. How could such evils be condoned for years even by great religions like Christianity and Islam? Why was there no Christian theological stand or condemnation of this evil by churches in Europe?[49] A cloud of silence descended upon the men and women of faith in Europe and America. Why did missionary activities, which started in Africa in the late 16th Century, stop for the 300-400 years that the slave trade lasted? Did the Christians of that era prefer the enslavement of the Africans to the redemption of their souls? The saints, heroes and heroines of faith maintained a sacred silence in what one would consider the worst institutional evil that affronted the authentic worship of God and service of humanity since the time of Christ. The evils of slavery made the Holocaust possible because it was the first time in human history that a particular race will be slated for destruction because they were seen as racially inferior and expendable. It is this mindset that gave birth to the persecution of Jews which was given concrete destructive impetus through the Nazis. All these past unspeakable evils and the terrorism of today are signs of a paradise lost: the lives of others mean nothing to perpetrators of evil and they are often led by a misguided religious zealotry that could only be properly called a bonus from the devil.

However, the greatest evil of the slave trade must be seen in the light of the onslaught on the human dignity of the African people—it ruined and stained the African personality. A person's dignity is a quality that goes beyond the consideration of man or woman. Human dignity is the quality of being human which has both a sacred and material content. A human person because of his unique nature is to be treated with utmost respect as a bearer of the image and likeness of God, and the meeting of the double horizons of transcendence and immanence, supernatural and material qualities. Human dignity is intrinsic to our nature and is prior to any accidents of color, sex, status, religion etc. Human dignity has a mysterious content because no person can be fully defined nor is our capacity for transcendence quantifiable according to any standard. It is because men and women are capable of loving; of willing or knowing and acting that we regard human dignity as essential to our nature. Our dignity is often seen in our ability to reflect the transcendental attributes of beauty, goodness, unity, love and peace. Deep within each heart lies this desire to respond to a higher call, which is often seen in various religious traditions as coming from God, who is the ultimate term and object of our longing. Our dignity shines through when we reflect the highest values that we are capable of and when we go beyond ourselves in acts of charity and self-sacrifice; we blight our dignity through acts of wickedness and selfishness. It is this content of personality and individuality which is both irreplaceable and irreducible that was violated by the enslavement of Africans. In that sense, the slave trade was also deleterious to the religious life and traditions of Africans and the rest of the world. According to Jean Jacques Rousseau, "the right to enslave is non-existent; it is not merely illegitimate, but absurd and meaningless as well."[50] The philosopher, John Locke denounces slavery as unreasonable since "labor being the unquestionable property of the laborer, no man but he can have a right to what that is joined to..."[51]

The Trans-Atlantic slave trade was evil and its effects have not been wiped out many years after the abolition of this ignominious trade. African-Americans still suffer many inequalities, injustice, and pain as a result of this evil, which placed them in a land that they did not choose, where they have to fight for their civil and economic rights. Many of them have died in the cause of securing their civil rights and even now many have remained on the margins of life in the most prosperous country in the world. African Americans have remained the underclass whose lot only comes to the fore in election years; many of them resort to the entertainment industry and sports where social or institutional barriers no longer prevent them from rising to the top. The face of the African continent must then be seen in great measure in the light of the effects of the slave trade. Africans must, however, work to achieve their liberation. This demands a journey into their authentic historical moorings and a realization of their unique personhood, which is an irreducible quality, conferred on the substantial nature of the human being. The progressive liberation of the African continent from the chain of poverty and the yoke of slavery would be a battle that may, if need be, demand new martyrs of Africa, who would fight against both the imperial lords and their local mimickers who parade themselves in shining armor of statesmanship.

1.4 Colonialism

> *I have listened to your words but can find no reason why I should obey you- I would rather die first. I have no relations with you and cannot bring it to my mind that you have given me so much as a pesa (fraction of a rupee) or the quarter of a pesa or a needle for a thread. I look for some reason why I should obey you and find not the smallest. If it should be friendship that you desire, then I am ready for it, today and always; but to be your subject... I do not fall at your feet, for you are God's creature just as I am...I am sultan here in my land. You are sultan there in yours. Yet listen, I do not say to you that you should obey me; for I know that you are a free man... As for me, I will not come to you, and if you are strong enough, then come and fetch me...*[52]

This dispatch from Macemba, the Chief of Yao people in present day Malawi, in 1890 to a German imperialist, Herman Von Wissman, is evidence of the position of most African leaders and people at the beginning of the colonial rule in the later half of the 19th Century. There have been many wrong assumptions that Africans did not have a cohesive society, that it was a lawless continent without form or shape and that colonialism was a good thing for the Africans. The greatest problem in understanding and properly articulating the phase of Africa's history before and after colonialism is that most documented evidence about Africa, was written by colonialists, who had an abbreviated and selective sense of African history, and attempted to reshape her civilization. The present crises in Africa are only indications that the African continent as it is today formed in the image and likeness of the Western world, cannot survive unless new models of development and democracy are adopted that are consistent with Africa's multi-cultural traditions.

The period of colonialism in Africa is dated from the end of the Berlin Conference (November 15, 1884 to January 30, 1885) to the post-Independence years of the late 1950s and early 1960s. Before this conference, convoked by German Chancellor Bismarck, there had been rival claims by the European countries for African territories. Before 1880, most European powers were not interested in the colonization of Africa. In the first place, their interests were best served by the slave trade. Secondly, before 1857 when the anti-malaria prophylactic, quinine was introduced by the Europeans to treat malaria, Europeans died in great numbers in Africa as a result of this deadly disease, because they did not have the immunity against it like most Africans. Furthermore, the Europeans had richer and more attractive territories that served their economic interests in places like Canada, New Zealand, and Australia. The Russians had a sphere of influence in the East Asian territories, while Spain was spreading its sphere of influence in South America and some parts of Asia. The United States of America was preoccupied with colonizing ever-widening frontiers of North America towards the West. It was also recovering from its Civil War and only became a stable polity after the victory of the states of the North in 1865. Germany and Italy did not exist as united nation-states until 1870, and both areas were troubled with revolutionary movements and European wars. France suffered from constant instability as a result of revolutionary movements (1830, 1848, and 1870) and her national constitution was not established until 1879. "Before 1870 new forces were wrecking traditions for the European race; democracy, nationalism, liberalism and socialism had produced an unstable ferment."[53] The British nation was the most stable of all the European countries, at this point in time, and her commercial and military powers were very diverse and needed some expansion. It was not surprising, as Mazrui had observed, that the greatest slaving country became the greatest imperial power in the late 19th Century. The British interest in penetrating the heartland of Africa was driven by economic interest in the post-slave trade era. She was not alone in this struggle for Africa's land, peoples and resources.

The Germans who were the leading military power in Europe, at the end of the Franco-Prussian War, began reluctantly to challenge the British claim to territories in Africa. This was happening after 1870, when Europe achieved a new stability.[54] In that year, the Prussians defeated the French armies and overthrew the regime of Napoleon III. This was followed by the proclamation of the German Reich. Within the same year (1870), the unification of Italy was achieved with the seizure of Rome that effectively put an end to the Papal States and the gradual loss of the power of the Church in the political life of the Italian nation.[55] However, France continued to assert herself in Africa with some measure of national stability, consequent upon the ascent of the Republicans to power and the ousting of the Bonapartists and the monarchists.

Belgium under King Leopold, an ambitious and clever man, entered into the fray. Leopold obviously wanted to have a personal empire in Africa. He veiled his ambition with philanthropy and so started a scheme of cooperation with the Africans under the International African Association. So deceptive was this scheme at its early stages, that President Chester A. Arthur of the United States, in a speech to the Congress, said this of Leopold's African Association: "The rich and populous valley of the Kongo is being opened by a society called the International African Association, of which the King of the Belgians is the president...Large tracts of territory have been ceded to the Association by native chiefs, roads have been opened, team boats have been to places on the river and the nuclei of states established...under one flag which offers freedom to commerce and prohibits the slave trade. The objects of the society are philanthropic. It does not aim at permanent political control, but seeks the neutrality of the valley."[56] What followed the formation of this group by Leopold is one of the saddest pages in the history of the exploitation and colonization of Africa. He used the group to gain the sympathy of other Western powers and recognition of his control of the Congo basin. Leopold was one of the most disliked imperialists in Africa, because of his culture of deceit, his recourse to violence and senseless brutality and his total lack of respect for African traditional institutions and value system. Most African modern-day dictators, like Mobutu Sese Seko, Kamuzu Banda, and the late Gnasingbe Eyadema are often referred to as Leopold's scions, because like Leopold, they perfected the art of deceit, violence, and disregard for local sentiment.

The presence of all the major European powers in Africa in the second half of the 19th Century created a lot of competition among them, and also revealed the struggle for power in Europe at this point in history. Britain, Germany, France, Belgium, Portugal, and Italy all had some commercial interests in Africa. The competition among them was not helping their commercial interests. In addition, commercial and cultural penetration without some form of political control, backed by force was not conducive for the growth of the businesses that the Europeans had in Africa. Already, there had been pockets of resistance among the Africans against the presence of the mainly British commercial companies in some parts of Africa. There were also visible signs of competition among the European powers in places like Egypt over the control of the Suez Canal, to which both France and Britain had invested. The Anglo-Portuguese Treaty of February 1884 over the control of the mouth of the Congo River had alienated Belgium and France, while the struggle for the heartland of East and West Africa raged on between France, Britain and Germany (which was reluctant to become a colonial power preferring instead to be the dominant power in Europe). Germany also vacillated in the fight for the possession of Egypt and Sudan in the face of the resistance by the indigenous *Mahdist* fighters.

The Berlin Conference is often referred to as the Berlin West African Conference because it had its origins in the events in West Africa. The other European powers wanted to destroy Britain's claim to the Congo and Niger rivers, which were the most important avenues to tropical Africa. The Conference set the standard for the acquisition of African territories and proposed the peaceful negotiation among the European powers for territories. It also established that the basis for territorial claim would be 'effective occupation' which meant the establishment of administrative, political and military presences in territories to which any European power laid claim. "When marking out the boundaries of their new territories, European negotiators frequently resorted to drawing straight lines on the map, taking little or no account of the myriad of traditional monarchies, chiefdoms and other African societies on the ground. Nearly one half of the new frontiers imposed on Africa were geometric lines, lines of latitude and longitude, other straight lines or arcs of circles. In some cases, African societies were rent apart: the Bakongo were partitioned between the French Congo, Belgian Congo and Portuguese Angola; Somaliland was carved up between Britain, Italy and France. In all, the new boundaries cut through some 190 culture groups."[57] There was no single African at this conference where their future was sealed. It marked the forceful loss of independence for Africans; it also inaugurated the large-scale destruction of lives, property, and works of arts, monuments and artifacts in Africa. The Berlin Conference gave birth to colonialism in Africa.

Colonialism has a long history. Assyria for instance dominated and colonized the rest of the 'world' for many centuries; there was the *Pax Romana* which signified the era of Roman colonial domination of the world. There was also the *Pax Britannica* which marked the era of British imperial hegemony in world affairs. Spain at some time also was a colonial power in South America and some parts of Asia. Colonialism has always defined the spread of the culture of the colonizing power. The Greek writer Herodotus once noted that the weak should bear the weight of colonialism as a natural evil, while Thucydides in his *History of the Peloponnesian War* asserts that human rights can never be a question among the unequal, for the weak suffer what they must and the strong do what they can. Colonialism, in his view, was the inexorable consequence of inequality among the peoples and races of the world. The Libertarian, John Stuart Mill advocated that despotism and colonialism over backward people or barbarians is acceptable to save them from infra-civilization. Mill argues that, it is justified to colonize people, who are not yet mature enough to engage in the practice of representative government.[58] Aimé Césaire in his *Discourse on Colonialism* notes that it was unfortunate that European merchants and politicians came into contact with Africa at a time when Europe was at the lowest level of ethical consciousness. Accordingly he argues that, "...no one colonizes innocently, that no one colonizes with impunity either; that a nation which colonizes, that a civilization which justifies colonization—and therefore force—is already a sick civilization, a civilization which is morally diseased, which irresistibly, progressing from one consequence to another, one denial to another, calls for its Hitler..."[59]

Colonialism in Africa can only be seen as a residue of the dark side of Western civilization and never brought any substantial good to Africa. However, it would be wrong to attribute all Africa's problems to colonialism since many countries in other continents also suffered colonialism and have, over time, taken their destiny by hand and redefined their future. However, the nature of colonialism in places like Australia, United States of America and New Zealand was markedly different from the African experience, in both the nature of the interaction and the structure of oppression and suppression adopted. Besides, the racial factor cannot be discounted in the appreciation of the contempt with which the Africans were treated by the colonial powers.

Colonialism in Africa has been interpreted in various ways by many Africans. In the words of the late Nigerian political thinker Mokwugo Okoye, colonialism is by definition dictatorial rule and robbery by violence. Arthur Nwankwo sees colonialism in Africa as the most vicious dictatorship ever used by man for the oppression of man, while Richard Onwuanibe sees it as the subjugation of a people for economic gains.[60] Frantz Fanon conceives colonialism as a system that understands only the dialectics of violence and for the late Nigerian president, Nnamdi Azikiwe, colonialism denies people their God-given freedom and rights. These sentiments by Africans who lived under colonial rule are best summarized by the Tunisian Memmi, "The most serious blow suffered by the colonized is being removed from history and from the community. Colonialism usurps any free role in either war or peace, every decision contributing to his destiny and that of the world, and all cultural and social responsibility."[61] Colonialism in Africa was the imposition of a foreign rule on Africans, for the good of the colonizing powers and without the support of the Africans. It was a lopsided relationship that created a master-servant divide between the Africans and the officials of the colonial countries.

It was not a relationship in the right sense of the word, for there was no contact between the colonialists and the Africans, except the issuing of orders and the execution of the mandate of the colonial masters by the native Africans. It was a system of exploitation that was hidden under the veil of philanthropy, which benefited the Western colonialists, with degradation and suffering for the Africans.

The treaties of friendship that came after the Berlin Conference were not entered into freely by the Africans, but were foisted on them by Western powers. In many cases, Africans resisted the loss of their freedom to determine their future destiny. This resistance was widespread from the *Mau Mau* in Kenya to the *Ekumeku* movement in Nigeria, from the Mahdist in Sudan to the Algerian and Tunisian nationalists (Habib Bourguiba in Tunisia and Hadj Messali in Algeria) and fighters in the deserts of North Africa; and from the John Chilembwe's uprising in Blantrye (Malawi) in January 1915 to the Aba women's riot (Nigeria) in 1929. African kings like Kabaka of Buganda, Shaka the Zulu, Jaja of Opobo and Nana of Itshekiri (Nigeria), the Hereroes of Namibia, and Madume of Ovambo (Angola) were renowned for mobilizing their people against the invading forces of the Western colonial nations. Some of these resistance were spontaneous, but there were some sustained wars like the four month siege on the British occupation force in Kumasi, Ghana, the 8 year war which Samori Toure, the founder of Mandingo empire waged against the French, the war between the Ndebele and Shona against White settlers in Rhodesia (Zimbabwe), and the Nandi of Kenya who were subdued by the British after 6 brutal expeditions.[62] The most significant of these battles for freedom was the battle of Adowa (Ethiopia) led by Emperor Minilik (1889-1913). The Ethiopians with an army of about 100,000 men with small arms defeated the Italian forces led by General Baratieri in 1896. In that battle, more than 6,000 Italians were killed, 1,500 were wounded and 3,000 were taken prisoners. This defeat of the Italians effectively put an end to Italy's colonial ambition in Africa and her presence in Eritrea and Somalia was subsequently downsized. Ethiopia, as a result of her victory over Italy, maintained her independence and sovereignty. Ethiopia was the single African country that was never colonized besides Liberia, which was a country created by the United States for African slaves, who were liberated from the plantations of North America. The point we wish to make here is that Africans did cherish their way of life; it served them at that point in time and they wanted to preserve their civilization. There is no reason that could be given to justify colonialism, nor is there any reason to dispute the fact that the Africans could have found their anchor in the historical process without Western invasion.

The argument was that to abolish the slave trade, there was the need to establish some form of administration in Africa. The colonial powers pretended not to be interested in taking away the independence of the Africans. They claimed that abolishing the slave trade required the establishment of law and order in Africa, and the creation of a peaceful environment for free and legitimate trade. British colonial apologists reasoned that the creation of Sierra Leone for the resettlement of liberated slaves was what brought the British to the West African coast. Many African chiefs, who refused to sign the so-called treaty of protection, and/or resisted the Western pacification, were often branded as slave dealers and surreptitiously eliminated or sent into exile. These treaties and protectorates established by the colonial powers were the means through which they secured the 'consent' of the local people, to move into their land, rule and dominate them. The real ambition of Western colonial presence was the continued exploitation of the Africans.

In the first place, the Industrial Revolution in the West produced surplus goods that required new markets; it also made many Europeans jobless and created the need for raw materials. The Western world needed Africa and wanted to enter into 'legitimate commerce' with her peoples. Slaves were no longer needed in Europe as a result of the mechanization of agriculture and industrialization. "The slave trade might be a sin and the work of the devil for the missionary, to the economist it was a wasteful and unnatural system of production, less efficient than wage labor, and one which hindered the proper economic development of African produce which could be utilized in British industry."[63] The abolition of the slave trade was not to be the triumph of the recognition and respect of the dignity and rights of the Africans by the Westerners. It was rather, the end of one phase, and the beginning of another in the progressive exploitation of the African people. One of the leading figures in the anti-slavery movement in the United States and the rest of the free world was Abraham Lincoln. He was widely revered as the symbol of Christian compassion and democratic sensibilities and an icon of America's democratic and liberal values. When it came to matters about the Africans (then called Negroes), he represented, in the words of Ali Mazrui, America's spiritual vision and racial blinkers. He is quoted to have said in a speech in Charleston, Illinois on September 18, 1858, "I do not understand that because I do not want a negro woman for a slave I must necessarily want her for a wife (cheers and laughter)...I will to the very last stand by the law of this state, which forbids the marrying of white people with negroes...I will say then that I am not, nor ever have been, in favor of bringing about in any way the social and political equality of the white and black races (applause)-that I am not nor ever have been in favor of making voters or jurors of negroes; nor of qualifying them to hold office, nor to intermarry with white people."[64]

The battle for the economic health of the West through the slave trade did not stop because of a more morally healthy Western world, but rather because colonialism offered a better economic well-being at this point in time to the West than the slave trade. In addition, the abolition of the slave trade, also helped to further the pacification of Africa even as it unified the West in her strive for global dominance. Furthermore, colonialism more than slave trade offered more power to the West and helped her to lay more claim to some kind of universal hegemony. Europeans at this point in history saw themselves in the words of Albert Beverbridge as the 'custodians under God of the civilization of the world.' Rev. Muller, referring to the perceived backwardness of the Africans before colonialism, was quoted as saying, "Humanity must not, cannot allow the incompetence, negligence, and laziness of the uncivilized peoples to leave idle indefinitely the wealth which God has confided to them, charging them to make it serve the good of all."[65]

Africans were regarded as racially, culturally and religiously inferior to Westerners. For many of the colonial officials and ideologues, the Africans typified all that was heathen, backward and detestable. Driven by a rabid ethnocentrism, these imperialists set about the destruction of the social cohesion of the Africans and the inner bond that held them together for ages.[66] As Frantz Fanon asserts, "The native is declared insensible to ethics; he represents not only the absence of values but also the negation of values...he is the depository of maleficent powers, the unconscious and irretrievable instrument of blind forces."[67] With this assumed racial superiority, the West regarded itself as the guardian of civilization and presented its presence in Africa as a humane way of spreading human civilization to the uncivilized and dark world of the Africans.[68]

There has also been the argument that colonialism helped to spread the wealth of the Western world to Africa, that the presence of Western colonialists was for the mutual economic development of Africa and the West. It is obvious that people rescued from the unnatural condition of enslavement would accept any form of administrative structure that guaranteed them peace, stability and security. However, the Western colonial powers did not regard the Africans as equals and never entered into any mutual economic relations with them. The emergence of free trade, which replaced the slave trade, was because of the changed demands of the Europeans for new forms of merchandise. The Europeans needed cotton, palm oil, rubber, gold, lodes and skins, timber, and ivory, which they took from Africa in exchange for cheap goods like gin, gunpowder, textiles, and toilet soap.[69] In addition, the colonial authorities established a system of direct taxation, in which Africans were forced to pay to the colonialists in the currency of the colonizers. This they could do by working to produce the goods needed for the 'mother country,' or by being employed by the colonial lords in administrative works and in the plantations.

In some cases, forced labor was also used, and those who refused to work for the colonialists were either sent to jail or sometimes eliminated. Forced taxation and forced labor, coupled with the violence of the colonial lords, were the causes of many uprisings in Africa. Most significant was the Aba women's riot of November 24, 1929, when a group of Igbo women rose up in protest against the colonial taxation policy, fearing that they were also to pay taxes for goats and chickens. The riot was the first popular revolt in Nigeria against colonial rule. In 1947, over 42 miners in the coal city of Enugu in Eastern Nigeria were brutally murdered at the hands of colonial police and soldiers, when they revolted against the forced labor and the inhuman working conditions in the colonial coal mine. It is significant, that the colonial lords took control of all the mineral resources of the African continent for the good of the 'mother country.' The colonial Governor General of Nigeria, Lord Lugard called this economic policy a *dual mandate* when he argued, "Let it be admitted at the outset that European brains, capital and energy have not been and never will be, expended in developing the resources of Africa from motive of pure philanthropy; that Europe is in Africa for the mutual benefit of her own industrial classes, and for the native races in their progress to a higher plane."[70]

This was only a theoretical maneuver and did not represent the true face of colonialism. What Africa got instead was nothing but the destruction of her social life, the impoverishment of her populace and the disruption of her cultural, economic and political life. Basil Davidson agrees with David Fieldhouse that the imperial lords 'squeezed and exploited their colonies in Africa.'[71] Fieldhouse has debunked the idea that the European colonialists helped Africa by presenting some statistics of the condition in some colonial countries: the money spent by France in Africa was insignificant when compared with the profits that accrued to her manufacturers in the post-World War II era. Britain between 1945 and 1951 spent £40 million in her colonies in Africa, but extracted about £140 million worth of minerals and raw materials from the colonies. By the 1950s, the Belgian government and Belgians in the Congo basin controlled 95% of total assets, 82% of the largest units of production, and 88% of private savings in the country. Reflecting on these facts, Davidson writes, "The point of recalling these facts is not to rebut the myth of imperial generosity or to lament its dishonesty.... The point is to emphasize that the extraction of wealth from an already impoverished Africa was in no way halted by the 'transfer of power.' A transfer of poverty continued as before, even while the means of transfer were modified or camouflaged."[72] In doing this, most Western colonialists were convinced that if all that Africa represented were to be obliterated from the face of the earth "the world would lose no great truth, no profitable art, and no exemplary form of life. The loss of all that is Africa would offer no memorable deduction from anything but the earth's black catalogue of crimes."[73]

The colonial policies of the British and the French exemplified the pattern of exploitation of the colonial governments. It also left the African continent with a system of government in post-colonial era that was fundamentally flawed and weighted against the interest of the common people. The British adopted the indirect rule policy, while the French adopted the doctrine of assimilation. The indirect rule policy of the British has been defined as, "A system of administration under which traditional rulers were allowed to rule their people under the supervision of British officials."[74] Under this system, African chiefs were directly responsible to the District Officers in performing their duties which consisted of collecting taxes, carrying out the order and proclamations of the 'mother country,' organizing the people to welcome colonial officials, mobilizing the people for forced labor and enlistment in the army, etc. The African traditional rulers had no power except that given them by the colonial officials. The tribal chiefs were rubber stamps and mere pawns on the complex and exploitative network of the colonial nations of Europe. The indirect rule was disruptive rather than integrative; it was disrespectful of the African rulers who were coerced or deceived into an alliance against their people. The indirect rule tried to legitimize colonial rule through the backdoor under the woven hands of the traditional rulers. It consequently retarded progress of self-government, polarized African communities between the African rulers who were seen as birds of the same feathers with the colonial masters and the African people. In egalitarian societies in Africa, with advanced democratic principles and stable and progressive social organizations, like Igbo land in Eastern Nigeria, the colonial officials imposed leaders arbitrarily on the people, and destroyed their socio-political life.

Reflecting on this, Mokwugo Okoye, writes that indirect rule was institutional hypocrisy and advanced training of the African leaders in deceit and irresponsibility.[75] The emergence of African elites in the post-World War II years created a lot of division in African societies between them and the British-made local rulers. This was because the African educated elites saw colonialism as immoral and barbaric, while the local African leaders who had been 'elevated' by the colonial masters thought otherwise in most cases. The colonial officials detested the intellectuals and preferred the tribal leaders, who they had easily won over by various arm-twisting measures and subterfuges. Lord Lugard said this of the African educated elites, "I am somewhat baffled as to how to get in touch with the educated native…I am not in sympathy with him…His loud and arrogant conceit are distasteful to me…His lack of natural dignity and courtesy antagonizes me…Education seems to have produced discontent, impatient of any control and an unjustifiable assumption of importance in the individual…"[76]

The greatest evil that colonialism brought on Africa is that it destroyed African culture and civilization. It led to Africans homelessness. Paulo Freire has written of the impact of cultural conquest on a people when he observed, "Cultural conquest leads to the cultural inauthenticity of those who are invade; they begin to respond to the values, the standards, and the goals of the invaders. In their passion to dominate, to mould others to their patterns and their way of life, the invaders desire to know how those they have invaded apprehend reality-but only so they can dominate the latter more effectively. In cultural invasion it is essential that those who are invaded come to see their reality with the outlook of the invaders rather than their own; for the more the mimic the invaders, the more stable the position of the latter becomes. For cultural invasion to succeed, it is essential that those invaded become convinced of their intrinsic inferiority."[77] This cultural invasion was brought out more in the French assimilation policy. The French were, as Basil Davidson observed, "systematic in their racism while camouflaging its reality behind Jacobin verbiage that promised much and meant, in practice, remarkably little."[78] The indirect rule system, which the British adopted in their colonies, disregarded the African way of life and demeaned the traditional institutions of the people. The French, on the other hand, took this cultural destruction to new heights. On this point, Fanon writes, "The constantly affirmed concern with respecting the culture of the native populations accordingly does not signify taking into consideration the values borne by the culture, incarnated by men. Rather, this behavior betrays a determination to objectify, to confine, to imprison and to harden."[79]

The French policy of Assimilation was built on the premise that French culture was absolutely superior to the African culture and that African culture was lacking anything worthy of preservation. Hence, there was the attempt to 'Frenchify' or make Africans native Frenchmen. Towards this end, attempts were made to "substitute their indigenous culture with French culture, language, law, civilization and religion."[80] This policy collapsed because of its own inner contradictions. Africans refused to become Frenchmen. On the other hand, the French themselves did not accept the Africans as equals. As one French Parliamentarian, MP Meyer, argued in the French National Assembly, the integration of the African peoples into mainstream French culture and civilization made the highly-valued French culture susceptible to corruption at the hand of the lowly-bred Africans. The resistance to French colonial policies in Africa was the most violent because of all the colonial countries in Africa (Britain, France, Portugal, Germany, Belgium, Spain, and Italy) it was the most reprehensible and bold attempt to wipe out Africa's past and to recreate Africa according to the mind of the French.

A comparative analysis of the two colonial policies of the French and the British reveals many negative aspects of the colonial policies. Colonialism was a negation of the dignity and rights of the Africans. It was based on a structure of damnation and domination.[81] The structure of domination is the whole machinery of the colonial system in which there are foreign investors and the local producers and consumers. The structure of damnation was the moral component of the colonial rule. There has been serious debate among Africans on whether Christianity and colonialism were two sides of the same coin. In many instances, the colonial master was also the missionary or his or her closest collaborator. Christianity came to Africa in the vessel of Western culture, which at the time of missionary activities in Africa, was purveyed by the colonialists. Many Africans, still see Christianity as an imposition for the very reason that missionaries and colonialists were not easily distinguishable. The *Mau Mau* in Kenya put this school of thought this way: "At first, we had the land and the white men had the Gospel. Then the missionaries came and taught us to close our eyes and say our prayers, while the white men were stealing our land from us. And now we have the Gospel and they have the land."[82]

Christianity was brought to Africa not because of colonialism but because Christian Europe was interested in planting the seed of faith in Africa. The European Christians believed in the power of the Gospel to change any society, including African society. There were obviously many things that the missionaries did, which in the light of today's thinking would be considered inappropriate. Whatever way of life or custom the missionaries did not understand they often condemned in Africans as fetish and pagan. However, the missionaries were driven neither by any imperial ambition nor economic gain, but by the desire to bring the Christian communion of faith, hope and love to the Africans. African culture like all cultures had its own dark sides, like the killing of twins, human sacrifice, and the subjugation of women among others. Some of these were transformed by the presence of the Christian missionaries. However, the missionaries' perception of the Africans as those who lived in 'the valley of darkness' and who were caught in the dark forces of ineradicable evil was not the right way of evangelizing a people.

There is today, a growing awareness, among Christians, that the religious institutions of non-Christian religions can serve as the launch pad for Christian missionary activities. This is because, such traditions, are worthy vessels for receiving the Christian faith. The feeling of religious superiority can never lead to any meaningful encounter and exchange between people of different religions. Religious pluralism, however, does not make missionary activity nugatory. It is also not religious condescension to offer one's religious belief to a person of another faith for his or her acceptance or rejection. However, religious conversion should take place in an atmosphere of freedom so that religious experience becomes a meaningful, self-transcending and self-transforming experience. The missionaries did not respect African traditional values and in many cases, offered Christianity as a superior Western way of life. They failed, however, to appreciate the fact that many Africans were already 'anonymous Christians' (Karl Rahner), in the sense that they lived the life of Christ even without knowing him personally. They only needed their eyes to be opened in the light of the Christian Gospel, so that they would have discovered in the expanding and transcending horizon of Christianity, the person of Christ the univocal term of their history and destiny. Many African theologians believe that the Christian faith in Africa can never take a firm root, unless Africans allow the faith to take flesh in the vast cultural trajectory of the continent.

When Pope Alexander VI proclaimed a Bull in 1493 authorizing the sending out of Christian missionaries from Portugal and Spain to the New World and Africa, he had wanted "that the barbarian peoples in these lands may be reduced to submission and brought to faith."[83] Critically appraised within its historical context, this call for mission was founded on motives of pure religious faith and not for any economic or political reason. However, the way the colonial nations implemented their repressive colonial policies; and the way they used the missionaries to win the submission of the Africans can only be interpreted as the wrong use of religion. History has shown that anytime religion is hijacked to serve political interests of politicians, it works like a double-edged sword and the final outcome depends not so much on the motives and dealings of the political actors, but on the commitment of the religious men and women to keep faith with their religious motives.

In the colonial era, the missionaries did not use the Christian religion to advance the cause of the colonial lords; rather the colonial officials used the missionaries to advance their political end. The line of contact was grey, but at the end of the day many Africans came to accept the Christian faith and rejected the colonial masters. There is always the clarity of vision which comes from religious truth, and there is always the detestation that comes from a clear evil like colonialism. In the abuse of the Christian religion for colonization, one would agree with Mazrui that colonialism represented a structure of damnation. This damnation can, however, not be attributed to the presence of Christianity, since the Christian faith offered itself wholly as one which would save people from existential and ultimate damnation. Albert de Jong summarizes the complex relationship between the missionaries and the colonialists this way: "The mission recognized the legitimacy of the colonial state and approached it on a 'de facto' basis. Owing to this, a great deal of realism and pragmatism had been calculated beforehand in its attitude towards the colonial regime. On the basis of this there was on the one hand, cooperation in the field of educational and medical work; on the other hand there was criticism, which was sometimes increased to antagonism. These different forms of stance towards the colonial government did not necessarily alternate with each other but overlapped sometimes. By and large we can say that the mission aimed for independence as great as possible from the colonial regime, while it wanted to maintain the functional contacts with it."[84]

In assessing the impact of colonialism, one would not forget its wide-ranging social and political consequences. Socially, colonialism tried to re-organize African society. This it did above all through the colonial schools which were aimed at brainwashing the Africans into accepting colonialism. The colonial schools produced Africans who served as interpreters, cooks and administrative assistants to the colonial officials. Education, in the colonial era, was not universal. It was selective and subsequently created an African 'upper class' that identified with the intentions and ambitions of the 'mother country.' They also saw themselves as privileged because they found themselves receiving some perks from the colonial officials. They also looked down on their fellow Africans and despised them as uncultured following after their Western teachers' worldview.

The colonial schools in retrospect were centers for the negation of African values, citadels for the indoctrination of Africans on the inferiority of their cultures, and the need for them to enter into the higher and exclusive portals of Western civilization. The colonial schools were also the bases for the loss of African identity and the rejection of African languages. It neither produced authentic Africans nor authentic Europeans, but a class of alienated Africans. These Africans teased their own destiny and true identity in the anvil of resistance and in the threatening miasma of personal and group extinction.

At the end of the day, the nationalists that rose up against colonial rule in Africa were not the products of the colonial schools. The nationalists were mainly veterans of the two World Wars and Africans who were educated in the Western countries, whose eyes were opened to the injustice and inhuman set up that characterized colonial rule in Africa. There was no genuine effort in the colonial schools to churn out literate and educated elites for fear of competition or an incipient drive for political emancipation, which education usually engenders. The understanding of education as mere clerical competence, which was introduced in the colonial schools continued even in post-colonial Africa. The kind of education in Africa during the colonial era and today is one that will never introduce Africa into the technological age nor will it help Africans discover their artistic, scientific, technological and creative genius. It will not unravel the beauty of the African continent and her people. In this sense, colonial rule was very destructive of the cultural identity of the Africans. It left Africans with, "A culture without economic autonomy or strength; a culture without political power; a culture with no flowering of the arts or the intellect…of incomplete synthesis; a culture without inner unity."[85]

Colonial rule was very violent. The colonial nations sequestered the best land, and used administrative fiats to tilt the land tenure system to their advantage. Africans were made beasts of burden, sources of cheap labor and instruments in the intricate chain of exploitation as teachers, interpreters, catechists, laborers, prison guards, court clerks, etc. When Africans resisted this master-slave divide in their fatherland, their actions were condemned as "feckless, idle, irresponsible, brutish, ignorant, crafty, treacherous, bloody, thievish, mistrustful and superstitious."[86] The resistance was usually crushed violently. Frantz Fanon asserts that colonialism was preceded, inaugurated, and upheld by physical and psychological violence for, "it is violence which has ruled over the ordering of the colonial world, which has ceaselessly drummed the rhythm for the destruction of native social forms, and broken up without reserves the system of reference of the economy."[87] The colonial condition created social injustice, political domination and estrangement which led to "racial inferiorization, psychological brain-washing and a bewitching of the soul…and the animalization of man's noblest virtues and impulse."[88] This same pattern of treating the opposition has taken root in contemporary

African society where the winner takes all, while the opposition suffers all kinds of persecution.

Modern Africa is left with an overarching colonial mentality. The leader in most African societies is the one who is to be served, and who offers rewards and punishment to the citizens, according to their loyalty. The leader is the master, who like the former colonial lords enjoys all the privileges of the state. The leader is the epicenter of power and privileges, those who wish to get any share of the bounties of the state must fall before the leader in homage and sycophancy. The people are to ingratiate themselves into the heart of the leader, in order to get any consideration in the provision of the social amenities of the state. The leader is to be shielded from the people by a long chain of bureaucracy and security because the leader should not be in touch with the people.

This kind of colonial arrogance has defined leadership in Africa today at all levels. Any form of position now attracts all forms of cult of personality, which effectively marginalizes the ordinary people and elevates the leadership. To hold a leadership position is to be a master; the do-gooder who sniffs incense and who must be appealed to always by the people over whom one is placed. The workers, for instance, have to beg the government for fair wages; the rural communities have to beg the government for the provision of the basic amenities; the subordinates in most offices have to treat their superiors like demigods who have right over life and death. In Nigeria, for instance, almost every person who has some means employs a coterie of attendants: drivers, cleaners, gate-attendant (one who opens the gate when the 'big man' comes and when he leaves the house), cooks, bodyguards, etc. This is one form of living that betrays a colonial mentality that sees positions of authority whether it is social, political, religious, or economic as a claim to be a master.

This master-slave relationship in African society has created an underclass that is rooted in colonial experience. Applying this specifically to politics, Richard Joseph writes, "The historical association of the term 'prebend' with the offices of certain feudal states which could be obtained through services rendered to a lord or monarch, or through outright purchase by supplicants, and then administered to generate income for their possessors…refers to patterns of political behavior which rest on the premise that such offices should be competed for and then utilized for the personal benefit of office holders as well as of their reference or support group. The official public purpose of that office often becomes a secondary concern, however much that purpose might have been originally cited in its creation or during the periodic competition to fill it."[89]

The other form of colonial mentality in Africa today is the rejection of anything African by some Africans. The colonial experience has left some Africans with a sense of inferiority. Many Africans think that nothing good can come from the continent. In Nigeria most people prefer foreign-made goods to locally produced ones. Everything foreign is good and everything local is inferior. If one bought a low quality shirt in Europe and brought it to Nigeria, many people would prefer it to a superior quality shirt produced in Nigeria for the fact that 'made in Italy' for example is preferred to 'made in Nigeria.' This can be replicated in many instances. It is always better to go for a medical check-up abroad than to do it in Nigeria (Africa) even if the machine to be used for the check-up in Canada is the same as that used in Nigerian hospitals. In Nigeria, the oil market is controlled by foreigners who do not have more scientific or technological competence than their Nigerian counterparts. A friend of mine working in a foreign oil company in Eastern Nigeria told me that his boss, a Westerner, does not have a degree or expertise in engineering, but he is placed above this Nigerian who has a master's degree in petro-chemical engineering. This Nigerian does the entire job and even taught his boss how to apply some computer software in their work! These examples can be applied to many other circumstances. Many Africans simply think that something is inherently wrong with their societies and would rather prefer to leave Africa for the Western world.

On the economic side, Africa was drained of her resources. Colonialism was unprogressive, rapacious, and exploitative and above all, prevented colonized society from developing by disrupting her history.[90] Africans received lower salaries when compared to their European counterparts, and on the other hand, put in more labor hours. Colonial apologists may point to roads, hospitals, railways as positive signs of colonialism, but these are tangential in scope against the backdrop of the massive wealth taken away from Africa to Europe. Nigeria's coal, Ghana's gold, Kenya's copper, and Sierra Leone's diamonds all went to the 'mother country' for nothing. Commenting on this, the late Ghanaian nationalist and president, Kwame Nkrumah wrote, "The colonized are thus a source of raw materials and cheap labor and a dumping ground for spurious goods to be sold at exorbitant prices."[91] The irony of all these was that the Africans were pauperized and pulverized by colonialism. They suffered poverty in the midst of wealth.

The Africans had no stake in the production and export of the raw materials found in their land. In 1939 for instance, the colonial powers in Kenya through the Coffee Plantation Ordinance forbade the native Africans from growing coffee privately. This was to prevent competition between the Africans and the Western farm-owners, who controlled over 80% of coffee plantation holdings in Kenya. Africans, on the other hand, were obliged to provide cheap laborers to the colonial farms. In all colonial Africa, Africans were not allowed to export any goods abroad.[92] In the midst of all this, there was widespread disease, unemployment, and no care for the old and the sick which reflected economic injustice. Colonialism in the words of Osita Eze was the most putrid carrion that ever rotted under the sun. He summarized the colonial situation thus: "They assumed full charge of the economic and political life of the country, monopolizing professional, large-scale commercial and administrative activities, exploiting the agricultural and other resources of the land and remaining socially aloof."[93] Colonialism made Africa economically rootless, because it did not initiate nor sustain any economic development. Any economical benefit that came with colonialism for the Africans was only an unintended consequence.

Colonialism obviously denied Africans' human dignity, for it made them a means to an end and injured their self-fulfillment and self-esteem. Human dignity demands that "man's self-fulfillment is an indispensable goal of all human life, and that society is backward, unjust, even evil that does not promote it."[94] In colonialism, Africans were treated with contempt by the colonial officials. Think of the quality of education offered to the Africans, the absolute denial of their freedom and right to self-determination; think of the economic strangulation brought about by the colonial lords which left newly independent African countries with heavy debts. What happened in Africa in terms of economic peonage is being replicated in Iraq. Africans never invited the West to Africa nor did Africans negotiate the terms and conditions of the relationship with the Western world. However, the colonial lords invaded Africa's living space; when they had got all they needed in Africa, they gave the Africans the bill in terms of debts for services the Africans neither wanted nor enjoyed. The colonial countries imposed a debt on the new African countries based on what the Western nations calculated as the quantum capital expended by the 'mother country' in the development of African societies in the colonial era.

No analysis of the African condition is adequate unless it embodies the evil effect of colonialism on the poverty of Africa. This is more amplified in the emerging complexities of globalization. Indeed, the beginning of the integration of African economies into the international market started with colonialism and that chain of exploitation and dependency has continued even now. Colonialism laid the foundation for globalization by introducing and squeezing Africa into the international market where she was not even a marginal player but an outsider. There are some African intellectuals who think that any discourse on colonialism is a waste of time, because Africa has moved on beyond the historical circumscription brought about by the events of the last 50 years. I do, however, hold a different position. I do not see any real difference between colonialism and globalization. The only difference is that during the colonial era, the Western countries were physically present in Africa, calling the shots and widening the horizon and senselessness of their exploitation. In the present era, their faces are not visible, but their reach has become more extensive and their impact more profound. This is because they can force an Ivorian to produce and export the cocoa he or she needs and starve for lack of carbohydrate because he or she cannot buy imported chocolate. They have forced Nigerians to export the crude oil they need and to suffer a chronic national oil crisis. They can force the Southern Africans to sell off their right to water and then spend half their monthly income on water and hydro. There are many of these instances and any serious African thinker or leader must not think that these phenomenal global structures that have perpetuated poverty and suffering in Africa would disappear over night. They have a history and are part of a global structure that should be dismantled because they cannot be transformed. Colonialism utterly destroyed Africa's history and civilization.

The problem of evolving a constitutional democracy in African countries can also be attributed to colonialism, which institutionalized new forms of social and political organizations and political systems that were alien to African socio-political conditions. Democracy can never be imposed as the colonial nations did in Africa, but colonial power negated the social and political values of the colonized and denied them all human qualities.[95] Any form of political domination of a people is a form of injustice, but many Westerners today believe in the normative universalism of Western values. Such Western chauvinists believe that people throughout the world, "would embrace Western values, institutions and culture because they embody the highest, most enlightened, most liberal, most rational, most modern and most civilized thinking of humankind."[96] The colonial heritage in Africa has been seen by most African social scientists as the most elemental cause of the problems of modern constitutionalism in Africa. This is because the colonial structure negatively affected the process of social integration, externally imposed new political and social structures. This brought together ethnic groups with diverse histories and forms of social organization into artificial contraption that mimicked true nationhood.[97] The political instability in African countries and the rampant civil strife are the fruits of the colonial structuring of the African society. Governments in most African countries are still colonial in being and operation, totally alienated from the people and non-responsive to the yearnings and aspirations of the people. The governments of Africa are often alienated from the people and totally out of touch with the condition of the ordinary people.

Colonialism created the problem of border disputes among some African nations. Ali Mazrui believes that France, like most European colonial lords, will withdraw her influence from her African territories. A claim that is doubtful when one sees the interference of the French government in Cote d'Ivoire and Togo to mention but a few. This is because in the face of the socio-political and economic problems created by the unification of Europe at the end of the Cold War, most European countries will be turning their attention to Eastern Europe. The result, according to Mazrui, is that France's West African influence would be filled by Nigeria—a more natural hegemonic power. In light of these emerging realities, Nigeria's own boundaries are likely to expand to incorporate the Republic of Niger with a Hausa link, the Republic of Benin with the Yoruba link and then Cameroon with historical links. This kind of thinking was no doubt predicated on the post-Cold War euphoria in the 1990s. There was the feeling then that African nations were moving towards a more united continent, with the consequent crumbling of artificial borders imposed by the colonial powers, who disregarded the political, tribal and economic affinities of the indigenous peoples in their division of the land and peoples of Africa. Indeed, as the borders of African nations were expected to collapse, there was also the hope that the new calligraphy of poverty and disease drawn in Africa as the new map of a land wars, drought, neo-colonialism, political instability and the debt burden, would be redrawn by the joint efforts of all Africans in the reinvention of the continent.

However, the most significant conflict between African nations in the post-independence era has been dispute over national borders. In 1986, Burkina Faso and Mali went to war over a disputed border area.[98] Following a ceasefire, both states went to the International Court of Justice of Arbitration, which ruled in favor of Mali, basing its judgment on cartographic evidence from the colonial period; and on the Cairo Declaration of the African states on respect of colonial boundaries. In 1989, Guinea-Bissau and Senegal also went to the same court over the delimitation of their Maritime borders. The case was resolved amicably by the two nations, following the inconclusive ruling of the International Court. In 1993, the International Court also ruled in favor of Chad in the disputed strip of territory along Lake Chad, between it and Libya, which had led to incessant skirmishes. Nigeria and Cameroon are still sparring over which country owns the oil rich Bakassi peninsula. In the Great Lakes region, there have been countless wars of attrition between the governments of Uganda and Rwanda on one hand, and between the governments of Uganda and Sudan on the other. In all cases, the respective governments have been supporting rebel groups in their neighboring African countries.

The Great Lakes region which comprise roughly of Uganda, Western Tanzania, Rwanda, Burundi, and the north-eastern part of the Democratic Republic of Congo has become a conundrum of a sort: a region rich with human, natural and mineral resources but which abound in crises. René Lemerchand has argued that tension between the ethnic groups in some parts of the region, who were arbitrarily parceled out into different countries by the colonialists, is sending seismic shock waves across the rest of the region. This has created what he calls a 'kin country syndrome' wherein people of the same ethnic region in different countries identify with their ethnic groups in troubled countries in the region. "Where ethnic fault-lines cut across national boundaries, conflict tends to spill-over from one arena to the next, transforming kin solidarities into a powerful vector of transnational violence. An action-reaction pattern sets in whereby victims in one setting become aggressors in the other. Such, in a nutshell, is the essence of the kin-rallying syndrome behind the escalation of violence in the region...Refugee flows can best be seen as the vehicles through which emotions are unleashed, ethnic ties manipulated, collective energies mobilized, and external support secured. What is at stake here in not simply the physical survival of human beings, but the political survival of specific ethnic communities."[99]

The former United Nations Commissioner for refugees, Sadako Ogata points out that the refugee situation in the Great Lakes region has not been helped by the fact of the 'kin country syndrome': "The large presence of Hutu refugees in the Kivu region of Zaire as well as the Tutsi prevalence in Rwanda had a profound impact on the political process in the Great Lakes region, in particular on Zaire. The complex ethnic composition of the Kivu population, the acute question of citizenship in the Zairean constitutional process, and the rising tension between Rwanda and Zaire altogether undermined the possibility for any solution to the Rwandan refugee problem. In the end Rwanda, in close alliance with Zairean rebel forces that organized themselves and formed the Alliance of Democratic Forces for the Liberation of Congo (AFDL), attacked the refugee camps in Kivu and forced the return of a large number of refugees in November

1996. The remaining refugees headed west to escape being attacked or forced back to Rwanda."[100]

The same arbitrariness was displayed in West Africa which continues to hamper the stability of African states. Many West Africans of the same ethnic origin were arbitrarily separated from one another by the colonialists, who divided them into different countries and in some cases with a different language (like the Yoruba who are found in English-speaking Nigeria as well as in French-speaking Togo and Benin). It is only natural that any conflict in which the Yoruba of Nigeria are involved would attract some sympathy from their brothers and sisters in other African countries. The weakening of the link between African nations is perhaps the greatest threat to economic and political growth and integration of the African continent and one of the saddest legacies of colonialism.

All of these negative effects of colonialism are to be taken into consideration in understanding the African condition. When one looks at the effect of colonialism in Africa, we are looking at the disruption of the history of a people; we are looking at the interruption of a natural progressive movement in Africa; we are considering the ontological onslaught on the form and shape of a whole race. Africa lost all her precious works of arts and monuments to the colonialists and all the precious artifacts and historical documents on Africa were all stolen away and have become the best secret of Western governments and agencies. Africans have been enriched one way or another by her contact with Western civilization, for each civilization has something to offer other civilizations. The problem is that the Western colonialists did not respect African civilization and went ahead to destroy it.

This destruction is still continuing. Africans have in a great measure contributed to the demise of their history and civilization, by cooperating with foreigners to ruin their countries economically and politically. However, it would be wrong to say that colonialism totally and absolutely determined the course of Africa's history. This would be an attempt in historical reductionism and paternalism. In terms of the economic and political future of Africa, colonialism was decisive. There are obviously many other factors that contribute to Africa's underdevelopment and political crises, which in addition to the colonial heritage include: "... social pluralism and its centrifugal tendencies, the corruption of leaders, poor labor discipline, the lack of entrepreneurial skills, poor planning and incompetent management, inappropriate policies, the stifling of market mechanisms, low levels of technical assistance, the limited inflow of foreign capital, falling commodity prices and unfavorable terms of trade, and low levels of saving and investment."[101]

However, viewed in its totality, colonialism was an evil of incalculable proportion. The five major benefits that colonialism brought to the Africans in the words of the Kenyan nationalist, Odinga Odinga, were "the inoculation against the plague from which the children ran in fear. There were the tax collections. There was the order to the villagers to work on the roads. There were the cloths, *kanzu*, the long robes copied from Arab garb at the coast, given free to the chiefs and elders to wear to encourage others in the tribe to clothe themselves in modern dresses. There were the schools, which came later, and to which, in the beginning, only the orphans, foster children, poor nieces and nephews and never the favorite sons were sent...["102]

1.5 The Evil of Apartheid and Racism

> *It was during those long and lonely years that my hunger for the freedom of my own people became a hunger for the freedom of all people, white and black. I know as well as I knew anything that the oppressor must be liberated just as surely as the oppressed. A man who takes away another man's freedom is a prisoner of hatred, he is locked behind the bars of prejudice and narrow-mindedness. I am not truly free if I am taking away someone else's freedom, just as surely as I am not free when my freedom is taken from me. The oppressed and the oppressor alike are robbed of their humanity...To be free is not merely to cast off one's chains, but to live in a way that respects and enhances the freedom of others. The true test of our devotion to freedom is just beginning.* - Nelson Mandela[103]

> *Apartheid provided the whites with enormous benefits and privileges, leaving its victims deprived and exploited. If someone steals my pen then asks me to forgive him, unless he returns my pen the sincerity of his contrition and confession will be considered to be nil. Confession, forgiveness and reparation wherever feasible, form part of a continuum...For unless houses replace hovels and shacks in which most blacks live, unless blacks gain access to clean water, electricity, affordable health care, decent education, good jobs, and a safe environment—things which the vast majority of whites have taken for granted for so long, we can just well kiss reconciliation goodbye.[104]*
> - Desmond Tutu

South Africa adopted majority rule in 1994, but the legacies of the apartheid era and racism are still haunting the South Africans and many Africans the world over. But racism is not just an evil that only the Blacks suffered and still suffer; it is an evil that is still embedded in the world's institutions and governments. Racism is the ultimate human disease. It is the cancer of the human soul and eats away at those who accept it as a way of life. It is the path to darkness and closes the door to any authentic human relationship. Racism is the darkest manifestation of human wretchedness and self-conceit; it is the worst prison for those unfortunate men and women who accept it as the lenses through which to see people of other races outside their own. The racist lives in a very small and suffocating world with blinders and blinkers. It is by considering the way the apartheid regime in South Africa was run that we can appreciate the depth of this disease. It would also give us an opening into the condition of those Africans who suffered racism in America and many who still suffer racism in the world of today because of the accident of color.

Apartheid became the official policy of the government of South Africa in 1948, with the coming to power of the Nationalist party. Apartheid is an Afrikaner word meaning separateness, but is a name that carries with it a bag of iniquities. Chukwudum Okolo defines apartheid as the social, economic, political and sexual or biological segregation of persons on the basis of race.[105] P. F. Wilmot defines it as "the most intense form of exploitation and degradation of African masses, the most entrenched and developed form of Western imperialism, the ultimate in neo-colonialism."[106] What is important in appreciating the apartheid policy is, according to the anti-apartheid activist Allan Boesak, the fact that people are seen not as created in the image and likeness of God, but by virtue of their racial identity which confers on them rights or denies same to them. Donald Wood would thus see this obnoxious system as "a carefully calculated, meticulously planned network of racist laws whose viciousness is unequalled."[107]

As a system, apartheid was based on the principle of racial superiority, and so was comparable in principle and operation to Nazism. As Rev. Jan Vorster says, "Hitler has given the Germans a vocation and a fanaticism that permitted them to retreat from no one. We must follow their example...to carry out our vocation."[108] That vocation was to dehumanize, suppress, destroy and objectify the Africans in order to secure the safety and well-being of the Whites of South Africa. In a sense, apartheid was motivated by the most primordial of all fears: the fear of the other. It was a system that was built on fear. In that context, the perpetrators of the apartheid system were cowards and felt inferior that they could have lost if they were to compete with the black South Africans. Hitler had argued that the law of nature is that of perpetual separation of races when he wrote, "The most portent principles of nature's rule is the inner segregation of the species of all living beings on this earth."[109]

Charles Darwin had earlier in the 19th century postulated in his *Origin of Species* that there are variations in nature and that through the process of natural selection, the stronger appropriates to itself the good things of life, while the weaker dies off. David Hume was the first Western thinker to assert that Blacks are naturally inferior to Whites because they had no indigenous manufacturers among them and no arts and sciences. Levi-Bruhl characterized the traditional man as having a pre-logical mentality, which does not fall within the canons of logical reasoning. Levi-Bruhl argued that in traditional societies, there is clear evidence of an indifference to the law of contradiction. This was an attempt to present the so-called traditional institutions like Africa as backward and intellectually inferior. Thinkers like Evan-Pritchard have debunked Levi-Bruhl's findings as baseless and a mere assumption.[110] Racial superiority biologists like Madison, Grant, and Arthur Jensen had come out with highly suspicious and controversial findings that Blacks are genetically inferior to Whites. Supporting this claim, H. C. Menchen observed that the 'Negro' brain is not "fitted for the higher forms of mental efforts, his ideals no matter how laboriously he is trained and sheltered remain that of a clown." Researchers on DNA evidence are proving that many people who thought themselves White may be Black and those who think themselves Black may actually be White. They also report that every living human being can trace his or her DNA to the Mitochondrial Mother, an African woman who lived 2,000,000 years ago.[111]

Today, these theories have few admirers, because the reality on the ground about equal mental capacities across the races does not validate any racial mental superiority theory. The White supremacists in South Africa introduced the apartheid policy because of their fear of the Blacks outnumbering them and to protect their economic interests. In addition, there was a religious dimension to apartheid. The Dutch Reformed Church with its own perverted Christian credo justified apartheid as ordained by God. "Apartheid and the racial superiority which underlies it as a system was born not only by race and economic power but also of faith-religion."[112]

South Africa is a melting pot of different races: Afrikaners, Asians, Indians, the "Coloreds," and the Blacks. Their coming together was a matter of historical accident, but their co-existence was marked by the attempt by the Whites to dominate other races especially the owners of the land, the Black South Africans. The aim of the Whites in South Africa was, according to Cecil Rhodes, the Premier of the British Cape in 1894, "to be the lords of this people (i.e., the Blacks) and keep them in subject position." This passion for domination gave birth to structural, physical and mental violence. The structural violence refers to the apartheid laws, which allowed the Bureau of State Security (BOSS) and the *Broederband*, an organization similar to the Ku Klux Klan, to freely unleash violence on Africans. "Apartheid is a system of racial discrimination built atop an immense foundation of economic exploitation, political repression, and cultural obliteration, established and maintained by ruthlessly organized and executed violence of Europeans against Africans."[113] The physical violence relates to tortures, police terrors, massacres in Soweto (June 16, 1976) and Sharpeville (March 21, 1960), etc. The mental violence refers to the loss of hope, loss of a sense of self-esteem and worth, which according to the philosopher Sartre, is "a person's attitude towards the precious privilege of doing what he wills from the innermost depths of his ego."[114]

Apartheid was a system founded on the separation of the races; it was a policy to prevent racial contamination of the Whites by the Blacks. This was supported by the Group Areas Act and the Influx Control aimed at keeping Africans in their separate areas. In this way, each race would develop differently according to their conditions: the White in an upward swing of prosperity and peace, the Blacks in the downward slide of poverty and violence. The segregation of the races was necessary according to the architect of the system, Dr. D. F. Malan, "to ensure the safety of the White race and of Christian civilization."[115] Africans were as a result forcefully ejected from their original land of habitation. They were swarmed into ghettoes in independent homelands (Bantustans) like Transkei, Bophuthatsawana, Kwazulu, etc., and confined into the so-called Black 'townships' like Soweto. These Black areas were really slums that mocked the humanity of the Black South Africans. They were "impoverished rural ghettoes with no industries, no major towns and cities, poor communication—in practice they will amount to little more than a chain of labor reservoirs to which White South Africans will send requisition orders for workers."[116]

Black South Africans were compelled to carry references or passbooks, which contained personal information about them. Anyone who violated this rule was liable to an automatic six months imprisonment or more. There was also forced labor as well as brutalities upon arrest for breaking the pass law, among other legal restrictions imposed on the Blacks. The Blacks were not only socially segregated, they were also deprived of their fundamental human rights—they could not express their opinions, they were not allowed to vote or to be voted for; they could not move in and out of their country; they were not allowed to fall in love with or marry the Whites and could not choose where to work or the kind of work they would do.

"Suffering indignities and deprivations, the African lives in intense contradiction with the political and economic structures in which he discovers himself as a result of history. His consciousness is of his unfreedom."[117] Violations of human rights could be in the form of official racism, totalitarianism, and the deliberate refusal to satisfy basic human needs. The South African government or her agents, according to the post-Apartheid Truth and Reconciliation Commission, was guilty of intentional killings, mutilation or humiliation of a distinct racial group (Blacks), detention without trials, miscarriage of justice and other abuses of human rights.[118]

Economically, the Blacks were a disinherited lot, for 'breathes there no man, with soul so dead who never to himself hath said this is my own native land.' The Blacks constituted 70.0% of the population but were given 13% of the land, while the Whites with 17.8% of the population had 86% of the land. Africans, during the apartheid days, were not true citizens of South Africa. They worked in mines and plantations with low pay, and while working in White areas under the Influx Control were housed in settlements without their wives and children. Under the Master and Servant Act, Native Labor Regulation Act (no. 15) and the Native Service Control Act (no. 24), Africans could not resign their jobs for any reason except with the consent of their employers. This means that even if one was not satisfied with the condition of work, as was always the case with the Black Africans, they could not quit the job unless they had worked for upward of two years.

While Whites got 70% of the country's income, Africans got only 17%. While the Blacks had no access to well-paid jobs, to prevent them from quitting their jobs, the apartheid government outlawed idleness (not having a job). Thus, anyone who resigned his job would most likely be regarded as idle and could be fined, conscripted into forced labor, or imprisoned. The logic of apartheid was repressive and unreasonable and betrayed the worst inhumanity to which Africans were subjected in their native land. "To keep apartheid going, an untenable position had to be made tenable, oppression has had to be followed by oppression, and repressive laws have had to be followed by more repressive laws."[119]

Apartheid is obviously an onslaught on the human dignity of Africans. In the first place, the method of punishment in the apartheid enclave degraded the personality of people. One could be 'listed' and thus banned from being quoted or from disseminating any kind of information. One could be confined to one's home for years or even imprisoned for opposing the regime, as was the case with Nelson Mandela and some leaders of the African National Congress. There were various other inhuman punishments like the 'wet towel treatment' which could cause partial or complete asphyxiation; there was the electric shock in the mouth, nipples, genitals, and eardrums. There was also the solitary confinement with blindfold and the dropping of a heavy weight from a cord tied to one's genitals. All these treatments according to Winnie Mandela were meant to "crush your individuality completely, to change you into a docile being from whom no resistance can arise, to terrorize you, to intimidate you into silence."[120] Apartheid tied a color tag onto one's humanity. One had a dignity because he or she was White and one had no dignity because he or she was Black. To have a dignity you have to become White and because you cannot recreate yourself, you had to bear the burden of being treated as an outcast. Apartheid systematically destroyed the dignity of Black South Africans.[121]

The pain suffered by Black South Africans was also felt by the whole Black race the world over. As elementary school kids in the 1980s, we sang in praise of Steve Biko, the founder of the Black Consciousness movement, who was killed under suspicious circumstances in detention for his opposition to the apartheid regime. Nelson Mandela, Winnie Mandela, Desmond Tutu, Walter Sisulu and many others were idolized in many parts of Africa for they represented the face of the suffering of Black Africans in South Africa. At the same time, Africans all over the world also saw the humiliation of the Blacks in South Africa as the humiliation of the Blacks all over the world. Many people still wonder why the world could allow such evils for so long. What happened to the conscience of many men and women of good will in the West? There were random words of condemnation of the evils of apartheid but there were no concrete action to tear down this evil empire.

Apartheid was a more evil system than communism and fascism, but it best served the interest of the Western powers hence they turned their eyes away. Even the application of sanctions by the United Nations was opposed by United States of America and Britain who preferred an ineffective and quixotic 'constructive engagement' policy with the apartheid regime in South Africa. We do not negotiate with evil; there was no negotiation with Nazism and there is no present negotiation with the agents of terrorism. In accepting to negotiate with the apartheid government and in tolerating this evil for over half a century, the West sullied its social conscience and showed a lack of real compassion for the African race. The lesson of apartheid, in my estimation, is that evil has a life span that is either short or long depending on what the men and women of good will do. Evil will never triumph over the good. However, when evil rears its ugly head, men and women of good will should rise up in one chorus of condemnation and take action against it. If our estimation of evil or the way we react against it, is determined by how it directly affects our lives, humanity can never make real progress in the fight against evil. Any act of evil in any part of the world, threatens goodness and good will all over the world.

Racism against the Blacks the world over has not ceased. Many years ago, Frantz Fanon, one of the most perceptive commentators on the African condition, with regard to racism and colonialism, observed that for most Africans the only way to be human beings is to become White or to accept the values of White people. This mentality is born out of the experience of inferiorization under the iron rule of colonialism and slavery, which invaded Africans' living space. This is seen often in Africans' "constant preoccupation with attracting the attention of the White man, his concern with being powerful like the White man, his determined effort to acquire protective qualities—that is, the proportion of being or having that enters into the composition of the ego." [122] The truth is that I cannot change myself to be any other kind of person; I love myself as a Black man for that is the great gift that God has given me. However, if someone hates me because of who I am, it is not my problem but that of the person. I may though start wondering whether there is something wrong with who I am. For some Africans, this fills them with a sense of inferiority, frustration and aggression; for some others it makes them pity and resist the racists.

The desire for acceptance, respect and recognition is a basic human aspiration. This is what all Africans wish to give and receive from people of other races. Unfortunately, there are some Africans who are yet to come to terms with this reality: they want to bleach their color to White and surgically alter their faces to look like White people; they want to have hair like Whites; they want to speak like White people and they want ultimately to leave Africa and be in the White man's land, which for them is the ultimate human triumph. For such Africans, Frantz Fanon offers this advice: "there is no White world, there is no White ethic, any more than there are White intelligence. There are in every part of the world men who search...I am a part of Being to the degree that I go beyond it. And through a private problem, we see the outline of the problem of action...I do not have the right to allow myself to be mired in what the past has determined. I am not the slave of the slavery that dehumanized my ancestors."[123]

Humanity must fight against the modern expressions of racism, especially those directed against Africans and people of color. This is manifested in various forms of condescending attitudes and the hubristic cultural arrogance and superiority complex of non-Africans towards Africans. They also manifest in the false sympathy that many Africans experience from non-Africans, who see Africans as unfortunate people, and in the various stereotypes which are used to interpret the African person and condition as if the peoples of Africa can only be understood as suffering and trapped. Also in sports, especially soccer, many Black players still receive racial taunts in form of monkey sounds which degrade the persons who make them. There are many men and women out there who need to be liberated from racial prejudice and hate. When we see the increasing violence in Black neighborhoods in Chicago, New York, Los Angeles, Toronto and Paris, we ought to wonder: Why is this happening to Blacks? Why are Blacks the underclass in many Western cities? Why were Blacks allowed to suffer the worst form of devastation in New Orleans when Hurricane Katrina struck? It is worth noting that after the initial outrage about the abandonment of the Blacks of New Orleans, it has become business as usual, while the reasons why the African Americans suffer in this way are never addressed from the root in the United States. Racism in its new and most pervasive forms against Blacks is still alive and active even in the world's richest democracy.

Racism against Africans comes from interpreting the African people in categories, which sometimes question their rationality, congeniality and conviviality. These breed prejudices and fears and even some derogatory conclusions. Many religious traditions and our common human experience point to a common humanity. Science confers validity on this conclusion in its genetic theories. No one should therefore be excused for being a racist. The racists of this world should be pitied for they have eyes but do not see. They should be resisted through pro-active means and punished to the extent that it makes it impossible for them to continue in their evil and inhuman mentality and way of life. Unfortunately, some of these racists are in positions of authority in many international organizations and Western countries, and their warped and biased perspectives have given birth to many unwholesome policies that have negatively affected the African continent and her peoples, who live either in Africa or in the Western and industrialized world. The gift of "who we are" is not a privilege, which we receive from others; it is a right, which God has conferred on all of us. They precede the recognition of anyone. Our racial differences, which are complementary, should be celebrated and not detested.

This is true for all races like the Africans, the Jews, the Aboriginals, religious minorities, and unsettled migrant peoples who have suffered massive destruction because of who they are. In order to conquer racism, we need sound and inclusive education that opens the mind of the young to the variety in creation and frees the old from prejudice. We need a massive campaign to enthrone love in the world and to remove the conditions that make it possible for people to hate each other. However, "to eradicate racist behaviors of all sorts from our societies as well as the mentalities that lead to it, we must hold strongly to convictions about the dignity of every human person and the unity of the human family. Morality flows from these convictions. Laws can contribute to protecting the basic application of this morality, but they are not enough to change the human heart."[124] The world should hear anew the message of Martin Luther King Jnr that humanity can no longer be tragically bound to the starless midnight of racism and war. Racism should become a bypassed phase of our human history.

1.6 Immigration and Second Slavery

> *The new migrational trend, reminiscent of those of over one hundred years ago now raises very complicated questions for the future of Africa in the new world order. Now as before, it is some of the best, the most virile who, having been trained with the resources of the state are now either being killed in coups and counter coups or they are compelled to flee in search of better and greener pastures abroad. How shall we cope as we try to rebuild our lives? When will the best now running for safety return home, will our lives be reduced to glorified exile? When will our new slavery come to an end?*[125]

These complexities raised by Matthew Hassan Kukah, represent the concern of many Africans today about their future. There are more Africans wanting to leave their continent than those that wish to live and work for a better future for their respective countries. Failing economies, unemployment, human rights abuses, armed conflict, and inadequate social services added to the better living condition in the industrialized world have been identified for the outward migration of African professionals and non-professionals. According to *Africa Recovery* magazine,[126] industrialized countries are in growing need of two types of immigrant labor—those willing to do poorly paid, dirty and dangerous jobs that their own nationals scorn, and highly specialized professionals such as software specialists, engineers, doctors and nurses.

The World Bank estimates that over 70,000 of Africa's most qualified professionals leave the continent each year and that the continent spends $4 billion replacing them with foreign expatriates.[127] In South Africa alone, the loss of more than 82,000 skilled personnel over an eight-year period between 1989 and 1997 is estimated to have cost the country US$5 billion. The United Nations Conference for Trade and Development (UNCTAD) quantifies US saving of over US$3.86 billion in training costs as a result of importing 21,000 Nigerian doctors over a ten-year period.[128] The United States, for instance, has 126,000 fewer nurses than it needs and government figures show that the country could face a shortage of 800,000 registered nurses by 2020. Such shortages lead developed nations to embark on massive recruitment of Africans. South Africa in 2003 appealed to the government of Canada to desist from enticing her healthcare personnel with better salary packages than what is being offered in South Africa. In the rural province of Saskatchewan, Canada, more than 50% of doctors are foreign-trained and at least 1 in 5 of the 1,530 doctors are African-trained. More than one third of Africa's skilled manpower has moved over to Europe and North America since 1987.

The recruitment of professionals from one country to another is an acceptable international practice. African professionals are serving in different capacities in many countries especially in Canada, United States of America, Spain, United Kingdom, and France. Most of them receive decent and equal treatment with the citizens of their host countries albeit with some restrictions. In the face of declining number of priests in churches in North America and Western Europe, many African clerics have been invited to take pastoral and missionary responsibilities in churches in these countries. These African clerics enjoy a great measure of respect and equal condition of service in most cases as their Western counterparts. Most of them have been signs of the validity of the co-dependence of humanity on each other for mutual and enriching common living. However, as the uprising by Blacks in the suburbs and slums of Paris in the Fall of 2005 showed, many Africans who emigrate to Europe and North America, are neither integrated into Western societies nor do they rise above poverty and second class citizenship.

The fundamental concern here is whether these professionals are working outside Africa because they are not needed in Africa on one hand, or whether their services are in higher demand outside Africa. Are they outside Africa because they want to escape to the so-called better world? The doctor who closes down his health clinic in a rural African village where he is the only source of healthcare for over 30,000 people to work in the United States, where almost everyone has access to healthcare, is a great loss to Africa. The African-priest doctorate degree holder, who prefers to work as a junior priest in a parish in Europe or North America is a great loss to Africa. The university professor in Africa who leaves his teaching post to take up a junior position in a Canadian university is a great loss to Africa. The commercial farmer in sub-Saharan Africa who abandons his farm to live in the slums of Rome as a drug dealer is a big loss to Africa. The high school teacher in a village school in Africa, who leaves her job to be a prostitute in Naples, Italy, is a big loss to Africa. The list goes on. I believe that African professionals must make a clear distinction of the motive of their services outside the African continent vis-à-vis the relevance of their work to their host countries.

In addition, African professionals who work abroad, must not lose sight of the fact that the task of transforming Africa can never be accomplished unless Africa's human and material resources are developed and used for the betterment of African society, before consideration for other parts of the world. This is because Africa is in deep crisis and cannot afford to continue to suffer a pervasive brain drain, which is working against her development. Some of these Africans, however, are professionals who negotiate suitable and dignifying conditions of service in Western countries. However, most Africans who leave for greener pastures abroad would rather settle for anything. These are the ones who typify the second era of African slavery.

Africa's second slavery has come to signify three realities: (1) the voluntary acceptance by Africans to live as second class citizens in Western countries, (2) the tendency of the average African who 'escapes' from Africa to do all kinds of menial jobs or indulge in shameful criminal activities abroad to survive, and (3) the tendency of African professionals to accept lower status or position or to discard their professional life altogether while living abroad because they are desperate to make money and to survive. In the first era of slavery, Africans were forced against their will to work on the plantations while their task masters treated them as if they had no humanity or dignity; in the second slavery Africans voluntarily give up their freedom and accept any kind of condition and treatment in Western countries. In the first era of African slavery, Africans longed to return to their beloved land but in the second slavery, Africans would rather live in sub-human condition and resist any attempt to return to their native countries. Most Africans would deny their nationalities; make bogus and false claims to escape repatriation when their claims for refugee status fail. In the first slavery, Africans did not know the condition to which they were to be subjected and had no choice, in the second slavery most Africans know what their conditions will be in Europe and North America and prefer it over anything as long as it offers them 'escape' from Africa. The second era of slavery for Africans has come to signify the ugly face of Africa. Africans deny their identity and declare themselves refugees in Western countries. Africans will literally do anything imaginable and unimaginable to live abroad. The degrading conditions of some Africans who live in Western countries are very worrying and it is a big embarrassment to fellow Africans and decent men and women the world over. These conditions give rise to all kinds of unwholesome practices among the Africans.

Migration is as old as the human race. Hospitality is one of the most priceless human assets. Among the Africans, hospitality is a cherished value. Africans believe that the stranger is one's brother or sister hence it is a great evil to harm a visitor. The visitor usually brings blessing and if he or she comes with evil intentions the spirit of the community will prevail against the visitor. The visitor or stranger in African communities demands the highest respect, protection, assistance and support. Most Africans who leave Africa as refugees usually get disappointed when they do not find this African sense of hospitality among their hosting countries or when they experience any form of racism. The Jews having experienced the pain of exile also recognize hospitality as a great virtue. Hospitality is central to the Jewish religion. A passage from the Hebrew Scripture teaches, "You shall not molest the stranger or oppress him, for you lived as strangers" (Exodus 22:20). The Christian faith also emphasizes the virtue of hospitality. The Lord Jesus in his preaching on the judgment on the last day teaches that the way Christians treat strangers will be one of the measures with which they will be judged on the last day, "I was a stranger and you made me welcome" (Matthew 25: 35). Christians see in the foreigner the face of Christ himself who once was a refugee in Africa (Egypt) as reported in the Christian scripture (Luke 2: 4-7; Matthew 2:13-23). The Greeks recognized hospitality as one of the criteria of civilization, so that, from one point of view, the measure of the community's approach towards a fully civilized polity was given by the theory and practice of hospitality maintained therein.[129] Writing on how best to treat immigrants, the Greek philosopher Plato, recommends in *Laws*, "*As regards the alien, we must remember that compacts have a peculiar sanctity...For the alien, being without friends or kinsmen, has the greater claim on pity, human and divine...What anxious care, then, should a man of any foresight take to come to the end of life's journey guiltless of offense towards aliens.*"[130]

Human history and civilization have been defined by migrations often caused by diseases, natural disasters, ecological and geographical factors, religious consideration, poverty and adversity of all kinds. The geography of North America was altered permanently because of the massive migration that came in the wake of the two world wars. In a certain sense, most of the Europeans who fled to North America during the two world wars were welcomed with open arms and given all necessary assistance to emigrate and settle down. This obviously was more out of their racial kinship than the unacceptable conditions in Europe in the 1930s and 40s. Today many of these migrants have become notable men and women in Canada and the United States.

Migration has always been a way of escaping from a bad condition of life to a better situation of things. This is not only natural but also human. The human person has the capacity to change and adapt to new situations of life in order to improve his condition and gain fullness of life and fulfillment. Migration then is not ethically wrong. The causes of migration today are the demographic changes that are taking place in countries that were industrialized first, the increase in inequality between north and south, grinding poverty in some parts of the world, the existence of protectionist barriers in international trade, which do not allow emerging countries to sell their products on competitive terms in the markets of western countries and, finally, the proliferation of civil wars and conflicts.[131] Indeed, the world over, according to a BBC report, it is estimated that migrants sent over $72.3 billion in 2001 from the developed to the developing countries. Senegal earns 2% of her national income from her citizens abroad, while Nigeria earns 4% from the same means. In the United States of America, many migrants from Mexico and Cuba sustain their families in their home countries along with other chains of dependants.[132]

The sad thing, however, is that the Western world is closing her doors on Africans. Any African who goes to any Western embassy for a visa knows that his or her application might be turned down despite the genuineness of his or her motives. The search for visas to travel to Western countries has become a nightmare for most Africans. Africans face all forms of visa restrictions in Western embassies. This is true for professionals and non-professionals alike. All Africans have become tarred with the same brush and are often suspected of having ulterior motives for traveling to the West. It must be admitted, that there is a high percentage of Africans who travel to the Western world with forged documents and false motives. There is also increasing concern globally about terrorism. There is greater vigilance the world over especially in Europe and North America over the kind of people that are being allowed into these countries. These might explain to some extent the reason why many Africans are denied visa application in many Western embassies. However, this does not justify the inhuman and insulting treatment that many Africans are subjected to when in search of visas or even when traveling at many international airports. There must be a clear standard of treatment to be established and benchmarks for visa applicants. In its present state, the whole process is not only arbitrary but also discriminatory against Africans.

The reason Africans are denied visas is not because they do not have legitimate claims to enter the Western world, but rather because they are not wanted. Germany, Holland, and Italy have all abolished their immigration camps and placed stringent conditions for obtaining refugee status or permanent residency. According to a report by Andrew Duffy in *The Toronto Star*[133] there is a growing opposition to new immigrants entering countries of Europe. This is reflected in the policies of extreme right-wing groups and political parties in Austria, Holland, Belgium, and France. A survey conducted in the Dutch city of Rotterdam shows that 62% of the residents support new limits on immigration. The feeling in Rotterdam is that new immigrants make up a high percentage of the underclass in the city and in the growing fear of terrorism some of these immigrants, especially those from Muslim countries of North Africa and the Middle East, could be easily lured into the faceless terror network that is growing by the day. In the early spring of 2004, European leaders sparred over the proposal made by the German Interior Minister, Otto Schily, on how to stem the flow of African migrants by building a 'holding center' in North Africa. These centers would facilitate the deportation of Africans and ensure that they made claims for asylum outside of Europe.[134] This represents a growing unease about the presence of Africans in Europe especially the fact that they represent what Dutch historian Paul Scheffer called an ethnic underclass detached from Western culture and society.[135]

In the early 1970s, Nigerians did not need visas to enter the United Kingdom. This was not only because Nigeria belonged to the Commonwealth but also because Nigeria was very rich at that point in time with a currency that was stronger than the US dollar. The same was true of countries like Zimbabwe, Ghana, and Kenya. The French-speaking Africans were allowed to travel and live in France without legal restrictions. Over 30% of the French population is Black because of this policy. The Netherlands in the 1970s, actively recruited North Africans and Turkish citizens for her industries and factories. Canada is the only Western country, whose immigration policy to Africa has been consistently open and compassionate. Canada's largest city, Toronto, has an immigrant population of 1.25 million (44%), and a significant percentage of these immigrants are Africans.

Much has changed since the 1990s, when the mercenary-motivated Structural Adjustment Program in Africa brought Africa's economies to their knees. At various embassies and international airports, there are usually separate lines for those from Africa, developing countries and the Middle East, and those from Europe, the United States and Canada. There is a clear discrimination against Africans, which has everything to do with racial and economic factors. The West does not want Africans except to use her professionals or to exploit her non-professionals as workers in factories, risky lines of production and other menial jobs. While most Westerners do not need visas to enter other European and North American countries, Africans must obtain them. This way, the number of Africans who enter the Western world will be monitored and curtailed through legitimate and non-legitimate means.

Humanity must, however, understand that we make up a single family of God, and we should take responsibility for one another. The search for security should begin primarily with human security, which guarantees that human communities are in a position to flourish and enjoy their fundamental rights to well-being and a good life and the actualization of their God-given talents. Security among nations will constantly be endangered if the primordial human security is not preserved. "A true culture of peace must therefore be based on a correct conception of the nature of the human person and his or her inherent dignity as well as understanding of the fundamental interdependence of the human family."[136] Peace cannot be imposed by denial of visas to Africans, for instance, or other immigration restrictions on developing countries. Peace is not a gift to the world by the G-8 countries or the work of the exclusive club of the wealthy nations in the UN Security Council. Peace requires the acceptance of the mutual implication of the entire humanity in the wealth and poverty of some parts of the world; and the opening of the global space for those peoples and nations who are suffocating in the heat of poverty and political crisis derived from the deliberate acts of injustice by the developed countries.

It is because of immigration restriction and discrimination against Africans that many of them adopt all kinds of illegal methods to evade the very stringent conditions for entering the West. Joseph Winter[137] of the BBC has chronicled the perilous path taken by thousands of Africans to cross over to Europe across the Sahara, the Libyan coast and the Spanish enclave of Ceuta or Sicily in Italy. Every day, over 2,000 Africans (especially from Nigeria, Gambia, Mali, Guinea-Bissau, Ghana, Cameroon, Algeria, and Morocco) attempt to cross over to Europe illegally and 10% of them get marooned or die on the way. Within the last decade alone over 5,000 Africans died in their risky journey across the Mediterranean or the Sahara desert into Europe. There are many Africans who travel to the Western world with forged documents and fake identity. Most of these Africans live comfortably by African standards but they feel that traveling to the Western world is like going to paradise. If many people in Africa knew what their African brethren suffer to get to Europe and North America and the kind of work they do, many would not be as willing to leave Africa.

In February 2002, I took a tour of five European cities as part of my research for this book (Rome, Brescia, Amsterdam, Berlin, Frankfurt and later in 2003 I traveled to London). My concern was to see how the Africans lived in these cities. In Frankfurt, I visited the refugee camp in Hanau, which was about to be closed down and met a few Africans who looked desperate, depressed and despondent. Most of them made false claims for asylum, which were denied, and most of them had fake passports obtained by fraud. Some others were shopping for some agents who could help them with an arranged marriage with a German or holder of EU passport for them to extend their stay in Europe. The practice was to obtain the passport of those countries of Africa that have some political or economic crisis in order to use that as a basis for seeking asylum. In Berlin, I met a Senegalese who had an arranged civil marriage with a German woman to get the residential permit to stay in Germany. Strolling down Friedrichstrasse in the rich galleries of Lafayette, I met some African ladies who were busy buying some expensive cloths in the Potsdamer Plaza. I introduced myself as a newcomer in town looking for a way of survival. These ladies told me that they are preparing for business (prostitution) and that I should go to the Berlin central train station and I would see many Africans like myself who are homeless and they would tell me how to survive. I spent that night at the Berlin Central Station and was shocked to see many Africans who clearly had no mission or destiny: some were begging for alms, some looked hungry and others were jobbers looking for some means of sustenance either by hook or by crook.

It was, however, in Italy that the condition of the Africans in Europe really hit me. I visited a jail in Perugia in the Umbria region of Italy, just a few meters below the Gothic-draped Piazza Italia. I was shaken by the presence of so many Nigerians and Ghanaians who were imprisoned for crimes ranging from drug and currency trafficking to robbery and human trafficking. In my short-lived romance with an Italian secret agency, I was to discover that the organized criminal class in Italy was an international network that included elements from Nigeria, Albania, Russia, Romania, Italy, and Afghanistan among others. One of the African prisoners told me that he had no regret for peddling drugs because that was the only way he could take back from 'White men' the wealth they took away from Africa. Most of the Africans who make money from these crimes do not tell their African families the source of their income in order to discourage this shameful blot on the escutcheon of the African continent. The situation in Africa has, however, made it very difficult for people to ask for the source of wealth of anyone. The man or woman who is able to provide for his family and friends is the local hero and people care less about how the person makes his money. This has marked a radical change in the ethical template of the African world.

The greatest source of shame to the Africans in Italy is the high number of African prostitutes. By the year 2000, it was estimated that there were over 50,000 African prostitutes in Italy alone. Sister Bonetti, and over 250 Italian nuns have volunteered for over a decade to help stop the abuse of African women in Italy with minimal success. These prostitutes are usually young teenagers who are lured away from their African countries (mainly Nigeria, Benin, Cameroon and Ghana) to Italy by a prostitution network that is invisible but strongly connected. I have seen numerous young girls half-naked on lonely streets in various Italian cities in sub-zero temperature during the winter. I have spoken with a number of these hapless girls and have not personally recovered from the nightmare of their sad stories. Most of them did not choose to be prostitutes but were forced into it by these gangs. They were deceived by their recruiters in sub-Saharan Africa to leave their respective countries for a better living but upon arrival in Italy everything changed. They live under the tutelage and dictatorship of some heartless women called 'madam' (most of them 'liberated' African prostitutes who have now been 'promoted' to 'madam' because they have served their terms). They are forced to answer to a new name. They are made to sleep with a certain number of men every day. They are denied any identity but assume only a number. They daily face threats of being eliminated should they do anything that jeopardizes 'the business.' Because these girls are too ashamed to return to Africa without 'making it,' they choose to remain in this bondage until they are able to escape from their mistresses and masters. The prostitution chain in Italy is a real shame to the Christian heritage of that country. The continued exploitation of African girls by fellow Africans and their European "clients" is an affront on our common humanity; it haunts and hurts anyone with any modicum of human sensibility.

I spent two nights with Africans in 'little Senegal,' a slum in the Northern Italian city of Brescia; I spent five days respectively with some Africans in Belma South Oest (Amsterdam Spot) Amsterdam, one week in North London, and three days in the Jane and Finch area in Toronto, and was traumatized by the living condition of the Africans with whom I freely mingled. Africans who live abroad suffer a lot to provide for their families as well as to take care of their relatives and friends living in Africa. Some of them spend sleepless nights working to earn some extra money to survive; some of them do a lot of odd jobs to survive. A majority of them do not have any decent jobs and also become consumed in some very unwholesome habits and lifestyles. The African section of Termini in Rome could compare with any slum in Dakar or Conakry. It is poverty that has driven most Africans to this kind of lifestyle. In some cases it is also greed and pride that have pushed some into very risky undertakings. I do, however, believe that a better way of living abroad is still possible for Africans and that this rush to leave Africa is unhelpful for the African continent in the long run.

The ordinary African does think that it is better to be a slave in the West than a king in Africa. Changing this orientation is a very important challenge, especially given the flamboyant lifestyle of Africans who live abroad when they return home for Christmas and other community celebrations. Here again we are dealing with the effects of poverty. People who have nothing will easily be intimated by those who flaunt their wealth like many foreign-based Africans do in their local villages. Africans must take time to think how this kind of living would advance the cause of their continent. Africans need to develop a think-home philosophy and a sense of responsibility and contentment. The African problem is not one that will be solved through *flight from* Africa but rather through *engagement in and with* Africa.

In the final analysis, the African era of second slavery represents another aspect of Africa's homelessness. This is because it hits at Africa's identity crisis. Who do we say an African is in the world of today? What does the African certified accountant who prefers to beg for alms in Berlin or the 20 Africans who share a single bedroom in Paris think of themselves and their self-esteem? What does an African medical doctor who works as a cleaner in a London clinic think of himself? What does an African leader who prefers to buy mansions in Paris think of himself and his continent? What does an African nurse who prefers to roam the streets of Amsterdam as a prostitute think of herself? These are fundamental questions for the Africans and the fact is that these incidents are not isolated but have become a pattern of life. Millions of Africans are wishing that they left their countries. Most Africans who live abroad are always bombarded with requests by their friends and family members as to when they will bring them over to the 'the heaven on earth' that Europe and America supposedly are. It must, however, be said that a world that has pushed a large percentage of Africans into this kind of desperation is unjust and the governments of Africa that have sunk their citizens into the nadir of frustration and despoliation should be seen for what they are: failed leaders and traitors of the hope and aspiration of the African race. As I wrote this section, I read a scriptural commentary by Martin Luther, which represents the Christian attitude to refugees, migrants and the poor in general, which resonates in most religions, "You are not to kill: This commandment is violated not only when we do evil, but also when we have the opportunity to do good to our neighbors and to prevent, protect, and save them from bodily harm or injury, but fail to do so. If you send a naked person away when you could clothe him, you have let him freeze to death. If you see anyone who is suffering from hunger and do not feed her, you have let her starve…it will be of no help for you to use the excuse that you did not assist their deaths by word or deed, for you have withheld your love from them and robbed them of the kindness by means of which their lives might have been saved. Therefore God rightly calls all persons murderers who do not offer counsel or assistance to those in need and peril of body and life…It is God's real intention that we should allow no one to suffer harm but show every kindness and love."[138]

1.7 Understanding the African World of Today

> *Africa's socio-economic development has become more dependent than ever on its ability to plan for the future. Confronted by turbulent international markets, uncertain flows of aid and other external financing, as well as political instability, African governments and economic actors are becoming increasingly aware of the need to better forecast future opportunities and constraints and to strengthen their capacity for long-range planning. Short-term crisis management is inadequate for what is generally seen as long-term process of recovery and development.* - Africa Recovery, November 1995.

The story of Africa has no single strain, but it adds up to a single condition: historically born challenges, persistent and present difficulties, and hope among the ordinary people who wish to see a better and brighter future.

Many people see an aspect of the African story and draw a precipitate conclusion that Africa is a land of crises. Others see the stories and identify the strains as forming a wider picture of a land of people whose complex problems demand a broader and integrated approach. Africa's identity crisis, economic paralysis; the historical problems of slavery, colonialism, apartheid, poverty, political instability, globalization; and the immigration restrictions on Africans by the industrialized nations make up a single picture of Africa seen in a wider and integral perspective.

This integrated vision of the African reality is related to what Martin Nkafu has called 'African vitology' that is, that life and reality is one in Africa. Every effort that is made in addressing the African condition today has to be comprehensive and synthetic. African vitology is "a conceptual vision of the whole of reality, where there are no spaces for irreducible dichotomies between matter and spirit, religious commitment and daily life, soul and body, the world of the living and the world of the dead…each concept, scientific field, cultural aspect is a value, which is found within a whole."[139] My proposal is that the variegated challenges of African countries should never be addressed in isolation. I argue along the lines of the *African Futures Initiatives*, that "long term development programs are useful in helping African countries achieve some equilibrium, but they cannot provide lasting solutions unless they are integrated within the long term framework."[140] *Short-term emergency reaction must integrate into it a new narrative of the bases for the structural conditioning of African society, which give rise to the emergencies.*

Each challenge is a symptom of something more fundamental. The water crisis in Africa, for example, cannot be treated in isolation from ecological factors, the exploitative monopolization of the sources of water in Africa by some Western companies, glaring mismanagement of resources, and failed government policies. Some charitable organizations that I work with, who have tried to dig wells in Africa, discover that there are many other things which should have been addressed that could have prevented the water crisis. This example could be ramified to all aspects of life in Africa whether with regard to the structures of African societies or natural disasters.

There is, for instance, a total breakdown of the social and economic fabric in most countries of Africa when they face outbreaks of epidemics like the Ebola disease outbreak in Congo-Brazzaville or environmental disasters (Congo, Madagascar, Ethiopia, Chad, Cameroon, etc). This is because the social, economic and political structures are not strong enough to withstand any crisis. In addition, these countries that have a history of earthquakes, volcanic irruption (Goma, Congo-Kinshasa, Lake Nyos in Cameroon), drought (Horns of Africa), and flooding (Madagascar) do not have any workable crisis response to these problems.

The question is always raised whether Africans can effectively manage their countries and the challenges that come in the path of nationhood. The answer is that Africans can manage their own affairs. The micro-level of social organization in Africa is vibrant and strong. At the village level, the Africans maintain robust and workable structures that protect and preserve the common good. The idea of nationhood understood as an amalgamation of diverse tribes and religions into one political entity, is one that has to be properly understood and forged into the culturally robust social structures at the micro-level. At this level of life and social organization, people of African origin enjoy some stability and order; but at the national level they swim in the turbulence of chaos and identity crisis.

In Nigeria, people identify themselves more by their ethnic origin than by their national identity. One is first a Yoruba, Ogoni, Hausa-Fulani, Igbo, etc., then a Nigerian. The priority of the ethnic identity in Africa over the national identity is ontological as well as historical. People can connect with their ethnic identity in terms of their personal history, their cultural traditions, their language, way of dressing, customs, etc. What is referred to, for instance, as a Nigerian culture is a nebulous concept. It is true of other African countries. This is also applicable to the question of who an African is. Many Africans are identified as such by non-Africans who do not often understand the cultural diversities of Africa. If I went to my village and told them that I am an African, most people would think that I am crazy because it makes no sense to them. I do think that the concept of African is more meaningful for the Africans in Diaspora, especially the African-Americans, because it shapes their identity. These Africans have somehow lost their ethnic origin and so can rightly identify with the historical concept of Africa as a single entity. The people who are referred to as Africans do not always see themselves in that category, except in relation to other people who are not identified as Africans. There is nothing, properly speaking, which could be called African culture or, for instance, an African language, but rather an ethnic language in the African continent. I am first an Igbo tribe's man, then a Nigerian, then an African in that order. What is primordial and fundamental is that I am an Igbo man, because that is the first world into which I was born. The other identifications, like Nigerian and African are secondary in my identity, because they can be dissolved and I still remain who I am: an Igbo man.

In other words, Nigeria can cease to exist today, but my being an Igbo man can never become history in my consciousness. The ethnic identity is always prior to the national identity in Africa.

African identity at the political level is more historical than ontological, but at the cultural level it is more ontological than historical. This means that defining people as Africans has more to do with historical factors of slavery, colonialism, the introduction of Christianity, and the emergence of the post-colonial modern states in the African continent than any other factor. When Africans speak of African culture, African religion etc., they are refering to common elements of culture, religion etc., found among different African ethnic groups. I do agree with those who like Basil Davidson believe that the predicament of Africa is the curse of the nation-state and its often unworkable ethnic components. This is because ethnicity in Africa is to a large extent synonymous with western nationalities. Reflecting on this, Samuel Kobia writes, "The nation-state in its current form and substance, especially in Africa, must be subject to an ethical critique. How does the nation-state respond or correspond to the question of human dignity? What are the ethical criteria for its existence? Is the nation-state absolutely the necessary institution that alone guarantees organizing for sustenance of life on planet earth? It is within the context of the African experience that we seek to comprehend the meaning of the nation-state and why it should exist at all."[141] Being an African person in its varied ethnic expressions is more meaningful than the political entities created in Africa by foreign colonialists.

This is a significant insight, because the challenges of the countries in the African continent may sometimes appear to be the same, but each carries its own uniqueness according to the ethnic components of each country and its geographical conditions. Each ethnic group has its own unique characteristics; the attempt to collapse these identities in order to achieve an idyllic national character has proved to be a will-o-the-wisp. These identities have to be respected and harmonized in the light of clearly articulated common aspirations. There should be a unity in diversity, which the colonialists did not recognize and which has proven to be a recurrent challenge to African countries. Understanding the strengths and weaknesses of the ethnic units of each African country, is a vital step in understanding the African world. This basic understanding would help to open up infinite horizons, on what needs to be done to establish a partnership model between the government and the people on one hand, and the international development agencies and the peoples of Africa on the other. This model of understanding is proving to be most helpful and productive in South Africa (the so-called rainbow nation), which recognized in her political, economic and social policies the racial and ethnic diversity of the country.

I do believe that Africans should be determined to go for the 'long haul' and ask the necessary questions about the nature and structure of their countries. However, this determination is lacking because of the leaders (political, religious, etc) who are reaping political and economic dividends from the crises in Africa. This also has some consequences on the governments we have in Africa and the policies and programs they pursue. Most governments prefer short-term policies to long-term programs, which should have brought about sustainable development. As one African observer notes of governments in Africa, "they set up projects that have no economic rationale whatsoever. They entered into all kinds of shady deals to set up industries most of which never took off. They realized their mad dreams of grandeur but only through monumental waste. Choices of technology, location of industries, and products were either completely arbitrary or reflected a highly idiosyncratic understanding of how industrialization takes place. Rarely did they reflect anything at national interest."[142]

Most of these policies are not keyed into a wider picture of a broad-based national policy. In most cases, the policies are driven more by political expedience than by any other factor. Most often, African governments work for the interest of a particular group and not the whole nation. Governance has, therefore, become the basis for the selective distribution of the scarce resources of the country, other than the agency for re-engineering the people and steering them to build up wealth and the collective economic, political, and social pool from which all could draw. Sometimes, governments in Africa prefer to ask and receive relief from international organizations, instead of plotting a new development graph, whose outline and evolution in a concrete way could be supported by international organizations. It is obvious that some governments and voluntary groups in Africa would prefer to maintain the beggarly status of Africa because it offers them an infinite pool of foreign aids, which in the final analysis they siphon for their selfish ends.

In Nigeria, this was the case at the time when the reckless and heartless regimes of General Babangida and General Abacha respectively rode rough shod on the country. These two oppressive regimes had a dictatorial stamp that brought incalculable harm on the national psyche and destroyed the inner fabric of the country. However, within that time, the nation witnessed an unprecedented outflow of support from the international community for the building and sustaining of civil rights activities in Nigeria. There were many genuine pro-democratic civil rights movements and NGOs in Nigeria, some of whose members were ready to die in the defense of popular democracy. Some of these groups sincerely used the foreign donations they received to fight the evil empire of Nigeria's military dictators, Babangida and Abacha. There were, however, many of these groups who were mere pretenders and whose leaderships were divided overtime by disputes over the distribution of the 'booties' acquired from pro-democracy activism! This also applies to election monitoring in most African countries.

The truth is that most of the crises in Africa are man-made and so can be addressed and averted through the agency of Africans. Sometimes those who are fighting abroad in Western countries for the good of the ordinary people in Africa may not necessarily be genuinely interested in the plight of the ordinary people in Africa. This is why any Western agency that is genuinely interested in Africa's development, should make a genuine effort to understand the continent and work directly with the people, especially at the grass root's level. Some individuals, who were 'mobilizing' abroad against military rule in Nigeria in the 1990s, are today military apologists who are even calling on discredited dictators like General Babangida to make a comeback to power. When one interprets these kinds of social dynamics, one would no doubt need to re-evaluate where the priorities of the African nations lie at any critical moment, and what actions would best promote positive changes in Africa.

The response to problems in Africa, either by Africans or international organizations, has always been to provide relief, which I refer to as the *crises reaction approach*. I do agree that we need an efficient crises response in Africa as in most parts of the world. More importantly, however, unless we sincerely address the factors that generate these crises, we would be building on shifting sands. Seeing the true picture of Africa is essential for both Africans and non-Africans. This appears to be the new thinking among young African thinkers and some perceptive Westerners interested in Africa. They believe that what Africa needs, is the conscious promotion of the capacity of the ordinary Africans to realize their human potentials, so that they can optimally develop their natural resources for the good of their communities.

The key to understanding the true face of Africa is to take an integral and broader picture of the African world. The bane of development policies in most of Africa is this lack of a broader and integral perspective on development. Most of the challenges facing Africa today are rooted in the very history of the various African nations and they will continue to generate tension, civil strife, and antipathy in these countries unless they are broadly addressed and responded to from the root. This complexity could be seen clearly in the conditions of many African countries that are at various stages of liberal democracy. This process has constantly been dogged by difficulties and failures, because the countries of Africa have not laid a true foundation for enduring democracy. There is a misconception of the reasons why democracy and development fail in Africa. Many Westerners think that the reason for the failure of democracy in Africa is that elections are not free and fair or because of corruption in government. The question is not asked why elections are always 'do or die' battles in Africa and why the governments in some of the African countries are corrupt.

The answer to the first is found in the answer to the second. Governance in Africa is big business and perhaps the highest investment anyone could make. Winning an election is like winning a big lottery, which could change and perhaps guarantee one's financial future. As a response to electoral crises, millions of dollars, which should be used to build schools and hospitals, are invested by Western donors to monitor elections, which do little to prevent electoral malpractice. The 2003 national elections in Nigeria were said to be the worst elections in the country's history, yet there is evidence that these same elections were the most monitored elections in the nation's history. Many foreign election observers came to Nigeria and many Western nations sent millions of dollars to support election monitoring. What happens in fact is that most of the local groups that monitor elections are smiling all the way to the banks after the elections, because it affords them a good source of financial support from abroad. The cars and buses used for the election monitoring are quickly converted into public transit for more moneymaking, while the local agencies for election monitoring wait in hope for the next election for another windfall.

According to the United Nations Millennium Project Report, *Investing in Development*, corruption and bad government are not the main causes of poverty and underdevelopment in Africa. The report calls for a deeper and broader understanding of the African situation. According to the report,[143] while there is a highly visible sign of poor governance in places like Zimbabwe, widespread war and violence in Angola, Democratic Republic of Congo, Liberia, Sierra Leone and Sudan, there are many well governed countries like Ghana, Malawi, Mali and Senegal who are caught up in the same grinding poverty like the badly governed African countries. Using formal statistics from organizations like Transparency International (corruption perception index) and Freedom House ranking (democracy ranking), Jeffery D. Sachs argues that relatively well-governed and less corrupt African countries failed to prosper, while extensively corrupt countries in Asia like India, Indonesia and Pakistan enjoyed rapid economic growth.[144] According to the World Bank indicators, Africa's governments are not worse on the average than other governments elsewhere in the world, nor is Africa's corruption worse than what is found in many parts of the Western and non-Western world. There is, therefore, the need to take a more comprehensive look at the African situation and the unexamined assumption that Africa is a land of corruption and misrule. It should not be assumed that all the 53 countries in Africa are all corrupt and that all of them are reeling under the iron fist of bad leaders. As we shall argue in the final part of this work, corruption negatively affects Africa and because of unstable structures it perpetuates Africa's poverty and weakens and even destroys the fledgling structures being laid for sustainable development.

The point that we wish to emphasize here in understanding the African situation is that one cannot lay the cause of the present unacceptable situation of Africa on one factor. Corruption and misrule in some parts of Africa should be seen as symptoms of a deeper problem. This is well presented in the Millennium Report when its authors argue, "Our explanation is that tropical Africa, even in well governed parts, is stuck in a poverty trap—too poor to achieve robust and high levels of economic growth, and in many places simply too poor to grow at all. More policy or governance reform, by itself, is not sufficient to break out of this trap. Africa's extreme poverty leads to low national saving rates, which in turn lead to low or negative economic growth rates. Low domestic saving is not offset by high inflows of private foreign capital, such as foreign direct investment, since Africa's poor infrastructure and weak human capital discourage private capital inflows. With very low domestic saving and low rates of market based foreign capital inflows, there is little in Africa's current dynamics that promotes an escape from poverty."[145]

The inflow of aid and Official Development Assistance to Africa must take into consideration the specific goals to be achieved and the peculiar challenge of each African country. Five structural reasons have been established as the causes of the failure of Africa to realize the Millennium Development Goals; these factors also make Africa vulnerable to poverty and they include: very high transport cost and small markets, low-productivity agriculture, very high disease burden, a history of adverse geopolitics and very slow diffusion of technology from abroad.[146] It is, therefore, important that aid to Africa should be targeted towards addressing these five structural factors which undermine the bases for sustainable development in Africa. This also points to another truth: resolving the present situation in Africa demands a multi-faceted and multi-pronged approach since no single factor could explain the African condition nor could one reduce the solution to one factor. Identifying the structural bases of poverty in Africa, the historical factors at play as well as the international structures of injustice at work in each African country, is a necessary step for any serious engagement with Africa by non-governmental and international agencies. Aids and handouts should not be thrown to Africa without regard to context, and without a clearly articulated vision of how these would respond to the structural context of each African country, and thus stimulate the base for sustainable development.

The foreign donor agencies that spend millions of dollars supporting election monitoring in countries like Nigeria, Zimbabwe and Ghana do not appear to understand African society as presently constituted. Election monitoring does not have even a tangential bearing on building political institutions in Africa. Political education can not succeed in a society where a greater majority of the people is illiterate; or where the people are so disempowered by poverty and the political elites that they do not connect with the political process and the leadership it produces. Establishing democracy in Africa has been one of the greatest sources of civil unrest, division and war, because elections are usually the only key to getting access to the nation's resources. The winner takes all. Elections often lead to many unresolved questions, and leave the losers abandoned and neglected by the winning party.

The reason for the failure of democracies in Africa, according to Claude Ake, is that "the self-appointed agents of democratization in Africa are implausible. They are not so much supporting democracy as using it. For instance, the African elites support democracy only as a means to power, the international development agencies support it as an asset to structural adjustment and Western governments support it ambiguously, torn between their growing indifference to Africa and their desire to promote their own way of life. What is foisted on Africa is a version of liberal democracy reduced to the crude simplicity of multi-party elections. This type of democracy is not in the least emancipatory, especially in African conditions because it offers the people rights they cannot exercise, voting that never amounts to choosing, freedom which is patently spurious, and political equality which disguises highly unequal power relations."[147] Nigeria has often come close to national implosion as a result of failed elections. The civil war in Nigeria was fought as the long awaited consequence of a failed election (which had led to military rule that preceded the war).

When Nigeria fought a civil war (1967-1970) that claimed over a million lives, there was a major international humanitarian supply coming in randomly and selectively to the country to help the war victims and refugees. However, none of the international bodies or Western agencies and governments asked the fundamental question about why the Nigerians were killing each other. If these questions were asked it would have helped avert future conflicts. Since the end of the Nigerian civil war, there are still conflicts among the ethnic groups and different religions, and between the fortune-seeking political elites and the suffering masses of our people. According to a news report in *ThisDay*, Nigeria's daily newspaper (07-10-04), over 55,000 Nigerians have lost their lives in communal and religious violence in the country within the last three years alone! This number is higher than the number of Iraqis and coalition soldiers killed within the first year of the Second Iraqi war. It is obvious that the cycle of violence in Nigeria will never end unless there are fundamental questions raised as to the basis for the existence of the country. The nationality question has yet to be resolved, and many of the minority tribes in the oil producing areas of Nigeria, whose future was a constant cause of worry even during the colonial era, are still suffering unspeakable injustice. The National Conference held in Nigeria in 2005 was a huge parody and an inexcusable waste of public fund. Its convocation, deliberation and recommendations do not reflect the sentiments of majority of Nigerians.

If Nigerians took time to address openly and freely the reasons for the civil war and if the international community raised the issue of the inchoate structural ethnic 'dis-configuration' of Nigeria at the time of the war, the Nigerian federation would have redefined her place in the world and restructured according to the complex ethnic structures of the land. Imposing a false democracy on various ethnic groups in Nigeria and using it for their own selfish ends, has been the most heart-wrenching evil brought upon the country by political elites. What has emerged is that more than 45 years after Independence, "Nigeria is no closer to being a viable state in the 1990s than it was in the 1960s when the country gained its independence. Indeed, the state-building project must now be pronounced a failure, inasmuch as the state has lost the bid to be the repository of the primary loyalty of Nigerians to ethnic and national groups as well as local communities."[148]

There is a tendency among the international community to *react* to *crises* in Africa instead of addressing the reasons for the revolving cycle of crises. This is based on a wrong reading of the story of Africa. Africa would cease to be a continent of crises and cries if the fundamental structures of African nation-states are addressed, with the recognition in national constitutions of the unique characteristics and identities of each ethnic component. The international community cannot continue to send aid to

Africa without reaching her limit. The greater need is to make the presence of international groups bear fruit by fundamentally addressing the *constants* in Africa (e.g., education, economic development, creating employment opportunities for young people, agriculture, and building of social and political structures), while trying to manage the *variables* (e.g., crises of political, economic, ecological, or health kinds). If African countries worked towards the education of their populace, agricultural production and building up their national, political, and economic structures, with or without help from outside Africa, they would realize that they would be reducing the causes of crises in Africa. What Africa needs is "capacity-building" and not the constant inflow of aid and emergency reliefs. *These aid only respond to problems that result from the failure to build up the capacity of African countries to help themselves in the first place.* Africans should become the agents of the transformation of their continent. They should not be the objects of Western sympathies and aid but active subjects in the shaping of the destiny of this great continent. Empowering Africans to do this is the most fundamental challenge facing African countries and those countries and international organizations who are genuinely interested in a coherent, ordered and gradual building up of Africa from scratch.

All development initiatives in Africa must be directed towards capacity-building, which demands that random problems should not be seen in isolation of the whole complex question of the general orientation and direction of African society. Capacity-building "encompasses the country's human, scientific, technological, organizational, institutional and resource capabilities. A fundamental goal of capacity building is to enhance the ability to evaluate and address the crucial questions related to policy choices and modes of implementation of development options, based on an understanding of environmental potentials and limits and of needs as perceived by the people of the country concerned."[149]

In ordinary language, capacity-building would entail helping someone to help himself or herself, by understanding the person's real needs and empowering him or her to pursue those needs himself or herself. This cannot happen if Africa's goals and objectives are not clearly articulated by Africans or if the African condition is interpreted with categories that defy and disregard Africa's cultural history and evolution. On the other hand, the international community and donor agencies, should see the broader picture of the African continent, and engage the people in a development partnership that prioritizes capacity-building over any other intervening variable. All kinds of paternalism that tend to treat Africans as helpless and directionless or immature and lacking in self and group direction because of a misconceived absence of self and group consciousness, should be abandoned by non-Africans working in Africa. This is not to say that understanding Africa demands a sole concentration on social analytical tools derived from the African reality, but rather that it is impossible to understand the African continent and her complex present condition, without integrating a narrative based largely on the tools of African social and cultural analysis.

There is, however, a major difficulty for the Africans given the ongoing contagion of globalization, the dead weight of debt burdens, the effects of slavery and colonialism, and the many years of mutual hostility among some of the ethnic groups. Many of the countries of Africa are still reeling from the pain that has accompanied their national life since gaining independence from their colonial masters. Capacity-building for the Africans would first begin by Africans setting an agenda for their future. The Western world and international agencies cannot define the agenda for Africa nor should they dictate the tone for the Africans. Any assistance to Africa that is based on some conditions and targets set by factors and currents outside Africa would ultimately fail. Western agencies and governments working in Africa must also be sensitive to the fact that ordinary Africans are huddling through the cold of night in rubbles of pain and poverty, because there is a democracy deficit which encloses their political and economic structures within the self-serving caesura of political and religious leaders in Africa. Donor initiatives should, therefore, be targeted at the grassroots through village heads and tribal leaders, whose positions are upheld by their intimate attachment to the spiritual fountain of the community.

African countries must, however, prioritize food production. A continent that cannot feed itself is really caught in an intractable web of dependency. African peoples must be able to feed themselves by tilling their lands. Based on what I saw growing up in Eastern Nigeria, agriculture even of a non-mechanized kind can provide food for Africans. As children growing up in the Eastern part of Nigeria, my parents practiced subsistence agriculture to supplement their salaries. We learnt how to cultivate the land and, for the most part, our farms provided our family of eight with most of what we ate. Subsistent agriculture in most of Africa has died. Part of the reason for this is because big international conglomerates that fight against the subsidization of agriculture by African governments have destroyed small-scale farmers. In fact, the removal of subsidies has always been an essential platform of mercenary-motivated economic policy in Africa like the Structural Adjustment Program. Africa is one of the most fertile lands in the world. Despite this reality, about 200 million Africans suffer from chronic hunger according to the UN Food and Agriculture Organization.

The reason for this situation in Africa is low farm productivity, grinding poverty, unstable domestic and international agricultural markets, and a decline in agricultural development assistance from the industrialized countries to Africa from $4 billion to $2.6 billion in the 1990s.[150]

There is no reason that can justify the hunger in those countries of Africa that have had good climate with no major ecological and political crises within the last three decades. Poor economy is not the reason for the failure of agricultural initiatives in Africa, but rather the result of a failure of the agricultural project. The same could be said of poverty in Africa. Failed governments are not the only factor that leads to poverty in Africa. Countries like Zambia, Kenya and Tanzania that have had democratic governments since Independence continues to wrench in poverty. Why is it that most African countries cannot feed their citizens even in countries like Nigeria, Ghana, Burkina Faso, Egypt, Kenya, Senegal, Tanzania, etc., where there have not been any major ecological or climatic crisis within the last three decades? Why is it that most African democracies are ticking time bombs that have no real foundation? Why should international donor agencies spend millions on foreign aid and personnel to monitor elections in most African countries, while they fail to understand the reasons for the failure of democracy in Africa?

The main reason for this kind of scenario is that Africans are not responding appropriately to the most pressing needs of the continent. The international community also is not seeing the African condition in its broader picture. For instance, if you monitor elections how do you monitor the people elected? When one monitors the people in doing something as important as national elections, then the conclusion must be drawn that they are not politically mature enough and thus cannot practice democracy. The reason that African democracies are crumbling is that they are not true democracies.

The bane of the African condition is institutional collapse, the crumbling of social structures and a cultural hemorrhage that started with slavery and continues today within the unjust structures in national governments and the international community. There is a total absence of any core center of national life around which the life and loyalty of the citizens should revolve. The state is still external to many people who have no emotional attachment to it and hence patriotism is not always a desire for the good of the country, any more than it is a desire to get a piece of the national pie for one's tribe or reference group. It is often the case that in most countries of the sub-Saharan Africa, development is uneven in the sense that some parts of the country are more developed than the others, because they have more people in government by sheer population dominance, political sagacity or strategizing. The greatest challenge then in arresting Africa's rapidly receding political and economic life is the building up of institutions and prioritizing education. The crisis-reaction approach to Africa's problem is not only unhelpful but also counterproductive. More importantly, the broader quest for sustainable development in Africa demands an integral interpretation of the African condition.

The ***total picture approach model*** for Africa's development responds appropriately to the emerging challenges that face the African continent. Fundamentally, this model sees the present crises in Africa within a comprehensive analytical picture, which demands a comprehensive approach beginning in the areas where there is greatest need. At the same time, it proposes that the evolution of Africa should be systemic, gradual and proactive, and not reactionary and episodic.

There are many major elements of development, social cohesion and progress which should be constantly placed on the agenda of African countries, namely food production, poverty eradication and education; and building and strengthening of the core institutions that relate to family, political organization, economic and social life. Concentrating on strengthening these core elements would help to avert the crises that arise intermittently in Africa. These should be the areas of highest priority for international groups working in solidarity with Africans. These elements hold the promise for a stable and vibrant African continent.

At the same time, there must be a genuine micro-level approach that responds to the various health, political, economic, ecological and social crises in Africa that have literally wiped away the middle class in African countries, created refugee problems in over 13 African countries and led to declining health for the Africans. *What this model of approach achieves is that it places human and cultural development as the permanent and most primary requirement for the future of Africa.* This is consistent with the recommendations of the **Practical Plan** to Achieve the United Nations Millennium Development Goals which states, "To achieve the Goals in Africa, significant investments in human resource development are needed urgently, since health, education, agricultural extension, and other critical social services cannot function without cadres of properly trained staff. HIV/AIDS, years of public sector wage ceilings and hiring freezes, outward migration, and poor working conditions have stripped Africa of the human resources needed to deliver needed interventions.... To build Africa's capacity to deliver the services and interventions to achieve the Goals, major coordinated investments in pre-service training will be needed to build a qualified work force of service delivery staff. These will need to be complemented by in-service training for existing staff, adequate salaries, and human resource management systems."[151] This model sets out to constantly address the challenges facing Africa relying on a multi-dimensional approach that builds on the resources of the Africans. It also reverses the current trend wherein micro issues (e.g., war, hunger, refugees, diseases, etc.)—consequences of failed or non-existent foundational policies at the national and international level for Africa—take precedence over the macro-level basic issues.

The micro-level refers to the consequences (e.g., wars, HIV/AIDS, refugees, debt burden, etc.) of the failed attempt to build basic foundations in Africa. These micro-level issues often drain the resources of the African governments and international organizations. In addition, they tend to determine the development priorities of African nations and donor agencies. I, however, propose that they be seen as the micro-level component, which should not make the Africans and the world abandon the basic and broader issues that lead to these crises, which I identify as the macro-level developmental dynamics in Africa. The concentration on the micro-level is a misplacement, which diverts the attention of Africans and non-Africans from envisioning the future and addressing the real issues that impact African development. There is the need to respond to the random crises in the continent, but there is a greater need to address the basic issues, which lead to the crises. The crises are symptoms of a disease; dealing with the disease and treating the symptoms are basic to this total picture approach model of development. This model points to the need to address the broader question of promoting education and awareness (self-consciousness) and institutional building on one hand, and the identity and structural constitution of African society on the other.

This model is based on a comprehensive interpretation of every sector of the African life. Thus, when there is any challenge to be addressed in the social, economic or political spheres, the question that should be raised is: What are the issues around this particular challenge? For instance, with the crisis in Darfur the first priority should be to provide relief for the refugees, but that should not make the international community forget to address the fundamental structure of the Sudanese country that led to the crisis. Addressing the immediate needs of these unfortunate Sudanese is as important as addressing the reason for the crisis. What happens is that a crisis like this is often seen in isolation of the whole picture of the structures of societies like Sudan, where there is the real and ongoing evil of xenophobia against the native Africans on one hand, and injustice against the Christians on the other, which perpetuates this kind of crisis.

The same could apply to the intermittent drought, locust invasion and starvation that face the African Sahel region. In the summer of 2005, the world was shocked by the starvation of millions of people from Niger who faced untimely death as a result of acute food shortage caused by drought and locust invasion during the lean season. However, while providing food for the hungry should be the immediate objective, finding a lasting solution through an early warning system should be the ultimate goal. The questions that should be asked are: Why does the Sahel region suffer from desert locust infestation and drought? What food security could be provided to the most vulnerable part of the African Sahel? Why is Niger most vulnerable to this condition? By applying the total picture approach model, we can see that it is not enough to provide immediate relief but rather that preventative and anticipatory steps could be taken which in turn demands a broader understanding of the geographic, political, economic and social situation of a country like Niger. Such insights set into motion a multi-faceted and multi-pronged approach to the needs of Nigeriens for food, health care, and adequate water among others. The problem is that once the food emergency is met to a minimal extent and the searchlight of the media zooms on another dark spot in Africa or other parts of the world, the international community forgets about the country, while the main issues that generate the crisis are left unaddressed. They will only be woken from slumber few years later when the same crisis emerges again from the ruins of the past.

The advantage of this model is that it helps the groups within and outside Africa to enter into the history of the people and to gain a firm hold of the dynamics on the ground. This model emphasizes closeness over distance, and long-term planning over expedience. In addition, it draws the line between those international organizations and nations that genuinely wish to support an ongoing development for Africa, and those that only come in when the abandoned task of building up the continent manifests itself in the form of a crisis. Any international organization or donor agency that wishes to contribute to sustainable development in Africa must proactively work at the macro-level of the African condition. It depends, however, on the resources available, because the macro-level approach, which the total picture approach model proposes, is capital intensive. The groups that have a low capital base can make a real and meaningful contribution at the micro-level in supporting the various crises response efforts to address issues like the scarcity of water, HIV/AIDS, child trafficking, child abuse, gender equality, etc. We propose then that for any challenge in the life of any African country, there is always an inter-play between the constant (the macro-level) and the variables (micro-levels) in the societies. Responding to the *variables* which are always what is reflected in political, economic, and social crises in Africa, should never blur the main challenge of addressing the *constant*, which I have defined as the need for education, food production and institutional building.

117

CHAPTER TWO
THE TWO FACES OF AFRICA

Who sees your face Mother Africa?
I cannot bear to look at your face,
I cannot admire your face this way,
This is not your true face:
War and famine, violence and destitution,
Hunger and suffering, pain and sorrow,
Diseases and scarcity, deaths and destructions,
Woes and groans reaching beyond the horizon.
Laughter is gone,
Hope has taken a sprint off the land of Africa.
This is but a myth; this is not true;
I long for the true face of Africa,
I want to see this beauty today,
I hear the cry of the children for a future,
Faith fills the hearts of all men and women of this land,
They are stubborn to despair, but held back by some hand.
Time has come
The dark days are gone,
Get up Africans let us go
Rise, let us build
This land of dream
This land of beauty
This land of possibilities
Must shine once more
Beyond the shadows of the night
To the morning dews of life
The True face of Africa.

2.1 The True Face of Africa

It was a quiet night, and the day, though long, had been rich in social interaction for this village that never goes to sleep. We had attended the naming ceremony of a neighbor's son. I was eight years old, and that was the first such ceremony I had been allowed to witness. The ritual was short but full of symbolism.

Chinonso (God is near) was born after four successive stillbirths. When he was safely delivered, his parents gave him a name that represented their joy at God's answer to their prayer for a child. *Nonso*, as the boy would later be called, was to be the sign of a new beginning of blessing for this frightened family. His parents, I learned, had prayed to God for a child for many years. They had been visited by the tragedy of having to bury three of their children before they were five years of age, but they never lost faith in God. Indeed, the mother's successive pregnancies were signs that God's blessing was coming. But they needed some stroke of good fortune to unwrap the mystery that surrounded this blessing. They had consulted with many oracles to find out if their life was 'clean' in the sight of the gods. The oracles did not reveal anything negative. They also wanted to know if their failure to get a child was because of any evil done by their ancestors, but found nothing against their family. There was also no sign of any spell cast on them by anyone in the village.

This family, according to my mother, was still practicing African Traditional Religion. They believed that every effect had a cause and that one who lived righteously and had a good disposition towards the neighbors had no cause to fear evil. No marriage within the traditional Igbo society could be seen as successful without children and having a large family was a sign of prosperity and blessing. It is the hope and joy of every woman to have a child as children are seen as the crowing jewel on womanhood. The same is true for any man. An unmarried man has no status in Igbo society and a man living in a fruitless marriage is perhaps the saddest person you could ever meet, because he lacks fulfillment that comes from the consciousness that one's generation will continue after one's death.

There was a clear sign of joy and an atmosphere of festivity on this special day for Eze's family, as they performed the naming ceremony of their son. The women's group of the village was well represented. None needed any invitation for this ceremony because the child in most African societies is seen as a gift to the community and not just the son or daughter of a particular family. It is not uncommon to see adults correcting and punishing a child who misbehaves in public. The child in question always accepts such corrections, and the parents will later thank the adult who offered it.

Thus, on the day of the ceremony, the whole village was gathered. Each person came with a gift for the newborn child. There was the white powder at the entrance of the family home, which everyone who entered had to rub on their face, as a sign of purity of heart and good wishes for a bright future to the newborn. They also gave their gifts to the newborn child in exchange for the white powder, which in itself was a gift from the newborn baby. It signified the life, purity, goodness, and innocence which every baby carries into the world. As we came in, I noticed that there was much to eat and drink. Everyone was happy and everyone knew each other. There were exchanges of hearty signs of love, hugs and shaking of hands.

As the festivities picked up with the arrival of nearly all the villagers, the father of the newborn baby came into the midst of the crowd, called all to attention, and solemnly announced the name of the child. This announcement was followed by clapping and chanting by the women who sang praises of the newborn and the wonderful future that awaited him. The father had gone out for some time prior to the announcement to confer with the elders, his wife, and some of his relatives on what name should be given the child. Sometimes when the baby is a girl, the mother may be given the privilege of announcing the name of the child. When the name was announced, they said prayers, and the eldest member of the *Umunna* (family group that traced its origin to a common ancestor) poured libation onto the family shrine for the good of the baby.

Many factors are taken into consideration in naming children in most African societies. Sometimes a newborn baby is named after the market day. Among the Igbo there are four market days (*Eke, Oye, Afor,* and *Nkwo*), which are the equivalent of the weekdays in Western society. If one was born on *Eke*, he could be called *Nweke* (son of *eke*) or *Mgbeke* (daughter of *Eke*).

Children can also be named after their great grandparents if in the traditional calculation, the son or daughter in question is a reincarnation of the great grandparents. Sometimes a child is named after the river or streams, or even after the local deities according to the signs of the times during his or her birth. More often than not, a child is named according to the circumstances, or conditions of the family, or the times around which the child is born. In times of adversity, people are often given names that reflect a family or communal wish like *Onwudinjo* (death is bad), *Ogugua* (console us), *chichekwa* (God, defend us), etc.

I enjoyed a great deal of the food given to me by my mum, at whose side I sat on this solemn occasion. As evening came, the crowd started to disperse but each family made a solemn journey to the new mother in order to wish her and her new son God's blessing and to assure her that no evil will come her way. I watched the glow in the eyes of *Nonso* and with my little mind I wondered, as I often do today when I perform the christening of a new baby, what God has in stock for our humanity when he allows a child to be born.

On our journey home, in the company of the other relatives and friends, I heard an elder explaining to some of his grandchildren the significance of a newborn to the community. I do not remember very well all that he said, but I was to find out from my own experience that the child in our traditional society was a sign of continuity for our community. Every child born in an African society is considered a gift for the community. Life can only be meaningful for the elderly if they could look forward to the future because of the great hope that they see in the children. For Africans, human life is to be prized and not priced; indeed there is an understanding of life as a spiritual chain of growth and development that begins in the spiritual realm, then through the womb and continues after birth, and beyond death.

In traditional African society, even miscarriage is seen as a curse and abortion is perceived as an unspeakable taboo that wounds and sunders the spiritual bond of the family and the community. To be pregnant is to be in the hands of God, since the pregnant woman is seen as a messenger of God because of the sacral quality of the gift in her womb. Thus, the preservation and protection of human life from the womb to the tomb is an essentially demanding and rewarding responsibility. It is the duty of each person to preserve and serve the interest of the child; to give the child a chance to live and to offer to the child the best possible values and resources of the community, if the community is to survive.

The appreciation of the giftedness of the human reality as shown in every living person, especially as manifested in the newborn child, is the condition for both being authentically African and properly oriented to live in society or to participate in tribal life. This message has never left me. It has also offered me the key to seeing the true face of the African world. It is in this understanding of life as a mystery, a gift, an offer, and celebration that one can fully appreciate the misrepresentation, which the often-distorted picture of Africa as a land of crimes, deaths, violence and diseases offers to many Africans and non-Africans. The typical African is a lover of life and a lover of community.

It is strange that in Africa today, many lives are wasted through violence and disease, civil wars and adversity. This, to say the least, is the very antithesis of the worldview of Africans. When we see, as has often been the case in post-Independence Africa, the bloody wars in many African countries, the increasing violence in, and the intrigues and killings that have come to characterize the acquisition and maintenance of power in some African countries, we ought to probe further into the underlying currents that set the stormy ripples cascading through the sea of life and love that should flow through the land and clime of Africa. Some African clerics, frightened by the massive and inexcusable rapine and human destruction that rocked the African continent, which led to myriads of deaths in the early 1990s, said in a statement, "We find ourselves in a situation of contradiction and paradoxes. We, as Africans, are reputed to love solidarity and we practice division; we love life and we disseminate death; we pursue brotherhood and we take part in fratricidal activities…"[1]

The question is often asked among the community of humanity about the meaning and goal of life. Our perception of the value of life should shape the way we live and relate with each other. That would also determine how people make choices and pursue their ordered ends. Obviously, any look at the face of the African continent would reveal some strange tendencies, which do not chime smoothly with the African way of life. How does corruption in government, for instance, relate to the African worldview on the primacy of the community? How does the spread of HIV/AIDS, which is mainly transmitted through sexual relationship relate to the often-held claims by Africans that they have a higher sense of morality than Westerners? How does the killings in many African countries, the tribal violence, the religious conflicts among Christians and Muslims on one hand, and between these religions and the practitioners of African Traditional Religion on the other, relate to the African world of respect for the sanctity of life, religious tolerance, good neighborliness and hospitality?

Africans place the highest premium on the community. The human person in the African society is seen as a 'being-with,' caught up in an intricate and intimate web of relationships with others and with nature and the transcendental spiritual world. One's identity in African society is inconceivable outside the cycle of community beginning from the family line. This idea of being-with is appropriately reflected in the fact that each person is a corporate personality who carries on his or her shoulders the burden of the community in a spiritual bond that finds its expression in a coherent pluralism.

This is opposed to Western philosophy that insists on the absolute originality and concreteness of the person as a "being-for-itself" (using the term of the French thinker Jean-Paul Sartre). Commenting on Sartre's philosophy of Western individualism, the African thinker, Bénézet Bujo[2] noted that Sartre elaborated more on a philosophy of the human person rather than of ontology. Sartre understands existence as the de facto existing and acting of the human person, who achieves his identity through action. Existence precedes essence in such a way that the human person not only possesses full freedom, but also has absolute freedom. Freedom is for Sartre a burden and the existing person can only be defined in the absolute act of being. Since Sartre's man admits the non-existence of God, the human person defines himself in the arc of history, and determines his value as the absolute author and maker of all things.

Bujo quotes Sartre in *Les Mouches* (*The Flies*): "There is nothing more in heaven, neither good nor evil, nor anyone to give us orders, because I am a human being, Jupiter, and each human being must invent his own path."[3] Admittedly, Sartre's thinking is not a Western paradigm, but it represents it to a large extent. It is a kind of morality that collapses the constitutive commonality of humankind; it negates the transcendental content of truth and being, and places the human person in the shifting sands of individual whims and caprices. It would leave the world at the mercy of human foibles, which even though deriving from freedom, leaves men and women vulnerable to those who do not realize that freedom is synonymous with truth, goodness, love and beauty and not some egotistic end. This perfection of being is God who is the 'beyond' in our midst and who summons us to make a leap into the higher portals of freedom with responsibility for the good of others, since we are the true stewards of a common humanity and of nature around us.

This kind of Sartrean individualism, enthrones personal choices and libertarian ethics as a monarch, and sublets a transcending moral regime and with it the common ethos that should govern life and social interaction. This mentality is at the root of capitalism. Capitalism is individualism writ large in the canvass of a thoroughgoing economics of enlightened self-interest, whether it is a group-based dynamics or individual pursuits. Humanity in this day and age, faced with the failure of policies and principles which are founded on individualism, needs to find an answer to the primordial instinct of survival, which when taken to the corporate, nationalistic or racial levels muddies the collective pool from which all should drink as from a wellspring. In looking at the face of Africa then, we see the steady but gradual rise of individualism especially in the higher levels of society among politicians, professionals and captains of industries.

The basis for the disintegration of African societies lies in the progressive exploitation of the ordinary masses of our people by these elites even, unfortunately, in some religious settings.

I think that the present situation of Africa has everything to do with the failure of leadership and smacks of a cultural crisis of incalculable negative proportion. This is because when people in leadership positions at the highest or lowest levels fail to bring the values of their culture to bear on their life and action, the people they lead can only wander in a dry desert of confusion and dysfunctional value syndrome. Unfortunately, those who suffer from all this is the 90% of the population that is honest, and driven as they are by a high ethical consciousness, which positively affects the content of their character. These archetypical Africans who are rarely seen but always exploited are often wounded, because in their fragility and vulnerability; they are like lambs that are prey to ravaging wolves that make up most of the political leadership in some African countries.

There are obviously various stances people can take with regard to life. In most African societies, life is highly esteemed and this does not only apply to one's own life but all lives. The basic concept of life and social relations in Africa is "that we are because of others." Africans believe in the creative value of each life, whether it is the poor who may never know the meaning of their gift, the old who are dying away in the rot that has come to characterize most African societies, the young who look to a future whose concreteness continues to recede, or the wealthy who might think of themselves as little gods when they are the only oasis of wealth in the vast desert of suffering and pain. The true face of Africa is the face of *Nonso* whose smiling little face greeted mine some 24 years ago.

As we gathered around the village square that evening under the bright moon for our moon-night dance, we sang lullabies for the newborn child, which we hoped would put him to sleep even as he was nestled, some distance away from us, in the warm comfort of his mother's bosom. We listened to a wonderful story told by one of the oldest of our group, who even at thirteen had mastered the art of story-telling. It is an important tribal quality to tell the fables of the land; it is a sign of wisdom if one can communicate to others through anecdotes, proverbs, figures of speech and didactic lore. The one who speaks plainly is seen as a greenhorn. The arsenal of oratory is the communicative power of adapting one's ideas in the often-uncommon folktales of the land and allowing the audience to figure out the lessons and message. African traditional speakers often do not speak plainly; they speak in symbolic language. This often shows the sophistication of the African mind and the interpretative edge that is demanded in entering the African world.

Many people rightly believe that the fading use of the native languages of most African countries is perhaps the greatest evil that colonialism caused in the continent. In many African societies today, it has become a sign of civility to speak and communicate in foreign languages. Most so-called high-class families prefer not to teach their children how to speak the native languages, which in certain circles in Africa are seen as a sign of primitivism. Many Africans who live abroad often come home to bemuse their fellow Africans who have never traveled outside Africa with their often-phony foreign accent.

How many Africans today think in their African languages and build mental categories along the lines of their rich cultural heritage? There are many Africans today who wrongly interpret development and civility in terms of adaptation to Western lifestyles. Our cultural identity or rather our African identity is the only reality and gift that we carry in our relationship with others; if that is eroded we cannot build an African civilization nor actually relate to others from a certain perspective. If we are rooted in our African tribal traditions we would have a base to relate with others and a locus of safety in the cultural crisis which has set the world on a confusing moral bazaar during the last four decades.

It is only these essential values that we can bring into our reality today. The decline in the use of the native African languages has brought an erosion of the collective memory of the people; with that loss most Africans' thought-patterns have become warped. With it the sacral and ethical content of speech and response are being lost. When *Udo* began to tell his story that evening, many of us listened because knowledge in the traditional African setting is more informal, a transmission which only took place in the chain of inter-relational communication and exchanges among people. It was said that *Udo's* grandfather was a consummate narrator, who would hold his audience captive for hours with interesting stories, folk tales and fables in which the collective wisdom of the tribe was hidden. The morals of *Udo's* story that day was the need for each person to be contented with what God has given him and the danger of seeking to acquire more things for ourselves.

"In the land of the animals," he began, "there lived a great crocodile who lived both on the ground and in the water. He was a wicked and vaulting creature who had poisoned spikes which he got from a malevolent spirit. With his spikes he killed and destroyed other sea creatures. He could never keep a wife because he was notorious for killing his wives if they refused to make love to him. One day he caught a squirrel who wandered to the bank of the river in search of food. Before he could kill the squirrel, the poor creature appealed to the crocodile to leave him alone since he would not be enough food for the crocodile and would only stir his hunger. Instead, suggested the squirrel, the crocodile should go after the boy on the other side of the river who was fishing. Now the little boy had caught several fish and was not satisfied and so threw them back into the river because he was searching for a better and bigger fish. His hook caught this big fish that was too heavy for him to pull out of the water. This big fish on the other hand, had come to the bait of the boy because the fish was not satisfied with the little fish he could have eaten at the river floor. The crocodile left the squirrel who ran away for his dear life. Then the crocodile swam towards the boy. On reaching the other side of the river, the crocodile thought it was better first to eat the fish which was struggling on the boy's hook before reaching out for the boy too, but on putting his large mouth around the head of the fish, he was caught in the bait and with his heavy frame he pulled the boy into the water. The boy drowned in the water. The crocodile too died from the injury received from the bait and the fish died as well. It was only the squirrel who just wanted to feed at the riverside who survived. The squirrel was the weakest, no doubt, of all these animals but he was the only one that remained alive. The squirrel was also the one who was not greedy." We all clapped at the end of the story. We sang one short verse, which was our own response to the story: *O ji n'aka togbo....* (Drop that which you are holding.)

This song was meant to help us appreciate the lesson of the story that we should not hold on to things and that we should learn to share. Sometimes it is not the mightiest who win in battle, and life's crown does not always go to the swiftest or smartest person. Africans believe that God gives everything and we cannot really lay claim to anything unless God gives it to us. Hence, life is not all about victory and conquests but about love and sharing. Even today as one looks at the world's scene and the condition of many people in the developing countries, I cannot but appreciate the morals of the story. It is not the richest of countries that have the greatest happiness. It is not the poorest of countries that experience the greatest expression of collective frustration. The suicide rate in the Western industrialized countries and Japan is higher than that in the developing world.[4]

When I shared the statistics of the suicide rate in the West with an elder in my community, he wondered, "Why should the White people commit suicides in such great number when they have everything they need in life?" Then he gave me an African proverb, *"nkita siri na ndi nwere ike amaghi etukwu ani"* (The dog says that those with seats do not know the best sitting posture…ever seen a dog complaining that he/she has no seat? Try comparing your sitting posture with that of a dog.) Greed is the ultimate human disease, which like a cancer does not often stop until it ruins the whole person. It is a fire that ravages without border and is a passion that drives the person beyond the limits of human comprehension.

That night as we were going home, I was so frightened because I guessed that the wicked crocodile could be crouching maliciously in some hidden place in the bush which encircled us like a cloud, and would eat me up. I feared that the crocodile must still be searching for the boy in the world of the dead. Greed does not stop even with death, I thought. That night, however, was very memorable because I learnt so much in a single night. This is the ideal in most traditional African societies. Life is an adventure that entails unending discovery and infinite engagement with people and conquests of nature. The young people are to learn the virtues of hard work and honesty; they ought to learn that life is meaningful when it is lived for the good of others, and that the only way to become an ancestor is in addition to writing one's biography through raising a family with children, being a person of honor, dignity and integrity. You can only outlive yourself in both time and eternity by living purposefully for the community and for your family.

I cannot forget the song my late granduncle used to sing when I accompanied him on hunting expeditions which translates like this: *"For every created person upon this land, death would have its time and place; the noblest death to have is for one to live and die for the good of his community and preserve the good creation of God."* The young people are to be trained to appreciate that life is a joint effort and that no one can live for himself or herself alone. Thus, the only way to live is to flow in the interconnected chain of community living in a right order of relationship, characterized by give and take. Hard work is to be glorified and indolence should be discouraged and condemned. Heroism does not mean the conquest of others but the conquest of self, for the true person of honor in the community is the one who has won the respect of all by righteous living. Evil is to be seen in those things that hurt the common good and those things that produce only a quantum good for a single individual.

I was to hear such lessons from my parents and grandparents and from my community's elders. It is this profound African sense of the common good, which fills me and many Africans with a sense of righteous rage against the leadership in most African countries, in their failure to place the good of their countries first before their selfish goals.

This is the face of the African world that many of us can see even in the present unacceptable reality of Africa. This is the beautiful face behind the ugly face that is often presented to the wider world in the negative news coverage that feeds on the sensational and the ugly. This core reality may have changed, but its essence can never be touched because it is the heart of the African cultural identity and personhood. Thus, as I look at the continent of Africa and watch the decay that has overrun the whole land like a mad elephant stomping roughshod through the farmland, I wonder at what has happened to our collective wisdom.

2.2 Poverty and the Dignity of the Africans

Many outsiders who look at our continent do not yet see the true face of Africa. What is often seen is the false face that has been contoured by years eaten by locusts. The former West and Central African Regional Director of UNICEF, Torild Skard has written of the deplorable ways in which the Western press presents Africa. She cites the example of the British Journal, *The Economist*. In the front page of the May 2000 edition the title of the cover was "Hopeless Africa." The paper describes the crisis in Sierra Leone as one in the catalogue of horrors which has plagued the African continent already reeling under the dead weight of many negatives: floods, famines, poverty, diseases and state-sponsored thuggery.[5] Such a negative cliché, she argues, disregards all positive aspects and precludes a further analysis of difficulties and possibilities. The face of Africa is the face of love and community; it is the celebration of togetherness as the essence of creation. It is the desire to be in a right order of relationship with God and with others.

Many Africans today wonder about the future of the continent when everything often said or written about Africa is negative. Many people in the Western world do think that the situation in Africa is so grim that there is nothing that can be done to save it. Some of this kind of thinking is based on the kind of information they receive through news agencies and NGOs about Africa. Many of them are developing donor apathy because they do not know when Africa and Africans will stop begging for assistance and take their future into their own hands. Western agencies who want to be involved with African development often paint a very negative and sad picture of the face of Africa in an attempt to get international support and sponsorship. It must be stated that the sacrifice made by many ordinary Westerners for Africa has never been fully appreciated. Many foreigners have died in this continent trying to light candles of love, and aglow with the flame of solidarity and compassion. They labored often in the most difficult circumstances and are indeed the living signs that this world with all its complexities can become a home for all. Their sacrifices have been a testament to the finest values and highest peaks of goodness that humanity is capable of attaining.

It must be admitted that Africa is the leaking basket-case of the world; it is a continent which is weather-beaten by myriads of problems. How can the international community be persuaded not to forget Africa? Is it by engaging them in the celebration of the worst side of the continent, or by letting them see the sunny as well as the seamy side?

Take some of the pictures we see in the Western media and in some presentations of NGOs working in Africa: A gaunt-looking child with flies all over his mouth! A slovenly and haggard woman with exposed sagging breasts trying to feed her baby, who with an inflated belly, apparently as a result of malnutrition, appears to be dying bit by bit! A bunch of naked African kids rummaging in dustbins like vultures! An HIV/AIDS victim who has been reduced to a walking skeleton, whose face is a living skull with a thin veil of wasted skin! The list goes on. I wonder if the civilized world needs the display of all these images of horror in order for men and women of goodwill to make some concrete commitments to help the poor in Africa.

Beyond all these, is the question of the dignity and respect that the Africans demand. There is a certain amount of respect demanded in any social interaction. Obviously, Africa as it is today might not relate with the rest of the world on an equal basis if she remains the sick continent of the world. This is, however, the law of humanity: unless you respect someone you cannot love the person or engage the person in a real and creative way. If the world engages Africa on the level of sympathy, Africa might never stand on her own feet; she will continue to be the 'disaster zone' of the world. If the world engages Africa as an equal, Africa will be allowed to assume responsibility for her future and will be given the necessary push to build up her structures and institutions. But if the continent is presented as dying, or worse, as the Dark Continent, we Africans will not win any kind of respect in the community of nations.

It must be admitted that Africa in a most obvious way is a poor continent. Poverty is perhaps the greatest insult to human dignity not only in Africa but also in the dark alleys of many cities in the world today. Poverty robs people of their humanity and disrobes them of their sense of self. Poverty inferiorizes a person. It degrades a person and reduces self-confidence. Poverty closes the door to life. It makes life a tale of pain and sorrow and a journey into the uncertain land of want and frustration. Poverty makes people powerless and voiceless; it denies them the opportunity to actualize themselves and invest in themselves for the enrichment of our common humanity. Poverty, in my thinking, is the greatest weapon of mass destruction in the present world.

Poverty, however, can sometimes be a gift in a reverse sense. There are some lives that become a gift because of what they bring to us, and some become a gift because of what they bring out in us. However we might see poverty, it is never part of the will of the Almighty God in his design for men and women that they should live through the skin of their teeth or that they should trek the long and winding journey of poverty to die unsung and unfulfilled. Reflecting on the reason people work hard to conquer poverty, Adam Smith writes, "The rich man glories in his riches, because he feels that they naturally draw upon him the attention of the world, and that mankind are disposed to go along with him in all the agreeable emotions with which the advantages of his situation so readily inspires him...The poor man on the contrary, is ashamed of his poverty. He feels that it either places him out of sight of mankind, or that if they take any notice of him, they have however scarce any fellow-feeling with the misery and distress which he suffers."[6] Commenting on this position, Francis Fukuyama notes that there is a level of poverty where economic activity is undertaken for the fulfillment of basic natural needs, such as in the drought-stricken African Sahel during the 1980s. Poverty, he argues, is a relative rather than absolute concept arising from money's role as a symbol for worth. The poverty in the United States represents a standard of living much higher than that of well-off people in certain developing countries. This does not mean that the poor in the United States have more satisfaction than the rich in Africa since poverty always is an affront on a person's self-worth.

John Locke observed in the 18th Century that the king in America feeds, lodges, and is clad worse than a day laborer in England. The king in America, Fukuyama argues, has a sense of dignity that is born of his freedom, self-sufficiency and the respects and recognition he receives from the community around him. The day worker in England may eat better but he has no worth in the eyes of his master for whom he is only something like a beast of burden, invisible as a human being. Poverty is always a robber of human dignity. This is what Engelbert Mveng means when he speaks of poverty in Africa as anthropological. According to Mveng, "When persons are bereft of their identity, their dignity, their freedom, their thought, their history, their language, their faith universe, and their basic creativity, deprived of all their rights, their hopes, their ambitions (that is when they are robbed of their own ways of living and existing)—they sink into a kind of poverty which no longer concerns only exterior or interior goods or possessions but strikes at the very being, essence, and dignity of the human person. It is this poverty which we call anthropological poverty. This is an indigence of being."[7]

In the Christian and Jewish religious tradition, the poor person is presented as: (1) the one who desires; the beggar, the one who is lacking something and who awaits it from another. (2) The weak one, one who is frail because he or she is exposed to the elements and is without care. (3) The person who is bent over, laboring day and night without any rest; one who is humiliated and one whose labor does not gain him or her enough sustenance. (4) One who is humble before God. (5) The one who does not have enough to sustain life; one who is lacking in the basic necessities of life and so cannot subsist on his or her own. Poverty is presented in the Christian Scripture as a great scandal; an evil of injustice which demands immediate action to put an end to its dehumanization of God's people. The scandalous condition of the poor anywhere is condemned in the Christian Scripture which presents God as one who is on the side of the poor. God makes a preferential option for the poor to lift them up to enjoy the dignity and fullness of life worthy of the human person, made in his image and likeness.[8]

The international community has set a benchmark for establishing the meaning of poverty. "For technical and statistical purposes, poverty is usually measured by establishing a poverty line, set at some multiple of income necessary to purchase a basic food basket that provides sufficient nutrition for an active, productive life. People whose income is below the level necessary to purchase even that basic food basket are called absolutely poor, or in deprivation."[9] Jeffery Sachs observes that one sixth of humanity is caught in a poverty trap which makes it impossible for them to escape from extreme material deprivation; they are trapped by disease, physical isolation, climate stress, environmental degradation, and by extreme poverty.[10] Sachs distinguishes between three degrees of poverty: extreme or absolute poverty, moderate poverty and relative poverty. Extreme poverty exists when households cannot meet basic needs for survival and are chronically hungry, unable to access healthcare, lack the amenities of safe drinking water and sanitation, cannot afford education for some or all of their children, and lack rudimentary shelter, clothing, shoes, etc. Extreme poverty unlike moderate and relative poverty occurs only in developing countries. Moderate poverty occurs when basic needs are barely met, while relative poverty is generally construed as a household income level below a given proportion of average national income. The relatively poor in high-income countries according to Sachs, lack access to cultural goods, entertainment, recreation, and to quality healthcare, education and other perquisites for upward social mobility. The World

Bank uses the income of $1 per day per person, measured at purchasing power parity to determine the number of people in extreme poverty, while income between $1 per day and $2 per day can be used to measure moderate poverty. Sachs argues that based on this grading, half of Africa's population is deemed to live in extreme poverty and it continues to rise in absolute numbers. The statistics bear this out.

According to an assessment report, *Investing in Development*, by the UN Development Group on how the different regions of the world are working towards reaching the Millennium Development Goals, in sharp contrast to Asia's progress, most of Sub-Saharan Africa faces significant challenges in meeting the Millennium Development Goals on almost every dimension of poverty. Many African countries are falling behind all other regions. Africa's average per capita national income is one third lower than the world's next poorest region, South Asia. Between 1990 and 2001, the number of people living on less than 1$ a day rose from 227 million to 313 million and the poverty rate rose from 45% of the population to 46%. In other words, half of Africa's 880 million people live on less than $1 a day. The precipitous decline in Africa's per capita income is such that some countries of Africa enjoyed a higher standard of living in 1960 than they enjoy today. Indeed, according to Martin Meredith, the entire economic output of Africa is no more than $420 billion, just 1.3% of the world's GDP. Its share of world trade has declined to half of what it was in 1980, amounting only to about 1.6%, while its share of global investment is less than 1%. Africa is the only region where per capita investment and saving has declined since 1970.[11]

The African continent has a more than fair share of the poor of the earth. In the 2004 *Human Development Report* published by the United Nations Development Program, African countries by all indices are in the lower rungs of development. The report looks at such issues as life expectancy, educational attainment, adjusted real income, access to water, food and social amenities and the all round choices open to people the world over in terms of the quality of life. The Index shows that of the 20 countries that suffered reversals since 1990, 13 are in Sub-Saharan Africa. While life expectancy in Norway is 79 years, that of countries like Angola, Central African Republic, Lesotho, Mozambique, Sierra Leone, Swaziland, Zambia and Zimbabwe has fallen to 40 years or less.[12] While Norway has a per capita Gross Domestic Product of US$36,600 (adjusted by purchasing power parity), Mali has a GDP of US$753.

Of the 35 poorest countries in the world, 32 are in Sub-Saharan Africa and the five countries with the lowest levels of human development in the 2004 rankings are all in Africa: Burundi, Mali, Burkina Faso, Niger and

Sierra Leone. Twenty out of 53 countries in Africa have been witnessing a frightening and heart-wrenching decline in the standard of living of their citizens since the 1990s. The average people in these countries are poorer now than they were in the last decade. In 11 African countries, more people go hungry than they did a decade ago. It is a tragedy that many people live in Africa without water, electricity, education, healthcare services and food; it is a tragedy that the margins of the life of comfort in the Western world merely intersects in a parallel way with the squalor that is witnessed in many African societies.

The attempt to engage Africa must flow from a degree of respect for the African people no matter how bad the situation in the continent is. The dignity of Africans should be determinative in the way the African condition is presented and in the way that Africans are treated in the international community. As the existentialist thinker Gabriel Marcel wrote, "We cannot succeed in preserving the mysterious principle at the heart of human dignity unless we succeed in making explicit the properly sacral quality peculiar to it."[13]

No matter how poor the lives of people in Africa are presented, they remain human persons who have in their hearts the desire for a future, and who carry the spark of God with his image etched in their beings. The human person has an absolute value of his own independent of his condition of existence. His value as a person is not susceptible to the calculable indices of a certain quality of life. Human life is to be willed and loved as an end and not as a means. This determines how we treat people whether they are poor or rich.

Human life is not quantifiable in terms of productivity or utility but in terms of the essential nature that each of us carries as the image of God and a gift to the world. The myth of utility and physical efficiency has been the greatest negative current that has made contemporary society evaluate people in terms of what they can offer or produce. This is the reason for the kind of treatment that seniors receive in Western societies: "The factors that conspire to consign many older people to the fringes of the human community and civil life are many: evasion of responsibility at the institutional level and consequent social inadequacies; poverty or a drastic reduction of income and of the necessary financial resources to secure a decent standard of living and appropriate levels of care; and the progressive removal of older people from their own family and social environment. The most painful dimension of this marginalization, however, is the lack of human relations. Older people suffer not only by being deprived of human contact but also from abandonment, loneliness and isolation."[14]

There are repeated incidents of abuse and neglect of seniors. Some of these heroes and heroines who squandered their lives serving society are often treated with disrespect in the evening of their lives. Some of them are abandoned within the lonely and quiet walls of nursing homes and die without much love from relatives who may start fighting over their wills as soon as they are gone. A typical example was the deaths caused by heat waves in the summer of 2003 in France. About 450 seniors suffered and died during the waves, because their children and grandchildren forgot about them while having a good time on vacation. Some 400 bodies were not claimed more than one month after their deaths, because some of the family members did not even know where they lived nor did they know when they died.[15]

The situation of Africa today is not irremediable nor is it one that has had no precedence in the long and checkered history of humanity. Africa's dignity is at stake when the face presented to the outside world is one that shows the continent as a place where everybody is everybody's enemy, where people are fighting and killing each other, and where children are unsafe. There is hunger in the continent of Africa but more people find food and work for their daily bread than is presented today. There are diseases in the land, but over 90% of the African population is healthy and productive.[16] Africa is a beautiful land. It is filled with a lot of primary energies that will be the very bases for a renascent Africa.

The people of this continent are a hopeful and happy people, who believe in a better future because God is acknowledged and is seen as part of the historical process that is presently moving beyond shadows to reality. It is not an empty hope but one that can be seen clearly on the faces of the young people. I see the face of Africa in the emerging vanguard of the young and determined Africans who can no longer watch as their blessed land is desecrated by a few selfish leaders who have little or no African values in their life-blood, and who destroy by their selfishness the common good of the land. I see the face of Africa in African women who are emerging as the Third Force in re-engineering African society in a more positive and activist dimension.

I see the face of Africa in the sportsmen and women, in the creativity that is once more emerging in the arts and sciences and in the business sector. I see the face of Africa in the many volunteers of African origin who from one end of the continent to the other are mobilizing in fighting the scourge of HIV/AIDS and who are ready to go the extra mile for the good of others. I see the face of the African continent in those Africans who live abroad and who are determined to survive against all odds hoping that one day after their stay they would go home to Mother Africa to help build her anew. I see the face of Africa in the fact that this sleeping continent with its immense and unused spiritual, human, and material resources has not yet started her journey to the mountaintop. Since she has a lot of unused energies, she can be shaped for better or for worse. However, waking this continent from her sleep of ages demands the heroism which Africans must embrace. How to smooth the contours on the face of Africa is a challenge that remains not only for Africans but the whole world. Poverty in any part of the world is a threat to prosperity in every part of the world, just as an act of terrorism in any part of the world is a threat to peace in every part of the world.

2.3 The Lost Generations

"What do you want to do when you grow up?" he bellowed to the boy standing in the row in front of me. *Onye army* (military man), as we called our guard and trainer that year, was a tough-looking man. He had a burly frame, with broad macho shoulders that mimicked the effigy of the Ogun god of thunder revered among the Yoruba tribe of Nigeria, Togo and Benin republics. He also had firm and weather-beaten arms that were as broad as a double handshake. He was the undisputed strong man of our village. He was the wrestling champion for three consecutive years in the village. At the last wrestling competition, he displayed amazing skill, stamina, and raw strength by the way he made *Ibe*, nicknamed "the Leopard," look ordinary.

The villagers had all gathered at the market square for the match. The women were there in great numbers, for as the saying goes in traditional Igbo society, *"Umunwoke gbacha mgba, umunwanyi enwere akuko."* (When the wrestling is over between the men, the women's lot is to give account of the championship.) Women do not wrestle in Igbo society. However, they were the veritable cheerleaders and sang and entertained in the course of the championship. It was an opportunity also for the young ladies to know who their prospective husbands could be since it was a thing of joy to be married to the village wrestling champion. Who wouldn't like to have the village celebrity as a husband? In the traditional society, where agriculture was the main stay of the economy, having a strong man as an in-law meant also having some extra help during the farming season. It was, however, also said that unless the *Umuada* (women's group) prevailed on the champion, he might sometimes use his strength the wrong way by violently abusing his wife. The true champion, however, knows that it is good to have the power of an elephant but stupid to use it like an elephant. He uses his strength on hunting spree, to defend the village in time of war and to also defend the people should a wild animal attack the village. It is no wonder that today in contemporary Igbo society, people use *Ogbu agu* (lion-killer), a title used many years back to reverence the strong men of the villages who sometimes would confront the wild beasts and tear them to pieces like the biblical Sampson.

Onye Army took just about thirty seconds to pin *Ibe* down. He actually lifted *Ibe* up with much ease and flung him round several times before bringing him down with some compassion albeit with athletic finesse. Wrestling was one of those ways in which the traditional society in Igbo-land trained the young in the art of self-defense, the value of competition, the development of physical fitness and the spirit of fair play. It was also a training ground for future village warriors who were taught the value of bravery and courage. This wrestling competition was to be the last in the village, as many of our wrestlers were now leaving for the cities in search of some means of sustenance, since being a village champion, does not guarantee one any financial safety nor any sponsorship in contemporary society. *Onye Army,* however, remained in the village and decided to pass his knowledge and skills on to the younger ones. Besides, since he fought in the Nigerian civil war, he had also acquired some military training. Like many other discharged Biafran soldiers, he nursed deep anger and hatred for the Nigerian nation and hoped that one day the Igbo and other tribes that made up the Biafran secessionists would fight again and this time be victorious. He felt it was his calling to train the young ones in the military arts so that they would be strong and courageous enough to fight for their true land, Biafra.

Onye Army, therefore, turned this annual camping for the members of the age group who were entering puberty into something of a military training. The camping was meant to do three things for the young teenagers: teach them the morals of the land, especially sexual morality now that they have reached puberty and are capable of putting a girl in the family way; they were to learn the meaning and value of chastity; and they were to learn the ethical conduct demanded in their relationship with people like respect for the elders, respect for women and courtesy in dealing with people, and the value of gratitude. It was also an educational period of acculturation into the shared wisdom of the tribe. The third reason for the annual camping for these young people was to teach them the basic arts and skills required to live meaningfully like hunting, farming, crafting, painting, construction, etc. The youth of the village would leave home and go to a deserted place sometimes far from the village. They would learn endurance, hence, no food was provided for them—they would forage, fish, and hunt for their food. They learned the art of self-defense and wrestling, and even how to behave when confronted by a wild animal (how to suspend one's breath in dangerous moments when a wild animal would threaten one's life so that the animal would think that one was dead). The camping exercise was very exhausting and painful. It was the quintessential endurance test, but at the end of the day those who survived came home as small princes who deserved the respect of all.

This year's camping, however, did not offer us any of these, since *Onye Army* turned the camping into military drills. He was apparently enjoying the fact that he had an imaginary troop before him and was using the occasion to maximum advantage. He shouted at us all the time as if we were all hard of hearing. He would commandeer us to run around and to stand *'aatentshion!'* (attention), and would scream at any of us who dared put his hand on his waist in a sign of weariness. The first question he asked was about the choice of careers for each of us.

The first boy to answer his question naturally said he wanted to be a soldier. He thundered, "Good answer boy and why do you want to be a soldier?" he queried further displaying the characteristic steeliness that could send fearful shivers running down my spine throughout this gruesome week.

"I want to be like you."

"Good answer again, but you have to prepare to endure. Besides, remember that our forefathers taught us that there is enough space in the air for each bird; you've got to play your own unique role. We all need role models for unless children are taught the difference between a stone and a toad they would mistake a toad for a stone. Those who never learnt how to tie ropes around the neck of the cow to muzzle him would rather use a snake and perhaps get killed by snakebite. The fly that has no guardian would be buried with a decaying corpse."

He always spoke this way in proverbs and anecdotes.

"You," referring to me, "What job would you take up when you grow up?"

Well, I had learnt a few lessons that everything we did depended on God and how was I to be sure that another war wouldn't break out in Nigeria, so I answered that it depends on God.

At this point, *Onye Army* was visibly upset at my answer and he grimaced in obvious spite and then inveighed in symbolic language that carried arrogant cadence in its delivery, "What do you have between your two legs....? Did your mother consult with God before deciding to breast-feed you? Did you ever take breast milk or did you only drink the children's milk brought after the war by Caritas, which make modern children behave and reason from the anus? Now listen, our fathers told us that the ram once said that even though he does not know how to dance, if the musicians played in his father's doorstep he would rather jump around in harmony than remain quiescent. He whose house is on fire does not spend time chasing the rats and squirrels that might be running away from the inferno. No matter the size of a person's head the gods always give a strong neck to support it, so it does not weigh down on the neck. Now what job do you think God would like you to do?"

I guessed what he would like me to say and then I answered that I would like to be a soldier and he was now visibly elated and asked me why. I answered right from my heart not really intent on pleasing him as to let off my anger.

"I want to go into the military because I would like to avenge on the Northerners who killed my uncles and aunties and killed my father's foster father and burnt down my father's house during the Nigerian Civil war."

"You are a true son of your father for it is only a true son who seeks to destroy the enemy who destroyed his family, because unless a rotten tooth is pulled out, the mouth would chew with pain. It is an act of heroism to pursue and kill the wild animal that would destroy your family in your absence. The gods would only defend the courageous, but the coward will only live at the tip of his toes because fear is his only mantle."

Onye Army was one of more than 100,000 ex-Biafran soldiers who were not reintegrated into the Nigerian army when the Biafran secession failed in 1970. Many of his fellow discharged soldiers were jobless and constituted themselves into gangs that carried out sporadic crimes. Others just lived without hope for any future in an ever-revolving chain of debilitating poverty and frustration. Some of those who were injured and maimed during the war were left to their fate and have been kept in the shadows of suffering. It was always a source of pain to me seeing these men begging for alms along the Highway in my home county of Oji in Enugu State, Nigeria, where they have been abandoned to their fate.

The story of the Nigerian civil war is one that draws tears from many eyes. It was a war that should have been avoided. The main players in that war like Yakubu Gowon, the Nigerian war Commander-in-Chief and Odimegwu Ojukwu, the Biafran leader were in their early 30s, when the war broke out. Their decisions were typical of the rashness and brashness of youth; reflecting a calamity which could visit countless people when they fell in the umbrage of romantic idealism, which had nothing to do with concrete realities as espoused by the more innocent idealists like the Nigerian leaders in the second half of 1960s. These men were driven, no doubt, by a certain sense of mission and they adopted the path of war in the baneful pursuit of their goals.

The Biafrans felt a deep rage; the near genocidal ethnic cleansing of the mainly Igbo-populated East and of many other minority tribes like the Efik, Ibibio, and Ogoni, who lived in Northern Nigeria, generated a lot of concern and hatred among their brethren in the East, who survived the pogrom. Even today, many Igbo have never stopped mourning the loss of thousands of their kith and kin in a senseless show of vendetta by the Northerners that saw the Igbo officers led by Nzeogwu as enemies of Northern Nigeria because of their supposed selective killing of the crème of the Northern leaders. General Gowon on the other hand, felt it was his mission to safeguard the unity of Nigeria at all cost; what began as 'a police action' to quell a small rebellion in the Eastern region of the country in January 1967 turned into 30 months of hellish destruction of lives and property of the Easterners.

But more fundamental to the cause of the war was the fact that the British government brought together 250 ethnic groups and forced them into a federation to which no tribe had any affinity. Nigeria remains today a country whose existence lies constantly on a balance. The blame for the civil war in Nigeria must be placed on the doorsteps of the British government, who out of its own political interests created Nigeria, a country described in many derogatory ways by the early leaders of the country. The godfather of Northern Nigerian Muslim nationalism, Ahmadu Bello, would decry in a national debate in 1947 that "the mistake of 1914 [when Nigeria was created by the British] has come to light." The first President of the country, Dr. Nnamdi Azikiwe, would boast that God had proclaimed his Igbo tribe as the inheritors of the Nigerian patrimony; while General Gowon, the second Military Head of State of Nigeria, would say in 1966 that there was no basis for Nigeria's unity. Obafemi Awolowo, who came from the Yoruba tribe, and who despite his commitment to the Nigerian nation, was described as "the best President Nigeria never had," because of the ethnic factor which influenced the way he was seen by other tribes, described the country as a mere geographical expression.[17] Reflecting on the failure of the colonialists and the Nigerian nationalists to forge a truly united federation, the Nigerian nationalist, S. G. Ikoku writes, "At the constitutional conference table (London), a capitalist-oriented, ethnically-minded national leadership, lacking the support of the direct mass action which it helped to castrate faced a firm and wily colonial power. After Independence in 1960, political leadership set out to consolidate three Nigerias divided on ethnic lines—each capitalist-oriented, inward-looking and seeking a tie-up with foreign capital...Military interregnums since independence have sought to resolve the conflict created by the three

Nigerias hypothesis without destroying the external control and direction that lay behind such an arrangement."[18]

There is no basis for the existence of Nigeria today. The history of this country is one of the worst tales of a failed experiment. It is the country with the largest population in the African continent, and one out of every six black men on earth is a Nigerian. However, Nigeria remains an experiment to date. This great land of peoples and cultures; this land of lush vegetation and mineral resources; this land of heroes and heroines has become a land hunted by many tensile projectiles that hang over the country like the sword of Damocles. Nigeria is always in constant danger of implosion. It is a land of darkness and wastes; a noisy and boastful country where the best never happens but the worst is never inevitable.

As *Onye Army* explained the failed Nigerian state to us, I did not know that I would have cause 22 years later to mourn the inexcusable fate of this great land of Nigeria. He bemoaned the fate of the Igbo people; a condition which I grew up to find out was not peculiar to the Igbo people, even though their historical antipathy with the Nigerian federation, and the existential angst felt by the rest of the country in relationship with the Igbo, continues to simmer unabated. *Onye Army* said that he blamed the British Christians for helping the Northern Muslims fight and defeat the Christian Easterners. He said that British pilots and engineers were the saviors of the Northerners who were on the verge of being defeated by the mighty Biafrans. I was later to find out that even though the British and Russians fought on the side of the Nigerian government, the French and some Russians were on the side of the Biafrans. These Western countries sold weapons to the warring sides and supplied relief to those who were wounded and displaced from the force of the war.

All the Western countries avoided direct involvement in the war even though all of them had a stake in the war, which I now realized was fought because the British did not want the oil wealth of the country to fall into the hands of the Biafra, whose relation with the British government and businesses was unpredictable and who Britain feared was more French-oriented. Millions of Nigerians were killed because British and French companies like Gulf, Mobil, Shell, Texaco, Standard and Phillips were interested in the oil wealth of Nigeria, 75% of which were in the secessionist territory of Biafra. According to Hugh McCullum, forces were let loose on the Biafrans to subdue them so that their oil wealth could be controlled by Nigeria with which Britain and Russia had established a marriage of convenience. As a result, "The Nigerians, heavily armed by Britain and Russia (odd allies in that Cold War period), withheld food supplies, openly stating that food was a legitimate weapon of war. As the Biafrans were pushed back from the best agricultural land into their own barren heartland, and as crops and stores fell into the hands of the Nigerian soldiers, starvation and famine appeared, flapping their wings like the vultures that hovered over the feeding centers and refugee camps. Casualties were huge among civilians."[19]

It was the oil companies of Europe and Britain that decided among the Nigerians who would eat and who would starve, who would be supplied with guns from the apartheid regime in South Africa and who would be defenseless. In the end, it was decided that the Biafrans, for the sake of the oil business of European companies, had to be destroyed and with it the millions of lives of innocent people. It is significant that the first section of the secessionist territory that was penetrated was the oil rich Delta region.

Most wars in Africa are fought because of the economic interests of Western governments and businesses, who take sides with the warring parties based on economic interests. *Onye Army* told us that unless we fought against the Muslim North we would continue to be enslaved and marginalized and would be a wasted generation and eventually be forced to become Muslims. As I grew up and started to study the history of both Nigeria and Africa, I discovered that it was stereotypes like this one purveyed by *Onye Army*, who obviously had a truncated version of the history of Nigeria, that has continued to destroy humanity along the path of history. This has been particularly evident in Africa, where affinity to a tribe is often the strongest passion; the ethnic constitution of societies in Africa is infinitely divisible and so politicians do have an infinite capacity to infinitely divide the people along these multivariate affinities. Ethnic identity has been seen as even stronger than the baptismal waters among Christians as the event in Rwanda and Burundi showed, where people of the same Christian faith killed fellow Christians of the same denomination but from different ethnic affinity. What was more important was not whether you were Catholic or Protestant but whether you were Hutu or Tutsi. Ethnic affinity in Africa appears to be stronger than Islamic fraternity as the horrors in the Sudanese region of Darfur have shown, where Arab Moslems were killing fellow Moslems of African origin. Ethnic affinity is such a strong attraction that politicians in their demagoguery always played on these affinities for their own selfish end.

This position was clearly reflected in the civil war in Congo Brazzaville, where the main political actors, Pascal Lissouba and Sassou-Nguesso played the ethnic drumbeat to shore up their support base. Reflecting on this, the former UN Special Envoy, Mohammed Sahnoun, wrote in a report to the Security Council, "There is hardly any antagonism between communities or ethnic groups or regions. The violence here is largely the result of conflict between leaders whose ambitions know no limit and no decency. These leaders have around them some hard-core followers, armed to the teeth. They have made the entire people of the Congo hostages to their blind ambitions. It is not the people, their communities or even their political parties who are driving this confrontation. They are!"[20]

This was also the case in the civil war in Liberia. When, in 1980, for instance, Samuel Kanyon Doe, a member of the Krahn tribe, overthrew and then executed the affable President William Tolbert (the last in the line of the Americo-Liberians to rule this little African country of Liberia), there was a great outpouring of support from the native inhabitants of the land. The indigenous Liberians felt that they had been unjustly held in thralldom by the Americo-Liberians who had dominated the political and economic life of Liberia since their arrival in 1847. Doe's tribal kinsmen and women welcomed him with open arms even when he came to power in the whirlwind of unprecedented violence that saw the public executions of the top echelons of Tolbert's regime. He was to turn the same bloody eyes on people of his tribe whose cause and that of the native Liberians he claimed to champion. Doe's brutality was phenomenal and paled the horrors committed by the self-anointed Emperor Jean Badel Bokassa of the Central African Republic.

It was, however, the same tribal affinity that helped legitimize Doe's coup that brought him down when he turned the beautiful land of Liberia into a living nightmare. Doe turned against his own people and became a living monster, whose only legacy to Liberia was that he rode roughshod on the back of the people, stewed in the blood of his real and imagined enemies, until the country slithered into a civil war, the ashes of whose raging flames are still smoldering.

Doe was the very antithesis of the highest values that was found in the traditional African leadership. History has shown that the best way to rouse a people's support to a leader is for the leader to personify in himself the people's aspirations. Sometimes this could be done by the leader engendering in the people a sense of collective paranoia of some real or imagined enemy who would have to be eliminated if the people were to survive. The oldest form of fraud is to engender a fear of some kind of disease or problem whose cure one could provide if the person allowed for it.

This often happens even in the most developed country. Since the tragedy of September 11, 2001 in the United States of America, many perceptive thinkers have seen the ship of state in that country being steered in a kind of national paranoia keyed into the Bush doctrine of two worlds: the world of terrorists and the free and safe world—a bipolarity, which is non-existent. Robert Lufton argues that the immediate reaction of President Bush after the attack that America was at war, "had to do not only with the devastating dimensions of the attacks—and with longer-standing projections of American hegemony—but also with the president's own psychological style in relation to anxiety and threat...when national leaders respond belligerently, they may tap the collective potential of their people for amorphous rage, which can readily be transformed into war fever."[21] The Bush Manichean global vision could only lead the world into a ceaseless conflict and widening polarity, since the world would continue to have the violent and the peaceful, the good and the bad all in a productive creative tension.

The task of the better part of humanity—those with the incarnated spiritual qualities of goodness, truth, beauty and love—would be to help plant seeds of peace in the world even in those places and persons who might not appreciate them. These values have their own power which the forces of darkness cannot defeat no matter how noisy and threatening they might be. This is what Martin Luther preached when he said, "When evil men plot, good men must plan. When evil men burn and bomb, good men must build and bind. When evil men shout ugly words of hatred, good men must commit themselves to the glories of love; where evil men would seek to perpetuate an unjust status quo, good men must seek to bring into being a real order of justice." It is totally unrealistic to recreate the world into double loci that are mutually hostile and in an antithetical tension with apocalyptic consequences. This kind of categorization is merely emboldening the thin top-layer of misguided terror hawkers into a kind of universal ubiquity.

This type of thinking has given birth to all kinds of prejudice and hatred in the course of human history. This is always a major factor in the conflicts in most countries of Africa, be it the genocide in Rwanda and Burundi, the conflicts in Sudan, or the constant civil disturbances in Nigeria. There is always the tension between 'us' and 'they.' Thus, when as young children we were taught by some of our tribal leaders that the Northern part of Nigeria is Muslim territory, and that they were opposed to the Christian tradition that we had inherited from Westerners, we drank that idea and prejudice to the dregs.

However, as one grew up and became more discerning, one found out that the reality does not square with the prejudice. Prejudice is the ultimate human disease that blinds our vision and blurs our sense of judgment. Prejudice is the greatest cause of hatred and animosity. It makes us judge people without encountering them; it makes us fear and even long to destroy people whom we have never met. Prejudice closes the door to authentic human encounter and dialogue and diminishes our world and freezes us in some presumed little world of comfort or fear. The story is told of a lion that went to the stream to slake his thirst and saw a little lamb that was also on the bank of the stream. The lion said to the lamb, "Why did you insult me during the drought season last year?" The little lamb told the lion that he was not yet born last year since she was only four months. Then the lion said to her, "then it must be your mother that insulted me last year." The lion went on to devour the innocent little lamb. This is the way prejudice works.

If I had accepted and lived the prejudice instilled in me by *Onye Army* I would not have come to realize that the Northern part of Nigeria is not a Muslim North, 30% of Nigerian Christians live in the North and that even if the North is Muslim, there was nothing negative about living and working together with Muslims. I have found out in my interaction with Muslims that Islam is a religion that has been misunderstood by many non-Muslims mainly because of the kind of information and attitudes that are often built on prejudice. The same kind of prejudice has made many Muslim radical fundamentalists hate Christianity and Western civilization.

These prejudices are often the fruit of the kind of leaders we find among some of these religions who drive their adherents to the margins of inter-religious precipice. The passion for aggressive theocracy and the fear-hawking, terror-mongering and *fatwas*, which have been sustained by certain forms of Islamic fundamentalism, should never be understood as the true face of Islam, a religion whose other name is peace. No religion has a monopoly of violence, but in this age the world religions should work more towards building a culture of love and peace and educating their adherents on the values of true religion, which has nothing to do with war, terrorism, violence and hatred.

As I think of my childhood in Nigeria and the pain that we went through in the early 1970s, I can clearly connect with the condition of many Africans who do not have a childhood because of civil conflicts in their countries. In the early years of my childhood, we saw empty cannons scattered all over the place, and it was not uncommon to see unexploded bombs or to step on a disused shell. We actually played with empty shells and live bullets, which we exploded with nails and iron casts. It was fun but it was unfortunate because it was in a way a sad introduction into the world of violence from which some of my mates never recovered.

This is the situation in most of Africa today. Many children do not have a childhood or a positive introduction into the world. The world they come to know is the world of violence, hunger, poverty and crimes. In the Western countries, children play with toys and teddy bears, but in some of the 18 countries in Africa, which within the last decade have been through civil wars or are still fighting one, the children play with guns and bombs. These represent one wing of the so-called lost generations of Africa.

The American poet Gertrude Stein coined the term "lost generation." Speaking to Ernest Hemingway, she said, "You are all a lost generation."[22] The term stuck and the mystique surrounding these individuals continues to interest many people. The term was used of those intellectuals, poets, artists and writers who fled to France in the post World War I years. These gifted individuals were full of youthful idealism; they sought the meaning of life, drank excessively, had love affairs and created some of the finest American literature to date. There were many literary artists involved in the group known as the Lost Generation. The three best known are F. Scott Fitzgerald, Ernest Hemingway and John Dos Passos. Others usually included among the list are Sherwood Anderson, Kay Boyle, Hart Crane and Ford Maddox Ford.

Hemingway is arguably the leader of the pack of the Lost Generation in the adaptation of the naturalistic technique in his novel. He volunteered to fight along with the Italians during WWI. He was, however, to swallow the bitter pill of defeat when the Italians were crushed by the Central Powers at the battle of Caporetto. Hemingway was reported in the newspapers as having been badly wounded with shrapnel in his leg and yet he was able to help another man who was mortally injured. His post-war disillusionment was captured in his book aptly titled 'Farewell to Arms' (1929). If the lost generations in Europe and America were inspired to positive actions by the experiences of war, the lost generations of Africa as presently seen represent the low water mark of the African condition.

I will try to present three categories of the Lost Generations of Africa and recast in a more positive sense the way to see these generations of young men and women who are facing real challenges in search of a tomorrow that may never come. The first category would be the children who are lost to wars or who have been robbed of their childhood by wars and conflicts in which they were involved either as soldiers or victims.

2.4 The Children of Wars

At one road block a group of children with battered assault rifles forced us off the highway at gunpoint and began shouting at us furiously. The boy in charge could not have been more than fifteen years old. His eyes were deeply bloodshot, and the smell of the marijuana that Taylor's commanders supplied to the child combatants, along with harder drugs, hung thick in the air. I remained seated when he ordered us out of the car, and attempted to gently reason with him, trying to strike the right balance of self-confidence with respect for the authority conferred by his gun, but he would have none of it, and resumed shouting and waving his rifle.[23]

Godfrey lies in pain in the dressing room of St. Joseph's Hospital, in Kitgum Mission (Northern Uganda). I can see the terror in his eyes. In the evening of May 30th 2003, the Lord's Resistance Army (rebels fighting against the government of Museveni in Uganda) came to his home in Mucwini and subjected him to a most horrible mutilation which left him without ears, lips and fingers. It is the fourth such incident I have seen over the last month. His torturers wrapped his ears in a letter and put it in his pocket. The blood-stained piece of paper gave a strong warning to whoever wants to join the local defense force (LDU): "We shall do to you what we have done to him."[24]

This represents the face of many wars in Africa, from the ethnic cleansing going on for decades in Darfur, Sudan or the war in Angola which was until the cessation of conflict in 2001, the longest war in Africa, to the forgotten wars in the Great Lake regions in Northern Uganda, in Somalia and the Congos; from the silent human hemorrhage in the Saharawi Arab Democratic Republic to the killing fields of Cote d'Ivoire, and from the fighting over oil rights in the Delta region of Nigeria to the simmering flames of hatred that has seen the sad face of violence in Zimbabwe and South Africa. According to the United Nations Secretary, Kofi Annan,[25] since 1970, more than 30 wars have been fought in Africa, the vast majority of them intra-state. In 1996 alone, 14 of the 53 countries in Africa were afflicted by armed conflicts, accounting for more than half of all war-related deaths worldwide and resulting in more than 8 million refugees, returnees and displaced persons. The consequences of these conflicts have seriously undermined Africa's long-term stability, prosperity and peace. According to the Secretary General, "By not averting these colossal human tragedies, African leaders have failed the peoples of Africa; the international community has failed them; the United Nations has failed them. We have failed them by not adequately addressing the causes of conflict; by not doing enough to ensure peace; and by our repeated inability to create conditions for sustainable development. This is the reality of Africa's recent past."

The causes of conflicts in Africa are varied. African countries have different histories and different geographical conditions, different sets of public policies and different stages of economic development and patterns of internal and international interactions. The sources of conflicts reflect these dynamics. The first and fundamental cause of conflicts in Africa is that nation-building in most African countries is at a very rudimentary stage and the building of a consensus as to the nature of the state and its structure have often been marked by considerable conflicts which lead sometimes to full blown civil war depending on the issues that dominate each nation. This could be traced back to the effects of colonialism where the colonial masters brought by default many ethnic groups against their will to live together as one country.

Claude Ake, the foremost African social scientist, argues that African countries like many other countries that went through colonialism or that were forced into nationhood by strong-arm tactics like former Yugoslavia are never politically integrated. According to him, a political system is integrated to the extent that the minimal units (e.g., political actors, tribal groups, religious groups, etc.) develop in the course of political interaction a pool of commonly accepted norms regarding political behavior and a commitment to the political behavior patterns legitimized by these norms. A commitment to these norms channels the flow of exchanges—outputs and inputs, actions and reactions, expectations and responses—among interacting political actors. It gives coherence and predictability to political life.[26] Based on his theory, one could say that most of the African countries were malintegrated or minimally integrated after Independence, because the citizens did not share a common value orientation. They were held together physically without any political culture, political socialization and invariably no sense of obligation, duty, or loyalty to the political system and the country.

The building of a central government and the forging into one country of people of diverse ethnic origins have often led to dictatorship and the suppression of political pluralism which leads to conflicts. The existence of a dictatorship in any country always reveals some kind of volatile and divisive component parts, which have to be held in balance by the authoritarian hand of a dictator. Until the last decade, African countries were all caught up in the throes of dictatorships. Most of these dictators like Mobuto Sese Seko of former Zaire, Houphet Boigny of Cote d'Ivoire, Matthew Kerekou of Benin Republic, Omar Bongo of Gabon, Dennis Sassou Nguesso of Congo Brazzaville, Gnasingbe Eyadema of Togo,

Kamuzu Banda of Malawi, Siad Barre of Somalia, and Ibrahim Babangida and Sani Abacha of Nigeria left their countries in deep political crises and economic peonage, which often exploded into full blown war as in Somalia, the two Congos and in Cote d'Ivoire.

Some countries like Uganda, Ghana, and Burkina Faso were luckier that the dictatorships in their countries did not explode into full-blown wars, though people rose up in protest and in armed rebellion as was the case in Uganda when Museveni over threw the UNLA-led government of Tito Okello Lutwa and Basilio Okello in January 1986 (these Acholi officers had earlier overthrown the government of Milton Obote in July 1985). Museveni has remained in power in Uganda since then, transforming himself from a rebel to a democrat and holding on to power! African dictators besides maintaining a tight grip on power through violent suppression of opposition also have proven to be adept in corruption and instead of being gifted in statecraft have instead shown themselves to be experts in kleptocraft.

Government is big business in Africa. "In post-colonial Africa the premium on power is exceptionally high, and the institutional mechanisms for moderating political competition are lacking. As a result, political competition tends to assume the character of warfare. So absorbing is the struggle for power that everything else, including the quest for development, is marginalized."[27] Most African dictators have emptied their national treasuries and have run aground their national economy. A clear case is the late president of Togo, Gnasingbe Eyadema, who until his death in 2005 was the longest-serving dictator in Africa today, and who despite his failed Marxist policies, and his evident corruption failed to hand over the reins of government to younger and brighter people, who may have a better idea on how to move the country forward. Some of these dictators have sustained power through violence and killing of opposition leaders and critical journalists (Nobert Zongo, the assassinated publisher of the anti-government weekly, *L' Independent* in Burkina Faso, Dele Giwa the assassinated Editor of the investigative magazine, *Newswatch*, in Nigeria, etc.).

In those countries that have become democratized like Zimbabwe and Nigeria, elections have constantly remained a source of tension and bitterness. In Nigeria, for instance, two years after the national elections, there are still cases in courts challenging the validity of the elections at national and state levels. The Secretary General of the United Nations summarizes this in the following words, "The nature of political power in many African states, together with the real and perceived consequences of capturing and maintaining power is a key source of conflict across the continent. It is frequently the case that political victory assumes a 'winner-takes-all' form with respect to wealth and resources, patronage, and the prestige and prerogatives of office. A communal sense of advantage and disadvantage is closely linked to this phenomenon, which is heightened in many cases by reliance on centralized and highly personalized forms of governance. Where there is insufficient accountability of leaders, lack of transparency in regimes, inadequate checks and balances, non-adherence to the rule of law, absence of peaceful means to change or replace leadership or lack of respect for human rights, political control becomes excessively important and the stakes become dangerously high."[28]

Poverty is, however, the greatest source of civil strife in Africa. When people are hungry and lack the basic necessities of life, they are easily prone to violence. There is a lot of discontentment in many African societies. Most of the recruits in many of Africa's wars are unemployed youth. As J. F. Clark observed referring to the conflicts in the Congo, "Many of the malefactors in the ethnic violence were unemployed urban youth who had little hope of finding jobs. Recruits to the ethno-political militia in Congo found not only adventure but also economic sustenance and a sense of belonging in the armed groups that they joined."[29]

As a Chaplain assistant to the former Director of Military Chaplaincy in Nigeria in 1991, I lived for 6 months in Ojo military cantonment in Lagos and discovered that many soldiers in Nigeria at this point in time were in the military, because it offered them easy access to power and wealth. Many of the non-commissioned officers were living in abject poverty, while the officers' corps was really swimming in the ocean of wealth and opulence. The then Nigerian strongman, General Ibrahim Babangida, who described himself as 'the evil genius,' had given the donation of brand new Peugeot cars worth US$20,000 each to all the officers from the rank of Major and above to win their loyalty and support as he drove the country down the lower plain of the worst political crisis ever experienced since the Civil War. The experience of any form of poverty by the main corps of the military would have doomed his regime.

When Valentine Strasser seized power in Sierra Leone in May 1997, the first thing he and his henchmen did was to loot the Central Bank reserves. Members of the military could fight for their rights to a share of the national wealth by joining in overthrowing the government of the day. But what happens to the ordinary people of the land who have to suffer the agony of failed governments in Africa? What should the ordinary people in Africa who are caught in the ever-revolving chain of poverty, hunger and starvation do in the face of the betrayal and destruction of the common good by their fortune-digging leaders?

Robert Kapling[30] captures the situation well when he told the tale of the failed state of Sierra Leone at the dawn of the New Millennium, a tale which could be replicated in countries like Burkina Faso, Gabon, Somalia, Congo Democratic Republic (DRC) and Equatorial Guinea. Sierra Leone, until 2001 when peace was restored, was in civil strife that has never had any precedence in the West African sub-region, in terms of its ferocity and the extent of its horrors. Foday Sankoh, the rebel leader of the Sierra Leonian Revolutionary United Front, who died in 2003 in captivity, while facing trials for crimes against humanity, like his partner in horror, Charles Taylor, amputated and maimed many of his fellow citizens including children, to put fear in the people and to win power from the government of the day. He used child soldiers in their thousands and his soldiers used to rape especially the very young girls as a sort of comic relief from their bloody adventures. Sankoh was only following the shameful practice of child soldiering, which has taken root in Africa going back to the rebel groups in Angola and Mozambique.

Like Macbeth, Sankoh had stepped into blood too deep so that going back was as tedious as going forward, and so he continued his inhumanities until the hands of fate caught up with him and his underlings. It was unfortunate that he did not live long enough to face justice. The war in Sierra Leone was not so much an ethnic battle as it was a battle between the majority of the disaffected people who aligned themselves to one rebel group or another to get rid of their common enemy, the government. The renegade commanders of the government army or the splinter rebel groups always had some disaffected tribal chiefs who were willing to align with any winning side that offered them a guarantee for sustenance. It was a formless war, which had no defined enemies, and hence the degree of killings that went unabated. The rebels were supported and financed by Charles Taylor, who had his eyes on the diamonds of Sierra Leone, which he illegitimately acquired and sold to line his personal coffers even though it meant the deaths of thousands of people, especially women and children.

Sierra Leone, like Somalia, is a microcosm of what is occurring in a more tempered and gradual manner throughout Africa and much of the underdeveloped world: the withering of central governments, the rise of tribal and regional domains, the unchecked spread of disease, and the growing pervasiveness of war.[31] Over 400,000 Sierra Leoneans were internally displaced and 280,000 fled to Guinea and Nigeria, while over 100,000 fled to Liberia and were later to run back to Sierra Leone when the Liberian war broke out a year later. It is estimated that over 40,000 people were killed in the war and most of these were women and children.

Most civil strife in Africa is caused by the struggle for scarce resources, the control of national resources, and the restlessness of a betrayed and short-changed populace, whose cup of frustrations overflows in acts of violence usually articulated by some rebel leader or military tough brat.

According to Washington-based *Refugees International*, armed conflict is the leading cause of displacement of persons the world over. Today there are over 35.5 million displaced people worldwide, 11.9 million refugees and asylum seekers and an additional 23.6 million internally displaced people. The leading cause of the displacement is armed conflict, 70% of which is taking place in Africa. West Africa has an estimated 1-1.5 million refugees and displaced people who have fled their homes and countries. There are, according to Refugees International,[32] about 500,000 displaced people in the conflict in Cote d'Ivoire and 69,000 refugees from Liberia. In Guinea, there are over 6,000 Sierra Leonean refugees and about 89,000 Liberian refugees. For those who flee and those who stay behind, death is only one of the many grim consequences.

War always has the face of women and children. According to UNICEF in the document, *A World Fit for Children*[33], hundreds of millions of children are suffering and dying from war, violence, exploitation, neglect and all forms of abuse and discrimination. Around the world children live under especially difficult circumstances: permanently disabled or seriously injured by armed conflicts, internally displaced or driven from their countries as refugees; suffering from natural and man-made disasters, including such perils as exposure to radiation and dangerous chemicals; as children of migrant workers and other socially disadvantaged groups; as victims of racism, racial discrimination, xenophobia and related intolerance.

It is estimated that two million children were killed in wars in the last decade globally and of this number 70% of them were Africans.[34] Six million were seriously injured or permanently disabled; 12 million became homeless as they lost both parents through death or exodus. Children, for instance, who were displaced in Sierra Leone, "wore big eyes and a stomach like a balloon, or swollen elephant feet with a small petrified doll's face. It was nearly unbearable and these were those who survived and got food," the rest died and were buried in many unmarked graves without history. Apart from physical injuries, some of these children suffer post-traumatic depression and all forms of mental sickness. Skard reports this tale by a nine year old Liberian girl, "I saw 10-20 people shot, mostly old people who could not walk fast. They shot my uncle in the head and killed him. They made my father take his brains out and throw them into some water nearby. Then they made my father undress and have an affair with a decaying body. They raped my cousin who was a little girl of nine years."

It is estimated that over 100,000 children under the age of 18 served as soldiers in government or rebel forces in Africa in 2001 alone. There were thousands more who fought in battles in Congo and Sierra Leone some of them as young as eight or nine. Since 1987, when Joseph Kony, a school dropout who claimed to have inherited the spirit of Alice Auma Lakwena (her title meaning "messenger" in Acholi)—who started the Lord's Salvation Army, which since 1984 has been called the Lord's Resistance Army (LRA)—has committed serious crimes against children ranging from forced abduction and conscription, forced marriage and slavery for young girls, outright killings and mutilations.

This is how a 12-year-old boy described the condition of hapless children, who fell into LRA's horror chambers, to Human Rights Watch: "That night, the LRA came abducting people in our village, and some neighbors led them to our house. They abducted all five of us boys at the same time. I was the fifth one....We were told by the LRA not to think about home, our mother or father. If we did, then they would kill us. Better to think now that I am a soldier fighting to liberate the country. There were twenty-eight rows. After we were tied up, they started to beat us randomly; they beat us up with sticks."[35]

UNICEF estimates that of the 38,000 people abducted by the LRA (which was officially designated a terrorist organization by the U.S. Department of State in 2001), since this conflict began in Northern Uganda, 20,000 were children. The brunt of the war in Uganda like other wars in Africa was borne by the civilian population, especially children who are killed, abducted, brutalized, orphaned or raped; and left with no future.

The condition of the African child soldier is very pitiable. They undergo a lot of emotional and physical destruction. They are subjected to all forms of adult treatment including painful and bizarre initiation rites, harsh and hard trainings, starvation, violence, use of drugs and participation in unspeakable evils like killing and mutilations. The females are randomly raped and sometimes killed; others are used as spies and cannon fodder in the senseless and endless wars of some of the troubled countries of Africa. Some of the abducted female children in Northern Uganda were reported to be domestic slaves who fetched firewood for the soldiers, served their sexual appetites, became wives for the commanders and were sometimes made to bear forced pregnancies. These children are the lost generation of Africa, who do not have a childhood, and are being betrayed by society especially the adults and their leaders.

In many instances in Sierra Leone and Liberia, rehabilitating these hapless children has proven an enormous challenge. Some of these children are still in thrall to the commanders who abducted them and hooked them on drugs. Sometimes a cash amount of $300 is given by the United Nations Mission in Liberia (UNMIL) and the Liberian National Commission on Disarmament and Rehabilitation (NCDDRR) to these children to start life anew, but some of them use it to buy marijuana and other drugs that are plentiful in Liberia. These children are really in the throes of personal extinction. Robbed of any future, these children are living in a false and bizarre world torn apart by the adult society that has offered them bombs instead of books and drugs instead of food and chaos instead of care and emotional stability.

The stakes are so high for our children. In the early 1990s, after the end of the apartheid regime in South Africa, the lost generations of Africa was a term which referred to those South African young people who even as teenagers were in the anti-apartheid movement and who took up arms to bring down that evil empire. These kids were not offered opportunities for education by that regime and were more driven by violence and hatred for the whites than any other motive. They saw their parents humiliated and dehumanized and rightly felt 'a common hate' (to use the title of a poem by the South African writer Dennis Brutus) for the oppressive whites that had held them as slaves in their own land. These courageous Africans did not know what to do with freedom when apartheid was abolished and majority rule was introduced in South Africa in 1990. These young people had become advanced in their ignorance and violent behavior. Thus, in the absence of their common enemies, the white supremacists, these young people receded into the backwaters of street violence and gangsterism, targeted this time against their own people. The early 1990s was the most violent in South Africa. These young people are now being rehabilitated and reintegrated into society. They make up the lost generations of Africa who are now being recovered and rescued from a collective *Masada* complex.

Saving the children of Africa from violence will involve a real and genuine concern by leaders in Africa to remove the causes of war. It is also important that the international community create a 'zone of peace' around the children. It should be considered a crime against humanity to use child soldiers or to rape girls in war or in peacekeeping operations as has been reportedly carried out by UN peacekeepers in the Democratic Republic of Congo. War is always a failure of humanity and in war the best of our humanity is sacrificed for the worst in us.

The struggle for control of gold, diamonds, and other mineral resources in many African countries will continue to be a source of conflict unless the greed of some of the rebel leaders and governments in Africa are curtailed, and unless the African continent takes a bold step to consolidate on the many peace initiatives started at regional levels and at the African Union. There is still much illegal arms dealing going on in the backyards of many African countries, fuelling the conflicts in many parts of the continent. Sometimes these arms are illegally imported by African governments from Western governments bent on supporting rebel movements in other parts of Africa. There are many African leaders who have been variously accused of gun running in Africa. Whatever be the case, it is obvious to all that war is obsolete and human civilization cannot give any reason to justify any form of violence in the world today. Violence is always a failure of peace and war is a failure of dialogue and the consequence of injustice.

2.5 HIV/AIDS: Africa's Holocaust?

> Tragically, Mandisi's untimely death should have been averted, for she also succumbed to the disease that is unmercifully mowing down many of our people. - Mongosuthu Buthelezi, the Zulu Inkatha Freedom Party leader, speaking at the funeral of his 48-year-old daughter who died of AIDS, months after her 53-year-old brother died of the same disease.

'Prophet,' as he was called because of his claims to predict the future, was respected and revered by the Charismatic Christian movement in this part of Eastern Nigeria. He would spend many hours at night in silent prayer to God; he would mutter incomprehensible words in staccato fashion for hours on end. He was a 'prayer warrior' who was said to have exorcised many who were bewitched and could 'deliver' people who were under a spell. He was an Evangelical but very ecumenical that he accepted to pray for *Nkoli* who was a Catholic. *Nkoli*, a very attractive and intelligent lady had been struck by a strange illness since late 1993. She became sick shortly after her traditional wedding and her sickness was said to have been brought upon her by the water goddess, who did not want her to ever get married because the water goddess had betrothed her to a god in the spirit world. I had known *Nkoli* as one of my brightest students in the teachers college. She was the first child in a family of six and was determined to give life a shot, and worked and studied at the same time.

Her father was a peasant farmer who could not afford to pay *Nkoli's* school fees and her mother was a tailor who repaired cloths for a token fee. When *Nkoli* failed to come to school for a month, I was worried and enquired from her friend whether her new husband like some men was opposed to her completing her degree. I learnt to my greatest sadness that *Nkoli* was dying from a strange illness and that unless something urgent was done she would not survive from the sickness. She was not responding to any treatment and all the medical tests were said to have proved negative. The family had then concluded after consulting with the fortune-tellers that the sickness had a mysterious connection and needed to appease the water goddess if she was to recover. I wondered why the family, which was Christian, should consult with a diviner and why they should accept his conclusion and follow his instruction. Her father told me that this has passed the competence of the Church and that when the chips are down as in this case, there is no other alternative than to revert to African Traditional Religion which offered solutions to problems of this kind. He told me that it was better to do anything possible to save his daughter's life and that God would not mind as long as she remained alive. I appealed to him to allow me to bring in some Christian healer to pray over and heal her. This he accepted, hence my trip to Prophet's home.

Prophet accepted the invitation on the ground that any fetish item placed around Nkoli's bedside be removed and that all the members of her family went to confession to a priest as there may be a curse placed on the family. He also declared a day's fasting for the family and myself if I wanted to join in the prayers. We were all willing to do anything possible to make Nkoli live so we all fasted and waited for the day of prayer and deliverance.

Nkoli looked weak and gaunt. She could barely speak. She was a ghost of her former self and I could hardly recognize her. Her smooth beautiful face was wrinkled like the face of a 90-year-old woman. Her long shiny hair was so disheveled like that of a deranged woman. I could not hold back my tears as I looked at her so shrunk and shriveled like a cocoyam leaf exposed to perpetual Sahara sunshine. Prophet started to pray with characteristic mysticism. He would roll down his hand magically before the wasted frame of Nkoli. He would stop at the stomach area and would hold his hand steady with renewed agitation and greater mystical lyrics that went in tandem and tremulously with the navigation of his hand. Prophet in a symbolic combatant posture started to punch the air in obvious fight with the negative forces that held their dreary hand on this beautiful angel. This would continue for over an hour with Prophet obviously sweating profusely from the combative prayer, which was very strange but acceptable to all of us as long as it made Nkoli well.

At the end of the day, we wished Nkoli well and left with hope and trust in God that she would be well after the visit by Prophet whose prayers were so efficacious that it was never easy to make an appointment with him because people streamed to him. Unfortunately, Nkoli died two weeks later. I attended her funeral with some of her classmates who were all troubled by the circumstances of her death. I could not forget the dirge given by her mother who traditionally was not allowed to stay for the burial itself because in some African cultures a mother should never see the interment of her daughter. Nkoli's mother said something like this:

> "Whoever did this to you, it may never be well with him or her;
> Whatever deity that took you before your bloom, may the spirits take him back;
> I know that you are a fighter and so would fight on in the spirit world so that such a fate may never befall any of your siblings;
> I do not know why God allowed this but I cannot change anything now.….."

Throughout the funeral rite, Nkoli's new husband maintained an emotionless stance. He was distant, perhaps, hiding his grief or trying to 'be a man' as they would say in Nigeria. He was to die a year later under similar circumstances. I was to find out from my aunt who worked in the University of Nigeria Teaching Hospital where both of them died, that they both had died of AIDS.

I asked my aunt why the hospital did not tell the family, but she said it was not a nice thing to tell them that their daughter had been sleeping around and was punished by God with this terrible disease. Besides, she continued, nothing could have changed by revealing her status to the family since she would still die anyway. This incident, however, brought me face-to-face with the devastating effects of HIV/AIDS, and how little we knew about it in Nigeria as well as in other African countries. This was 10 years ago.

When the late Health Minister of Nigeria, Professor Olukoye Ransome Kuti, announced in 1997 that his younger brother Fela, one of Africa's foremost musician and Afro-beat proponent, had died of AIDS, it was unprecedented in the nation's history. It was considered unethical of him to have done that. He was, however, a pioneer in removing the stigma attached to this disease. Had the country followed his passion to fight the disease, Nigeria would not have about 2.3 million people living with HIV/AIDS today. The conception of HIV/AIDS as a strange ailment sent by God to punish the promiscuous and the stigma attached to it has not changed. To be struck by this ailment in Africa means receiving a death sentence. Churches in Nigeria now recommend, for instance, that couples that wish to marry should go for a screening to be aware of their HIV status before marriage. I have seen a couple who tested positive to HIV die within 6 months because they could not live with the stigma that goes with this disease.

Many African countries have awakened to the reality of this disease and are fighting it with renewed vigor. In sub-Saharan Africa, 40 countries have developed national strategies to fight HIV/AIDS—almost three times as many as two years ago and 19 countries now have National AIDS councils. Unfortunately, in many countries, especially in sub-Saharan Africa, competing national priorities inhibit allocation of resources to expand access to HIV/AIDS care, support and treatment. Unaffordable prices remain the most commonly cited reason for the limited access to antiretroviral drugs. Insufficient capacity of health sectors, including infrastructure and shortage of personnel are also major obstacles to health service delivery in many countries. The cult of secrecy around this disease is being overcome in many countries of Africa.[36]

People have become increasingly aware of the choices they have to make with regard to prevention and treatment of this disease. According to the Ugandan president Yoweri Museveni in an address to the African Development forum in December 2001, "When a lion comes to the village, you do not make a small alarm. You make a loud one. When I knew of this problem (HIV/AIDS), I said we must shout and shout and shout."[37]

Uganda and Senegal have proved to be two countries that took the epidemic as a national disaster and declared a total war against it. Uganda's infection rate has been reduced from 30% to 8% within the last decade.[38] In Senegal, as soon as the first case of the disease was detected in 1986, the country's government appointed a very gifted African woman, Professor Awa Marie Coll Seck, who mobilized the people and started a nationwide campaign that, as of 2004, has reduced the infection rate to 1%. The statistics on the spread of this disease in other African countries is, however, frightening.

Sub-Saharan Africa is home to just 10% of the world's population, but two-thirds of the people living with HIV live in sub-Saharan Africa. In 2003, an estimated 3 million people became newly infected and 2.2 million died, 75% of which are Africans.[39] An estimated 25 million people lived with HIV in Sub-Saharan Africa in 2004.

When compared with the 26.6 million people who were living with HIV in 2003, there appears to be stabilization, but this is mainly due to the rise in AIDS death and continued new cases of infection. New infection rates are still rising in countries like Madagascar and Swaziland according to the report of the Joint United Nations Program on HIV/AIDS (UNAIDS). Rates vary considerably across the continent ranging from less than 1% in Mauritania to almost 40% in diamond-rich Botswana and Swaziland. Southern Africa is home to about 30% of people living with HIV/AIDS worldwide, yet this region has less than 2% of the world's population.[40]

A priest friend of mine, working in the Transvaal region of South Africa, told me that he buries on average one person every week that dies of AIDS. In some African countries like Botswana, South Africa, Namibia, Lesotho, and Zimbabwe, the epidemic has assumed devastating proportions. In Lesotho and Namibia it has climbed to 30% and 23%, respectively, within the last decade that the decease was ever reported for the first time in those countries. The statistics of Zimbabwe placed the rate of spread at 25% by the end of 2003. In East Africa, there is a marked reduction in the spread of this disease, in Uganda as well as in Rwanda where the prevalence has dropped to 13% from 35% in 1993; in Ethiopia it has dropped from 24% in 1996 to 11% in 2003 among the pregnant women surveyed. In West Africa, surveys suggest that adult HIV prevalence is relatively low, being at 2% in Mali, and 1% or lower in Gambia, Mauritania and Niger. Ghana and Burkina Faso show some stable trends. Cote d'Ivoire appears to have the highest prevalence of HIV in West Africa with 9.7% of infection rate. Nigeria has a national median average spread of 2.8%.

From the available statistics, Africa appears to be at the epicenter of this global pandemic accounting for 80% of the 3 million fatalities worldwide. There has been a change in the statistical analysis of the number of cases of infection. Improved data collection and analytical tools have led these organizations to lower their estimates for infection and deaths in 2003 compared to those published the previous years. Under the new statistics the number of people thought to be living with HIV/AIDS reflects the midpoint between the lowest estimate of people infected, 34 million and the highest 46 million. Thus, African fatalities from the disease for 2003 set at 2.3 million actually represent estimates of between 2.2 million and 2.4 million. This could also apply to the Bangui definition of AIDS in Africa. The Bangui definition (named after the Central African Republic where the World Health Organization (WHO) officials met to determine their new approach to understanding and defining this disease in Africa) stipulated that a patient should be classified as an AIDS patient if he/she displayed two or more of these common ailments: significant weight loss, chronic diarrhea, persistent fever or cough (lasting for over a month), widespread skin rash, recurrent herpes infections and swollen lymph glands.[41]

Some skeptics ask whether the figures of African mortality and infection were deliberately inflated to breed negative views of the continent. Perhaps thousands of Africans are dying from the same diseases that killed their parents and grandparents. This line of thought, however, flies in the face of the reality. This was the kind of argument brought forward by President Thabo Mbeki, the President of South Africa: that HIV was not the virus that causes AIDS. This porous argument misled many of his countrymen and women who could have been saved from the deadly disease.

The truth must be told that Africa is in the midst of a continental calamity of apocalyptical consequences, if it is not controlled. HIV/AIDS is killing more Africans than the many wars fought in the continent within the last four decades put together. "The disease fractures and impoverishes families, weakens work forces, turns millions into orphans and threatens social and economic fabric of communities and the political stability of nations."[42] No meaningful and sustainable development can occur if the AIDS epidemic is allowed to drain the human resources of Africa. According to UNAIDS, if allowed to go unchecked, HIV/AIDS weakens the capacity of households, communities, institutions and nations to cope with the social and economic effects of the epidemic. Productive capacities—including the informal sector are eroded as workers and managers fall prey to the disease. Flagging consumption, along with the loss of skills and capacities in turn drains public revenue and undermines the state's ability to serve the common interest of development and human well-being.

This cycle is both dynamic and vicious. It is the poor who are edged further towards the margins and exclusion as the worsening social indicators in countries with serious AIDS epidemic reveal.[43] Unfortunately, the endless civil strife in many African countries is worsened by the economic and social crises precipitated by this epidemic. HIV/AIDS thrives amid social displacement and disintegration. The food emergency sweeping through Southern Africa highlights how vulnerable countries are to shocks that disrupt food production.

According to UNAIDS, almost 13 million people are at risk of starvation in six Southern African countries of Lesotho, Malawi, Mozambique, Swaziland, Zambia, and Zimbabwe. A combination of factors is at play here ranging from drought, floods and a lack of adequate manpower; there is also the lack of consumer protection, the selling of food reserves, misguided governance and political instability among others. With the alarming rate of HIV in these countries where human resources are critical in reenergizing and stimulating the agricultural sector, the fact that HIV/AIDS strips bare the farmer, the farm-worker households as well as the agricultural extension workers and the state personnel unfolds a scene of hunger, starvation and hopelessness.

In the hardest-hit countries, the epidemic has wiped out decades of progress made in health, education and social development. If the rate of spread continues in Africa, a majority of today's 15-year-olds will not reach their 60th birthday. In the six hardest-hit countries in Southern Africa, the life expectancy has plummeted radically to 49 years; 13 years lower than it was before the outbreak of this horrible epidemic. The epidemic affects all sectors of life in Africa, including the business sector which suffers from absenteeism in the number of people who are sick, organizational disruption, loss of skills, and the increasing cost of funerals. In Kenya, for instance, 400 people die everyday from AIDS. "With education and prevention program starved for funds, access to medications is limited to the very rich or the very fortunate, victimization of the infected all too common, Africa and the international community failed to halt the spread of this disease, or ease the suffering and economic and social devastation it has wrought."[44]

2.6 HIV/AIDS Has The Face Of Women And Children

African women are at greater risk of being infected with the HIV/AIDS disease than the men. Today, on average, there are 13 infected women for every 10 infected men in sub-Saharan Africa, up from 12 to 10 in 2002. The difference is more pronounced among the 15-24 year olds. A review compared the ratio of young women living with HIV to young men living with HIV. This ranges from 20 women for every 10 men in South Africa to 45 women for every 10 men in Kenya and Mali.

The *AIDS Epidemic Update,* for 2002, gives the reason why the epidemic has a woman's face.[45] Women and girls are commonly discriminated against in terms of access to education, employment, credit, health care, land and inheritance. With the downward economic trend of many African countries increasing the ranks of people in poverty, relationships with men (both casual or formalized through marriage) can serve as vital opportunities for financial and social security or for satisfying the basic necessities of life. In many girls' boarding schools in Burkina Faso for instance, older men lure high school girls into relationships with false promises of money and support for their schooling. In many poor countries in Africa, such an offer for poor girls is often too difficult to resist. Older men would most likely be able to give financial securities to the younger girls. Besides, in some African communities, it is believed that it is safer to make love to virgins who have less likelihood of being HIV/AIDS positive. In addition, their state of virginity is often attributed with the power of curing the older men of diseases like HIV/AIDS, and even to grant them some good fortune.

The increasing subordination and dependence of women on men makes it nearly impossible for them to choose with whom to have sex or to refuse to have relationships that carry the threat of contracting diseases. Lack of knowledge about reproductive health is still widespread in some communities and young girls are more prone to infection biologically (the cervix being susceptible to lesions) than older women. Statistics show that the rate of spread among younger women in the ages of 15-19 is very high. At the preparatory women's conference, held in Dakar in 1994, it was agreed that female power is Africa's vaccine against AIDS.

These millions of young girls who face an uncertain future make up the second level of the lost generations of Africa. With the failure of the international community to provide them with antiretroviral drugs, with the failure of their respective governments to prioritize the fight against AIDS and channel national finances to key health and social security sectors, these children might die without singing their special songs to the world. Most of these young women with their male counterparts are also among the orphaned generations of Africa. "In the past, people used to care for the orphans and loved them, but these days they are so many, and many people have died who could have assisted them, and therefore orphanhood is a common phenomenon, not strange. The few who are alive cannot support them."[46] This statement by a poor widow in Kenya aptly captures the situation in some African countries today. The sum effects of all these are that multiple deaths and widespread hardships are steadily dissolving the traditional safety nets that, in the past, enabled households and communities to weather periodic adversity.

Of the estimated 34 million orphans living in Africa, more than 11 million under the age of 15 living in sub-Saharan Africa have been robbed of one or both parents by HIV/AIDS. This represents 12% of the population of children in Africa. Seven years from now, according to UNICEF's estimates, their number will grow to 20 million, meaning that at that time on average about 20% of all children living in Africa would be orphans. "Orphaned children are disadvantaged in numerous and often devastating ways. In addition to the trauma of witnessing the sickness and death of one or both parents, they are likely to be poorer and less healthy than non-orphans are. They are more likely to suffer damage to their cognitive and emotional development, less likely to go to school, and more likely to be subjected to the worst forms of child labor. Survival strategies such as eating less and selling assets intensify the vulnerability of both adults and children."[47]

In the hardest hit countries of Southern Africa like Botswana, Lesotho, Swaziland and Zimbabwe one in every five children is an orphan and most of them double orphans because they have lost both parents to AIDS since naturally if one parent has the virus, he or she would transmit it to the partner. According to UNICEF, in sub-Saharan Africa, the HIV/AIDS epidemic has deepened poverty and worsened dependency and deprivation of the most vulnerable of society. The responsibility of caring for the orphaned children is a major factor in pushing many extended families beyond their ability to cope. With the number of children that require protection and support soaring by the day, and more adults falling sick with HIV/AIDS, the extended family network that is characteristic of African societies have become stretched beyond limits. In some African families we are seeing families headed by children (below the age of 18), women, grandparents, and great-grandparents.

HIV/AIDS usually wipes out the most productive sector of the economy. The families of orphans are usually left with little financial base to carry on with life, as the sickness that took their parents and funeral costs would have drained the finances of the family. In cases of paternal orphans, the widows are often denied the right of inheritance, as is the case in most African countries where women do not yet have the right of inheritance. Many children are forced into abandoning school to do many odd jobs to provide for themselves, because with the death of their parents, they are abandoned in the lower rungs of a broken social network that has no welfare and social package for children. These orphans are among the lost generation of Africa. They are faced with searing emotional trauma living with the stigma that their parents were promiscuous hence their deaths through AIDS.

I met with some of these orphans in a little parish in Eastern Nigeria and noticed a palpable sign of shame and lack of dignity from some of them, because they felt abandoned by God and betrayed by society. Some of them suffer the injustice of their inheritance being forcibly taken away from them by vaunting and greedy relatives; some of them suffer from forms of child abuse from older adults who might take advantage of their vulnerable situation. The situation of these children totally affects their integral development and denies them access to education, health care, and a childhood that conduces to human dignity. It also jeopardizes their rights as enshrined in the 1989 Convention on the Rights of the Child. If the world does not take care of these children, it invariably jeopardizes the future development of African countries.

Addressing this crisis requires an integrated response that prioritizes food assistance; seeking effective ways of HIV/AIDS prevention, treatment and care services; provides more support to save the most vulnerable households from destitution and disintegration; and puts in place long term strategies that boost the lives and livelihoods of the rural poor.[48]

Sadly, none of these steps are being taken in some of the countries most hit by the disease, and in other countries like Nigeria there appears to be clear complacency in responding to this pandemic while a culture of silence and denial still reigns supreme. However, it is important to note that the way we treat children, especially the most vulnerable, is always a measure of the quality of any civilization and any leadership. Children are our most cherished assets and every child born into this world is a gift of inestimable value. Rescuing these lost children should be the central social policy of any government worth its name in Africa, and NGOs working in Africa should work outside the government's circle to reach out to these abandoned children. Many grants, given to the governments of some African countries to fight this deadly disease, usually end up in the private coffers of some senior government officials. These officials are like vultures that would feed on the carrion of the dying and whittling population of their countries. I did notice suicidal thoughts in some of the orphans I spoke with who were not connected to any community support. The community support network for children who have lost their parents from this disease has not been established in many communities in Nigeria, because people refuse to admit the fact that there is an HIV/AIDS crisis in that country.

In June 2001, the United Nations General Assembly Special Session on HIV/AIDS paid special attention to children orphaned by this epidemic and came out with a five-pronged framework for action:

- Strengthening the capacity of families to protect and care for the orphans and other children made vulnerable by the disease.
- Mobilizing and strengthening community-based responses.
- Ensuring access to essential services for orphans and vulnerable children
- Ensuring that governments protect the most vulnerable children.
- Raising awareness to create a supportive environment for children affected by HIV/AIDS.[49]

When we combine the suffering these orphans face and the fact that they too might also die as a result of the epidemic (95% of African children whose parents died of AIDS are thought to have the virus), or as the result of hunger, when we also admit the fact that malaria is the greatest killer disease in Africa after HIV/AIDS, and that many children of Africa die from this disease too, we would appreciate the extent of this crisis.

Every year, malaria, spread through mosquito bites, results in 300 to 500 million clinical cases and causes more than 1 million deaths. It is mainly children under the age of 5 who have not yet built up a strong immunity like the adults, who die of this disease, which kills about 3000 African children every day. Malaria also contributes to high maternal morbidity and mortality, and leaves most children and mothers who survive the sickness with other related ailments that hinder their healthy growth and well-being.[50] What can be done to avert the HIV/AIDS pandemic and save the future of Africa?

2.7 Why HIV/AIDS is Africa's Problem.

The UNAIDS *Epidemic Update* for 2002 notes that about 90% of the African population has not been infected by this deadly virus.[51] This is good news as well as bad news. It is good news, because it means that with concerted efforts keeping the rest of the population HIV/AIDS-free is a clear possibility. It is bad news in the sense that the 10% who are sick need help which they are not getting, and unless aggressive campaigning is carried out at a grassroots level, the number of infection cases will bourgeon in the years to come. There are many people who have the disease who do not know yet and who continue to spread the disease because they are afraid of having their blood screened.

Early detection of the disease and early treatment helps to save the lives of those who have the HIV virus. Countries like Nigeria, Ghana and Benin republics who have not adopted an aggressive campaign, risk having an explosion of the disease, which is now in its invisible stages. Unfortunately, this fact does not appear to impress many Western countries who subject all Africans to HIV/AIDS tests, against international convention, before giving them visas. For these officials, the face of Africa is the face of HIV/AIDS. Every African is seen as potentially HIV/AIDS-positive in the eyes of Western government officials unless proven negative. In a certain sense, we Africans should bear the blame for the inhumanity that we suffer as a result of this disease, which did not originate in Africa. Indeed, when people started to hear of this disease in Nigeria they called it a White man's disease. Unfortunately, while the 'White men' are getting rid of it, Africans are getting swallowed up in this terrible pandemic. This epidemic is spreading rapidly in Africa because of cultural, political and economic reasons.

Culturally, sex is never discussed in African communities. A teenage boy cannot move freely with his girlfriend without incurring the wrath of adults. This was a healthy way of preserving the sanctity of sex in traditional African society. Some communities in Southern Africa and Eastern Nigeria are now renewing the rite of virginity before marriage, which is administered to girls in praise of their parents for keeping them virgins until marriage. It used to be a thing of pride in traditional Igbo society for a husband to bring home to his mother-in-law, the blood stained veil that proved his wife's virginity, after their first night together. It is obvious that such a rite appears weighted against women since there is no way of determining the virginity of a man. However, given the fact that women always bear the brunt of diseases, poverty, and cultural restrictions in most traditional societies, one would appreciate the reason why this rite was restricted to women.

Things, however, have changed and many teenagers are now sexually active before their 16th birthday. The traditional African society is yet to come to terms with this transition, which does not bode well for the moral life of the people. HIV/AIDS is spreading in Africa because of Africa's cultural crisis. The sexual morality of the African communities was usually high in times past. There were sanctions for sexual promiscuity and those who got pregnant outside of wedlock were severely punished and suffered some kind of social ostracism. In some Igbo communities in Eastern Nigeria, children born out of marriage unfortunately are still denied the right of inheritance. Sex was only allowed within the context of marriage. Prostitution was a taboo and today those who sell their bodies have to leave their regions for another region or another African country because it is still considered a shameful and reprehensible abuse of womanhood.

Among the Mossi tribe of Burkina Faso, prostitutes are considered social outcasts. Unfortunately, the busiest street in Ouagadougou, the Avenue Kwame Nkrumah, now serves as a supply point of prostitutes for politicians, business moguls, irresponsible youth and some randy husbands. Rape was considered an act of madness, and any man who raped a woman was usually excommunicated from the community and underwent a rite of purgation to cleanse the defiled land and the defiled family line. Thus, young people were encouraged to maintain healthy relationships, but any kind of intimacy of a sexual kind was discouraged among them. These were values which kept the traditional society morally and socially healthy. Since, marital infidelity was frowned upon, the women, including the family-in-law, would go to great extents to sanction any man who was proven to be an unfaithful husband. He would be required to do a lot of symbolic acts to assuage the frayed spiritual veins of the holy covenant of marriage. There were definitely aberrations, but in general this was the moral order which was upheld.

The templates have, however, changed, and we are living in an era of widespread sexual activity. Pornography has become pervasive in many cities in Africa. Red light districts are now common in many major cities. There is thus a crisis of a cultural kind. How do we discuss sex today? What image of sexuality do we present to the children? How do we stem the banality of sexual relations without real commitment, which has been implanted in African society by some negative currents? This is the context within which we see the campaign on the use of condoms. The United Nations Secretary General, Kofi Annan, reported in an interview[52] a dialogue between him and two African presidents who refused to support the UN-backed campaign on the use of condoms in the fight against HIV/AIDS. When he told one president about the need to intensify the campaign with condoms, the president replied, "I can't utter the word condoms; I am the father of the nation. You can't ask me to encourage the youth to be promiscuous."

Another president told him to remember that he is an African (he is from Ghana) and that it would not be right to associate him in public with condoms. He should refrain from speaking about it publicly, the president advised him. The Secretary General said, "Mr. President, I've even written the Pope about it to see how we can work with the Catholic Church on prevention, on education, on treatment and care."

The president replied, "When it comes to condoms, the Pope and I are one."

"Mr. President," replied the Secretary General, "your people are dying. We are talking of saving lives. This is very serious business and God will understand."

The issue here is whether proposing the use of condoms to the people of Africa, especially the young, is the right thing to do; or whether there are other messages about prevention which are not being promoted as much as condom use.

Let me state that what our young people need in Africa is a culture of hope. The young people who are being driven into unhealthy practices need education to open to them infinite horizons so that they can develop skills and contribute to the development of their countries. There is also the need to inculcate in the young people a healthy cultural life that introduces them into the glories of authentic humanity. The young people need religious values that should shape their vision of life, morality and reality. Above all, they need to be propelled to dream dreams and thus chart the path for a better future for Africa. The idea that the continent is blighted and that there is nothing that they can do except to latch on to sex, drug addiction and crimes as substitutes should be combated as much as possible. This is why joblessness among young Africans is a great and grave condition, which governments and non-governmental organizations as well as voluntary agencies and religious institutions must address with urgency.

Many young Africans are driven to unhealthy practices because they do not see positive signs of a better future in their countries. Any young person who has a sense of purpose in life, and who believes in his or her place in the collective future of humanity, would see his or her life as meaningful and a diamond worthy of protecting. Knowledge, they say, is power and that is what is unfortunately not being given to the young people. Thus, at a preliminary level of analysis, my alternative to Africa's condom conundrum is more education, so that Africans can make the best choices for themselves in view of their understanding of the meaning of the human project, their vision of what their lives mean to them and their communities.

It must be stated in a most obvious way that the question of the morality of condom use has not been properly and objectively examined in Africa. This has hampered the need for openness and dialogue in addressing the complex issue of condom use in Africa across the lines. Many Africans do not believe that the prevention of this disease is simply the adoption of condom use as the official position of governments and religious institutions. Condom use is only one of many possible solutions to the prevention of HIV/AIDS. It should not be absolutized. It might not be totally true to say that the disease is spreading in Africa because Africans are not using condoms and that it will stop spreading if condom use becomes widespread.

Many people accuse religious institutions who propose abstinence as the most effective solution for the prevention of this disease of committing genocide. Such people fail to point out why abstinence should not be integrated into the public health policy in Africa, if it is a valid approach to fighting this pandemic. As Kingsley Moghalu had stated in a recent article, "Many critics of the abstinence message are social libertarians who believe that individual freedom should not be restricted on moral grounds, as was argued among the free sex, marijuana-smoking youth culture of the 1960s America. The Nigerian musician Femi Kuti, debunking the Untied States government's support for abstinence campaigns, recently argued in an interview with the American newsmagazine *Newsweek* that 'we were born to have sex'. He is entitled to his opinion, but I suspect that is not the advice many parents will be giving their daughters."[53] Moghalu argues that there are four elements to be considered in addressing the issue of condom use in Africa, namely, cultural factors, political leadership, gender concerns and religious obligations. Public health policy in Africa should integrate all these elements in determining the most effective means of combating this disease in Africa. Our concern here is however to appraise the position of the Catholic Church on the use of condom and see how it helps the fight against the spread of this disease and the challenges it must help to address.

The *Washington Times*, on June 17, 2004, described how Tsetsele Fantan, leader of the African Comprehensive HIV/AIDS Partnerships, sponsored by the pharmaceutical giant Merck & Company and the Bill and Melinda Gates Foundation, felt embarrassed on taking a visitor to a primary school in Botswana, whose walls had posters about using condoms and whose children sang songs about prophylactics. Fantan said, "At that age [approximately 12 years or less] they should have been singing about 'saying no' to sex."[54]

The message here should have been abstinence and not the wrong message of condom use, which terribly erodes African culture and promotes promiscuity and unfaithfulness. The fight against HIV/AIDS cannot succeed in Africa unless it is keyed into the cultural traditions of Africa, for there is no solution to any African problem that will succeed unless it has its legs on the cultural life of the people.

This view is shared by Helen Epstein, a visiting research scholar at the Center for Health and Wellbeing at Princeton University. In an article in the June 13, 2004 edition of *Time* magazine, Epstein had observed that many efforts aimed at stopping the spread of HIV have had disappointing results. According to her, ignoring the need to promote fidelity in sexual relations may well have undermined the efforts to fight the disease.[55]

In an important article, "Condom Promotion for AIDS Prevention in the Developing World: Is it Working?" Norman Hearst, a professor at the University of California, and Sanny Chen, an epidemiologist with the San Francisco Department of Health, argued against the undue emphasis given to condoms as prevention for HIV/AIDS. Measuring the effectiveness of condom use is nearly impossible they argue. The question raised based on evidence is that there are no clear examples of a country that has turned back a generalized epidemic primarily by means of condom use. UNAIDS has actually changed the campaign to *ABC*, that is Abstinence, Being faithful to a mutually faithful uninfected person, and Condom use, in that order, based on pressure from the Catholic church and the Islamic religion.

Uganda's noted success in reducing the prevalence of AIDS was due to a program that focused on delaying sexual activity among adolescents, promoting abstinence, encouraging faithfulness to a single partner and condom use. Condom use was the last in the order of importance. The substantial reduction of HIV/AIDS in Uganda and among pregnant women in Zambia and Tanzania was not due to increased use of condoms, but due to a substantial reduction in the number of sexual partners,[56] in cultures where having multiple sexual partners was the 'manly thing' to do. The most cultural thing to propose to the people is the revered African tradition of chastity before marriage and chastity within marriage. This value may have eroded like all other values offered by the traditional society for the healthy growth of the community, but it remains eternally relevant and urgently needs to be rekindled in African societies.

HIV/AIDS is, more often than not, a lifestyle disease and there is about a 0.09% chance of getting this disease through means apart from sexual intercourse.

I do appreciate the position of some Christian churches on de-emphasizing the use of condom as the solution to the problem of HIV/AIDS in Africa, because religious institutions would lose their value if they fail to set the standard of behavior for people. The issue is not whether condom is effective in prevention of HIV/AIDS (research done by the BBC on prostitutes in many parts of Europe and North America shows that condoms are effective when properly used; however condoms do not guarantee 100% protection as the labels in condom packages indicate),[57] but whether African families are training their children on the values of sexual responsibility, which demands learning to love people as persons to be encountered and not objects to be used for sexual pleasures.[58]

There is always a need to set the standard of moral behavior for the people of our day. There are various arguments for and against the use of condoms. I do see some merits in the position of the Catholic Church on sexual abstinence. No one can argue persuasively that abstinence is not the best answer to this epidemic. Those who do not wish to pursue the best solution should not blame the Church for offering it. The Catholic Church is in the forefront of the campaign for the prevention and treatment of this epidemic. She has actually launched a Marshall Plan to fight AIDS in Africa not by distributing condoms, but by preaching abstinence and providing quality care to those suffering from AIDS.

According to Archbishop Javier Lozano Barragan, President of the Pontifical Council on Pastoral Health Care, in an intervention at the

United Nations, the Catholic Church provides approximately 25% of all AIDS care in the world today. Through its ministries and many of its more than 110,000 healthcare organizations like Catholic Relief Services, men and women of love are providing relief, compassion and courage to those who are living with this deadly disease. It is because the Christian faith has a total vision of the human person and human dignity, respecting all persons in their wholeness and in the depth of their being (physical, psychological, spiritual, and moral) that it rejects the idea that people should abandon their lives to latex.

People are encouraged to embrace chastity, fidelity and sexual abstinence outside of marriage, behaviors that protect physical and spiritual integrity, preserve their true dignity, and promote true responsibility.[59] The Symposium of Episcopal Conference of Africa and Madagascar (SECAM) reiterates this position when it says, "Abstinence and fidelity are not only the best way to avoid becoming infected by HIV, or infecting others, but even more are they the best way of ensuring progress towards lifelong happiness and true fulfillment....We want to educate appropriately and promote those changes in attitude and behavior which value abstinence and self-control before marriage and fidelity within marriage. We want to become involved in affective and sexual education for life, to help young people and couples discover the wonder of their sexuality and their reproductive capacities. Out of such wonder and respect flow a responsible sexuality and method of managing fertility in mutual respect between the man and the woman."[60] The message we find in the Book of Deuteronomy is germane here: "I am offering you life or death, blessing or curse. Choose life, then, so that you and your descendants will live" (Deut 30:19).

The teaching of the Church against the use of condoms comes very close to traditional African morality. This is not to say that this position is totally acceptable to all African communities, nor is there a universal acceptance of the position of the Church even within the Church itself. Indeed, the extent of the epidemic in some countries of Africa has resulted in some kind of emergency response, which emphasizes what is pragmatic over what is moral; what is life-saving over what is life-giving.

This provides a complex scenario that does not lend itself to an easy moral calculus. What do we do when one of the partners is infected so that he/she does not infect the other partner? What do we do about people who are not married and who want to become sexually involved? There has been an argument led by the influential Belgian Cardinal Godfried Danneels, who was quoted to have told a local television, "When someone is seropositive and his partner says, 'I want to have sexual relations with you,' he doesn't have to do that, if you ask me. But when he does, he has to use a condom."[61] This position needs to be fully explored as it carries some message of hope to those who are sick with HIV/AIDS and whose lack of intimacy and love from their partners could help to harden the feeling of discrimination. In this case, the use of condoms is not for birth control measure, but to give life to the sick partner who would find life and love in the conjugal union. In this context, the use of a condom is for therapeutic reasons.

The fight that has engulfed the Western church over contraception since the publication of the papal encyclical *Humanae Vitae* (July 26, 1968) does not come into consideration here. This document, which could be called the *magna carta* of the papal defense of the culture of life and the generative process, continues to attract diverse response till date among Catholics and non-Catholics alike. Many Episcopal conferences in the then West Germany, Austria, Scandinavia, France, Brazil, United Kingdom, the United States and Canada were not totally in agreement with some of the directives of this document. The then Toronto Cardinal, Gerald Emmett Carter, defended the famous *Winnipeg Statement*, wherein the Canadian Conference of Catholic Bishops (CCCB) called on Canadian Catholics to choose the course which seems right in good conscience, if they were unsuccessful in following the directives of Pope Paul VI in this encyclical. According to Carter, "Our statement was definitely meant to indicate to the people of Canada that if they found, as we anticipated, and God knows history has proven us to be correct, that they couldn't follow the directives of the encyclical, then they were not to consider themselves cut off from the Church."[62] Africans accepted the papal teaching because contraception is also unacceptable in African culture. Today some Africans and non-Africans who are calling for the use of condom in the fight against AIDS in the continent, make it clear that condom use in Africa should be for therapeutic reasons and not as contraceptives. The Africans make this call based on their lived experience and history and the need to save lives, preserve family life, harmony and the unity and sanctity of married life. This is not based on an anti-life mentality but rather on a pro-life orientation: the prevention of death.

There are cases where actions, which are inherently evil like abortion, are permissible (e.g., ectopic pregnancy, cancer, etc.), where a pregnancy is terminated to save the life of the mother, when the lives of both mother and child are endangered. Hysterectomy is carried out on women who have cancer, which removes their uterus, which in Catholic moral teaching would have been considered wrong morally. There is the need then to keep the discussion on the use of condoms in perspective.

Furthermore, for anyone who is HIV positive, his or her seed is no longer a pure 'seed of life' but a 'seed of death' and consideration should be given to how to prevent this seed of death from destroying a seed of life that has already grown into a tree in the healthy non-HIV partner. The HIV/AIDS epidemic in Africa is an emergency and there is the need to walk finely the moral line with an eye on compassion, healing, conversion and the avoidance of more deaths. There is also the slippery slope syndrome, wherein, what is permissible for therapeutic reasons could be used for some other motives that go beyond the moral. This must be part of the discussion, which should be open-ended, because humanity has never been through the kind of death-dealing paralyzing puzzle, which the HIV/AIDS pandemic is playing out especially in Africa.

During my visit to some local communities in Nigeria in December 2003, I discovered that many people approve of the use of condoms which are freely available to the populace. At a seminar organized by the Canadian Samaritans for Africa, many of the women were asking questions not on the morality of the use of condoms but rather on their effectiveness as a protection against HIV infection. They wanted to stay alive by any means, as there is a real anxiety about the future in most communities in Africa over this epidemic.

Many other churches in Africa do promote the use of condoms. According to Dr. Vincent Bagame of *Ugandan Straight Talk*, "Abstinence is the main method we emphasize, but there are other methods…we are saying if you can't abstain, if you want 100% protection, please use condom."[63] This kind of condom campaign was among the issues raised by the leaders of the All African Conference of Churches, in a 2003 meeting in Cameroon. While the religious leaders publicly had themselves tested for the disease to encourage people to go for voluntary screening and to help remove the stigma about this disease, there was no consensus on the use of condoms. They were divided on the use of condoms and many of them noted that they would be in an odd spot if they were seen to be encouraging the use of condoms in their churches.

It is estimated that only about 3% of Africans who are sexually active use condoms. The issue is a complicated one. This calls for greater understanding of the cultural background that has led to the widespread resistance to the use of condoms despite the information about its effectiveness as prevention against HIV/AIDS. It is, however, important to give the people full knowledge about the degree of effectiveness and the risks in the use of condoms.

The more fundamental awareness is to make people understand that HIV/AIDS is not a punishment from God. Many religious leaders do preach that this disease is a punishment from God to warn Africans of the increasing rate of sexual promiscuity. I have seen and cared for some sufferers of this disease who kept on crying out to me especially in their moments of pain that they do not understand why God would punish them this way. This is the question many parents and grandparents are asking clerics in Africa today as they watch helplessly as their children and grandchildren die from this disease. HIV/AIDS has nothing divine in it and to associate it with God is to make God a wicked being that glories in the suffering and death of his creatures. I would rather think that this disease is the consequence of the use and abuse of human freedom and it can be reversed by the proper use of freedom.

This is a significant challenge to religious leaders, because in African thought any deadly disease is usually attributed to a punishment and curse from God. It is no wonder that many who are affected by this disease, believing that it has a spiritual origin, resort to traditional, Christian, and Islamic spiritual healers for a cure. Most of these people, who waste their scarce resources seeking help from spiritualists, die in impoverishment, leaving their children with little financial base to fall back on. In Nigeria, claims of scientific and spiritual healings for HIV/AIDS are rampant. I once visited one such healer, Dr. Agbalaka, in the wee hours of the night on the outskirts of Nigeria's capital Abuja in 2001. I saw hundreds of people lining up to see him, most of them came by very expensive cars betraying their status and wealth. They were all seeking a cure for their HIV/AIDS infection from this doctor, whose claims could not be validated by the scientific and political communities in Nigeria.

We ought to emphasize lifestyle change in African societies. My barber in Lagos, who was a Liberian refugee, told me that he loved making love to Nigerian ladies and admitted that he does not use a condom because he does not enjoy sex with a 'rubber.' I asked him why should he continue to have casual sex and he replied that it is the African thing to do! For such a person the choice is not between condom and abstinence, rather it is one of living responsibly and living without any real commitment to people and treating women as playthings. Those who have casual sex have already made a more fundamental choice beyond the use of condoms, so the question is not whether condom use is moral or not, but whether they should be having casual sex or not. My barber told me that he has a magical charm from his grandfather which he wears during sexual intercourse that prevents him from contracting any sexually transmitted disease (STD).

Many people in the continent still see the disease as a spiritual attack and consequently being infected is dependent on how you stand before God, and being cured would demand some kind of spiritual intervention.

When people resort to spiritual healing and live in denial of their HIV status, they lose time to seek proper medical attention; they also sometimes infect others and develop the opportunistic diseases through multiple infections and delays in receiving medical attention. It is no wonder that those who suffer from this disease are stigmatized, because they are seen as accursed by God for some of their evil deeds or because of the sins of their ancestors. It is because of this that most Africans find it hard and degrading to reveal their HIV/AIDS status.

There is an urgent need to educate people on the causes of this epidemic, and the different possibilities for prevention and treatment. The one that is more at home with Africans is the one that emphasizes chastity before and within marriage. Condom use should never be presented as the best means of combating this disease. Sexual responsibility should be encouraged. Many women in Africa are coming to the awareness that they are not sexual objects to be used at the whims and caprices of some hounding men who only 'use and dump them.'

HIV/AIDS is a threat to family life and spiritual well-being; it is a threat to community life; it is a threat to the fight against poverty; it is a threat to human dignity; and it is a threat to African cultural tradition. The churches and religious institutions must step into this fight, especially in the face of the ineptitude of the governments in Africa. This pandemic is spreading in Africa not only because of the cultural factors that we have mentioned, which also include levirate marriages wherein a man remarries the wife of his late brother and who might infect him with the virus if the late brother died of the disease. Poverty is also a breeding ground for diseases like HIV/AIDS, so it is not surprising that the African continent, the poorest continent in the world, has the highest number of cases of this disease.

The other factor that has led to the spread of this pandemic has to do with the failure of governments in Africa. Governments in Africa, more often than not, are not responsible enough to meet the needs of their people for education, health care, and water, etc. It would be a miracle if they responded to this emergency. Thus, the international community should work directly with tribal leaders and religious leaders at the grassroots level to help save the lives of millions who may die because of the failure of governments. This is what Stephen Lewis, the UN Secretary General's Special Envoy on HIV/AIDS in Africa has been doing for many years now with great success.

The churches in Africa have authority and strengths, and they are grounded in communities. This offers them the opportunity to make a real difference in combating the epidemic. To respond to this challenge, the churches must be transformed in the face of this crisis, in order that they may become a force of transformation, bringing hope, healing and accompaniment to those affected by HIV/AIDS.[64] The fight can be won. It is a fight that demands courage and determination on the part of all those who play any kind of leadership role: religious leaders, tribal leaders, political leaders, healthcare workers, family leaders, age-grade leaders, captains of industries, as well as the mass media. The pandemic is spreading in Africa because of ignorance; people need to know the challenges and dangers they face. Our families are being wiped away because of ignorance and lack of action; our children are being stigmatized for no just cause; our women are being wasted through no fault of their own and our youth are being abandoned in the mouth of a lion that would devour them without any mercy. HIV/AIDS is a ravaging fire that does not know any borders; it is no respecter of persons; the high as well as the low all fall to this terrible disease. However, it does not need to be the champion or to throw us all into existential hysteria. It strikes the most fundamental thing in our human world, which is the survival of our human species, which comes through the sacred act of sexual union. The conquest of HIV/AIDS will begin when people are able to use their freedom responsibly and choose the way of life that safeguards their lives and that of their children, family, and wider society.

In the struggle to overcome this disease, Africa needs help. No part of the world is safe from this scourge, unless all parts of the world are safe. The United Nations, through her numerous agencies, has done a great work for humanity in the efforts it has made to bring the danger to the epicenter of world politics and life. There has been the concern about making the antiretroviral drugs (ARV) available to the Africans. Father Angelo d'Agostino,[65] who is the medical director of Nyumbani, the Children of God Relief Institute of Nairobi, spoke on the day Pope John Paul II released his Lenten pastoral letter that centered its message on the challenge facing humanity in the face of the HIV/AIDS pandemic, condemned the failure of international pharmaceutical companies, to supply low-cost medication to persons living with HIV/AIDS in Africa. According to him, it is an act of genocide if the pharmaceutical cartels refuse to offer reasonable medication to Africa. Indeed, the refusal of these companies to lower the prices of their medication is a great moral evil, which sends thousands of Africans to their graves every day. Kofi Annan also decried this situation when he said in an interview with the BBC, "What is even more difficult is when you see somebody lying there dying who knows that there is medication and medicine somewhere else in the world that can save her, but she cannot have it because she is poor and lives in a poor country. Where is our humanity? How do you explain to her that in certain parts of the world AIDS is a disease that can be treated, that one can live with and function, but in her particular situation it is a death sentence?"[66]

Only a tiny fraction of the millions of Africans in need of ARV treatment are receiving it (according to WHO and UNAIDS only 50,000 out of 4.1 million Africans that are either living or have died from the disease within the last two decades).[67] Millions are not receiving medicines to treat opportunistic infections because they are poor and live in countries with a collapsed system of Medicare. This represents the unjust face of a world that cares less about Africa and that is reluctant to face the challenge of HIV/AIDS according to its scale and severity. The cost of treating this disease and preventing mother-to-child infection is estimated at US$10 billion annually, which is about the amount spent by British citizens to feed their dogs (£3.4 billion)[68] and less than 4% of the defense budget of the United States of America (The US defense budget for 2005 is estimated to be $450 billion). It is high time the international community declared the antiretroviral drugs as a 'social mortgage' in which case they cease to be private property, but part of the common patrimony of humanity, which should be used for the common good especially in the fight against disease, hunger, and poverty.

Perhaps the lives of the Africans living with HIV/AIDS are not worth much in the eyes of the international community. But unless something is done, the epidemic will become a modern day holocaust for the continent of Africa. The fight against HIV/AIDS is not an African problem; it has become a global issue as new areas of infection are being witnessed in Asia and Eastern Europe. Humanity has proven in the past her capacity to wrestle with negative forces that tended to destroy her, and I think that God equips us today with the necessary weapon to defeat this disease. What is lacking is the political will and the human determination to say yes to life and no to death.

The World Bank's $500 million loan facility under the Multi-Country AIDS Program (MAP) does not appear to be meaningful and realistic for most African countries already bludgeoned by debts and who are spending a greater part of their GDP on huge debt capital outlay. World Bank loans under its country assistance strategies make such assistance conditioned on economic reforms set by the Bretton Woods institutions. In addition, fighting the scourge of HIV/AIDS is not an economic regenerative venture, and so it would be immoral to finance such core health concerns with interest-bearing loans.[69]

The fight against HIV/AIDS in the final analysis would entail[70] a global coordination in combating the disease. In this regard, enormous pressure should be put on governments especially in the developing countries to make maximum use of the power and authority of the state in responding to the epidemic, and allocation of sufficient funding. There should be an integral education of the young on the value of life and the meaning of sexuality, love, marriage, and life, and an emphasis on the equal dignity of men and women, and the elimination of any form of discrimination against people living with this disease. In addition, there should be greater involvement of the international community in the fight against this epidemic.

The industrialized nations should show an involved commitment and solidarity to the plight of the African nations crushed by this epidemic; a maximum reduction of the prices of antiretroviral drugs should be aggressively pursued; and there should be a war against sexual exploitation of women in countries where such practices exist and the elimination of sexual exploitation through immigration, tourism, and international prostitution. The war against HIV/AIDS is one that humanity could either win decisively or lose collectively to our common peril.

2.8 Child Abuse and Trafficking

The last category of the lost generation of Africa refers to children who face many forms of child abuse. I wish to refer here to the phenomenon of child labor and child trafficking which have assumed a very shameful proportion in African societies. Also, to be noted, are the new forms of slavery and violent behavior being meted out to children in some African societies. In his poem, *The Chimney Sweeper*, William Blake, refers to the condition of children, which could apply to the abused children of Africa:

> Because I was happy upon the heath
> And smiled among the winter's snow
> They clothed me in the cloths of death
> And taught me to sing the notes of woe
> And because I am happy and dance and sing
> They think they have done me no injury

G. H. Ketterman defines child abuse as any treatment of a child that threatens his or her safety or leaves in them, physical or emotional scars.[71] Child abuse is thus to be understood as any deliberate action by an adult to deny a child his or her right in all its dimensions and any action or inaction that robs a child of the necessary endowments and provisions of life that prepares him or her for a future life that is meaningful, healthy, dignifying and creative.

Thus, any act of violence or exploitation of a child or any denial of a happy childhood should be seen as child abuse, whether it is caused at the institutional level by international or national governments, organizations, agencies or businesses, or whether it is caused at the microcosmic level by parents, relatives, communities, or rebel groups. The child needs to be protected and the child's needs should be considered as the first thing in the resources of society. The sign of decay in any civilization is the way it welcomes or treats its children, and what we see happening in Africa today is a sign of the collapse of an African traditional value system as well as the sign of a deep crisis of identity. An example of some of the worst forms of this abuse will help highlight its prevalence in African society and expose the sad fate of the lost generation of Africa.

Child Trafficking: The hunt for *MV Etireno* in West African waters, which ended April 17, 2001, brought to the consciousness of many Africans, the hidden but flourishing shameful trafficking of children in West Africa. This ship, owned by the family of Nigerian footballer Jonathan Akpoborie, was suspected of carrying about 400 children meant for plantations in Gabon. At the end of the day, it was discovered that only 23 children and 20 adolescents were on board the vessel. However, based on evidence from UNICEF, over 200,000 children are sold into slavery in West and Central Africa every year. These children are sold out by their parents for between \$US14-\$US18. The trafficking is usually from Mali and Burkina Faso to Cote d'Ivoire, and from Togo and Benin, through transit countries like Nigeria and Cameroon, to oil rich Gabon.[72] According to UNICEF, the trafficking in children is one of the gravest violations of human rights in the world today. Children and their families are ensnared by the empty promises of the trafficking cartels and networks of a better life, of an escape from poverty. These children are sold as mere pieces of wood into an uncertain future. Their survival and proper development are totally compromised and their right to a decent childhood, proper education, health, family life and social integration are denied. They face all forms of exploitation and abuse.

Article 32 of the 1989 UN Convention on the Rights of the Child states that, "State parties recognize the right of the child to be protected from economic exploitation and from performing any work that is likely to be hazardous or to interfere with the child's education, or to be harmful to the child's health or physical, mental, spiritual or social development."

In Article 35, state parties agreed to take all necessary national, bilateral and multilateral measures to prevent the abduction of, the sale of or traffic in children for any purpose or in any form.

The International Labor Organization (ILO) Convention No. 182 on the worst forms of Child Labor (1999) states that child trafficking is one of the worst forms of child labor, "All forms of slavery or practices similar to slavery, such as the sale and trafficking of children, debt bondage and serfdom and forced or compulsory labor, including forces or compulsory recruitment of children for use in armed conflict." The Palermo protocol refined this definition and made it more general in terms of whether the abduction was voluntary or not and the purpose of the act, "Trafficking in persons shall mean the recruitment, transportation, transfer, harboring or receipt of person, by means of the threat or use of force or other forms of coercion, of abduction, of fraud, of deception, of abuse of power or of a position of vulnerability or the giving or receiving of payments or benefits to achieve the consent of a person having control of another, for the purpose of exploitation. Exploitation shall include, at a minimum, the exploitation or the prostitution of others or other forms of sexual exploitation, forced labor or services, slavery or practices similar to slavery, servitude or the removal of organs."[73]

There are different kinds of exploitation that children face in Africa. Child trafficking starts with the kind of practice wherein some families send their children to live with other families in cities. The most prominent in Nigeria is the use of maids or 'house help' (as house maids are usually called in Nigeria) mainly female. These females are sent to the cities by poor rural families, who cannot provide for them, and who hope that they would be able to receive education or learn a skill before returning home. Unfortunately, these children are abused in many cases. A visit to most households in the urban cities of Nigeria for instance will show the condition of these domestic servants; one would notice that they are poorly clad and look withdrawn. They are not allowed to eat at the same table with the household; they are not allowed to watch television, nor are they allowed to sleep in the main house. There is usually a separate attached house, usually called 'boys quarters' where the house-help live. Some of these maids are physically abused by the 'madams' (mother of the house) and sexually abused by the *oga* (father of the house).

Some of these maids never get the opportunity of going to school. In rare situations where they are allowed to have some education, they do not go to the same school as the children of the 'madam,' but sometimes attend the evening classes. This is an abuse of a very wonderful African traditional way of reaching out to the poor. Under the African extended family network, the rich members of the family helped the members of the extended family (like cousins, nephews, nieces, even aunts and uncles) that were poor, by being like foster parents for their children and bringing them up. In many cases, these foster children are brought up to become responsible members of society. This African solidarity, which also encouraged people to pass on their skills to their relatives, is now being abused and exploited. Children are sent out by hapless parents to live with some family in the city where they suffer all forms of humiliation and discrimination. It is this kind of abuse that leads to child trafficking.

Many children are child workers, spending their childhood on farms, on the long water-routes to streams, on the highway hawking sundry items, and on plantations. In some cases, they are exploited by their own parents, but in most cases they are exploited by outsiders. The trafficking network is so strong and well entrenched regionally, nationally, as well as internationally, and it is gradually breaking through the security networks to carry these nefarious practices across West Africa's porous borders. It must be admitted that if there was not already a high level of child exploitation in Africa at very basic levels, there would not have been the international trafficking and exploitation that is challenging the African claim to placing a high premium on children.

The increasing rate of child labor and exploitation (29% in Africa)[74] exposes the quality of the provision made for children in Africa. Frightened by war, wounded by decaying healthcare, denied of access to education and social welfare, the African children are becoming a lost generation; losing their lives, health, and future to a society that brought them into being without a plan on how to unravel the mystery of God's love and grace carried by every child.

2.9 The Next Generation of Africans

What does the future hold for the young people growing up in Africa today? These young people belong to the so-called "Generation Y" or the *millennials*, those born shortly before the introduction of the first computers for homes, offices and schools by IBM in 1981. The children of the millennium are expected, at least in the Western world, to have longer life span than their parents and grandparents; they are expected to be more educated than previous generations. At no time in human history has humanity had such a vast horizon of infinite opportunities opening up for its young people. With improvements in the standard of living and a greater awareness of the dignity and equality of all men and women despite race, creed, or sex, young people of today have greater possibilities for personal development and a more meaningful life. They are also guaranteed better and more effective healthcare that will help combat all kinds of diseases that once held humanity hostage.

On the downside, most of them will be faced with a world in which there is dissolution of values. They will have to go through the gauntlet in search of firm foundations for life, family, society, and the economy in a world where there is a gradual and steady rejection of the foundations offered by religion and custom. This is particularly relevant to the *millennials* of the Western world.

The African *millennials* live in a continent that has failed to offer them the best introduction to the world of life and joy. The young people of Africa are asking their leaders for some responsible and responsive leadership. They are asking the international community for some justice in the market economy and for compassion and human sensitivity to the suffering of millions of ordinary Africans. They wish to know the meaning of what it means to be African in today's world. They want to know the glories of a renascent African culture that has in itself the seeds for the rebirth of new hope, founded on a sound culture of peace and hard work and built on the foundations of authentic human values.

They want to see an end to child abuse and neglect in their families, communities, and nations. The average young person in Africa has a dream of a future that is bright and fair. They believe in the rewards that come from commitment to work and to community and they want to be given positive leadership. There appears to be few stars in the African skies to lead the forlorn and wayfaring young people to the path of healthy and wholesome personal and community development. They do not have models, and they find themselves self-destructing because society has offered them nothing but misery and pain.

It is necessary to highlight that this situation is only the ashes of a new beginning. There has been some talk among many perceptive African intellectuals on the need for 'a second independence' or African equivalent of the Enlightenment, which would see the tumbling of the social, political, cultural, economic, and religious structures that hold Africans down. There is a crying need for a new vision which should give a sense of direction to many African countries. Unfortunately, there is a widening gap between the intellectuals and the political leadership and a yawning chasm between religious adherents and the ideals of religions in Africa. In the midst of this conflict, many young Africans are beginning to ask what the future holds for them in Africa. Why are they not like the rest of the world on the fast plain of development, education, science and technology?

When I look at the faces of my fellow young Africans, I see anger wrapped up in hope. I see the two faces of Africa, one of despair and another of hope. The young Africans are tired of failed leadership; they are tired of failed policies and worn out by Western exploitation. These faces may once more smile with the joy and happiness of a liberated people, whose desire for knowledge, security, and human fulfillment, closeness to God and to others will become reality. This can only happen when we address the reasons and factors that damage the beautiful face of Africa.

Chapter Three
The Challenges

Do not lie where you have fallen,
Do not bemoan that you have fallen,
Your legs are not broken,
Your spirit though stricken,
Your will not to weaken.
Africa, the land of heroes and heroines
Africa, the land of kings and Queens
Africa, the land of warriors and fighters
Africa, the land of peace and love
Is your spirit hovering in a cove?
Is your future hidden in a grove?
Let us all one and many
Think and think again
For deep within the heart of Africa
Lies the answer to our cries and woes
Together we work and walk to tomorrow
The challenge to face
The Cross to embrace
We must struggle and tarry
For the shrines of our fathers
And the hearths of our mothers
The gold and diamond in our children
The wealth hidden in this land
We must burrow again and again
We must search today for tomorrow
This great land to build
Our faith and hope in God are gain
Our friends abroad not to deny
Our friends abroad not to depend
Our wills never to bend
Today is for us the day
Tomorrow is hidden only in Today.

3.1 Removing the Structures of Sin and Injustice in Africa.[1]

> *These sins are the signs of a deep crisis caused by the loss of a sense of God and the absence of those moral principles which should guide the life of every person. In the absence of moral points of reference, an unbridled greed for wealth and power takes over, obscuring any Gospel-based vision of social reality...the best response to this tragic situation is the promotion of solidarity and peace, with a view to achieving real justice.* - Ecclesia in America, 56.

Many Africans and non-Africans ask in political, academic and religious settings whether it is possible to build a new kind of community in Africa. There is a real concern as to the possibility of a new kind of Africa, where there is law and order, respect for the dignity and rights of men and women and where all will have an equal opportunity to achieve their ordered ends. The fact that Africans and non-Africans are asking these questions is a positive sign. Many Africans and non-Africans interested in the African condition wish to find out the root causes of the problems of Africa, and ways of building communities where there will be justice, peace and integral development.

I have a strong belief that it is possible to build God's community in Africa. This will come about if we are able to dismantle the structures of sin, which make it impossible to promote and preserve the common good in the African continent. My proposition in this chapter is that a just order within African nations will offer Africans the irreplaceable assistance to realize their free personality and true destiny. I shall argue that there are ways of structuring society, which are inimical to human progress and personal and cultural development. I will subsequently define and identify these structures and outline how they negatively influence societies in Africa. I believe that religious and political institutions are the hinges on which life in Africa revolve and that the present situation in Africa reveals a failure of these institutions to rise to their glorious heights. I will conclude by offering a new Christian theological category, civilization of love, which can help rebuild African societies.

Structures of Sin and Injustice[2]

I have always wondered what is in the life veins of those African leaders who on taking the reins of government lose their sense of community.

When I think of such leaders like Generals Babangida and Abacha who institutionalized corruption and state violence in Nigeria; or of Mobutu Seso Seko who glorified graft as a new form of statecraft in Zaire; or of Emperor Bokassa of Central African Republic or Idi Amin (the so-called 'butcher of Uganda') both of whom canonized state terrorism, I wonder whether they came from the same continent as Nelson Mandela of South Africa, Julius Nyerere of Tanzania, Thomas Sankara of Burkina Faso or Samora Machel of Mozambique. I also wonder what type of state structure led to the emergence of such men and promoted their tragic long tenure in office. I also wonder about what type of political structure produced some of the leaders we have in some African countries who would watch their people die of hunger, the young die of disease, the youth waste away because of lack of jobs, and the very old go into the twilight of life with tears. At the same time, such governments continue to be 're-elected' in every new election. It is obvious that there is something fundamentally wrong with the structuring of a society that sustains such a government.

First, structures are not in themselves bad since they help to give form to society, and are vital in social organization. In addition, structures are the fruits of the actions of men and women. The radical mutation of structures cannot lead to social transformation, unless we reorient the values of the men and women of our continent and develop a social conscience and an ethico-social consciousness. These are values which are inherently built into the ethical framework of Africa's cultural life. Structures come alive in human actions. Thus, the corruption in high places in Africa, the state bureaucracy which destroys honest social life; the neglect of the common good, and the nepotism and partisanship which characterize party politics in Africa and the nagging problem of lack of gender equality in Africa, cannot be adequately addressed unless there is a radical conversion to moral integrity which is the necessary condition for the health of society. The process of structural reforms must run in tandem with moral regeneration. Our understanding of sin in this context is Christian. We shall use this understanding to expose the full breath of structures of sin and how they affect African societies.

Sin always entails the *exclusion of God, rupture with God and disobedience to God*.[3] The human person is made by the Creator to live a life of freedom and serve the cause of truth, love, justice, happiness, peace, and unity. Deep within each heart, there lies a real spark that ignites the desire for these afore mentioned ends, which make for a wholeness and fullness of life for the human person. However, human freedom as the philosopher Sartre has said can also be a burden because it involves responsibility. The exercise of freedom can either overwhelm people or lift them up to the glorious heights of personal fulfillment and liberation from self-imprisonment. In the exercise of his or her freedom, the human person is pulled between the forces of light and darkness, the desire of the spirit and the flesh, the good and evil, love and hatred.

Authentic freedom is the service of justice and truth, while the choice of falsehood and injustice leads to the slavery of sin which is rooted in selfishness. Sin is the rejection of the love of God for each and every one of us. It is saying YES to self and NO to God. To sin is to miss the mark set for us by God; it is also the failure not to become what we are meant to be by God. Sin always entails making a wrong choice. Sin is, in the words of St Augustine, "an utterance, a deed, or a desire contrary to the eternal law." It is an offence against God. It rises up against God in disobedience contrary to the obedience of Christ.[4]

Sin alienates the human person both from himself and from God, who is the principle of life and the object of the human desire for truth, happiness, and freedom. In disobeying God, the human person profoundly disturbs his own order and interior balance; he or she also harms the harmony of society and sunders inter-personal relationships.[5] Understood in its totality, sin is seen in traditional Christian teaching as contempt of God (*contemptus Dei*). This means the desire of a created being to escape from the dependent relationship to God similar to the desire of a child to escape the intimate relationship with his or her mother. Sin, therefore, creates rupture in the acting person and in society. To the extent that it wounds the inner thread of life at the personal level, sin ruptures the fabric of our relationship with others and with the world of nature. Any destruction of life or nature or any assault on the environment is also in this light to be considered a sin.

The ancient Christian writers often referred to sin as a turning towards the created things (*conversio ad creaturam*). Unfortunately created things are limited and can only give limited joy. There are people who believe that they could find joy through the elimination or domination of others, through the abuse and misuse of nature, through disregard of the law of nature, through the unreasonable pursuit of power and wealth, and the undue craving for pleasure. This quest for satisfaction outside of God gives rise to many unjust structures in the vast trajectory of human history in various local, national, political, religious, and international communities. Structures of exploitation and slavery, which threaten the common good in the world today, are 'visible monuments' of our sinful passion and the cumulative effect of personal sins. According to Pope John Paul II, unless we identify the root of evil in our societies with the moral failures that give rise to the structures of sin, we may not be able to solve the perennial problem of poverty, which hampers the development of peoples.[6]

Structures of sin result from the cumulative and interlocking effects of personal and moral failures in a people's value system, habits, and beliefs, institutional structures that intertwine in the historical process enabling the bourgeoning of injustice and destruction of the common good. Where such a situation exists, individuals in society share in certain 'solidarity' in the sins of injustice generated by these structures. Basic to the understanding of the structures of sin is the fact that they grow out of the personal sins of the members of society. "They are linked to the concrete acts of individuals who introduce these structures, consolidate them and make them difficult to remove. And thus they become stronger, spread, and become the source of other sins, and so influence people's behavior."[7]

The subject of sin is always an individual person. The responsibility for sin can never be transferred to structures, institutions, or societies even though the existence of such institutions or structures may diminish personal responsibility.[8] We cannot, therefore, excuse the sprawling corruption in government circles in some African countries on the ground that the structure makes it possible for those in government to be corrupt. We must emphasize that the pull of structures is quite powerful. Indeed, there are institutions and practices, which people find already existing, or which they create at national and international levels and which orientate or organize economic, social and political life, which are relatively independent of the human will, thereby distorting social development and causing injustice. These are, however, dependent on the actions of men and women and do not come about as a result of the iron will of historical determinism.

The analysis of the structures of sin opens a way to appreciating our involvement in the maintenance of those structures and the degree of culpability of each and every member of society both as victims of, and beneficiaries from, these structures. It is contrary to the will of God and a perversion of his plan that unjust and oppressive structures should hold many Africans down. This is why the Church and other religious groups in Africa should consider it a moral responsibility to proclaim justice on the social, national and international levels and to denounce instances where certain structures promote injustice and destroy the fundamental rights of people and their integral salvation. This is particularly true of those at the very margins of the good things of life: the low income earners, disabled, ill or infirm, the homeless or poorly housed, those in prison, the powerless and voiceless women and children in Africa, the refugees who are displaced by war, famine and natural disasters, the vulnerable, and the powerless. These poor of the Lord are the losers in this ethical crisis in a world characterized by the myth of physical efficiency, productivity, utility, and cost effectiveness.

Three levels of social sins are very significant in Africa and they relate to the failure of Africans on one hand and the negative external influence that hurt African development on the other. These are: social sins as they relate to women and children, social sins as they relate to institutions within the African society, and social sins in relation to the reality of globalization that have had far reaching negative effects on Africa.

3.1.1 The Condition of African Women

There is no sin not even the most intimate and secret one, the most strictly individual one, that exclusively concerns the person committing it. With greater or lesser violence, with greater or lesser harm, every sin has repercussion on the entire ... human family"[9]

African women are one of the greatest gifts of the continent. African women are beautiful and dutiful; they are hardworking and responsible; they have been the most vital element in the sustenance of a culture of love and community even in the midst of unnerving difficulties. African women may hold the key to the future of Africa if the process of women empowerment is realized in the continent.

The award of the 2004 Nobel Peace Prize to Wangari Maathai, a Kenyan woman, is a sign of the height which African women can reach, when given equal opportunities with men and when they are supported through affirmative actions. African women are coming of age. Besides their creative genius, which is being manifested in the arts and sciences and in the teaching and medical professions; they are also gradually gaining ground in the political arena. At the end of 2005, Ellen Johnson-Sirleaf made history in Liberia, when she became the first African woman to win a presidential election and subsequently the first African woman President. Early in 2004, Gertrude Mongella was elected the first female president of the pan-African parliament. Mangella, popularly called 'Mama Beijing,' is widely respected in Africa and beyond, because of the pivotal role that she played in energizing African women to present an African women's agenda for the 1995 UN International Conference on Women. In many parts of Africa, a new generation of African women is rising up in grassroots social movements to challenge the assumptions of established patriarchal, cultural practices in Africa. Women are the prime victims of such a mentality which sees them as expendable and irrelevant in society. This new generation of women is articulate, determined, purpose-driven and well organized in the fight for the liberation of African women.

They are fighting entrenched social sins in African societies that are evident in various political, social, economic, and religious institutions. There is still a lot of work to be done in Africa in reforming the unjust and deleterious mentality, which sees women as instruments for the selfish interests of men or as objects for pleasure.[10] Africans must critically appraise the ways and means in which entrenched cultural practices have made it impossible for women to participate fully in the life of the community at all levels. Certain customs and traditions should no longer be considered sacrosanct if they do not correspond to the demands of human rights and dignity, and the needs of the modern world.[11] Cultural traditions are not ends in themselves, but means for realizing certain ends. When they no longer serve the goal of human progress, they should be abandoned. I agree with Musimbi R. A. Kanyoro that, "The witness of the Church in Africa will not be credible unless the Church takes into account the traumatic situation of the millions of women and the perilous conditions of the outcast of our societies. What meaning can faith have in churches that seek to be liberated without sharing the people's battles with the forces of oppression assaulting their dignity? ...These questions frighten churches and communities with long established traditions and practices of injustices to women. They threaten our institutional comfort as churches, our invested privileges, our secure situations and they threaten the security of our judgment of what is right and what is wrong."[12]

There are four levels at which social sins affect women in Africa: marriage/family, education, health care, and participation in social, economic and political groups. I will discuss these briefly trying to point out how the social structures contribute to the abuse of the rights of women.

The African marriage tradition as constituted today represents a real challenge for women liberation. Women liberation, in my conception, consists in the full realization of the dignity of women so that each woman is able to realize her ordered end, without any cultural, economic or political restrictions. Women liberation does not mean collapsing the gender differences; rather it entails the destruction of the sociological bar that makes women inferior to men. This means the rejection of all andocentric, sexist and patriarchal cultural practices, which have made it impossible for most African women to pursue their ordered ends. The liberation of women in Africa demands that the rights of women should not be seen as privileges or mere concessions to women, according to the whims and caprices of male-dominated societies. About 50% of women in Africa are married by the age of 18 and one in every three women in Africa lives in a polygamous marriage; the fertility rate for women in Africa is about 5.7 children per woman.[13] A greater majority of African young girls marry before they are 18 years of age. Indeed, teenage pregnancy accounts for half the number of maternal deaths in Africa. According to the findings of the Western Nigerian based Muslim Students Society of Nigeria, more than 40,000 Nigerian teenage girls lost their lives within the last decade due to pregnancy. It is poverty, ignorance, and cultural factors that lure young girls to early marriages, which puts an abrupt end to any kind of professional life for the young girls.

Understanding Women Liberation

The proposal, which I make for the recognition and acceptance of gender equality in Africa, is based on a theological and anthropological model which views humanity as made up of 'man' and 'woman' in equal and complementary relationships. We are human only through being woman or man. Humanity, therefore, cannot be complete unless both ways of being human are equally acknowledged and respected in both its substantial and relational aspects. The differences are not accidental but substantial, though they are mutually complementary. It is a difference of kind and not of degree. As the female theologian Edith Stein argues, "I am convinced that the species of humanity embraces the double species man and woman; that the essence of the complete human being is characterized by this duality; and that the entire structure of the essence demonstrates the specific character. ...Man and woman are destined 'to rule over the earth,' that means, to know the things of this world, to delight in it, and to develop it in creative action."[14] This differentiation is part of creation. Humanity can only subsist if these two forms of being human are fully realized in relationships and responsibilities of all kinds. At the level of co-generating life, we see a clear distinction of the two genders. There are obviously some schools of thought about the distinction between sex and gender. According to Pope John Paul II, "The creation of woman is thus marked from the onset by the principle of help: a help which is not one-sided but *mutual*. Woman complements man, just as man complements woman: men and women are complementary. Womanhood expresses the 'human' as much as manhood does, but in a different and complementary way...Womanhood and manhood are complementary not only from the physical and psychological points of view, but also from the ontological. It is only through the duality of the 'masculine' and the 'feminine' that the 'human' finds full realization."[15] Maleness and femaleness are substantial forms of being human; gender distinction is based on maleness and femaleness, but it is at this level that cultural and religious factors tend to blur the lines of distinction. Sexual differentiation is not a functional distinction, but an ontological distinction, hence, what a man can do and what a woman can do should not be interpreted in terms of functional differences founded on sexual differentiation, but in terms of the ontology of the two sexes which are mutually implicated in the fullness of what it means to be human. Thus, what a man does and what a woman does is not distinct for humanity; both make up what our humanity is capable of doing and realizing for the good of the human race. If a substantial part of our human race (women) is denied the opportunity of fullness due to a wrong interpretation of gender differences, our humanity is impoverished. This is why Oduyoye argues for a revisiting of the anthropological self-understanding of the human person in Africa so that a new basis will be found for the transformation of the human relations in which it is assumed that the man takes precedence over the woman.[16]

In terms of functions and responsibility both sexes play equal roles. Other aspects of social, economic and political life do not necessarily need these distinctions, because in terms of performance and productivity one does not see any essential functional disparity. In child rearing, both man and woman play complementary and equal roles. However, because the mother carried the baby for nine months there is a more natural tendency in women to have more affinity with the child as both a child-bearer and a child-trainer than the father. This is why it is said that one can be a father in the sense of one who procreates and a father in terms of one who brings up. Both motherhood and fatherhood are related in an intimate way, "every element of human generation which is proper to man and every element which is proper to woman, namely human 'fatherhood' and 'motherhood' bears within itself a likeness to, or analogy with, the divine 'generating' and with that 'fatherhood' which in God is 'totally different,' that is completely spiritual and divine in essence, whereas in the human order, generation is proper to the 'unity of the two': both are parents, the man and the woman alike."[17] Any form of cultural practice which promotes this kind of model, to my mind, is healthy for the human species.

African family life is often not based on this kind of model, because a man and a woman in a marriage are not considered equal partners in African societies. This is the basis for the abuse of the rights of women in marriages in Africa. The argument given for this kind of unequal treatment of women is that it is the man who marries the woman and not the other way round; it is the man who pays the bride price and not the woman. It is through marriage that a woman gains a dignity, hence, she is *someone* because she is married and she *is nobody* outside marriage. In addition, in Africa it is the woman who leaves her family to be with the man—this is seen as a new form of identity, which is conferred on the woman. *A woman acquires an identity through marriage to a man.* There is one major and fundamental transition in a woman's identity-journey, that is, from *'whose daughter?'* to *'whose wife?'* Women and children are part of what a man owns in African traditional society.

This kind of conception has three main consequences for a woman. Already a number of African women theologians/social scientists (Mercy Amba Oduyoye, Teresa Okure, Kanyoro Musimbi, Uchenna Ugwueze, Wangari Maathai, Elizabeth Amoah, Letitia Adu-Ampma, Ama Ata Aidoo, Buchi Emecheta, Rosemary Edet, and Felicia Ekejuba, and Ayesha Imam among others) are increasingly challenging the Christian and Islamic presuppositions used in Africa to sustain attitudes and structures that militate against the liberation of African women.[18] In the first place, the woman has no rights within marriage. She cannot easily divorce her husband, because that would rob her of her identity. When an extended family member of mine divorced her husband because of repeated domestic violence and celebrated infidelities, many people did not support her decision because it was considered some kind of cultural suicide. Many women like her who refuse to live in abusive relationships are seen as women of easy virtue by the ordinary African. A woman who divorces her husband in most African countries loses everything because there are no claims for a wife who divorces her husband. Actually, it is the man who divorces the woman and not the other way round. In my native Igbo tribe, *igba alukwaghim* (to divorce), *ichuna nwanyi be nna ya* (to send back a woman to her father) is properly an act or decision to be taken by a man. For the woman, she can never divorce her husband, she can only 'run away' (*igbapu be di*) from her husband's house. Naturally, she is expected to go back to her husband, because once married to a man she can only 'run away' not 'break away' from the marriage. There is no law in most African countries to protect the woman's right to divorce, because it is something that should never happen. It is usually the case that most women have to literally beg their husbands to be faithful to them and have no reprisal against an unfaithful husband.

Exploitation of Women

In the second place, marriage is seen as an absolute for African women and, hence, they are beings-oriented-to-marriage, no matter at what age and at what cost. There is, however, one positive aspect of this attitude. Because both the man and the woman in an African marriage understand their union as spiritual and eternal, there is always a commitment to marriage and family life that is so deep and sacrificial. Not only the two partners in marriage, but also the families of the two and the entire community help to make the marriage work in such cases of serious family problems. Through the same agencies, different kinds of remedies and sanctions could be applied to stop any form of abuse or injustice to women in marriages. I have been touched many times at funerals when a wife or husband symbolically hands over his or her wedding ring to the late spouse (placing it by the heart of the deceased for custody in the spirit world) before the final burial. In a certain sense, this practice in some African Christian communities is a sign of the fundamental understanding of marriage in Africa as a union beyond death. If people do love each other beyond death and believe in a continuity of their conjugal life beyond death, one can understand the low rate of divorce in Africa. It is, however, important that such a cherished tradition is not sustained at the expense of the women. Measures should be taken to remove any form of abuse that women suffer in marriages.

Many African wives are more like domestic servants than equal partners to their husbands—they do the laundry for the man, prepare his food, go to the stream to fetch water for the man in places where there is no public supply of water and, at the same time, take care of the children. According to a survey of nine African countries by the Food and Agriculture Organization (FAO) in 1996, about 80% of the economically active female labor force is employed in agriculture. Food production is the major activity of rural women and their responsibilities and labor inputs often exceed those of men in most areas in Africa. Women also provide much of the labor for men's cultivation of export crops from which they derive little benefits. Women are responsible for 70% of food production, 50% of domestic food storage, 100% of food processing, 50% of animal husbandry, and 60% of agricultural marketing.[19] The same woman who goes to the farm with her husband in the morning is the one who in the evening goes to the market to buy the family groceries with money made by selling sundry products. Some African wives have to live silently with domestic violence, domestic enslavement, marital infidelity, and the drudgery of household work as part of what it means to be a wife, a mother and a woman. This is the way the cultural condition has defined their roles. Such cultural situations have no basis in any sound anthropology and are the fruit of successive acts of men to dominate and defeat the genuine aspiration of African women to become the kind of persons that God made them to be.

Polygamy and Widowhood Practices

One of the worst social realities with regard to family life that still negatively affects most African women is their being yoked into polygamous marriages. Polygamy is still widely practiced in Africa. Polygamy is, however, not peculiar to Africans. It is a common practice among Muslims and was widely practiced among the Ancient Near East peoples. Polygamy existed in many Western societies until recently. The philosopher, Plato, recommended that wives should be common among the Greeks. Nicolaus, one of the deacons in early Christianity, also recommended that Christian men should have wives in common.[20] There are some Africans who argue that polygamy (polygyny) is a good thing and is not meant to oppress women, but to support them. This is because women outnumber the men in African societies. African women are hardier and survive infancy and other health risks more than men. Polygamy provides the women with husbands, this way they become part of a family, have employment and social security, for which there is no alternative in rural societies of Africa.[21] The question is: Why are the women not working for themselves, if they are strong enough to work for their husbands? Is marriage a means for sustenance or rather an institution, where a man and a woman enter into equal covenant of love for the good of society and the procreation and education of children? We must look beyond the veil of this argument to expose the underlying conception of womanhood, which makes polygamy still prevalent in Africa today.

Polygamy is still rampant, because having a large family of multiple wives and children is still considered a sign of wealth and honor for a traditional African man. Many African men accept the cultural myth that African men are polygamous and marital infidelity among some African men is usually excused as part of this cultural practice. Polygamy also exists when a first marriage is childless or when it produces only female children. Most African families prefer having a baby boy to a baby girl. A boy child guarantees the continuity of the family line, while a girl child will be married away to become the 'property' of another man and thus her identity is not tied to her parents' family. This is also the reason why women do not have a right of inheritance in most African countries. This denial of the right to inheritance is most prominent in many Muslim countries where women are invisible and silent without rights of any kind.

Most widows do not have any claim to their husbands' estate. The property and estate of their late husbands usually reverts to the family members (brothers and uncles) and not the widow. The widowhood practices in most African societies, which denies the woman the right of movement for over six months, and places many social restrictions on her, is still rampart and destructive of the humanity of women. Most African widows remain single for the rest of their lives, even if they were widowed at a very tender age. This is because in Africa, marriage between a woman and her husband does not end with death. It is the duty of the late husband's family to take care of the widow and children of the dead relative. 'Taking care' of these widows exposes them sometimes to sexual exploitation by men, even from within their late husband's family. It is curious that most widowers remarry after the death of their wives—there are always two different standards and practices in marriage for men and women respectively.

However, it is polygamy that insults the dignity of women and in the face of HIV/AIDS exposes women to all kinds of health risks. The woman who lives in a polygamous relationship is a wounded woman; her love for her husband is not full, because she is one of many such loves. She is a woman who has to share her love with other wives and she nurses in the depths of herself a certain sense of inadequacy. She is a humiliated woman who may see herself as a sexual object or a domestic slave of her husband with whom she shares little in common. The wives of a polygamous man take turns to sleep with him and to prepare his food and sometimes fight each other to please their husband. Most polygamous families are never homes of peace; there is always a feeling of partiality and injustice among the wives and between the siblings themselves.

One of the worst aspects of polygamy is the treatment given to women when they grow old. These wives are relegated to the background and the new wife, who would definitely be younger, sometimes as young as the children of the oldest wife, takes center-stage in the heart of the polygamous man. Many people will argue that no one forces any woman to become a second wife and that women accept polygamy, especially if a second wife could 'produce' the male child preferred by the man, and if the husband respects and takes good care of them. I do think that the whole cultural situation creates a certain mindset and superstructure that encourages women to think the way they do. Many African women still accept this kind of stereotype and continue to live with the obvious humiliation which the cultural forces put on them. However, no one can seriously maintain that most women find fulfillment in polygamous marriages or that a woman would willingly share her man with other women in any normal situation.

Health Risks to Women

Women in Africa today are faced with all kinds of health risks. In 1998, I lost my beloved sister from pregnancy-induced hypertension. She held a first class graduate degree in English and was teaching in a high school at the time of her death. In 2003, my late sister's good friend also died soon after childbirth. She had a degree in Administration. I remember with pain my high school biology teacher, a wonderful woman in her mid-30s, who was doing her master's degree in biology, who died in childbirth in 1987. According to the news we received, she was told by her doctor that since she has had three successive Caesarean sections, it was unsafe for her to bear any more children. However, she wanted to have a baby boy for her husband (the other three pregnancies led to three baby girls). In the process she lost her life. These were well-educated women, open to the best form of medical attention and well-informed on health issues about women. The cause of their deaths is mainly a poor healthcare system. Imagine the fatality rate among uneducated women in Africa!

According to a survey conducted by the Grassroots Action for Sustainable Health and Rural Development in Nigeria (GASHRUD), 1 out of every 5 pregnancies in Nigeria ends in the death of the mother. In the whole of Africa, maternal mortality is very high—for every 100,000 children born in Benin Republic, 1,500 of their mothers die. In Guinea, it is as high as 1,600 and in Sierra Leone 1,800 mothers die for every 100,000 births.[22] Maternal mortality is very high in Africa, because of poor healthcare, illiteracy on the part of women, and the cultural factor which forces African women to raise large families.

Large families are in themselves a blessing if the parents have the means to raise their children to realize their full potential. However, most African parents who raise large families do not have the means to train their children. This results in child labor and the exploitation of women who have to go the extra mile to provide for them. Many African women spend most of their time on farms when they are not pregnant or nursing their babies. There are situations where women are still bearing children in Africa when they are over 40 years of age or where they do not have adequate antenatal health services. In religious institutions in Africa, women who are pregnant often turn to rituals and prayer sessions for safe delivery. These prayers and rituals cannot save the women unless adequate medical attention is provided. My sister's death was not necessary and this is true of most women who lose their lives in Africa during childbirth. Such a noble vocation like childbearing should not be a short cut to the grave for African women.

Another health risk that women face is female circumcision or female genital mutilation (FGM). This practice is still rampart in most African societies—this practice is a cultural way of preventing promiscuity among women. This in itself is one-sided: How do you keep men from being promiscuous? Among women in Mali, there is a myth that without FGM, the child would die during childbirth. This practice is very evil and inhuman. It has claimed the lives of millions of women. In February 2003, a number of female activists in Africa gathered in Addis Ababa to proclaim a 'zero tolerance' on FGM, a practice which they noted has led to an intolerable number of women being mutilated, abused, abducted, battered, maimed, and bruised all in the name of tradition. The UN General Assembly, in January 2002, adopted a resolution on traditional or customary practices affecting the health of women and girls and characterized female genital cutting as a serious threat. However, despite all these national and international efforts, female genital mutilation practices persist in many sub-Saharan African countries like Mali, Ghana, Sierra Leone, Nigeria, Benin, and Kenya.

There is no justification for the pain inflicted on young women who undergo this mutilating procedure without anesthetic. Many Africans justify this practice as a way of making women capable of childbearing, but these justifications are myths without any scientific connection. Cultural practices are in themselves expressions of a people's worldview. Female circumcision expresses the way women are perceived in most traditional African societies. Women are made for the men; they exist as domesticated beings that have no role in the public; they are prepared for marriage in the most 'moral' way. Marriage and childbearing is the destiny of women and anything that threatens this is prevented from the root. This is why they have to be subjected to the horrors of circumcision, symbolically, to prepare them for womanhood.

Since women in Africa are regarded as inferior to men, building up the capacity of women is often not considered a priority. This is why female education in most African countries is low compared to men. In many professional bodies, except in the teaching and healthcare sectors, African women are still far behind the males. The level of political participation of women is still very low and their involvement in decision-making, even in matters that concern their future, is marginal. Indeed, as Rose Uchem argues, the situation of women in Africa is not just a matter of marginalization but of subordination: "Women's subordination refers to cultural claims and customs, which maintain that men are primary and pre-eminent, and that women are secondary, subordinate and under men. It is a belief, which excludes women from public leadership of family, Church and society, most especially, from decision-making and from officiating at cultic/ritual and political leadership positions. Subordination is distinguished from marginalization, in that the latter is an offshoot of the former. Thus, women's marginalization amounts to their being relegated to the periphery and margins of society economically, socially and politically, as a result of subordination to men."[23]

Exploitation of Women in Religious Institutions

The question of the involvement of women in religious leadership evokes a lot of passion and debate, which sometimes ignore the pains suffered by women and blurs a deeper understanding and appreciation of the different positions of churches and other religious bodies on the question of inclusiveness. In the Catholic Church, the teaching authority of the Church has settled the matter of women ordination officially by stating clearly, that the Church has no right to change a law on the ordination of women which she did not make. Female ordination, according to the Catholic teaching authority (Magisterium) is inconsistent with the teachings and practices of Jesus Christ, the early church and Christian tradition.[24] There are some opposition to this teaching from within the church, especially in Europe and North America. However, in Africa, the question of female ordination to the priesthood does not relate to the immediate concerns of women in Africa for gender equality. However, in those churches that allow women to be ordained or to preach in the church, the participation of African women is still very marginal. In the Catholic Church, African nuns have not been given the chance to play leadership roles in the Church as befits their training and professional competence. Many still wonder whether the nuns are stewards to the clergy or whether they have distinctive roles to play or whether they play their roles at the mercy of the clergy.

Lamenting on the marginalization of women in the Church, George Ehusani writes, "We must recognize that there has been widespread victimization or subjugation of women. Though they form the overwhelming majority in most of our churches, they are not often considered for appointment into decision-making bodies."[25] It must be stated in a very obvious way, that women are equal members of the church with men; they are called by Christ to follow him and to bear fruits in the world. They are a majority in most churches and often raise all the money needed for all kinds of work in the church. They need to be respected, affirmed and given due recognition in terms of offices and duties that befits every child of God with due respect to the requirements and rules of different religious institutions. Chukwudum Okolo points out that the Church in Africa is "challenged to liberate African women in the society and in the Church. To spearhead this struggle for liberation of African women, the African Church should start the battle from within, since liberation like charity must start at home. Certain questions for self-reflection seem crucial to the African Church at this point in time such as: How far is the Church herself an obstacle to women enjoying their *freedom* in the Church? How often does she conscientize women on their rights in the society and Church or make them aware of their full responsibilities and rights? More importantly, is the Church fully aware of the characteristic modes she uses to exploit and oppress women or deny them their legitimate rights?...The Church's graver responsibility towards African women, is to liberate them from customs and traditions which oppress them or bar them from active membership in the Church."[26]

It is, however, left to women and men of goodwill to constantly put this concern in perspective. What is worrying, however, is that in many African churches, women are still being treated as if they are the repositories of evil forces. I have gone to many spiritual healing sessions and have always been curious as to why most of the people who are being exorcised are women. Is the devil still attacking and seducing women as was the case with Eve or are these clear religio-cultural biases and burdens that women are 'made' to bear as manifested in the creation narrative? Elizabeth Amoah has shown in her well-documented article that cultural and religious institutions in Africa tend to disrespect women's body, taking liberties to touch particular parts of a woman for amusement and for excitement. In addition, according to Amoah, women are also seen as carrying in their bodies maleficent forces. She goes on to say that: "Over a long period of time the belief has been held that witchcraft, which is essentially perceived as evil and destructive, is associated with women. Thus forms of inhuman acts of violence are meted out to women who are accused by the system of being witches. Even in most recent times in Ghana, there are some villages described as witchcraft villages, especially in the northern part of Ghana, where any woman accused of witchcraft is sent away and confined. Such women are kept in very small rooms where they are denied some of the basic necessities, including visitors and hygienic conditions. It is not unusual for deaths, or mental and physical disabilities, to occur among such women."[27]

This practice has also become prominent in many Christian churches in Africa. Many women undergo different 'deliverance' sessions to free them from evil spirits that made it impossible for them to bear children or to be obedient wives. It is not unusual to see women being exorcized for bringing misfortune to a family after marriage, for being a princess of a water goddess and for being the cause of suffering and pain. I do think that this is one issue that demands a deeper reflection with regard to the theology and anthropology that sustain such archaic and unchristian thinking. It is an insult to African women for them to suffer these painful rites in the name of demonic possessions. It is also a rejection or denial of the power of God working in them, which in Christian tradition, regards all baptized Christians as temples of the Holy Spirit.

Sexual Exploitation of Women and Prostitution

Most women in Africa cannot advance in their chosen professional careers without being subjected to all forms of sexual abuse or restrictive cultural influences. For instance, most working class ladies in Nigeria are reluctant to buy a car, because it is a liability for them in terms of getting a husband. I have often heard some nubile young men say that they will never marry women who already had a car or who belong to some profession like medicine, law or academia. Some women fall into this mindset wherein they lack self-confidence and depend on men for everything. The very traditional African woman is one who is dependent on men even for the things she can do for herself. Unfortunately, in many African countries there are no provisions for legal recourse for women who are exposed to sexual exploitation or harassment in offices. Indeed, there is a feeling in most male circles in places like Nigeria and Ghana that any successful woman in the public or economic square must have some *bottom power*, a conception that betrays the andocentric bias of African societies.

Finally, a great evil, which is taking root in some African societies, is prostitution, especially resulting in the trafficking of young African teenagers to Europe. According to **Zenit News Agency** (March 28, 2001), Caritas-Italy sources revealed that the sale of Nigerian women as prostitutes in Europe is controlled by a Nigerian bank. Volunteers of the Italian Church's aid organization in Salerno have gathered the testimonies of several young women, whom they have rescued from this "slavery," with the help of the John XXIII Association of Rimini, headed by Father Oreste Benzi. The director of the "Caritas Group Against Trafficking," who has rescued nine women in one year from the hands of organized crime, explained that about 10 or 12 volunteers constantly risk their lives

Christianity.[35] There is in Africa a tension between the received faith and the African Traditional Religion. Indeed, in many African societies, African traditional religious beliefs, worldview and practices still govern the way of life of the people. Christianity and African Traditional Religions are coming together to form some new elements on one hand, while the Christian traditional framework is providing African Christians theological tools to re-interpret their original beliefs and practices. At the same time, there are many Africans who are abandoning the Christian faith because they do not believe that it is superior to African Traditional Religion; besides they think Christianity is culturally alienating.

If Jesus were to come down to Africa, today will he see their Christian churches filled with converted hearts? Will he see the societies in which they live transforming and transformed? Will he find them transcending the particularities of cultures, ethnic groups, greed, war, violence and religious intolerance and selfish attachments to things and persons? Will Jesus be silent over the millions of Africans who are dying of AIDS and other diseases every year, over the millions who are starving to death every year? Will he accept a Christian faith that has not given justice to all and not protected the rights of women, children and the weak? Will Jesus be satisfied with the lip service which is so often the case in some African Christian faith? Will he be pleased with the religious leadership in some African churches that lives above the people they serve? Will Jesus be satisfied with Christian religious grandstanding, that is sustained through the exploitation of the ordinary people, through shallow prophetic ministries and claims of miracles, deliverance from diseases, witches, unfortunate deaths, accidents, demons etc? Will he accept the syncretism of some African Christians? Will he accept the offerings and dancing of the people without justice, righteousness and peace rolling down from the heavens?

Religion is the most important thing for the African because the world is seen through the eyes of faith. Any other variable in the transformation of African society can only work if it is integrated into the religious life of the people. For Africans, "life belongs to God. It is he who summons it into being, strengthens and preserves it. We find that in Africa, the real cohesive factor of religion is the living God and that without this one factor, all things would fall to pieces...living it and practicing (i.e. religion)...connects the past with the present and upon it, that which they base the connection between now and eternity with all that, spiritually, they hope or fear."[36]

Of the African it could be said that every effect has a religious cause and every life puzzle can only be unraveled through religion. "Because traditional religions permeate all the departments of life, there is no formal distinction between the sacred and the secular, between the religious and the non-religious, between the spiritual and the material areas of life. Wherever the African is, there is his religion: he carries it to the fields, where he is sowing seeds or harvesting a new crop; he takes it with him to the beer party to attend a funeral ceremony; if he is educated, he takes religion with him to the examination room at school or in the university; if he is a politician he takes it to the house of parliament."[37]

The expression of religious sentiments in Africa takes different forms: in the mode of greetings, in the signs and symbols of religion that surround the people, in the various forms of prayers and in the deep reverence that Africans show to religious places, religious objects and religious men and women. However, the height of the African religious experience is often found in the rituals that characterize religious worship and religious ceremonies. Rituals are the form of worship which assumes a higher religious tenor, because they are characterized by different elements of worship that embody and transform both the worshippers and the objects used in the religious ceremony.

Rituals in this regard, within the African religious experience, are forms of sacrifice; which go beyond the external rites of worship because they enfold through the objects used in the worship, the interaction between the human and the divine. Whether the object is a human being (in ancient African religious rites) or an animal or even an inanimate object, the important thing is that those objects play a role in the efficacy of the worship and the divine exchange between God and the worshipers. Ritualism, as the high point of religious experience, and the ultimate mode of obtaining divine favor or remission of evil deeds remains relevant to contemporary Africans. Even among some African Christian religious groups, these rituals have been clothed in Christian categories and symbols. There is still much to be understood among African religionists about rituals and how they operate. However, the use of ritual sacrifices and sorceries to gain undue advantage over the other, or to harm individuals and their interests, has become a worrying concern among many discerning Africans.

Recently the Tanzania Football Federation (TFF) banned the rampant use of witchcraft and juju to win football matches. According to a BBC[38] report, football clubs in Tanzania spend over $5,000 for witchcraft services in a bid to win matches. In one match involving teams Simba and Yanga, the players cast strange powder and broke eggs on the pitch and some urinated in the pitch to reduce the efficacy of the *Juju* (magic) power from the opposing teams. This is a common spectacle in some parts of

Africa. As children playing inter-school football championships, we feared that the opposing team would use charms to win matches. Sometimes, we perceived some pungent smell around the players because they had performed some rituals prior to a match. So strong is the African belief in *Juju* power that the present president of Nigeria, Olusegun Obasanjo, called for the use of *Juju* power to dethrone the apartheid regime in South Africa in the 1980s. Religious syncretism and superstition still prevail in many circles in Africa. There are many incidents of sorceries and bewitching even among political leaders.

As editor of a university's official magazine *The Wisdom Satellite* in 1996, I had the sad task of writing a cover story of the ritual killing of an 11-year-old boy in the Eastern Nigerian city of Owerri. Little *Okonkwo* was selling peanuts when he was lured into the *Otokoto* hotel and satiated with a bottle of coke and then dragged to a location where his head and penis were severed as part of a moneymaking ritual. This grisly crime was committed by highly-placed 'Christians' who continued to go about their business, as if nothing happened. Reporting that news woke me from a certain reverie that Nigeria was not quite the kind of religious land that I grew up to believe. Rituals of all kinds are ongoing in Africa. The discovery in 2004 of over 60 human skulls (killed through ritual acts for money-making or because they failed to keep to certain strange oaths) in a shrine in Eastern Nigeria again brought home the point that there is a glaring abuse of religion in some parts of Africa. There are still some strange religio-cultural practices, which are still prevalent among the people that clearly violate human rights.

In my native Igbo tribe, the existence of an *Osu* caste system is the clearest sign of the failure of the Christian religion to pull down deep-seated cultural practices, opposed to the requirements of human rights and the dignity of the human person. The *Osu* person is an outcast who cannot intermarry with the rest of the tribe's people. He or she can only marry a fellow *Osu* caste member. These castes are descendants of people, who were either dedicated to deities, or flew under the protection of deities when faced with personal threats and challenges, which they could not meet. The *Osus* of today are discriminated against by fellow Christians who attach more importance to this religio-traditional segregation than to Christian fraternity and communion. I believe that if the Christian faith continues to subsist this way in parts of Africa, it may not withstand any strong current from either cultural and/or ideological factors that are opposed to the Christian faith or even the attacks from non-Christian religions and movements.

Many Africans are hybrid Christians torn between their established African way of life and the received Christian faith. In many parts of Western Nigeria and East Africa, the death of a king and the enthronement of another are accompanied by rituals, which involve the eating of the heart of the late king (*Oba* in Yoruba land) by the new king. According to *Oba Sikiru Kayode Adetona*, the *Awujale* of Ijebuland, "When an *oba* dies in Ijebuland, as in most other parts of Yoruba land, his remains are immediately taken over by the palace ritualists and their leader the *Agunren*. The body is traditionally cut into pieces with the heart and some parts retained for special preservation. The pieces are buried at various locations within the town, but the head is reserved and later given to the *oba*'s family...for preservation in a special chamber where it is venerated by the family and succeeding *obas* yearly....The Yoruba tradition holds it firmly that ascension (to the throne) is incomplete without a would-be-king eating the heart of his predecessor."[39]

A poll conducted in 2004 by the BBC of ten countries (United Kingdom, USA, Israel, India, South Korea, Indonesia, Russia, Mexico, Lebanon, and Nigeria) indicated that Nigeria is the most religious country in the world! The same country is also the third most corrupt country in the world with a high rate of religious violence. One wonders how these statistics square up and what the people who conducted the survey understood as religion. Religion does not mean the expression of religious sentiments or the presence of large congregations and big churches and mosques; religion is faith and works, expression and action. For the Christian theologian Thomas Aquinas, religion becomes a lie when that which is expressed in outward signs of religiosity is in discord with the truth.

Anthony A. Akinwale argues that, "while a just nation is an aggregate of just citizens, there is something pernicious in a country that is said to have the highest level of religious belief when in fact it is plagued by crimes and utter disregard for the rule of law on the part of its leaders and citizens...when prosperity or materialism becomes the major driving force of religion, as can be seen in the mode of prayer of many Nigerians, it becomes clear that one is dealing with idolatry...the sign of a true religion is in a belief system that transforms human action because it transforms the human person into a loving object."[40] Among Africans, the aspect of religion that deals with rituals, witchcrafts and sorceries that endanger people's interests represent an abuse of religion. Rituals in themselves are signs of some interaction between the living and the 'spirit world,' but if they are directed to money-making, bewitching of people, and other false motivations, they should be condemned in unmistakable terms.

Our goal here is not to judge these acts, as we shall devote more time to these kinds of issues in another work, but my aim here is to point out that these sentiments should be used in a more positive way since they are very powerful religious phenomena.

Because religion plays such a vital role in the evolution of the moral and spiritual life of African people and in interpreting the historical process, religious leaders in Africa command enormous influence. Religion in Africa could be the vital source of the positive energy needed to generate radical changes. Every event always starts with a prayer and ends with the same; every social and political function has some religious angle. Thus, religion in Africa can be a real force for change in all aspects of life in Africa. The religious sentiments of the Africans are ecumenical and tolerant. This is why the Africans accepted Christianity and Islam. Religious traditions in Africa are not totalizing, but open-ended (your deities are as good as ours, but we all have the same allegiance to one God represented to a lesser or greater degree in various deities and shrines). The Africans believe in one God, hence, they do not accept the conflict of religions; local deities are only channels towards God and people of one tribe can come to another tribal deity to worship God without being impeded. Africans are pragmatic with regard to religious affinity: if one deity is more powerful than another, people come to worship God in that deity and make intercessions notwithstanding that it may be a deity from a different tribe. What is important is that religion should connect people to God and to one another and the community.

Traditional African societies did not fight religious wars. A Western observer of African Traditional Religion captured this very well when he wrote: "All the local religions and cults show a friendliness to one another which is remarkable as to the liberality and entire freedom of thought permitted to individuals. Considerations towards the convictions of others and respect for their sacred symbols are expected from strangers and are naturally accorded by these. This tolerance in religious matters is one of the Negroes' most attractive qualities."[41]

This openness of religious sentiments in Africa, and its ability to adapt to new forms of worship, based on new interpretation of reality, is perhaps one of its strong points, as well as its weakest point. In the contemporary period, it has made the people very gullible and superstitious. When this is the case in a poor and problem-ravaged society, religion really becomes an opiate and not a genuine journey to God and neighbor. It is not surprising that religion today in some parts of Africa has become a bazaar of different competing options valued for their problem-solving ability, especially with regard to the Christian faith.

These complexities and contradictions, which we find in religious and political institutions in Africa, lead to some forms of exploitation that are ingrained in these institutions, and carried out consciously and unconsciously by their leaders. Social sins arise in religious and political institutions, when those at the helm of affairs, use these institutions to advance personal agenda, that often do not reflect religious and spiritual goals. When religion does not lead people to conversion, personal and group transformation and transcendence, it leaves much to be desired. When the political system does not promote the common good but serves as a means for the promotion of the selfish interests of the political elites, then it becomes an obstacle to peace and progress. These social sins flow from the triumph of the self over the others, and the misuse of politics and religion as means for moneymaking and a status symbol. They concern interpersonal and corporate relationships in social, political, and religious institutions, which stand against the demands of justice and social transformation. They arise from the use of institutions as a means to something other than that for which they were meant. How does a religious institution that is meant to promote the worship of the true God be a breeding ground for social sins?

Religious institutions by virtue of what they symbolize are supposed to be agents that lead individuals to a deeper communion with God and neighbor. However, religious institutions find themselves embedded in societies that are culturally determined. At the objective level, it is often difficult for religious institutions to represent and project the evils of exploitation and injustice. Indeed, abstracted from the personal agency of individuals, religious institutions may not be the proper subjects of moral acts. However, at the subjective level, religious leaders have sometimes introduced into religious institutions their own worldview and moral failures, which radically subvert the original direction of the religious institutions in some way. It is obvious that unjust structures are the product of wrong and selfish goals, self-serving ambition and value system, which are often introduced into religious and political institutions by individuals who play leadership roles. Such leaders use the institutional framework of the religious group, to advance their selfish agenda, and in some way 'convert' many others—in leadership or membership—to think and act as they do. When the 'personal sins' of the leaders of a religious organization affect the orientation and aim of the religious group, therein we find a structure of sin. In that sense, the religious group ceases to have a transforming effect on the wider society and unilaterally adapts itself to conform to it. The religious group then accommodates the prevailing culture instead of rising above it; it ceases to critique the prevailing ideology but rather mirrors it.[42]

The structures of sin in religious and political institutions in Africa arise from the exploitation of the poor and the weak by the strong economic and political elites, who use the people as pawns on their political chessboard. There is a strong case to be made against the way some religious and political leaders in Africa conspire to exploit the gullible, ordinary people. In Nigeria, for instance, many religious leaders visit the president and state governors regularly to have 'prayer sessions' for their well-being. There is even the competition among clerics to become spiritual directors and chaplains to political leaders. There is nothing wrong with praying for one's leaders; however, what prevents the leader from going to the Church? Why should such prayers be so publicized? Why should religious leaders be the first to endorse a leader and call for support for him even when there is obvious evidence of misrule in such a leadership? How do these constant prayer sessions explain or legitimize the failed leadership of successive governments in Nigeria?

Religion in Africa, specifically Christianity, has not become an effective means for social transformation, especially within the last decade. There have been numerous resolutions by various religious organizations in Africa on how to promote integral development through their different agencies but none has yielded any lasting fruits. In the late 1980s until the early 1990s, religious leaders in Africa played a very active role in shaping the political process and redefining public discourse. Today, they appear to have docilely returned to their rectories and chanceries, or to be at home with the leaders of the day, as long as they receive some perks from the government. What fruits is Christian religion producing in Africa? We must hold religious leaders accountable for the kind of fruits which the faith is producing in Africa. Religious leaders in Africa, especially the new religious leaders in places like Nigeria, Uganda, Kenya, Ghana, Cameroon and Benin, have not properly interpreted the religious experience in Africa. They often live above the level of the people they are meant to serve. Religion has become an institution in Africa, which is affected by the structures of sin. These ought to be identified and healed so that authentic religious practices will take root in Africa and save the land.

The structures of sin in religion can easily be traced to the religious leaders who have not brought out the best values of religion in the faithful through exemplary and selfless leadership. A situation where the religious sentiments of the people have not given rise to conversion, transformation and transcendence, or manifested honesty, righteousness, love and justice, does not evidence the presence of authentic religion. We are then tempted to question the impressive religious sentiments that we see in many African countries.

Religious sentiments in themselves are value-neutral, being natural tension towards the divine. What is important is what is done with these genuine sentiments. Most often religious sentiments arise from a genuine hunger for God, a search for meaning to the complexities of life and for some foundations for life in the present and assurance for the future. In some parts of Africa, what we often see is that religious leaders have diverted the religious sentiment of the ordinary people to serve the often distorted vision of the leaders. Africa has become a breeding ground for different Christian religious sects with various degrees of claims to deliver the people from their bondage. This is particularly troubling with regard to the new churches in Africa. The established churches like Catholic, Anglican, Methodist, Presbyterian, Lutherans, and Baptist do have some form and direction. However, most of these established churches, have not clearly articulated a social agenda, nor have they become involved in the political process in a very active way, that could help change the present status quo. They appear to be in a comfort zone. The reason that many people from these mainline churches are leaving to join the Pentecostal, evangelical, and African Independent churches (AICs) is that they feel the mainline churches do not often offer them the answers to the pressing social, economic, religious, and political concerns of the day. The established churches sometimes lack a sense of African communal life, where everyone is known by name and they often tend to proffer abstract solutions to concrete problems, which demand pastoral flexibility and creativity.

Christian worship in some of the new churches in Africa has, however, become theatrical and bizarre in some cases. This appears in the very limited and sometimes fundamentalist interpretation of Christian scripture among the new religious leaders. Faith is seen through the lenses of miracle and some exaggerated claims of the fantastic and the sublime. Christianity is now all about casting out demons, spiritual combat against some real and imagined enemies, and negative forces against people's progress in life. It also involves the finding of marriage partners for singles, making childless women pregnant, healing from HIV/AIDS, finding jobs for the jobless, and food for the hungry and making the poor 'instantly and suddenly rich'. Some of these points of prayer are basic necessities, which the government should provide for the people. The people do not need to pray for the government to give them water or light; those are their rights. They should rather work for the establishment of a good government. An active social consciousness among the Christian faithful would help bring about a better government or bring down a bad one. It is not enough to condemn the corruption in government, it is more important for the churches to do something to remove bad governments and to set the hearts of the people aflame with righteousness. The concern should be whether the authentic message of the Christian faith is proclaimed and not the benefits, especially financial or political, that should accrue to one from authentic Christian living. Fidelity to the authentic Christian message is more fundamental than immediate success or profit that may also come from following Christ.

It is painful to see the poor people who flock to the churches encouraged to give all they have to meet the flamboyant lifestyles of some religious leaders. Today's churches in places like Nigeria have become lucrative businesses and religious leadership has become a way out of poverty, conferring on clerics the right to join the privileged class of the rich and honored. Some religious leaders in many African countries where Christianity is growing have become members of the exclusive club of the rich. They have not stood tall in moral excellence and in the active cause for the poor and the marginalized. When the Christian faith engages in social action like building schools, hospitals, or homes for the destitute, it shines through with the values of Jesus Christ and wins more people for Christ. In Africa, this is not happening at the same pace with which the churches approached these issues in the past. This is a season of anomie among the churches for reasons which are hard to identify.

Destroying the structures of sin with regard to this situation demands that some of the religious assumptions in Africa should be put to theological and philosophical scrutiny. There is a crying need for a new kind of theological reflection on the African reality. "The African situation requires a new theological methodology that is different from the approaches of the dominant theologies of the West...African theology must reject, therefore, the prefabricated ideas...defining itself according to the struggles of the people in their resistance against the structures of domination. Our task as theologians is to create a theology that arises from and is accountable to African people."[43] There is also the need to properly articulate the variegated religious experience of the people and the motives of the increasing number of priests, men and women of God, prophets, and ministers of God who are being 'called' to religious leadership in Africa. It is not enough to presume that these signs of religiosity are genuine, healthy, and life-giving; nor is it enough to interpret these religious sentiments via some form of abstract theology that is distanced from concrete life of real people and from history. Theological reflection must try to interpret these new realities in a profound way. At the same time, this scrutiny cannot refuse to engage these realities at the concrete contextual levels, with a view to giving direction to genuine religious sentiments of the people, and isolating the negative dynamics that have historically accompanied these sentiments.

Why is it that the growth in religious consciousness has not led to a radical change in the orientation and direction of African societies? The reason is the presence of the structures of sin, which we find in the religious institutions that make institutional religion in Africa today (Traditional, Christian, and Islamic) a complicated reality. According to Theophilus Okere, the churches in Africa cannot heal the society because they too have the same problems that plague the wider society. "In the dioceses, bishops and priests often have a master-servant relationship with flattery, sycophancy, and adulation of bishops galore, since they are vested with absolute power over everything, absolute power that itself also corrupts absolutely....This corrupt use of power helps to swell the ranks and vaulting ambition of priests who themselves would be bishops themselves, who then get entangled in the unseemly and unholy race for power in the Holy Church of Christ. So in many ways, the Church is quite as corrupt as the environing society and worse, since *corruptio bonorum pessima*."[44] There is the need for a renewal of the Christian faith in Africa in light of authentic Gospel values of Christianity. These values are already accepted by a majority of the people, but in the area of practice, they lack moral leadership and direction. If this is done, Africa would assume the leadership in the revival of the Christian religious traditions.

As Chukwudum Okolo has perceptively observed, "Although Christianity has been in Africa for hundreds of years and in spite of the large numbers of confessing Christians; giving an optimistic vision of Africa as the last hope of Christianity in the world, the Christian faith is still on trial in Africa. It has neither penetrated to the roots of the African culture nor have Africans gone beyond nominal Christianity. Bishop Peter K. Sarpong of Kumasi, Ghana, in his frank analysis of the state of Christianity in Africa warned, 'but I think it would be a sad mistake for us to be complacent. All this seems to be superficial. In fact Christianity and Christian conviction are merely skin-deep in the lives of Africans."[45] While this appears to be a very harsh judgment, it contains some warning as well as some hope for the future for African Christians. I am very optimistic about the future of Christianity in Africa, because there are strong indicators that the basic tenets of the Christian faith have been accepted by African Christians. What remains however is for these to translate into some form of social, moral, economic and political surplus of fruits, that can change and orient African societies to realize the ordered end of everyone. The Christian faith has to become culture in Africa for it to have any deep and lasting impact in changing the face of Africa. This is why one agonizes over the failure of religious leaders in Africa, who have largely failed to understand the African religious experience and cultural life. As a result they have failed to steer the people to the golden heights of the worship of God and selfless service to their neighbors. The ordinary African Christians are enthusiastic about the faith and have a lot of spiritual potentials waiting to be put into use for the transformation of the continent.

We cannot deny, for instance, that the church in Africa needs to wake up to her prophetic calling. Church leaders in Africa have been too quiet in the face of the growing misrule in most parts of the continent—they have not been prophetic enough. Church leaders have attended the rallies of ruling parties in some African countries, they have domesticated the liturgies on occasion, tailoring them to suit the interest of corrupt officials who come to their churches on rare occasions; they have sought and received unnecessary financial donations from corrupt government officials and politicians without asking for the source; they have facilitated structures in the Church that parallel the hegemonic and authoritarian civil structures; they have not demanded transparency and accountability from governments nor questioned the sit-tight leaders in some African countries who have failed to produce successors after many years in office. Many a time, the rigging of elections, the abuse of the rights of women and children, and the ceaseless harassment of civil rights activists in many African countries have not received the needed public condemnation and action from church leaders.[46]

3.1.3 Transforming Political Institutions in Africa

The blame for the present situation in Africa also must be laid on the quality of her political leadership. This is where the structure of sin looms large in African societies. The cumulative result of all these is that many African countries are failed states.

The movement from the politics of ethnic sentiment to the politics of issues is a paradigm shift which most African countries find hard to make; it is also the main reason for the state failure which in turn is the symptom of the failure to grapple with the issue of national identity. An understanding of the intricate connection between the demands of justice founded on the common good, and the desire for positive and focused leadership should not be lost to Africans, because we have become used to failed leaderships, failed policies, and unaccountable governments. Obviously, it is becoming a common refrain in most countries of Africa and a settled political behavior that politics should begin and end with the settlement of interests, even when these conflict with the national interest. However, a more important problem is the definition of what constitutes the national interest in African countries. Is it the good of the individual, the tribe, one's religious group, the entire nation, or the Black race?

This is a real problem, because the cobweb of selfish glorification, personal interests and gains by successive leaders, makes it impossible for the good of the nation to direct their mode of thinking and acting. This is the context in which we must draw the fine line of distinction between what is the common good and what constitutes the parochial interests of a few individuals and groups. Most important of all, is the distinction between the often-confused interest of the political class and the wider and more important good of the nation. There is the urgent need to raise, once again, the question of the common good and the ways and means of preserving, protecting, and promoting it in the African continent.

The question of the common good should be a common thread, running through the political discourse of African countries, and should be determinative of the quality and caliber of persons elected into positions of leadership. What will promote the happiness of ordinary Africans? How can we develop every section of society and bridge the gap between rural and urban dwellers? How can we manage the differences in religion and ethnicity without suppressing minorities like women, children and castes, whose unique but diverse cultural heritages form a yarn in the fine tapestry of the rich identity of the African continent? How can the human and material resources of Africa be harnessed for the good of all? How can we stop the scandalous unjust condition that makes the lines of contact between the very poor and the very rich run parallel in the same society? What steps must be taken to stop the flight of capital from our land due to the corruption and short-sightedness of governmental policies?

The common good is at the heart of the existence and sustenance of every society. The common good represents the highest aspiration of a people for well-being and survival. It colors national identity and it gives form to actions and initiatives of individuals and groups; it is the propelling shaft around which decisions at the executive level and laws at the legislative level must revolve. The common good has to do with those commonly held values and goals that promote the quality of life of all members of society. It must include a blueprint for the promotion of the highest good of the highest number. This is the basis for the existence of society. "The principle of the common good, to which every aspect of social life must be related if it is to attain its fullest meaning, stems from the dignity, unity and equality of all people.

According to its primary and broadly accepted sense, the common good indicates the sum total of social conditions which allow people, either as groups or as individuals, to reach their fulfillment more fully and more easily. The common good does not consist in the simple sum of the particular goods of each subject of a social entity. Belonging to everyone and to each person, it is and remains 'common,' because it is indivisible and because only together is it possible to attain it, increase it and safeguard its effectiveness, with regard also to the future. "[47] Each individual left on his or her own cannot attain the destined end of happiness and self-fulfillment. The social thinkers who reflected on the political concept of social contract argued that, left alone, men and women are the worst of animals, but when integrated into society where there is law and order, there is the mutual reinforcement of shared values and the harmonization of individual talents and qualities for the building up of the commonweal. The duty of the government is to promote these shared values and to govern the production of goods and services.

The fact that each member of society makes a contribution to the common good is a basis for distributive justice, which makes it possible for each to receive what is due to him or her. This demands that every member of society ought to work to promote the common good. Structures of sin are usually perpetrated by the government, when it exploits the political institutions for the selfish ends of politicians and officials of the state. "The political community…exists for the common good: This is its full justification and meaning, and the source of its specific and basic right to exist. The common good embraces all those conditions of social life which enable individuals, families and organizations to achieve complete and efficacious fulfillment."[48]

The task of making Africa a renascent continent demands the courage of both ordinary and uncommon heroism. It demands also the transformation of the political institutions in Africa. A central problem is that most countries of Africa are still at the very rudimentary level of nationhood; and for a long time have been tottering on the shaky walls of statehood. Therein lies the need for the redefinition of the basis for the collective existence of the peoples and nations of Africa.

The evolution of a healthy, progressive, and self-sustaining African continent founded on the principles of community and solidarity, a land of justice and peace; a bright and fair land of equal opportunities, where men and women, irrespective of their religious or ethnic backgrounds, can pursue the purpose of their creation, demands a conscious collective decision founded on a strong moral and mutually shared vision. This is why, I think, most African countries should go back to the drawing board and re-establish the bases for staying together as one. Many African leaders like Ghaddafi of Libya propose that the solution is the establishment of an African union that collapses the present African nations and merges them into one entity with different ethnic and racial groups. This may not be feasible, but at least it is one of the various options, which should be placed on the table. Unless Africans forge a realistic vision for a better tomorrow they will continue to existentially sail in the storms.

A great percentage of our people are totally frustrated with the present situation. There is no visible sign that elections, and changes in leadership in some African countries, will produce the men and women who have the courage to address the nagging national questions. This is because the present political structures will only produce the same people whose short-sightedness, selfishness, ethnocentrism, and intolerance have kept many African countries from reaching even half their potentials.

Successive elections in African countries have produced the same kinds of political realities. This is because political identification on the part of the citizenry is usually based on ethnic factors, religious affinity, and the personal gratifications that one derives from aligning with any politician. Voting is not done on the basis of issues, because there are no policy options or viable alternatives/oppositions to ruling governments in Africa. What have emerged are structures of patron-client relations between the politicians and the people who support their political aspirations, with the subsequent neglect of the interest of those outside the ruling party's political circumference.

Many Africans see the problems of their countries as the failure of leadership at all levels especially in the national governments. When the African nationalists won independence for African countries, they idealized their future and failed to appreciate the complexities of the present, and thus set their respective countries on a rollercoaster ride with random highs but more persistent lows. The leadership needed in Africa is not only political but also religious, cultural, economic, and social. Africa needs realistic visionaries who will properly understand the movement of history. Africa's march is not to catch up with West, but rather to realize her unique identity and destiny, which is not necessarily Western.

Progress in Africa should never be measured comparatively in Western standards. African leaders must become people of insight and not slavish imitators. I refer here to all forms of policy initiatives to be taken by Africans in all spheres of life: the march is not towards Westernization but Africanization. Diverse cultural identities are needed to counterbalance the present movement of history at the cultural, scientific, and ethical levels towards secularism and relativism of Western countries that presently threaten human civilization and the worship of the true God (as opposed to the worship of pleasure, science, wealth, etc). As Laurenti Magesa has opined, "It will not do for the African continent to imitate blindly the meaning of development, ushered in by the Industrial Revolution in Europe during the eighteenth century; or that of the Marshall Plan, imposed upon many African states, since the middle of this century. Whatever else may be the apparent benefits of the European or American model, it is too materialistic, relativistic, unilaterally expedient, individualistic and grasping. It is, thus, from the point of view of both the Christian faith and human reason unacceptable. There should be no hurry for Africa to catch up in this sense with Europe and America. As a matter of fact, it is possible to assert: judging by widespread attitudes in Europe and America, that at some sober moment, the Western world will need to re-evaluate its mode of development, probably to change it—assuming that it would not by then have reduced the whole world to moral, spiritual and other forms of bankruptcy."[49]

The political leader is determinative in the overall sense. The leader is always the rallying point for the people. *He or she is the personalization of the highest aspiration of the people. He or she is the man or woman of the people who feels the heart beat of the people and understands their joys and sorrows. He or she is one who is not bogged down by the negative sub-culture of the people he or she is leading. He or she is with the people and does not rely on second-hand information to know the feeling of the people because he or she is one with them. He or she is a person of vision with a clear mission and sees himself or herself not on a selfish project but on a path of sacrifice to create a better society. Indeed, he or she does not see governance as an extension of his or her business empire nor a means of livelihood. He or she has a sense of history and wishes to make his or her contribution to the betterment of the life of the majority of his or her people. He or she sees governance as service, which can only be met by patriotism and heroism, such that, at the end of his or her service he or she will perpetually receive the honor and adulation of a grateful populace as a statesman. No nation ever reached its historical destiny without such courageous tall men and women in the saddle of leadership. However, such people cannot emerge unless they are imbued with a sense of moral worth and without the people of Africa desiring and working towards bringing them in the saddle of leadership.*

Many corrupt dictators have served African peoples the cup of suffering to saturation point and have often dashed the ardent hopes of Africans. These leaders as Martin Meredith has rightly pointed out are like gate-keepers for foreign companies and hold on to power for the purpose of self-enrichment. While I do not agree totally with his sweeping condemnation of African leaders, I think he is quite right in stating that the face of Africa is contoured largely because of the quality of the leadership in Africa. According to Meredith, "Africa has suffered grievously at the hands of the Big Men and its ruling elites...The patrimonial systems they have used to sustain themselves in power has drained away a huge proportion of state resources....Much of the wealth they have acquired has been squandered on luxury living or stashed away in foreign bank accounts and foreign investments. The World Bank has estimated that 40 percent of Africa's private wealth is held offshore. Their scramble for wealth has spawned a culture of corruption permeating every level of society."[50]

Africans are asking their governments for selflessness and imaginative leadership, which yields tangible and immediate results in the improvement of the quality of their lives. Such leaders cannot emerge if the present structures that promote election rigging, corruption, state terror and other acts of injustice to the poor and the minorities continue to persist. In the final analysis, Africans are to blame, to the extent that they conspire in maintaining these structures of sin either by a conspiracy of silence, through complicity, indifference, or a lack of courage to stand for truth and righteousness. In the fight for the soul of Africa and the demolition of the structures of sin, all Africans must be prepared to make sacrifices and, if need be, to die in the process of serving the cause of truth, justice and love.

Social groups and movements like trade unions, ethnic militias, and political parties also perpetrate social sin, for example, when labor unions immoderately use strikes to paralyze social and economic life contrary to the requirement of the common good, and thus wounding the life of the community; or when victorious political parties practice the politics of exclusion through party patronage; or when ethnic militias fight for the parochial interest of their ethnic groups. The life of society is a chain of interconnected relations; efforts at protecting the rights of a social group should be aimed not only at furthering the interest of the group, but safeguarding the common good of the entire society. We need the emergence of robust social movements in Africa to hold African governments to account. These groups will properly articulate the concerns of the ordinary Africans, for the dismantling of the structures of sins which have held them in domestic slavery in the midst of infinite possibilities in Africa.

3.1.4 The Pain of Globalization and the Debt Burden on Africans

> *Three years ago, former Tanzanian President Julius Nyerere asked the question 'Must we starve our children to pay our debts?' That question has now been answered in practice. And the answer is 'yes'. In those three years, hundreds of thousands of the developing world's children have given their lives to pay their countries debts, and many millions more are still paying the interest with their malnourished minds and bodies...Today, the heaviest burden of a decade of frenzied borrowing is falling not on the military or on those with foreign bank accounts or on those who conceived the years of waste, but on the poor who are having to do without necessities...on the women who do not have enough food to maintain their health, on the infants whose minds and bodies are not growing properly...on the children who are being denied their only opportunity ever to go to school.* – Peter Adamson, *The State of World's Children, 1989.*

"Globalization" has become a buzzword since the 1990s, but globalizing tendencies have always been with humanity since the eon of time. This tendency, in a positive sense, reflects a common origin of humanity, which establishes a shared sense of concern and mutual implication in the pains and joys of others. Interaction among peoples and races is as old as humanity. The exchange of goods and services among them has always been marked by considerable competition and strains with some benefits, especially for the most powerful. Universalizing tendencies whether with regard to religion, economics, or politics have always been with humanity. However, the bases for such claims to universalization are not discussed, because the forces that drive them and benefit from them presume that they are good for all. The history of humanity has been one of domination of the weak by the strong; and the unending conflict for political and economic ascendancy over others, between individuals and groups, and among nations and races. The battle for survival becomes even more pronounced in the present global setting, where human security and national security have been defined in the narrow lenses of those whose interests are being served. The world is badly divided along different lines: ideological, economic, cultural, and religious and even in terms of rationality (knowledge is a key issue in globalization debate).

There is no clear definition of the meaning of globalization. A workshop organized in June 2004 by the Center for the Study of Globalization and Regionalization of the University of Warwick, United Kingdom,[51] came out with some very interesting conclusions. In the first place, different disciplines have had different trajectories of globalization studies. In sociology, globalization studies developed as a reaction against world-system theory as a framework of thinking about trans-national social structure and world-scale social change. In international relations, globalization would entail a study of the state-centric orthodoxy of political realism. In economics, the concern in engagement with globalization is on the dynamics and operation of the forces of international trade and finances buoyed by neo-liberal currents.

The definition of globalization depends on contexts. The context within which I define globalization is my own weather-beaten pain like that of most young people in Africa in the early 1980s. I will never forget the suffering we underwent in the mid '80s as junior high school students. It was in the heat of the devastation brought on Nigeria by the Structural Adjustment Program. Life was so difficult for all Nigerians. There was widespread suffering, the intensity of which still horrifies me. Those of us who were privileged to go to school found life very unbearable. Schools in Nigeria, like many other African countries, have come to mark clear signs of economic polarity. The poor usually go to the state-run public schools, which are lacking in the most basic learning facilities like library, laboratory, teaching aids, computers, and well-motivated teachers. Private schools are meant for the rich and privileged. I was, however, fortunate to have gone to a seminary run by the Catholic Church that admitted people based on merit and not on social or economic status; however, we all felt the hard pains of globalization.

The government withdrew all subsidies on most products including petroleum; the national currency was devalued; scholarships were withdrawn for students while school fees increased beyond the reach of the average Nigerian. Government workers were owed salaries for over 6 months. The universities in Nigeria closed down for one year, because of the hike in school fees, and the government's failure to pay the salaries of university teachers and subsidize education and research. Those of us in high school did not have enough food in residential schools and ate meat once a week. We were later unable to eat meat at all or even to have enough food for our little stomachs. Bread, which was the commonest and cheapest food in Nigeria, went beyond the reach of the ordinary people. This was the stage at which the middle class in Nigeria started to disappear (a disappearance that has literally been completed now). Any person who lived in Nigeria at that time as well as in present day Nigeria, no doubt, saw (sees) the ugly face of economic globalization understood as the attempt to integrate Africa into the global market. Those years were years of devastation and destruction. At the same time, the oil producing communities in Nigeria continued (and continue even today) to suffer the worst forms of environmental devastation and ecological disaster ever known in history. Everyday, in the oil-rich Delta region of Nigeria, oil spillage/flaring continues to wreck untold harm on the health of the people, destroying the fauna and flora of the environment, and poisoning the air and water for the people. The full horrors of this ecological disaster are yet to come into the open, because the foreign oil conglomerates and their Nigerian turncoats continue to put a veil over the eyes of the international community. At the same time, they systematically destroy the growing consciousness and movement of the people of the Delta area to fight for a better kind of world for themselves and their children. However, underlying this fact is the truth that globalization means different things for different people.

The Western oil companies in places like Nigeria, Gabon, and Algeria and the new economic hawks that are flooding into Libya, would glory in globalization, because it yields billions of profit for them, to the detriment of the local people. Globalization for most people in Africa has been a story of injustice, pain, neglect, dictatorship, and poverty. Africans are not global citizens for they do not count in the economic and political equation of a globalizing world. As a young high school student in the late 80s, I wondered how we could suffer so terribly in Nigeria, a country that abounds with wealth. I still continue to pose that question. However, I am now beginning to see the answer everyday. Nigeria, like most African countries, is a primary producer. Nigeria exports crude oil and imports gas, petrol and kerosene; Ivory Coast exports cocoa, but imports chocolates and other cocoa-related products. Globalization has made African countries consumers of finished products and exporters of primary agricultural products and (raw) mineral resources.

However, African leaders must take some part of the blame for their failure to take control of their natural resources and their usurpation of the oil wealth of their land for their selfish end. Referring to how national governments waste the oil wealth of their respective countries, Friedman writes, "As long as the monarchs and dictators who run these oil states can get rich by drilling their natural resource—as opposed to drilling the natural talents and energy of their people—thy can stay in office forever. They can use oil money to monopolize all the instruments of power—army, police, and intelligence—and never have to introduce real transparency

223

through power sharing. All they have to do is capture and hold the oil tap."[52]

According to Max L. Stackhouse,[53] globalization claims a more integrated and a more variegated historical interaction of people and societies. This interaction has wide-ranging implications for the movement of history, for it makes claims of religious and cosmic kinds, and paints a picture that has implications for the biophysical planet, for the economic and political futures of vast numbers of people, and for creation as a whole. In addition, as Jonathan Sacks points out, "Global capitalism is a system of immense power, from which it has become increasingly difficult for nations to dissociate themselves. More effectively than armies, it has won a battle against rival systems and ideologies, among them fascism, communism and socialism, and has emerged as the dominant option in the twenty-first century for countries seeking economic growth. Quite simply, it delivered what its alternatives merely promised: higher living standards and greater freedom."[54] According to Sacks, today the time frame is considerably shorter than a single life span. Change has become the texture of modern life. This change is often interpreted in some circles as progress, which gives credence to the charm and power of neo-liberalism to order the world in a certain way. However, many Western thinkers and the harbingers of the glories of globalization have not often interpreted the intentionality of the forces of globalization. What does one understand as progress in a world where over 22 million children go to bed without food and 840 million people are starving; in a world where over a billion people lack water and 1.2 billion others lack adequate housing; where the wealth of three richest individuals on earth surpassed the combined annual GDP of the 48 least developed countries of the world; where 15 richest individuals in the world enjoy a combined assets that exceed the total annual GDP of Sub-Saharan Africa[55]; in a world where millions of women do not have a right to authentic human existence; and in a world where there is an inversion of morality in politics, international relations, and in economics?

Progress could only be found in such a world through the lenses of autistic thinkers, who do not feel the pain of millions in Africa and Asia; and the minority and disempowered groups and peoples in Western industrial nations, who suffer because of historical factors and the presence of unjust structures globally and locally. According to Taye Assefa et al., "Rather than benefit all actors relatively equally, by its very nature, globalization tends to produce gains for the powerful at the expense of the relatively weak. The economic inequalities and power imbalances among different actors in the global economy, translate into the uneven distribution of opportunities, constraints and vulnerabilities. Side by side with the inequitable distribution of wealth and power is the inability of the poor and weak to influence world affairs since the decision-making arena is usually a monopoly of the powerful."[56]

The hegemony of globalization has become increasingly questioned in many forums. The optimism engendered by this phenomenon in so many parts of the world and the predominant ideology of neo-liberalism (e.g., science, technology, rationality, wealth, power, and human triumph), which is the propelling shaft around which globalization revolves have come under increasing scrutiny. This has been pioneered, especially in groups like the World Social Forum, Jubilee Coalition, Global South movements and counter-globalization voices in the West, who argue that an alternative world is still possible. This alternative world will be one that rejects the ideologies of a free market that has left African countries with over $345.2 billion debt representing a daily repayment value of $379 for every man and woman living in Africa.[57] Given that most Africans live on less than $1 a day, it would take over 400 years for Africans to repay these debts to the multilateral or bilateral lending institutions and governments. Africa's debt represents 180% of her exports; for every dollar that Africa receives in foreign aid, the continent sends back $1.51 in debt repayment. The quantum debt servicing profile of most African countries has gone beyond the money they borrowed in the first place. Nigeria, for instance, borrowed $5 billion and has paid by mid-2004 $16 billion and still owes $32 billion.[58] The idea of progress brought on as a result of globalization does not make sense to me as an African, nor does it offer any hope for a better future for Africans, as we shall demonstrate.

As Noreena Hertz has argued so well, African countries like other developing countries cannot make any significant progress with the albatross of debt hanging around their neck: "Botswana, in which 40 percent of adults are now HIV-positive, pays more today on debt servicing than it can afford to pay on health care or provision. Niger, the country with the highest rate of child mortality in the world, continues to spend more on debt servicing than on public health. Countries that can't afford to provide basic health care, education, or shelter to their people have to use their pitiful resources, including, in many cases, all their aid flows, to repay debts typically racked up by authoritarian, unelected regimes long since gone. Children in Africa die every day because their governments are spending more on debt servicing than they are on health or education."[59]

One cannot engage globalization discourse without understanding its claims and inner logic. That means understanding its various manifestations; the sometimes deceptive logic around this phenomenon and its unjust structural rough edges. According to Stackhouse, globalization is not only an economic phenomenon, "globalization is in fact a vast social, technological, communications, and structural change laden with ethical perils and promises as great as those brought about by the ancient rise, and subsequent fall, of the ancient empires, the later development and then demise of feudalism, the still later rise of modernity with its nationalisms and recent industrial revolutions, and their decline."[60]

Globalization as a phenomenon cannot be easily defined—references to it are often connected with its manifestations. Globalization is not, for instance, a policy of any organization, nor does one read a blueprint on globalization by governments (even though policies of empire-building can reflect underneath them a globalizing tendency as could be seen in the unilateralism of the administration of George W. Bush). There is no given definition of the content of globalization by organizations and agencies and the powerful financial institutions like the World Bank, World Trade Organization (WTO), and the International Monetary Fund (IMF) described by Richard Peet as 'unholy trinity.'[61] International conglomerates that spread the evils of neo-liberal capitalism around the world also offer no definition of globalization.

Globalization could only be described as the reality that is emerging in which the whole world in the words of Roland Robertson *is becoming one place*. This goes beyond economics. Globalization currents generate a vast, world-wide complex of extremely diversified, highly unpredictable, rapidly changing dynamics that comprehend and transform every particular contextual reality and creates the fragile prospect of a global civilization, one more complex and differentiated than the world has ever known, one that adopts traditional diversities into its ever-extending net, one that has no obvious singularly, coherent center.[62]

In the light of the foregoing analysis, we should adopt a hermeneutics of suspicion in interpreting this phenomenon in Africa. I do not think that globalization is the cause of all the problems of Africa. However, there is no African problem today that can be understood without engaging globalization discourse. The man or woman on the streets and village alleys of Africa would blame the run-away inflation that is squeezing the life out of the populace on the government of the day. While one should hold African leaders responsible for their failed leadership, one should also observe that some of the factors making it possible for African leaders to be the kind of leaders they are can be traced to the forces of globalization. The kind of harsh economic conditions that the IMF and the World Bank impose on African economies can only be applied in dictatorial regimes that are not accountable to the people.

According to Susan George, "over the past twenty years, the IMF has been strengthened enormously. Thanks to the debt crisis and the mechanism of conditionality, it has moved from balance of payments support to being quasi-economic policies, meaning of course neo-liberal ones. The World Trade Organization was finally in place in January 1995 after long and laborious negotiations, often rammed through parliaments, which had little idea what they were ratifying. Thankfully, the most recent effort to make binding and universal neo-liberal rules, the Multilateral Agreement on Investment, has failed, at least temporarily. It would have given all rights to corporations, all obligations to governments and no rights at all to citizens."[63] It is significant that most of the African countries that accepted the Structural Adjustment Program (SAP) were under dictatorships. It is also to be noted that these mercenary motivated fiscal policies and death-dealing measures were imposed on the people without their input and with a clear disregard of their condition of life. The 'new heaven and the new earth' that globalization promises for Africa brings instead plagues and curses. Indeed in a sense one would say that globalization is still leaving after shocks in Africa. These shocks will continue into the future, unless Africans reject it and work a new and integrated development that is based on dynamic African cultural traditions.[64]

There are six main claims of globalization in Africa, which have shaped the direction of African development since the post-colonial era. I will outline these claims and then focus on how these claims have been framed into economic policies in Africa, using Nigeria as an example, while engaging other African voices in the dialogue.

1. *Integration into the Global Market.* Africa needs to be integrated into the global market so that she can claim her place in the new world order. To this end, the economic recommendations of the *Washington Consensus* are applied with determination by the World Bank and the IMF in Africa. These recommendations include privatization, lower tariffs, devaluation of national currency, increased foreign investment, less inflation and tighter budgets. M. A. Mohamed Salih points out that this kind of reasoning is built on a neo-liberal capitalist paradigm, which holds that the global economy, regardless of social or political consequences, will be most efficient in the long-term if dominated by free market forces. He points out four characteristics of neo-liberal economic globalization[65]: (1) a relentless advocacy of market efficiency as a foundation for social order, conceiving market forces as more objective than social values; (2) an apparent unease with social justice and welfare, which it views as a hindrance to market freedom; (3) a critical posture of state intervention to correct market

failure, which it considers a limiting factor to what it perceives as the more efficient market forces; and (4) a disenchantment with subsidy, which does not allow for the control of the prices of basic needs making it impossible for the poor and vulnerable to suffer from the run-away prices of essential goods and services, which are left to the insensitive free market pricing regimen.

These characteristics are framed into all forms of attempts to enthrone a privatization policy that effectively destroys the possibility of survival for the weak and the poor, while maximizing profits for corporate interests and global financial institutions. Salih argues that the interest of Africa is not protected by these economic proposals. On the contrary, free market competition within the global market is structured to protect the interest of the formidable regional trading blocs like the European Union, the North American Free Trade Agreement (NAFTA) and the G8, with their UN-based major multilateral actors normally referred to as the international community. He concludes by noting that the attempt to integrate Africa into the global economy has adversely affected African economies and societies leaving it with, "worsening living standards, high and rising poverty and malnutrition levels. In human terms, Africa's economic crisis also meant declining social sector expenditures, falling schools enrolment ratios and the persistence of a high rate of infant and maternal mortality."[66] Africa can only be integrated into the global market when it can promote the human security of her people and when she meets these three prerequisites: when she can sustain a high level of economic and industrial development satisfying the basic human needs of her populations; when she has developed a global economic and technological reach; and when she has acquired the capacity to compete in the international market, because her economies are no longer susceptible to the crushing power of economic pressure exerted on the global market by the big powers.[67]

At the G8 Summit in Gleneagles in the summer of 2005, it was agreed that successful development in Africa requires sustained and consistent progress across a range of areas, which were identified as impeding the integration of Africa into the global market. The core areas include strengthening peace and security, better governance, improved healthcare and education, enhanced growth, access to markets and capacity to trade. These relate to the main areas identified by Salih and which we have also pointed out constitute the macro-level dimension of the total picture approach model to the African condition.

Unfortunately, the G8 has always been long in proposals and short in concrete action. Since the Birmingham Summit in 1998, the G8 has always presented itself as addressing Africa's problems and that of the developing world, but it has failed to address the structural basis of poverty and inequality in the world, which is rooted in the various agencies that serve the interest of the G8 (IMF, World Bank, and WTO). The G8's call for good government in Africa is always an attempt to divest the control of basic services like water, healthcare, agriculture, and manufacturing into the hands of private Western companies or the propping of dictators in Africa as long as they danced to the tune of Western powers. Many Africans have not forgotten that great African visionaries like Patrice Lumumba of Congo-Kinshasa, Kwame Nkrumah of Ghana, Murtala Muhammed of Nigeria, Thomas Sankara of Burkina Faso, and Sylvio Olympio of Togo were all assassinated by Western agents working with their African turncoats, who in turn replaced them with dictators. In the case of Patrice Lumumba, his body was melted in acid as a reminder to future African revolutionaries of the fate that awaits an African leader, who stands in the way of Western economic interest, which are introduced into Africa under different guises.

In an impressive article in *The Guardian* (London), George Monbiot decried the deceptions of the G8 with regard to the African condition. He exposed what many Africans are long convinced of: The West does not care about true and lasting peace, progress and development in Africa whether with regard to debt cancellation, trade promotion, immigration restriction, industrialization or capacity-building. According to Monbiot, nine days after the G8 Summit in July 2005, the United States announced a pact with Australia, China and India which undermined the Kyoto Protocol on climate change; on August 2, 2005 leaked documents from the World Bank showed that the G8 had not in fact granted 100% debt relief to 18 countries (14 of which are in Africa), but had promised enough money only to write off their repayments for the next three years. On August 3, 2005, the UN revealed that only one third of the money needed for famine relief in Niger, and 14% of the money needed by Mali had been pledged by the rich nations.[68] The underlying truth here is that Africa should not be blamed for her failure to prosper like the rest of the world, when there are structures of sin and injustice in the global market that make it impossible for Africa to stand before she can even walk and work with the international global hawks.

2. Institutional Reform. This claim holds that internal factors in Africa are largely responsible for Africa's underdevelopment. Africa, therefore, needs a radical reform of her institutions at all levels for her to 'catch up' with the rest of the world.[69] This is perhaps one of the most deceptive claims of neo-liberal capitalists. Many Africans and non-Africans have also bought into this kind of mindset that Africa's institutions are largely to blame for the failed development models in Africa. The New Partnership for Africa's Development (NEPAD), for instance, is conditioned on both institutional and economic reforms—another word for structural adjustment. However, these institutional reforms being recommended are often interpreted as Western-type democracy or economic orthodoxies of the World Bank and the IMF. These political models are proposed to Africans without regard to contexts and with utter disregard of established patterns of politics and economics.

Globalization is a continuation of Western imperialism that goes back to the slave trade. This becomes more painful when it has ramified into cultural and anthropological discourses that deny African identity and an authentic and differentiated African way of life. Globalization is based on a wrong anthropology that the human person is what he consumes, produces or possesses. The African institutional structure advances the whole community and is built on a *universal-specificism* that accepts the primacy of the community (universal) but respects the particular.

The kind of governments that we have in sub-Saharan Africa is not built on participatory democracy as we have argued. Institutional reforms cannot come about with the emergence of *constitutional democracy* but a *participatory popular democracy*. Such democracy has to be worked out in African countries through dialogue and not by any Western blue print. African countries all had constitutional democracies after independence, but they all failed, because they were not participatory democracies. The constitutional democracy which is being proposed in most African countries by the international financial institutions is the one that disempowers the people. Thus, the government is neither accountable to the people, nor do the people take part in the formation of policies that affect their lives. It is this kind of constitutional democracies that produce capitalist champions in governments who can literally buy their respective countries, and parcel away their national interest and wealth without due consideration for the suffering of the people and the future of the children. The same could be said of the economic reforms being proposed by the IMF and the World Bank.

According to *Trans-Africa Forum on Globalization Monitor*,[70] all economic reforms proposed in Africa within the last two decades by SAP, the Heavily Indebted Poor Country program (HIPC), the Poverty Reduction Strategy Papers (PRSP), and the US Africa Growth and Opportunity Act (AGOA) have the same kind of logic: a treadmill of endless structural adjustments and debt burden; the belief that Africans do not have the sophistication to draw sound policies and so need to be helped by the IMF and the World Bank; and a glaring disregard for the local conditions and cultural life. The result has been that young people are being pushed into working as unskilled, low-income earners for Western companies in Africa; the best land in Africa is being used to grow cash export crops like cotton, cocoa, tobacco and flowers and not for growing much needed food crops. According to Jean—Marc Ela, it is this kind of situation that makes it possible for Cameroonian peasants to become mere objects in the hands of international conglomerates: "In that tropical region where farmers reap but one harvest a year, where sowing is always difficult, and where women and children live in a state of chronic famine, thousands of peasants are being forced to pull up millet that is just sprouting and to plant cotton in its place. In societies where millet is the staple, that deed forced upon landless peasants is a veritable dagger in the heart. It is all done so quietly, under the watchful eye of the agricultural monitors employed by a large development company investing in cash crops."[71]

Governments in Africa, in order to meet their debt obligation and earn some foreign exchange to maintain the barest basic services, have to promote this kind of economic order in Africa. Africans are then blamed for failed economic policies, while in effect these policies, in their conception and execution, were doomed to fail, because of their inherent contradictions and unjust superstructure. All Western-induced economic policies in Africa are doomed to fail because they are not development paradigms directed at grassroots development, but are top-bottom policies that are aimed at redressing economic imbalance and forcing Africa into the global market to 'be like the rest'[72] of the world, when she is not yet ready for such integration. They do not address the development needs of Africans, nor do they have any relevance to the integrated vision of development, which the total picture approach model that we proposed in the last chapter advances.

3. *Globalization is an irreversible process* that needs to be confronted not by withdrawal but by engagement if Africa is to progress and 'be like the rest of the world' and, as a result, reverse the marginalization that she has endured since the late 1960s.[73] This is perhaps one of the strongest and most unrealistic claims of the agents of neo-liberal capitalism. There is no economic process in the world that is irreversible or perfect. Capitalism has a history that is rooted in the triumph of property and capital over the human person. Ownership of property and capital conferred power over those who did not own much. Feudalism and monarchy thrived well under capitalism. David Hume, who advocated the existence of government in order to guarantee the rights of people to property and capital, and avert the 'war of all against all' in the battle for survival, would be turning in his grave

to see how most international financial institutions and conglomerates, squabble with each other for interest, without any governmental control to the detriment of the ordinary people. The most undemocratic institutions in the world are the Security Council, the IMF, the World Bank, and the WTO, because they make decisions that affect the lives of a majority of the people in the world, with no semblance of democracy or participation of the people whose fate they shape. Unfortunately, many governments in Africa have bought into this argument and are mortgaging the future of the continent by joining an international market system that has no place for Africa except to be 'hewers of wood and cutters of grass.'

4. *Setting Goals for Development.* The United Nations Millennium Development Goals (MDG) are aimed at bringing the gains of globalization to all countries of the world, especially in Africa. I would say that I find it hard to fit the UN into one trajectory of globalization or another. Viewed in one light, it has been the greatest sign of the possibility of humanity to work together for the common good of all. It has been a center for the articulation of shared concerns and for mutual action for the poor and weak against the wealthly and the strong. However, viewed in another light, it represents the negative side of globalization because the main decisions of that body is made by the Security Council, especially the five permanent members, whose decisions on war and peace, trade and security are determinative of the shape and movement of the world. The UN is largely to blame for the failure of humanitarian aid during conflicts in Nigeria in the late 1960s, in Saharawi Arab Republic and Chad in the 1980s, in Rwanda and Congo in the 1990s, and in the Sudan in the past four decades. The scandals that rocked the UN in early 2005, exposing the corruption in the Oil-for-food Program for Iraq, the acts of rapes carried out in Congo-Kinshasa by UN peacekeepers, and the sexual scandals that rocked the UN's humanitarian agency, show also that the UN, like all other human institutions, is not error-proof. Its proposals for Africa should always be chewed before they are swallowed by Africans.

The UN has failed to stem the rampaging devastation of the IMF, the World Bank, and the WTO. It appears that the UN was not formed with Africa in mind, because by the time it was established, most African countries were under the domination of the same Western powers, who use the UN to advance their national interests. The war in Iraq, which the US carried out without a UN mandate, is a clear example of the weakness of that international body. Unfortunately, as Robert Kagan rightly observes, "This enduring American view of their nation's exceptional place in history, their conviction that their interests and the world's interest are one, may be welcomed, ridiculed, or lamented. But it should not be doubted. And just as there is little reason to expect Europe to change its fundamental course, there is little cause to believe the United States will change its own course, or begin to conduct itself in the world in a fundamentally different manner....Absent some unforeseen catastrophe...it is reasonable to assume that we have only just entered a long era of American hegemony."[74] Globalization appears to have found its home in North America as well as in Europe and the emerging Asian economic bulldozers, i.e., China, Japan, Indonesia, Malaysia, India and Taiwan.

In Africa, many agents of international financial organizations and their African sympathizers, frame UN Millennium Development Goals within the terms of globalizing forces. The UN goals are sometimes unrealistic, but they help to energize nations to work for some positive changes in their countries by establishing some benchmarks. How this is worked out is often a big challenge in Africa, where no real progress could be made, because of the structural injustice of the global economy. This is a very fundamental issue. Trade barriers against Africa and government subsidies of local goods in the industrialized nations, make it difficult for African countries to compete in the international market. African countries have to devalue their currency and lower the prices of their products, which in turn destroy their economy. The redemptive infusion of capital into the African market by the IMF and the World Bank has been a chimera of economic recovery.

5. Implement Effective Systems of Support for Development. This claim holds that the decline in aid to Africa has been brought about by the failure of African countries to build an appropriate framework and system for working with the international development agencies. Africa is a failed partner with the international financial markets and donor agencies. There is no attempt made to expose the failure of these institutions, their lack of accountability, and their institutional framework vis-à-vis Africa. The IMF, the World Bank, and the WTO have internal structural incoherence; their modus operandi is flawed with regard to cooperation with African economies. However, the argument is aggressively pursued that they should be directly involved in private and public capital flow and supervising domestic policies in Africa. There is no single nation in Africa whose economy has been saved by these institutions and the blame should not be laid solely on the doorsteps of African countries.

6. Legislate Long-term Economic Policies. Africa needs a long-term economic policy, which would offer her sustainable economic development. Globalization offers African countries the opportunity of broadening their vision beyond the limited scope of immediate needs and disengagement from African regional groupings, which are collapsing because of the forces of globalization. African economic groups are indirectly stymied by these international financial organizations.

Globalization presents a lot of challenges to African countries. There is the mind pollution through the internet and the cable systems; there are the cheap encryption programs on the internet that make trans-national crimes a seething cesspool. Many people are worried at many phony emails purportedly originating from Africa, offering fake contracts and money transfers. Globalization has also wiped out the middle class in Africa and destroyed the moral fiber of young Africans, as it has spread unwholesome Western tendencies like pornography, online prostitution, and impersonal life styles to most of Africa's young people. Globalization[75] has not provided answers to a universal social justice agenda, the growing illiteracy in some developing countries, especially in Africa, or to the existence of dictatorial regimes in Africa and how to resuscitate decrepit state economies. There is also the challenge of curbing the power and magic of the media and the issue of threatened cultural traditions of people and disappearing national identity in many Africa countries and how to lift up the millions of Africans suffering from the time-crusted mud of poverty.

African governments and people must pay attention to the intentionality of this new reality, which is based on a superstructure of deception and on an anti-African ideology, which goes beyond the economic. Globalization and the debt burden in Africa are structures of sin, because they are invisible forces which promote unequal development; they take away the ability of African peoples to take control of their lives; and they sustain a well-tailored pattern of economic, political and cultural enchainment of the African peoples. They also destroy, invisibly, the lives of millions of Africans and spread poverty and suffering to peoples by subletting human needs for economic profits, making the rich richer and the poor poorer. Globalization has become a kind of monstrous behemoth defying control, rampaging economies of Africa and other developing countries in what Claude Ake calls 'antinomies of peripheral development.' It has become a giant spider at the hub of an inter-continental economic web of wheeling and dealing, with an over-weaning suction pipe placed at the fountain of African economic and cultural life. It has also distorted the aim of knowledge and education globally, making them serve the interest of economics and Western linear-progressive view of history, and undercutting the religious and cultural life of many people.

Globalization is not the measuring rod that will equalize the economic imbalances in the world, nor is it the moral antiseptic that will salve the decaying moral platform of the world. The trade liberalization and privatization advocated by agents of globalization have destroyed

African economies by leaving the fate of millions in the hands of greedy conglomerates. The world is not free from the dangers of an economic meltdown as a result of the absolute faith in the triumph of the free market. Similar financial complacency, in 1929, led to the Depression of that year, with the collapse of the US stock market and Wall Street. The free market cannot sustain a just world unless international financial organizations, multilateral agencies, and international conglomerates are globally held accountable. They should search for new ways that will allow peoples still under-developed to break through barriers, which seem to enclose them, and to discover for themselves in full fidelity to their own proper genius, the means for their social and human progress.[76]

In 1989, *African Alternative Framework for Structural Adjustment for Socio-Economic Recovery and Transformation*, a publication of the United Nations Economic Commission for Africa (UNECA), exposed the lies of the World Bank (in her publication *Africa's Adjustment and Growth in the 1980s* which tended to demonstrate the soundness of her economic policy of SAP for economic recovery). This has followed the same pattern in other parts of the world, because the World Bank and IMF have never been favorably disposed to other voices that challenge their neo-classical death-dealing economic theories for developing countries. A critical examination of these claims already reveals its lack of foundation. It does not take into consideration the local needs; it neglects the dynamic character of cultural traditions; it lacks a sense of history and is insensitive to the sufferings and poverty that suffocate the lives of millions of Africans. It is, to say the least, mercenary-motivated.

Claude Ake's **Democracy and Development in Africa**[77] is considered an African classical critique of the claims of globalization. His main argument is that democracy and development in Africa have not started. The institutional context of globalization in Africa is not so much the problem against globalization, but rather the reason why Africa does not need exogenous intervention in her economic life. The development paradigm from Western nations and financial institutions like the IMF and the World Bank fail in Africa, because they have an a priori negative conception of the African people and their economic life. The ideologies of globalization pay little heed to historical specificity and wrongly treat development as a way of connecting cultural, economic, institutional, and political contexts. These claims are the bases for different economic policies like the Structural Adjustment Program, the Poverty Reduction Strategy Papers, and the New Partnership for African Development, which have been offered to Africa. In addition, they interpret the African society in economic categories, without regard to other aspects of life in Africa such as ecological issues, gender equality, grassroots democracy, ethnic diversities, cultural, and religious traditions of Africa among others

According to the IMF, the Structural Adjustment Program targeted the integration of African economies into the global market as a way of solving the problem of poverty. The argument was that the root cause of poverty in Africa was found in the structural organization of her national economies. Among other things, SAP was supposed to help lower inflation rate, increase export, create an enabling environment for the development of agriculture and industrialization, relieve the debt burden, overcome public sector inefficiencies, and spread rationalization of many unwieldy and unprofitable parastatals.[78] Using Nigeria as a test case, one would immediately see the negative effects of globalization.

According to Ake, the economic policies of SAP reduced local control of the governments of Africa over their economies; it led to the production of primary agricultural products, which were exported while the local people suffered hunger. It reduced access to health care and basic social amenities with the withdrawal of subsidies from the government. It disempowered the small-scale farmers whose credit lines were cut by the national governments in order to check inflation. Basic services like water, electricity, and telecommunications were privatized making it impossible for the ordinary majority to benefit from them.[79] It is also significant that at the time of the implementation of SAP, most countries of Africa were under dictatorial rulers who, as in Nigeria, carried on with the austere measures of the IMF without regard to the groans of the populace. Indeed, this has been a constant tendency in Africa; the exogenous policies of the international financial institutions are often imposed on the ordinary people without their counsel or consent.

Since her attempt to be integrated into the vast expanding global economic network, Nigeria, like most African countries, has experienced the worst policy incoherence of any country in the world. Her external debts have continued to increase, while the oil industry, the main stay of her economy, has witnessed the worst decay ever known since oil exploration started in the country in the late 1950s.[80] By the end of 2004, the Nigerian government came out with the conclusion that the country can no longer sustain her debts and cannot fulfill her debt serving from 2005 and beyond. Ake concludes that the exogenous agents of development conceive it in the framework of the global capitalist economy of liberal democracy. He sees this as undesirable and detrimental to local conditions.

In terms of African development and economic growth, the attempt at integrating Africa into the global economy will continue to be a failure. Neo-liberal globalization has brought destruction to Africa. I agree with

Ake and many other perceptive African social scientists that Africa must take some steps away from the globalizing tendencies of neo-liberal capitalism, which tends to vertically connect Africa to the industrialized Western countries. Some of these proposals have already been adopted in the Lagos Plan of Action (1980) developed by African leaders and leading social scientists and economists from Africa (a plan rejected by the IMF as unrealistic). At that critical stage of economic crisis in Africa, this plan was a new development paradigm that was African-woven and grassroots-based and which bears a re-reading because it presents the vision of Africans for African development without Western interference.

According John A. Tesha, "Although Africa has the potential to be the richest continent on earth, its present and future, like its past, remain the object of international manipulation, exploitation and ridicule. The solution to Africa's development dilemma thus lies squarely with Africans themselves. External partners can only supplement the efforts of the Africans; they cannot replace the initiatives of the African peoples and their leaders. Africa's capacity to address its own problems was clearly demonstrated during the liberation struggles, when African leaders and peoples committed themselves and resolved to fight foreign domination in all forms including the dismantling of the racist apartheid regime of South Africa. The same determination and resolve should be marshaled to effectively respond to the contemporary challenges of globalization, marginalization and exclusion."[81]

We wish to propose the following steps as an alternative route to economic growth and poverty alleviation in Africa:

- A human-centered approach that rejects completely any mechanistic classical neo-liberal economic orthodoxy.
- A holistic approach to socio-economic change. Human development does not subsist only on economic variables; rather change should be situated within the social, political, cultural, and economic values and institutions of Africa. The most solid foundation for lasting socio-economic development and progress is the infrastructure of human skills, especially those anchored on emerging skills midwifed by locally based science and technology.[82]
- The validity of any economic policy in Africa should be dependent on the validity and legitimacy of the structural nature of the political economy of specific African countries. It is also to be amplified by its viability at the village and grassroots level. "The activist groups that are alleviating poverty the most are those working at the local village level in places like rural India, Africa, and China and to

spotlight and fight corruption and to promote accountability, transparency, education, and property rights."[83] It must be context sensitive and people-friendly. The application of economic paradigm without regard to context is destructive and defeats Africa's genuine thirst for integrated development.

- There is no 'ready-made' economic policy that globalization offers which can solve any of the problems of Africa. Any development in Africa that is not specific to African context will perpetuate the tragedy of Africa, which is the deepest and most protracted crisis of modern history.[84]

- *Africa's liberation from the negative effects of globalization will be in its ability to find its own unique voice and speak its own reality. There is the tendency in us all to lose ourselves and to compromise our identities in the presence of those perceived to be stronger than ourselves. The danger of economic globalization is that it so subtly, yet forcefully, defines for us who we are and what we need.[85]*

The search for the common good of African communities and humanity as a whole should be what is primary in Africa's engagement with the global market. Africans should use their experience of globalization as a starting point for a dialogue on a viable alternative to her present crisis generated by globalization. Unfortunately, most Western nations and international lending groups predicate the granting of financial remedies to Africa on the adoption of the economic orthodoxies of these groups. The reason is always that Africa needs to be helped through some of these stringent conditionalities so that she might repay her debts. What Africa needs is not a rescheduling of debts but unconditional cancellation of her debts so that she can begin a new journey to sustainable development. The world today owes Africa a debt in justice more than Africa owes a debt in capital. Why should the G8, the Paris Club, the IMF, and the World Bank propose the cancellation of Iraq's $145 billion foreign debt and the freezing of the debts of Asian countries affected by the Tsunami, while Africa's unsustainable debt burden is upheld with increasingly fiscal severity? Here again, we see the unjust structure of the world and the weaving of issues that deal with the life and death of millions of people around the world on the national interests of a few Western nations.

However, it is important that Africans articulate clearly their worldview and *reject any attempt to be framed into global situations that are destructive of African autonomy and self-understanding.* Globalization is a kind of cultural cloning that makes it impossible for Africans to think 'in *concreto*,' to explore the inexhaustible and unfathomable mystery of

God and creation in Africa, which is always in differentiation and in the plural. Globalization absorbs the individual and communities and makes them faceless even as it despotically determines their fate, without their involvement in the whole process.[86]

Globalization is not inevitable. Rooted as it is in materialism, profit-making, scientific and technological reductionism, with its claims of being a 'god' or a merciless behemoth that controls the lives of billions all over the world. A Christian social ethics could join in the counter-voices and convergence on seeking an alternative vision. The terms for this engagement can never be a prior determination, but rather should evolve from the historical conditioning of the people. Christian theology proposes the principles of subsidiarity and solidarity[87] as a response to neo-liberal capitalism. This is a starting point for discussion with other new voices rising in opposition to globalization.[88]

Thomas Rourke[89] has summarized four definite requirements of any social order that is free from the dark forces of structures of sin: The first, that its conception of the common good must be rooted in a strong sense of service and an efficacious desire to realize the good of all members of the community. Economic and political policies that proceed from self-interest of individuals and groups do not meet the requirements of justice and the good of all. The second, that society should reject consumerism and materialism; and should work to prevent them from becoming structures that shape the way people relate to each other or evaluate each other. The third, that profit-making and capital should not be the determining factor of economic policies rather the determining factor should be the good of all, especially the weak and the marginalized. *Any economic policy must put the interest of people first and must ask the question: Who suffers and who stands to gain from it?* The fourth, that a healthy society is one that is built around a moral vision that embodies the distribution of goods and services to all, especially the marginalized. It would reward individual initiatives but not at the detriment of the common good and the weak. It is this kind of vision that Pope John Paul II had in mind when he called for the globalization of solidarity[90] and the building of a new kind of world on the civilization of love. We cannot have authentic human progress when the frontiers of Western wealth merely intersect with Third world poverty.

The history of the future may be written by those who understand and engage the movement of the spirit towards 'a new heaven and a new earth,' which is possible for Africa, as well as for the whole world. It is in this regard that Nelson Mandela, in his last presidential speech to the South African Parliament on February 5, 1999, called on African people to defy the merchants of cynicism and despair and halt the flight of capital from

Africa to other parts of the world, without attendant benefits to Africa. He appealed for the courage *"to reconstruct the soul of Africa,"*[91] or to use the words of the late President Thomas Sankara of Burkina Faso, *"to reinvent the future of Africa."* This is a giant leap, which can only be made when Africans understand the forces against their progress and courageously confront them even if it involves present difficulties, seemingly unnerving challenges, suffering and pain.

3.2 Education and the Future of Africa

The African Situation

Education holds the key to the future of Africa. No policy initiative, locally or internationally, can succeed in Africa unless there is an integral education and intensive war against illiteracy in African societies. Educational aims in Africa must integrate the deep religious sentiments of the Africans as well as their local genius, rationality, and creativity in varied expressions. It must, in addition, embrace a classical-liberal education in its search for truth in multiple forms. Moreover, this search will be meaningful only if it is directed to the conditions and opportunities around Africa. Until recently, most Africans in high schools, universities and colleges, spent most of their time studying European history and theories of education. Some African countries still place the highest premium on 'transferring' Western technological know how to their countries with little success.

People who are mentally emancipated can climb to the highest level of human development. It is this realization that made Dr. Nnamdi Azikiwe, the founding father of the first post-independence university in Nigeria, frame the motto of that university, "To restore the dignity of man." Education is the only way to restore the dignity of the Africans; a dignity, which should shine through in a healthy life and vibrant economic, cultural and political life; and the flowering of the arts, science and technology, and authentic religious life.

The World Education Forum in Dakar, April 2000, produced a policy document, *The Dakar Framework for Action*, that assigned to the international community six goals for making universal education for life a reality:

(i) expanding and improving comprehensive early childhood care and education, especially for the most vulnerable and disadvantaged children;

240

(ii) ensuring that by 2015 all children, particularly girls, children in difficult circumstances and those belonging to ethnic minorities, have access to and completely free and compulsory primary education of good quality;

(iii) ensuring that the learning needs of all young people and adults are met through equitable access to appropriate learning and life skills programs;

(iv) achieving a 50% improvement in levels of adult literacy by 2015, especially for women, and equitable access to basic and continuing education for all adults;

(v) eliminating gender disparities in primary and secondary education by 2005, and achieving gender equality in education by 2015, with a focus on ensuring girls' full and equal access to and achievement in basic education of good quality; and

(vi) improving all aspects of the quality of education and ensuring excellence of all so that recognized and measurable learning outcomes are achieved by all, especially in literacy, numeracy and essential life skills.

However, three years after the Dakar Forum, the number of adult illiterates worldwide still stands at 868 million and 125 million children are still not receiving a primary education. Illiteracy nonetheless, has significantly diminished in relative terms and should continue to decline. The percentage of illiterates fell from 30.8% in 1980 to 22.8% in 1995 and should drop to 16.6% in 2010. But because of the increase in world population, the actual number of illiterates remained astonishingly stable between 1980 and 1995 (about 890 million) even if it has declined since then, albeit slowly.[92] Over 100 million children of primary school age do not attend school or simply have no possibility of doing so. In Africa, according to the 1995 Social Development Summit, on current trends, 54 million children (representing 57% of children in Africa) in Sub-Saharan Africa will drop out of school by 2015 and the speed in narrowing the gender gap in education in most African countries has been very slow, hence, 83% of all out-of-school girls in the world live in sub-Saharan Africa.

Most African countries were signatories to the policy document produced by the Dakar Forum, but the situation of education in Africa leaves much to be desired.[93] There is a general lack of commitment on the part of governments at all levels, which mirrors their failure to define their national goals and policies. The right to basic education for most people in Africa remains elusive. In Nigeria, for instance, the government estimates

241

that of the over 7 million children not attending school two thirds of them are girls. This raises the critical question as to whether the government is taking enough initiatives to increase the number of children and adults who are getting quality education.[94] This is very disturbing because Nigeria was a pace-setter in education for most other countries of Africa until the recession of the 1970s. However, with the onset of the years of the locust in a country characterized by economic mismanagement, lack of public accountability, wholesale corruption of sprawling proportions, irresponsible government and lack of a proper scale of preference in governmental policies, the educational sector, like other aspects of the national life, started to witness a glaring lack of direction. This led to poor visioning and strategizing and translated into a poor policy framework that lacks coherence, coordination, and integration. These problems led to disjuncture in policy initiatives, epileptic and unstable structures, and lack of synergy of both personnel and planners on one hand, and the people for whom the policies were intended on the other. Many countries like Tanzania, Mozambique, and Uganda have taken quantum leaps in their efforts to achieve education for all within the next decade. Indeed, in Uganda, school enrolment has risen from 54% to 90% within the last six years. This happened because the government of Uganda increased its funding for education from 1.6% of its GDP to 4%.

Education, which is a basic human right, takes a back seat in most countries of Africa. A country like Nigeria, considered the construction of a national stadium within two years, spending $300 million, and another bogus $90 million on a phantom space program,[95] and the hosting of the All-African Games, more important than funding education at all levels and empowering her citizens.

The right to education is enshrined in Article 16 of the Universal Declaration of Human Rights, as well as in Articles 28 and 29 of the Convention on the Rights of the Child. As the Director-General of the UN Educational, Scientific and Cultural Organization (UNESCO), Koïchiro Matsuura, stated on the occasion of Human Rights Day (December 10, 2003), the right to education is so fundamental for human rights in general, because only a person who is aware that he or she has rights can better strive for those rights, whether it be the right to a job, to obtain adequate food, shelter or medical care, to participate actively in political life, or to benefit from the progress of science and technology.

Girls and women are especially disadvantaged in education. This is particularly evident in Nigeria and other countries in Africa where female education is considered particularly unprofitable since there is the feeling among many Africans that a woman has more value in getting married, bearing children, and making the home, than being a professional worker—they are better seen than heard. In Northern Nigeria, for instance, as well as in many Moslem countries of Africa, the rights of women to education and basic freedom are still far from being realized. Addressing the present crisis of education in the continent is an urgent task. I will restrict myself to three issues: the need for a sound philosophy of education, the need for an integral education in schools, and the training of teachers. In these tasks, governments play a fundamental role, while churches and other voluntary organizations play complementary and essential roles.

A Philosophy of Education

Education opens doors that no other process can. It gives people a way to understand their world, to develop their self-identity and skills for working productively in order to support their families and contribute to the common good. Education is an important tool in alleviating poverty and addressing the inequalities within and between countries. Education is the key to national development and the path to the survival of civilizations. Education is not a commodity for sale to the highest bidder; it is a service provided by society for the benefit of her members, especially the young people. Education (formal and informal) is an ongoing dynamic, which should be open to both the young, as well as those adults who never had an education. However, we cannot educate the young unless we clearly understand the content and end of education. It is important that any educational process must take into consideration the cultural tradition of the people. This is what is lacking in many African countries. I contend that Western education, as practiced in African countries, must be brought into harmony with the specific challenges facing Africa today; it should, therefore, be weeded of its secular accretions and pass through the rich rarefied fields of African cultural traditions.

Writing on African education, Babs Fafunwa,[96] notes that there are seven characteristics of traditional African education, namely: physical training, development of character, respect for elders and peers, intellectual training, vocational training, agricultural education, trades and crafts, community participation, and promotion of cultural heritage. These meet the requirements of authentic educational philosophy. This is because they responded to the challenges that faced the traditional Africans at that point in time, which included establishing the preeminence of the community and social life, the intimate bond between social life and spiritual values, the multivalent character of formation to meet with diverse life situations, and the gradual and progressive development and formation of the physical, emotional, and mental faculties of the child. These should be integrated into the formulation of any philosophy of education in African schools today.

Since fundamental questions concerning the aim and nature of education are within the purview of philosophy of education, we ought to develop a philosophy of education that is native to us, receptive to other influences, yet strong enough not to lose its creativity and able to inform and form the mind of Africans. Any philosophy of education necessarily derives from a philosophy of life of the group. "A philosophy of life or worldview consists of a set of assumptions, beliefs, concepts and ideas (explicit or implicit) in terms of which one understands the world and interprets one's experience of it within that framework; and a set of values, principles and attitudes which influence how one chooses to act in it. A philosophy of life is an understanding of ultimate reality and life and one's place in it."[97]

An educational system is informed by the assumptions and beliefs on the nature of the human person, the ultimate purpose of life and human destiny, and the goal of common life among others. Two realities emerge from the foregoing excursus. The first, is that every educational system has a worldview that underpins it; and the second, is that those who are formed in that educational system are formed according to this worldview. The success or failure of any educational system can only be judged by its philosophy of education, and the applications of this philosophy in the educational enterprise.

Philosophy of education is concerned with ascertaining the purpose of education and the meaning of the key terms associated with the educational process. The content and character of education are determined by what one perceives to be its aims and purpose. This is further informed by the concept we have of the human person and his or her place in life and society. All educational systems, whether Western, Islamic, Christian, or African must revolve within a philosophical cycle, evident, or implied. Education is a process of transmitting cultures in terms of continuity and growth and for disseminating knowledge either to ensure social control or to guarantee rational direction of society or both.[98] Education is concerned with the formation and development of human beings, or as Jacques Maritain notes, education does not consist in adapting a potential citizen to the conditions and interactions of social life, but in *first making a man* and thus preparing a citizen.[99]

The goal of education should be the liberation of the internal and spiritual freedom of man, to be achieved by each person through knowledge and wisdom, goodwill, and love. The Jomtien World Conference on

Education for All recognized that it is the responsibility of governments working with other agencies to provide quality education. The kind of educational philosophy envisioned here is one that promotes the cognitive, social, physical, emotional, moral and spiritual development of the child.

The Nigerian National Policy on Education (otherwise called the 6-3-3-4 system), for instance, states that the philosophy of education in the country is to promote "a free, just and democratic society, a land full of opportunities for all citizens, able to generate a great and dynamic economy and growing into a united, strong and self-reliant nation" (No 8). The 1999 Constitution of the Federal Republic of Nigeria (18), clearly states, that the objectives of education is to eradicate illiteracy, offer free education to all, at all levels, and to promote science and technology. Missing in all these is the need for creating a morally-conscious citizenry, the promotion of the cultural heritage of the country and inculcating a culture of peace and tolerance in a nation that has witnessed civil war, a cycle of religious and ethnic violence, and other signs of lack of unity among the people.

The Inadequacy of Western Educational Model

The kind of education given in Western schools is a major cause of the crisis of civilization in the West. Education transmits culture. If a culture seems rudderless in the sense that a society absolutizes individual freedom, and aspires for nothing other than the satisfaction and promotion of economic ends, the young people are left in a moral and existential wilderness. There has been a lot of intellectual discussion and disagreements on the extent of the crisis in Western civilization and inter-civilizational conflicts in the world, since the publication of the work of Huntington, *The Clash of Civilizations and the Remaking of World Order,* in 1996. I do not think that Huntington's thesis of conflictual dynamics among civilizations should be normative; rather it is interpretative, based on the emerging world situation, especially in the face of rising fundamentalism among religionists, terrorism, violence and wars. Human civilizations are not meant to be in conflict. There is something human in every civilization, which connects all humans to all civilizations outside their own. From the heart of each civilization, re-echoes the highest ideals of the human spirit, that is, the desire for love, peace, happiness, justice, and the urge to be connected to the spiritual reality that transcends and defines us.

This is what is gradually being lost in the West. Pope John Paul II has constantly referred to this as the crisis of civilization, which has resulted in secularism and materialism of frightening proportions, wedded to a techno-scientific determinism. The loss of a value-center, which historically in the West has been Christian and Christ-centered, is the ground for understanding this crisis of civilization.[100] The Christian tradition, which informed and carried Western civilization, is in reverse gear. Today, the Christian message does not capture the imagination of many people in the West. The reason for this is the emergence of ideological education, the free market economy, and secularism since the Enlightenment.

The Enlightenment[101]

The Enlightenment was an international movement that included French, English, Scottish, American, German, Italian, Spanish, and even Russian schools. Voltaire and Montesquieu visited England and wrote and taught in its institutions. Benjamin Franklin and Thomas Jefferson visited England and France and maintained regular contacts with her intellectuals. It is not easy to date the period that we refer to as the Enlightenment, but one can put it as the period between the 1680s to the 1790s. The beginnings are marked in Britain by the Glorious Revolution in 1688, which provided a constitutional arrangement repudiating Stuart autocracy and ushering in religious tolerance, as well as the writings of Locke and the publication of Newton's *Principia*. The Revocation of the Edict of Nantes, in 1685, and the writings of Bayle and Fontonelle, in the 1680s, signaled its French beginnings. The end of the Enlightenment is best likened to the realization of its ideals in the revolutionary fervor that swept through America, France, and even England in the last quarter of the 18th Century, which in turn produced the romantic and conservative reactions in the early 19th Century.[102] What were the main intellectual trends of this period?

Immanuel Kant (1724-1804), whose writings are central to understanding the thoughts of the Enlightenment, outlines the goals of this era in his popular essay, *What is Enlightenment?*, "Enlightenment is man's release from his self-imposed tutelage. Tutelage is man's inability to make use of his understanding without direction from another. Self-incurred is this tutelage when its cause lies not in lack of reason but in lack of resolution and courage to use it without direction from another. **Sapere aude**! *'Have courage to use your reason!'*—that is the motto of the enlightenment."[103]

The central thought of the Enlightenment is the use of reason unassisted by faith or tradition. Everything, including political and religious authority, must be subject to a critique of reason if they were to commend themselves to the respect of humanity. This is what Thomas

Jefferson meant when he said, "We are not afraid to follow truth wherever it may lead, nor to tolerate any error so long as reason is left free to combat it."[104] The universe is not governed by a whimsical God, but by the laws of science, which are accessible to human beings through scientific method and experimentation.

This concept of intellectual progress and the power of the human mind are well represented in the writings of René Descartes, who is the father of modern philosophy. Descartes, in his *Meditations,* seeks for the *indubitandum,* the sure ground on which to base his knowledge of reality. He rejects as absolutely false anything he conceives with the least doubt. Indeed, the first law of sufficient reason for credibility is never to accept anything as true which one does not recognize clearly and distinctly as being so. His universal doubt of all things led him to discover truth only in the subjective, hence, the famous Cartesian method, *Cogito ergo sum—I think, therefore I am.* It is only the fact that the subject exists and thinks that enables the subject to exclude all grounds for doubt. Reason was the unifying and central point of this century, expressing all that it longs and strives for, and all that it achieves. It was an era of both qualitative but above all quantitative expansion of knowledge in an indefinite path.[105]

David Hume (1711-1776) was a radical empiricist and skeptic who denied the idea of transcendence and any metaphysical knowledge. He demonstrated in a dialogue that any religion based on miracles and the intervention of God is irrational. Even though he recognized the riches of sciences, this did not stop him in the universal denial of causality and of the existence of God. The succession of events does not in any way give us a link between two objects such as cause and effect, but are only a link built on custom. It was Hume who woke Kant from his dogmatic slumber and gave him the push to reconstruct philosophy and theology.[106] The Kantian attempt to reconcile the position of the idealists and the realists led to his novel system, which has shaped many philosophical systems.

In Kant's *Critique of Pure Reason,* he set out to establish the possibility of human knowledge. Accordingly, the mind of the human person has the capacity to unify experience. He used the structure of space and time to establish the way we come to know. Collin Gunton,[107] in his fine synthesis of Kantian position, notes that the development of Kant's thought was founded on the otherness of the world of our sense experience and its foreignness to all human values. Reason's function is not to discern what is imposed from outside. To receive our moral guides from God is as alienating and heteronomous as to receive knowledge from sense perception. The idea of heteronomy is central to understanding Kant's epistemology, as well as his idea of morality. His categorical imperative places the burden of choosing what is right or wrong on the inherent capacity of the human person to come to truth and be his own legislator.

The Enlightenment sought to replace God with the individual as the source of all authority. This is the idea with which the French thinker Voltaire defended his denial of God. Added to this, was the separation of the state from religion, which was pioneered in Locke's essay on tolerance. A religion removed from public life and public authority would be reserved for the private sphere of individual preference and individual practice. Jefferson is quoted as saying, "the legitimate powers of government extend to such acts only as they are injurious to others. But it does me no injury for my neighbor to say there are twenty gods, or no God. It neither picks my pocket nor breaks my leg."[108]

If religion was the villain of the Enlightenment, science was its hero. The 18th Century presaged the Western romance with science and technology. Science as Newton has shown in his works and Descartes in his methodic doubt embodies reason. This scientific worldview embodied a rational perspective freed from religion and superstition. Added to this, is the idea of progress, which was the *leitmotiv* of the Enlightenment. The eras before this period were adjudged as pre-scientific and uncivilized. Voltaire described history, before the Enlightenment, as "a long succession of useless cruelties and a collection of crimes, follies and misfortunes." The social contract theorists, Jean Jacque Rousseau, John Locke, and Thomas Hobbes looked at past social organizations and characterized them as representing societies in which life was short, brutish, and nasty. Progressive and perfectible, humanity disdained traditions and superstitious past and was entering then the pleasurable era characterized by happiness. This concept exploded into political ideals 'life, liberty and the pursuit of happiness.'

The Christian ideal of the good life was no longer assumed; each individual was to pursue whatever is good for him. This moral relativism sundered the connection of the individual to God and undermined the idea of a revealed religion. Indeed, Protestant thinkers like Barth[109] and other theologians of the Word, in an attempt to recover this connection, emphasized the wholly transcendent nature of God in revelation. Their positions were later modified by the First Vatican Council (1869-1870), which taught that God is not so transcendent that he cannot be immanent: it also taught that the human person can come to a rational knowledge of God, especially through created things, hence, the possibility of natural theology.[110]

The Enlightenment also gave rise to radical individualism. The individual was the author and creator of meaning and truth. This individualism led to political liberalism and intellectual freedom unencumbered and uncontrolled by political and religious institutional structures. The human person did not live to serve the temples of the gods or the dynasties of princes, but the individual's own self-interest. With this kind of disposition, came the intellectual and moral freedom that gave free rein to the limitless imaginations of the human person. Hence, higher truths and clerical and royal censorship were the lightening rods of the Enlightenment's contempt for institutions.

The rise of positivism and atheism in the writings of philosophers in the 19th Century and early 20th Century is no surprise to those who are familiar with the evolution of Western thought. Positivism, for example, found adherents among those empiricists dismayed by Hume and among those scientists who saw no need of any metaphysical underpinning for their works, and certainly were not lured by the intellectual scheme of Kant or Hegel. This is the state of affairs that gave rise to existentialism. Even though existentialism had a lot of influence on modern exegesis, we must state that the root of this influence reaches back to the Enlightenment, and its twin offspring: positivism and rationalism.

The Enlightenment was the intellectual trend that gave rise to a value-free liberal education. This kind of education was different from classical liberal arts, which had an integrated vision of education that respected the needs of the mind and the soul. On the contrary, it was characterized by individual liberty in the pursuit of truth, freedom to choose one's lifestyle, equality of respect, and consistent rationality. Liberal education encourages personal autonomy, critical openness, autonomy of academic disciplines, equality, rational morality, avoidance of indoctrination, neutral moral standpoint, absence of any conception of the good, and acceptance of diversity and pluralism.[111] Many people in the West, today, think that Christian education is a prescriptive enterprise, motivated by theological intent, its theories based on ungrounded a priori metaphysical abstractions that are seething with high doses of dogmatic conclusions and recommendations. Educational philosophy, they argue, should neither be metaphysical or prescriptive; it is, rather, an empirical and value-neutral enterprise motivated only by a disinterested search for knowledge and understanding.[112]

At this point in time, Western culture achieved a position of world hegemony and exported, or rather, imposed its educational philosophy on many colonial countries, especially in Africa. At the same time, it also effectively ceased to be Christian as the institutional framework of Christian culture was swept away by anti-church movements. Even though Western education came to Africa through Western missionaries, it communicated a dualistic education that served the interests of both the missionaries and the colonialists. For the missionaries, faith was what education should offer, and for the colonialists, competence was what education should communicate to native Africans who served as links between the colonial Lords and their exploited African workers. This kind of education contributed to putting African countries in the cultural crisis and political problems they face today. They offered Africans a more or less pragmatic education which is typically Deweyan in nature even though Christian in scope.

However, for a proper understanding of this whole question, it is worth noting that this liberalism, as articulated mainly by Locke, Montesquieu, and Rousseau, and further elaborated by Mill, had its origins in the English Puritan Revolution of 1640, culminating in the "Glorious Revolution" of 1688, which, in its turn, inspired the American and French Revolutions of 1776 and 1789 respectively. Locke, Montesquieu and Rousseau, influenced by Calvinism, were reacting against the absolutism of the Tudors and Stuarts in England, and the Valois and Bourbons in France. This absolutism, inimical to individual liberty and freedom of enterprise, continued the ancient imperial tradition of Persia and Rome and the revived Roman-Germanic Empire. However, Western civilization 'threw the baby (Christian faith) out with the bath water (education).' It is not surprising that in order to carry on the project of liberal education to its end, Church-owned schools were either taken over by the state or their course contents were radically altered to serve the new liberalism of the state. This explains the takeover of schools in Austria (Austro-Hungarian Law of 1868), Germany (Reich Law of 1872), France (1841), and Italy among others. England and Wales were to follow in the middle of the 20th Century. Although Western education lifted its civilization to an enviable height, and produced many marvels of science and technology and liberal arts, it is still deficient. It is in need of radical reform, if it is to produce more balanced and integrated men and women, who integrate classical liberal education with a deep sense of God's place in life and society.

In his study of the works of the godfather of Western liberal education, John Dewey,[113] Jacques Maritain reveals their hidden pretensions and limitations. Dewey denied the immutability of human nature and moral principles. For him, education is not a preparation for something, but an end. Education is important in so far as it is treated as an end in itself. Education treated as a preparation for external and future ends represents one great failing of traditional pedagogical methods.[114] His idea of progressive education was founded on a misplaced anthropology. Dewey was wrong to argue that education is an end in itself. A self-sufficient education places the human person on the margins and separates the subject of knowledge (the human person) from the object of knowledge (wisdom).[115] Referring to this kind of philosophy, Pope John Paul II wrote, "Rather than make use of the human capacity to know the truth, modern philosophy has preferred to accentuate the ways in which this capacity is limited or conditioned."[116]

The horrors of the Holocausts and the World Wars, colonialism, capitalism, apartheid, the gap between the rich and the poor countries, and the present scourge of insecurity in the world, show us the limit of liberal education precisely in its lack of a *sapiential* and ethico-transcendental cutting edge. The dissolution of the sense of right and wrong in Western culture is a result of a system of education that has no room for moral and religious education.[117] Africans need to distance themselves from this kind of liberal education model. Africa needs an education that responds to the emancipation of the whole human person, which also uplifts the continent from the cesspool of poverty, unending political crises, ignorance, disease, and undue dependence on Western technology.

Integral Education and the Role of Teachers, Governments, and Voluntary Agencies

Any true education must be integral. It must prepare young men and women for positions of rule and responsibility in the world; it must shape their minds with a sense of method, measure, and sober and subtle judgment. The key to the future of all nations is to be found in how the citizens of countries are able to make correct judgments about who they are; the meaning and value of life, the goal of society, and the ultimate human destiny.

Article 1 of the *Declaration of the Second Vatican Council on Education*, affirms that education is the inalienable right of every person irrespective of age, race, or condition. This is founded on the dignity of the human person. Education should not be value neutral; it should be suited to the particular destiny of the individual and adapted to their ability, sex, and national cultural traditions. The Declaration defines education this way: "True education is directed towards the formation of the human person in view of his final end and the good of that society to which he belongs and in the duties of which he will, as an adult, have a share."[118]

This definition is rich in meaning, and echoes the definition of Pope Pius IV in *Divini Illus Magistri*[119] that the whole purpose of education is to shape the human person in this mortal life, that he will be able to reach that final end for which the Creator has destined him. It needs to be observed that education is an ongoing human-divine reality. Education should aim at bringing all men and women to peace and unity founded on mutual fraternal relations. Education should lead men and women to appreciate the differences in race, religion, and worldview; it should lead especially the young to make sound moral judgments based on a well-formed conscience, and to know and love God more perfectly. There is also an emphasis on the proper integration of the advances in psychological, pedagogical, and intellectual sciences in the educational process and for a prudent, balanced, and positive education in matters relating to sex.

The Christian conception of education is based on the dignity of the human person and on the acceptance of transcendent truths in terms of which human life, morality, and existence are to be given some objective and absolute meaning. It also recognizes the primacy of the common good. The human person can only realize himself or herself within the community. The community finds itself by serving the human person and realizing that in every created person is the meeting point of immanent and transcendent horizons beyond the limited veil of social analysis, abstruse and purely scientific theories of education. The human person is a mystery, and education and life demand a double connection with human and divine realities as they relate to the full truth about human destiny and reality in general.

Integral education encompasses the ontology of the human person, *nihil humanun mihi alienum* (nothing human is foreign to me); in the same vein, nothing human is foreign to education. Religious education is not opposed to liberal education, but rather is against absolutizing liberal education and marginalizing the place of religion. Religious education demands that the whole process of education is religious in that the human person has a religious end and all his or her aspiration should be directed to his or her end. The task of building a more humane society, of conquering poverty, of implanting the dreams and glories of a better future in the hearts of the young, is necessary to the extent that it leads them to a deeper appreciation of the ultimate purpose of life, the meaning of life, the goal of society, and the final destiny of the human person. Religion offers the foundation for authentic science and technology and it provides a measuring rod for all authentic human projects. In the world of today, characterized by all forms of extremism, the young people, especially in complex societies of diverse religious and cultural traditions, should be led into appreciating the dignity of differences and the value of contrary worldviews.

In view of this acute need, it is then, regrettable that schools run by voluntary agencies were taken over by governments in some countries of Africa. This was a great act of injustice. Schools run by churches are essential components of promoting the common good of nations and do not threaten the secular status of any nation. From the earliest centuries of Christendom, churches and voluntary agencies have been great pioneers in education, especially in classical liberal education, which integrated a religio-cultural moral perspective. Christianity in Europe, North Africa, and some parts of Asia and the Middle East, has been the greatest agent for the preservation of human civilization, dating back to the monastic education of the 6th Century. Christianity teaches that human beings can grasp the truths about themselves, and by doing so, know their maker and serve their neighbors. Christian education then is not just education in faith, but education in culture, education in love, education for work, and education for the poor. We need to liberate our schools from the chain of state control, which has not helped to advance the cause of the continent, or improved the standard of education.

There are six areas of interest in education in Africa, where I propose that the state working with faith-based groups; churches and other religious groups; and voluntary agencies should play a major role:

1. Policy Formation. Educational aims in Africa should reflect African cultural values. This demands that the aims of education should reflect Africa's unique condition. They should integrate a liberal classical education that embodies the search for wisdom in science, technology, and arts with a religio-moral vision. Many years after independence, the curriculum and syllabus of schools in Africa were written by their former colonial lords who also set educational standards for African countries. This appears to be changing in some African countries who realize that most of these aims do not respect Africa's particular needs. The educated person in Africa is usually seen as the Westernized person and not the true African. Shortly before I left my country to study in Rome, my dad told me, "When you reach the Whiteman's land, try and know what they know but return to Nigeria a true Igbo Nigerian man." That explains what I mean by shaping educational policy to respect African cultural values. Africa needs to be open to the fruits of Western education, but she does not need to see Western education as the touchstone of educational orthodoxy.

2. A Keen Sense of African History. Every authentic education in Africa must embrace, in its totality, African histories both past and present. African history in this context includes political, cultural, scientific, technological, literary, religious, and educational traditions. A proper understanding of Africa's past before her contact with the West, her pains under Western influence, and the ongoing identity crisis of Africa that has also led to a crisis of development and Africans' homelessness, must be inculcated into young Africans. As elementary and high school students, we spent a greater time learning Greek and European history. No attempt was made to teach us African history. Schools in Africa should become centers for the recovery of the African past. The young people should be challenged to understand and appreciate their cultural identity and the sad and glorious epochs of Africa's past. A true sense of history is often the best motivation to face the future.

3. Context Education. Education in Africa should respect the context of the students. This is what Thomas Groome has called "consciousness raising" because it enables people to think contextually; to analyze what is going on in their lives and in their world and why and how historical circumstances shape their lives, society, and their future. Groome proposes four important questions, which every student should answer relative to context education: (1) What is really going on here and why? (2) Who is benefiting? (3) Who is suffering? (4) What is influencing my own perspective?[120] Research and reflections in our schools and learning among the students should revolve around the specific challenges facing each African country. Unfortunately, in most African schools, even in ecclesiastical studies, what is offered is far removed from the reality of the students. Many Africans cannot read and write in their tribal languages, while they boast proficiency in foreign languages.

The African countries, for instance, with mineral resources, should be training their citizens to take control of their natural resources. There can be no authentic development and maximization of profit from African mineral resources if foreign companies are controlling these sectors and transferring the profit home. The same applies to agricultural products. Unless Africans take control of their industrial, agricultural, and mineral resources sectors they cannot make any progress economically. This is where capital is needed by the African governments. Financing industrial development is very capital intensive. However, what is most important is for the government to encourage a new kind of educational process that is contextual; there are talks about the transfer of technology from the West to Africa, but that is not realistic. What is possible is the development of basic education in the direction of local needs, the discovery of local techniques and African rationality, supplemented by the educational heritage outside Africa such that gradually there could emerge a new crop of Africans that is sufficiently empowered to take control of the resources of the continent.

4. *The Quality of Teachers*. There can be no authentic transmission of knowledge and the unfurling of the latent powers of the young people of Africa without qualified and motivated teachers. Effective education requires qualified and motivated teachers, who will be role models to the students. Teachers are custodians of humanity, for they play a vital role in handing on the right kind of values and attitudes that make for a stable society. Unfortunately, teachers in African countries like Nigeria, are underpaid and overworked, hence, they lack enthusiasm for the work and eventually reproduce many unwholesome tendencies in their students. There are all kinds of examination malpractices, sexual harassment of students, bribery and corruption in schools and higher institutions of learning. Sometimes, students are exploited financially by their teachers, especially in universities and colleges. The teachers also lack adequate training, teaching techniques and educational resources like good libraries, computers, and internet services to help them enrich themselves as well as their students.

5. *Priority of Education*. African governments must make education, skills acquisition and literacy their first objective. Free education should be introduced in Africa at least at the primary school level. Many African countries like Ghana, Malawi, Uganda, Lesotho, Tanzania, Madagascar, Zambia, Benin, Cameroon and Kenya have all abolished school fees. In each of these countries, school enrolment went up considerably because parents in Africa want their children to go to school but most of them cannot afford to pay their school fees. No other issue in Africa is as important as education. There are many crises in the continent, which might make this objective appear impossible, but aggressive war against illiteracy is the only way African countries can move forward in this day and age. The civilization that can stand on its own, in the world of today, is the one that has perfected the art of transmission of knowledge, from within her womb, with capillaries and arteries in other educational traditions to enrich her own native genius.

6. *A Pedagogy of Hope*. This is a subtitle of Bell Hooks work,[121] which I find appropriate in capturing the kind of formation that students should

receive in African educational institutions. Schools in Africa should be centers for building a sense of hope, by making the students recognize the immense potential that God has implanted in them. Schools in Africa should make the students realize that they can contribute in making a change in the African society; that the future of the continent is in their hands. This is why the quality of education offered in schools in Africa is very fundamental. It should embody a sense of hope and inspire a progressive engagement of the students with the African experience and condition. It should empower the students to realize that their lives can help make a difference in Africa and that they have an infinite capacity for goodness and creativity which they can realize within their life time. Hopeful education is one that brings the students to the truth that life is worth living and dying for; that the community and the family are part of our history and demand our sacrifice, and that the future of African countries lies in their hands. Hopeful education is education that also inspires the people to work for justice, peace, and right relationship; to cultivate character; and to be purpose-driven. It also offers the students the prospect of infinite self-discovery and the encounter with history and people, which goes beyond the mere toleration of others to a healthy collaboration with them, to realize the common good of our societies and nations.

Today, the notion of literacy is no longer restricted to the three R's of reading, writing and arithmetic (numeracy): education must also offer access to skills and knowledge that enable the individual to take his or her place in society. It must also be a school of democracy, for the surest defense of the city is an educated and responsible citizenry. *True education will bear fruit if universal education is integrated in national development and poverty-reduction programs of African countries.* Today, the essential link between education, development, and poverty-reduction is universally recognized. Education, as Jacques Delors has stressed, is founded on four pillars: learning to know, learning to do, learning to be, and learning to live together. Education for all is the best cement for peace, both between and within nations; it is the road to prosperity and the surest guarantee of moral rectitude and technological advancement. The challenge is whether the governments of African nations can courageously pay the price for integral education and whether the international community is ready to help them achieve this aim. For those who say that education is costly, Abraham Lincoln was in the habit of replying. "Very well, gentlemen, let us try ignorance."

3.3 Water for Life

One recurring problem, in Africa today, is the lack of clean and affordable water. Africa demands some assistance in this regard from all men and women of goodwill all over the world. I, however, insist that Africans should not abandon their fate to Western donor agencies. The governments in Africa and religious institutions ought to re-engineer the African society and steer the people on the path to self-autonomy and healthy growth. Most Africans do recognize that Africa has a lot of primary energies in terms of her under-developed human capital, untapped material resources, rich cultural heritage, and a flowering creative genius in arts, science, and technology. There are also the wonderful natural resources which remain largely unexplored and unused. Indeed, the emerging world order would be enriched and the pressure on immigration and refugee agencies by desperate Africans reduced if Africa is supported in her bid to reclaim her future.

Unfortunately, sometimes the problems of Africa, like water scarcity and civil unrest, have become a source of cheap business for Western companies. The Pontifical Council on Justice and Peace, in its 2003 address to the 3rd World Water Forum in Kyoto, Japan, notes that water by its very nature cannot be treated as a mere commodity among other commodities. Water is a major factor in each of the three pillars of sustainable development: economic, social, and environment. On November 26, 2002, the UN Economic and Social Commission affirmed that: "the human right to water entitles everyone to sufficient, safe, acceptable, physically accessible and affordable water for personal and domestic uses." Article 19, of the UN Millennium Declaration, states the commitment of the international community to halving the number of people without safe drinking water by 2015. Water is an economic good and a vulnerable and finite resource essential to sustain life, development, and the environment. Indeed, water is essential to realizing other key elements of development in the social, economic, and political domain. Water, then, could be said to be essential to life.

Catholic social thought has always stressed that the defense and preservation of certain common goods, such as the natural and human environments, cannot be safeguarded simply by market forces, since they touch on fundamental human needs which escape market logic (cf. *Centessimus Annus,* 40). Many people living in poverty, particularly in the developing countries, face enormous hardships daily, because water supplies are neither sufficient nor safe. Women bear a disproportionate burden in this regard. In many African countries, most women spend a lot of time fetching water to provide for their husbands and children. For water users living in extreme poverty, this is rapidly becoming an issue of life and death. As Luc Coppejans, Executive Secretary of Africa-Europe Faith and Justice Network (AEFJN), has argued, the water crisis in Africa is the worst in the whole world and calls for some kind of compassionate effort to address it instead of the present exploitation of the crisis for economic gains by some Western companies. For instance, the French service provider groups, Vivendi-Environnement, SAUR, and SUEZ-ONDEO, which together hold 74% of the water market in Africa, have in recent years been contracted (some for concessions up to 25 years) for water and sanitation services in Côte d'Ivoire, Guinea, Mali, Chad, Mozambique, Niger, Morocco, Cameroon, Gabon, South Africa, Senegal, Burkina Faso, and Kenya. The fact that water and sanitation in Africa are essential elements of living, offer a rapidly growing market with an elite clientele, makes water and sanitation a sure source of wealth for some Western companies.

The problem of water scarcity in Africa was graphically presented by the former Nigerian Minister for Water Resources, Muktari Shagari, when he said at the informal meeting of African ministers for Water resources that, "The highest price for water scarcity in Africa is often paid by the poor majority of people in terms of money to buy small quantities of water, calories expended to fetch water from distant sources, impaired health, diminished livelihoods and even lost lives." Any person who has ever lived or visited the African continent would agree with this statement. According to the UN Water Development Report for 2003, Africa faces a water crisis: 250 million Africans, representing 21% of the population, have no access to clean water. With only 64% of the population having access to improved water supply, Africa has the lowest proportional coverage of any region of the world. The situation is much worse in rural areas, where coverage is only 50% compared with 86% in urban areas. Yet more than half of the urban dwellers also have inadequate provision. Given the fact that about 300 million Africans live below the poverty level, living on less than $1 a day, one can imagine the degree of suffering that many Africans face with this water crisis. About one third of African countries, especially in the Horns of Africa, the West African fringes of the Sahara Desert, and those in the Atlantic coast, also face some ecological disasters that worsen their water situation. In Ethiopia and Eritrea, the decreasing water level of Lake Alemeya and other rivers has led to drought with resulting hunger and starvation, especially of the most vulnerable members of society. Many dams and water catchments in these regions have become sandy basins. There are more than ten countries in Africa that face the threat of drought and famine in the Sahel region of Africa and in the Horn of Africa and surrounding regions.

The government of Tanzania made news in 2002 when it claimed that 70% of the population in its capital city of Dar es Salaam had clean water. This statistics appeared exaggerated given the scarcity of water in Tanzania. In Kenya, the price of a liter of water is higher than the price of a liter of petrol. This is similar to the situation in Nigeria, Niger, Mali, Chad, and Cameroon where there is severe water scarcity owing to corruption and official apathy. In some cases, this situation is worsened by adverse encroachment of the Sahara on arable land, which diminishes the water levels and endangers the ecosystem. In the North African Maghreb region, where it is believed that irrigation originated, the water problem has meant that countries like Algeria only meet half of their water needs, making water hawking a flourishing business for the massive sea of unemployed youth. Water hawking is a kind of unhelpful way of survival for many jobless young people in other parts of Africa, like Northern Nigeria and Cameroon. Both droughts and floods have increased in frequency and severity over the past 30 years. Over the past ten years, Africa has experienced nearly one third of all water-related disaster events worldwide, affecting nearly 135 million people, 80% of which was drought-related. In 2000, large floods hit southern Africa, leaving 850,000 people homeless, and almost 1,000 dead. Drought and cyclones have constantly ravaged Madagascar and destroyed her source of water. Runoff and water availability are expected to decline in the northern and southern regions of the continent, while the frequency of floods and droughts will increase. As a result, 25 African countries are expected to experience water scarcity or water stress over the next 20–30 years. Due to recurring droughts and chronic water shortages in many areas, the majority of African countries and their people pay a high price for water.

Many water borne diseases are home to Africa and are, perhaps, the greatest causes of sickness and death. Contaminated water causes gastro-intestinal illnesses, like diarrhea and the deadly typhoid fever. Vector-borne diseases cause bilharzias and malaria (which is the highest cause of death in Africa), especially in the sub-Saharan region. According to the World Health Organization, Africa accounts for 85.7% of the 1.1 million deaths caused by malaria worldwide annually; most of those who die from Malaria are children under five whose immunity is usually low. There are many countries in Africa in which whole villages have been wiped out due to water-borne cholera outbreaks. Guinea worm disease and *filariasis* (river blindness) are destroying the sight and lives of many people in Africa and ravaging many countries in sub-Saharan Africa, whose only sources of water are stagnant ponds and streams. When one realizes the poor healthcare system worsened by the HIV/AIDS pandemic, the grim situation and condition in Africa can be seen in its harsh reality.

With two thirds of the world's debt owed by African countries and with Africa producing just 5% of the income of the developing world, it is heart-wrenching when one thinks of how Africans could rise to the challenge of the water and sanitation crisis which she faces today. I often wonder what most Westerners who take water for granted, think of the African water crisis or what they think of the daily Tsunami disasters that are decimating Africans in their thousands and placing many of them in harsh and hard living conditions. I still wonder when Africa will rise from the shadows into the broad daylight of integrated development. Most Africans believe that Africans should put on the shoes of the long distance runners to make a break through. They also hope, however, that there will be some concrete acts of solidarity and genuine concern shown by Western countries to kick-start Africa's long walk to sustainable development.

3.4 Building God's Kingdom in Africa

If our Lord Jesus were to pass through the streets of Goma in Congo Kinshasa, he would no doubt be moved to action by the human hemorrhage that a volcanic eruption had wrought there; he would wonder why the government had done nothing to rehabilitate the displaced. The Lord would weep over the killing fields of Africa from the Angolan wasteland to the battlegrounds of Cote d'Ivoire, and from the vast windy plains of Darfur to the forgotten people of Somalia, Uganda, and the Great Lakes region. He would definitely wonder why African nations have done nothing to combat the scourge of diseases that has shortened the life span of many and made life for them an unbearable cross. He would definitely question the moral basis of such governments that sustain the kind of structure that subject the people of God to squalid poverty.

The Good News that Jesus came to proclaim had the message of liberation of both soul and body. The reign of God became present and operative in the person and works of Jesus and became perceptible and tangible in his saving powers. The kingdom, which the Lord came to establish, "is a kingdom of truth and life, a kingdom of holiness and grace, a kingdom of justice, love and peace." Accordingly, our hope for a better future should spur us to work for the establishment of conditions that are necessary for the emergence of the new heavens and new earth in Africa. Earthly progress is of vital concern to the kingdom of God insofar as it can contribute to the better ordering of human society.[122]

The theology of the kingdom of God is one that has generated a lot of theological discussion. Obviously, for a non-Christian, any idea of God's kingdom from a Christian perspective will be seen with suspicion as totalizing. However, my objective in this book, is to present, what I perceive, as Christian and African solutions to changing the face of Africa. Many other religious traditions also offer some rich solutions for a better world, which should be part of the discussion and dialogue that we are initiating here.

Is God's kingdom a reality here with us? Is it a reality that is wholly otherworldly and so demands our patient expectation? I do not intend to go into the very rich corpus of discussion on this topic, but I believe that there are marks of the kingdom (love, justice, compassion, solidarity, fraternity, righteousness, mercy, generosity, etc.), which could be incarnated in society. It is clear in the New Testament that the concept of the kingdom of God signifies the kingly rule and the sovereignty of God. Its basic intention is to affirm the fact that God reigns in all aspects of personal and social life.[123] When Christians pray in the Lord's Prayer, "thy kingdom come," what they indeed say is that there emerges here on earth a society in which the will of God is as perfectly done as it is done in heaven. The reign of God always emerges when the love of God incarnated in Christ is received by humanity as the term of our search for happiness and peace. This reception is followed by witnessing, through which we communicate this love to others in Christian activism for a better world. The reign of God will involve the presence of God penetrating all reality, persons, and nature in general. When we pray that God's kingdom should come, we are anticipating and expressing our willingness to be part of the process, for bringing about God's presence in all aspects of life and reality.

Therefore, it follows that to be in the kingdom of God is to do his will, both here and now and in the life to come. The duty of Christians is mainly to transform life within history, so as to bring it into total conformity within an ever-present dynamic will of God. This Christian responsibility is also the responsibility of non-Christians: to make the world a home for all, to remove the causes of conflicts, to build the structures of love and justice, and to seek and save the lost poor ones and the numberless many who are roaming the paths of life without any direction and any hope. It is a duty of which none should sit on the fence. God's kingdom can never be realized unless men and women everywhere are able to sing the hymn of love and enjoy the riches of wellbeing and goodness. The kingdom of God begins at that very point where one accepts the will of God.

The kingdom must come into the hearts of men and women before the kingdom will begin to come in the world. It is an inclusive kingdom, where everyone is known by name; where the wealth of the world belongs to all; where the pain and suffering of the majority becomes the concern and source of anxiety of the minority who control global wealth. It is the converted hearts, who have given up selfishness and greed; who have renounced violence and hatred; and who believe that, here and now, we all have a mission to restore the dignity of the suffering millions all over the world, who should answer the children of one Father and God of all. We all are called to reject all forms of structural injustice and to renounce any undue advantages and privileges which we enjoy that impoverish others. This call is particularly addressed to Western Christians and men and women of goodwill who hope for a better future for Africa. They must hold their governments and institutions accountable for the kind of policies they adopt towards Africa. Westerners also should deepen their knowledge of Africa to understand how they can better use their wealth to support Africa. Building a better society in Africa is part of the task of building the kingdom of God. The collective knowledge and resources of humanity that are hidden in Africa need to be tapped for the good of the Africans and the rest of the world. This is why it is important that Africa should be rescued from the entangled poverty web that holds her down. It is also the mission of the elites in Africa and in the Diaspora, who should consider themselves representatives of their brothers and sisters who are suffering and have a moral claim to their wealth and knowledge. We can work for the transformation of society by making the present unacceptable structures in the world to conform to God's will.

It is the mission of all Christians, and men and women of goodwill, to dispose their hearts to accept the values of the Kingdom of God, and to create a better world where there is justice, fraternity, love, and authentic freedom. It is the Christian responsibility to help incarnate the values of the Kingdom of God into the diverse structures of society. It is part of the Christian calling to resist the forces of evil and wrestle the negative forces that deny the people of God, especially the least of the brethren, of the good things of life. It is a mission which demands our full energy; our whole-hearted involvement, and, if necessary, the ultimate sacrifice. Indeed, the divine promise of total liberation, and the fulfillment of this promise in the death and resurrection of Christ, is the bases of the joyful hope from which Christians draw their strength. "The great lie of our age is that we are powerless in the face of compromises, structures and temptations of mass culture. But we are not powerless. We can make a difference. We belong to the Kingdom of the Lord, in Him is our strength, and through His grace we can change the world."[124]

The task of changing our societies in Africa demands the courage to build a new kind of society and a new kind of civilization—the civilization of love. This is the basis for building a culture of hope in Africa based on an African sense of solidarity.

The kingdom of God is the situation that emerges where no man or woman cries because of the wickedness, injustice or weakness of the other; a world where peace would be maintained not by force of arm, but by the force of universal love; it is the situation where children grow up in peace and the elders live with dignity and respect; and it is the presence of love as the dynamic that governs human relationship. The kingdom of God is the emerging new situation that renews the human spirit and brings about positive energies in the hearts of men and women. This kingdom will come about by the great strides in the positive direction by good men and women who I see everyday as I pass through the path of life. These are men and women who are rejecting the structures of sin in religious, political, international, and financial institutions that have sustained injustice, poverty and terrorism in the world. They are discovering convergences, not so much in institutions, but as in real human needs that must be met and evil forces that have to be defeated. This world is not an accident, otherwise our collective mistakes would have destroyed it permanently. There is someone who has placed us here to do some good; to make a difference and to be a light; no matter our station in life or our condition, there is someone out there who would and can intervene in our long nights and dark days. This person is God working in and through us. He calls us always to account in the direction of love and in the values of his ever-present and coming kingdom.

Chapter Four

Hopes and Dreams

Africans, especially, should re-discover positive aspects of their culture. In accepting them, they would give themselves a sense of belonging, identity and self-confidence.

All through the ages the African people have made efforts to deliver themselves from oppressive forces. It is important that a critical mass of Africans do not accept the verdict that the world tries to push down their throat so as to give up and succumb. The struggle must continue. It is important to nurture any new ideas and initiatives which can make a difference for Africa. - Wangari Maathai, Nobel Peace Laurette, 2004.

4.1 The Future of Africa: An Afro-Christian Vision of Hope

All peoples and civilizations cherish the vision of a better future. However, hope as a principle that sustains belief in the rich possibilities of the future, needs to be emphasized particularly in Africa, where there is a frightening decline in the living condition of millions of people. An Afro-Christian vision of hope is a theological category for understanding the Christian root of hope based on African cultural experience of salvation and liberation in Christ. The content of salvation positively entails the remission of sin and the removal of evil and the gift of new life, freedom of the children of God, of the Holy Spirit and of hope in eternal life (Raniero Cantalamessa). For St. Paul, salvation also embraces the final redemption of our bodies (Philippians 3:20). The salvation wrought by Christ also has a negative aspect that consists in the liberation from the forces of evil and the structures of sin and injustice, which negatively affect the lives of persons and cultures. Salvation is a reality experienced in life and celebrated in Christian worship. Built on the word of God and the sacramental life, believers feel they are living in the mystery of salvation realized in Christ. This salvation is realized in a gradual way and embodies grace, liberation, illumination, liberation from sin and evil, rescue from danger and life-destroying situations, overcoming limit-situations, divinization, and social transformation, among others. Salvation is both a revealed truth of the Christian faith as well as a lived experience, which plays a decisive part in leading men and women to the full truth about themselves, their society, the world, ultimate reality and above all about God.

Based on this Christian thinking, we can conclude that there can be no transformation of any society and no emergence of a culture of hope without the integration of a religious component into the whole reality. This is particularly true of African societies that are deeply religious, where the Christian faith is gradually taking root. Therefore, any proposal for a better Africa must integrate an Afro-Christian vision. This applies to the fight against HIV/AIDS, gender equality, good governance and democracy, development paradigms, neo-liberal globalization, child abuse and neglect, among others. Christianity always changes cultures and situations. If Africans are embracing the Christian message, one expects their societies to be transformed through the power of the Gospel.

The Afro-Christian vision of hope is built on the intimately linked reality of liberation and salvation. Salvation in Afro-Christian perspective is the redemption of the African men and women, from any situation of sin and evil especially at the personal and group levels. This will entail the transformation of the societies and cultures of Africa so that they can assume a redemptive value, capable of bringing life to all and serving the cause of human and cultural development. This will release the energies, human potentials and material resources of Africa to sustain life in Africa and outside the continent. Salvation in this context means delivering the soul of Africa from all that weigh on her and her peoples, and planting a seed of hope, which cannot be blighted by darkness of any kind in the socio-political and religious life of the people. Salvation will involve the removal of any aspect of African culture that is tainted by sin and any structure in African society that is manifestly evil in the fruits it produces in individual lives and in the life of society. Liberation in Afro-Christian perspective, is the conscious effort to free Africa from all structures of sin and injustice in all their dimensions.

Liberation of Africa in this sense means the elimination of the negative values and systems that make it impossible for Africans to live fully. Both desire for liberation and salvation in Africa stem simultaneously from African religio-cultural tradition of abundant life. This is supported by the Christian conviction that the structures of sin, which give rise to poverty, injustice, suffering and indignities, can be transformed by the power and presence of Christ in the heart of human cultures and in the lives of people. Christ in his person and work offers the possibility of abundant life. The immediacy of his presence in the search for meaning and life is felt within cultures and persons that come in contact with authentic Christian message, which reflects authentic human and cultural values. There is then a convergence of the African sense of ultimacy in terms of the realization of the abundant life in the historical process for one and all and the Christian message that the person, life, death and resurrection of Christ offer liberation and salvation to persons and cultures, especially those caught in the chain of suffering and fractured existence.

The deeper roots of an Afro-Christian vision of hope is built on the firm conviction that the future is not a dead end, but a reality that opens the power of the people and the creativity of cultures to a new life; a determination to reconstruct the socio-political structures to enhance the life of all and the health of society. This is sustained by a sharpened moral sensibility and social conscience that recognize the mutual implication of all in the good and bad actions of each member of society and our mutual solidarity with one another to remove the roots of evil, suffering and pain in order to plant the seeds of goodness, love and quality living. This vision arises from the heart of African culture and is raised to a new level in Christian faith-experience and life as the ultimate end of societies.

In other words, *an Afro-Christian vision of hope is the certain and concrete belief based on African Christian thinking, that there is a possibility of liberation in all aspects of life in Africa and the world from all negative factors that make it impossible for peoples and cultures to blossom with fullness of life. It is also anchored on the certainty of salvation in every aspect of life by the power and presence of Christ working in the lives of men and women, freeing them from selfishness and evil, so that in their lives and actions they rise above the imprisonment of immediacy and self-gratification and see the good of all. They are thus impelled to look beyond the shadows of today to the bright promise of tomorrow, which is possible through the mutual effort of all. This way, the life and well being of all is enhanced and every man or woman in society is thus given the offer of realizing their ordered end.* It is a vision which works for the removal of evil and injustice and the implantation of good and right order in the lives of members of society through positive steps to build up the common good. This way, the aspirations of members of society for a better tomorrow becomes concrete and immediate through individual and group life-affirming and culture-transforming actions in religious institutions, political establishments, economic life and social actions in diverse settings.

Africa's perception of ultimate reality is rooted in this desire for abundant life and the hopeful stirrings at the heart of their societies, which never abandons individuals and communities to themselves or to the vagaries of harsh and hard actions and inactions from within or outside, which stifle and destroy the fullness of being. Even in cases where evil is perceived to have come upon a people as a result of some negative action of a member or members of society, there is a strong effort to remove the source of evil because life must be lived fully if it has to be lived at all. This finds a resonance in the life and person of Christ who gives life to persons and cultures especially those caught in the cold hand of sin, death and decay. Christ came also to take away sin in its spiritual and socio-political dimensions.

The Afro-Christian vision has a great significance in interpreting the reason why Africans in spite of present difficulties in their continent remain strong and hopeful for a better future. Their worldview is built on a strong belief that the future will be better. This is captured very well in an Igbo tribal saying: *nkiru ka* (what the future holds is greater and better). This is not an illusion because this vision is what inspires Africans to work hard for a better future and to look beyond the shadows of present difficulties to a new face of Africa, which will emerge through mutual commitment to doing what it takes to bring the better future about. The vision is also a challenge to Africans to become that which they believe in; to live that which they glorify and effectuate in their societies and nations that which they really hope for. The bases of hope in Africa then can be seen in the light of the basic vision that within the heart of this continent and based on her spiritual traditions lie the tools for building a better future, which is coming about in Africa today. The question is whether the Africans still believe in this vision and whether they are capable of giving legs to this vision by making the necessary sacrifice for the emergence of a better future for themselves and their children?

There is hope for the African continent. According to the Kenyan born Secretary-General of the World Council of Churches, Samuel Kobia, "The courage to hope means that we [referring to Africans] shall refuse to accept our current experience of the human condition as permanent. We must negate the negation imposed by history that has created our status quo. Africans must be convinced that, despite all socio-historical factors, a better, brighter and more beautiful future is possible. We must convert our vision, aspirations and insights into a program, just as older generation did with regard to ending colonialism. We must defeat the Afro-pessimism that strangles nascent initiatives for transforming our present situation."[1] Hope appears to have gone on exile in Africa; but at the same time one can see signs of the resilience of Africans in the midst of great difficulties. This hope is well captured by Nelson Mandela when he said in a speech to the United Nations Habitat II, African Housing Ministers' Conference in Johannesburg; "The very specific challenge that

Africa faces is that of poverty; quite simply, most of our people are too poor for a pure market solution to the housing problem. Yet poverty does not mean hopelessness. The greatest single resource we have in solving this challenge is the energy and creativity of the homeless themselves. It is an energy that can be mobilized in an effective partnership that helps communities to help themselves."[2]

There are signs of hope in Africa. These might appear unrealistic for those who think that the African condition is very complex and intractable; but it is an imminent possibility for optimists who believe in the plan of God for all people and the innate goodness and power of the human person to auto or group transcend threats and challenges to their collective progress, happiness, and wellbeing. However, we need to look into the African continent to see the signs of hope. This hope lies in the power and strength of her people and her cultural tradition. The hope of Africa lies also in her untapped material resources. The determination and perseverance of Africans, especially the womenfolk in the face of spirit-sapping conditions, offer a real sign that Africans can overcome present difficulties. There is a deep sense of connectedness among peoples of Africa, which is beyond the calculation of economics or utility. People share in tragedies and rejoice in successes; there is a deep sense of family and community, which leads to the formation of cooperative groups and other group networking which at the lowest or highest levels of social organization galvanize the people. In the villages, age-grades, and social groups have a great capacity for generating positive joint energies to support the one with the resources of the other.

The idea of large multi-ethnic amalgamation, like the nation-state, to my mind, is largely unworkable, because it is alien to Africa's long held tradition of community-based (village-based) social networks. Ethnic groupings in Africa approximate, for instance, to being a Quebecois in Canada or being a Welsh in the United Kingdom. The big can only be relevant in the light of the small. Macro-economic policy and macro-social integration cannot work in African societies unless there is a basic grassroots action that energizes people for higher integration. This is one reason why I think that neo-liberal globalization is antithetical to African worldview with regard to social organization, wealth creation, and redistribution. As Adebayo Olukoshi proposes, "For macro-economic policy-making to succeed in advancing the frontiers of social policy in a manner that is equitable, just and inclusive, it would also require to generate growth without which it will not be possible to expand expenditure. The tragedy for Africa is that the structural adjustment years were characterized by a policy orthodoxy, which by its deflationary logic, stifled growth. The quest for a social state will necessarily, therefore, involve a revisiting of the macro-economic fundamentals that inform policy with a view to affecting a radical shift from a growth-retarding orthodoxy to a growth-promoting heterodoxy. In sum, the rebirth of a social state in Africa will also simultaneously involve a re-thinking of policy in a direction that could promote what some have conceptualized as developmental democracies on the continent."[3]

In my native Adu Achi village in Eastern Nigeria, people jointly share the burden of cultivation during the farming season. That means that they take turns working for each other. Thus, farmer **A** had his fields cultivated by five other farmers plus himself on Monday and the next day all worked for farmer **B** in that order until all six farmers' lands were cultivated. That way, the strength of one is supported by the many. This also applied to funerals wherein all the members of the village contributed food and drink for the ceremony. This practice has been applied now in the urban cities where neighborhood support groups are growing, as people seek to support one another in protecting their economic investments and security and in moments of emergency or disaster.

This is not an ideal for tomorrow, but rather a reality, which is already active among the people. There is a sense of solidarity, which has given rise to various forms of support networks that are weak because of economic and social strains in Africa today. These networks embody the highest values of African communal living: fraternity, concern for others, hospitality, respect for the elders, love for children, and a culture of work, responsibility, and accountability. Some people might think that this is a bypassed phase of African social evolution and cannot be actualized in the complexity of today's world. I do think, however, that this mode of relating is resurgent in modern African societies. Thirty-eight women from my community recently organized themselves and bought a palm oil pressing machine, which they would manage jointly in order to get some measure of financial independence from their husbands. Many women at the grassroots level use this kind of method to develop some economic viability; they also use the women's group as a means of social support for newly-married women, for first pregnancies, and for support of widows and their children. I do know many professionals in Nigeria who do what they call *ISUSU* in Nigeria, wherein each person contributes 10% of his or her monthly salary to a common pool, which in turn is given to each person in a rotational way every month. Thus, each person got a lump sum of money from the pool once every year, which he or she could invest in business or use for paying the fees for his or her children or settling outstanding debts.

There is also the 'street support contributions' made in big cities to address common issues that affect everyone like security, housing, sewage, bereavement, hospitalization, to mention but a few. There are many joint efforts, which are undertaken by Africans at this level with regard to home ownership, health care, job search, and apprenticeship. What is significant is that in spite of 'modernization' these networks continue to blossom and they have even grown in stature in village or community-based development initiatives which one can notice all over Africa. This has happened because, faced with the government's failure to take care of the citizens, each community decides to do something to help itself. These projects in Nigeria range from rural electrification, road construction, the building of schools, hospitals, and post offices, water projects, and neighborhood watch among others. It is because the ordinary people in Africa hope for a better tomorrow that these networks are growing and becoming a significant part of the social consciousness in African communities. These groups grow out of the cultural sense of community and mutual connection shared by most Africans.

The challenge for religious and political institutions in Africa is to seek to understand these groups and their inner workings, and to try to frame their activities into these groups. What is significant about these groups is that they are vibrant and strong; they have a robust structure that is maintained by built-in checks and balances. Membership is open to all members of the community or social group. Above all, these groups are also ways of monitoring and encouraging members to work hard and assume responsibility for their lives. A member who is not able to contribute to the *ISUSU* account for a particular month might incur the disaffection of the people and their disrespect for being irresponsible. The groups serve also to maintain some sense of connection among people because regular interaction leads to mutual support of each by all and helps to keep a tab on all members in terms of their professional and family life and even their religious life. Those who do not belong to these kinds of base groups are treated with suspicion and their religious affinity is usually sought before people's mind could be put to rest about their good intention or lack of it.

The strength of these groups lies in the basic confidence that each member has in the others; just as communal solidarity group and action help to sustain each member. When one is not involved in these groups there is always a genuine concern for the person's purpose and orientation in life. This does not mean an invasion of people's privacy but a sense of concern for as the saying goes 'the weakness of the snake is because of his failure to be in community.' Another significant sign of this group is that these neighborhood watches are made up of people of different tribes and religions and they cooperate and collaborate without any tension or intolerance. This is the kind of network of action that is demanded to build African societies from the bottom up. Indeed, it should be the duty of African intellectuals, thinkers and policy makers to discover the bases of the strength of these groups and their character and inner surviving capacity. These could form seeds for social movements, which could undermine bad governments and dismantle the structures of sin and injustice that perpetuate the suffering and poverty of ordinary Africans.

Another basis of hope in Africa is that Africa is a land with immense material, human, and spiritual resources. The management of these resources of Africa will be fundamental to the future of the continent. Twenty percent of the 18 million square miles of tillable land for agriculture in the world today is in Africa. Africa has many natural resources (e.g., gold, diamond, oil, uranium, etc.), not to mention the food crops and cash crops (e.g., cocoa, coffee, cereals, cotton, peanuts, etc.) that fill this beautiful continent. These are primary resources for the future development of the continent.

The face of Africa is contoured because of the failure in the management of her resources. The painful journey that we have presented in this book is the story of failure to manage the resources of the continent, i.e., human, political, religious, cultural, economic and historical. The human capital, for instance, has been badly managed making the African population a burden instead of a blessing. Today unemployment has become the greatest challenge facing young people in Africa. In Nigeria, university graduates are now turning into armed robbery to survive as the saying goes, "an idle person is a devil's workshop." It is a matter of grave concern that most of our young people are jobless; some of them lack the requisite skills to survive in the fast-paced world of today and so are wasting away without a sense of history and destiny. Millions of young Africans are roaming the streets of life as beggars and jobbers and they are ready hands for rebel groups, ethnic militias, political thuggery, street gangs, drug cartels and terror networks. The hope of Africa lies in her young people who must be equipped with skills and knowledge to become agents for the transformation of Africa.

Africa has a rich diversity of ethnicity which is not seen in any other continent. Indeed, many African social scientists and philosophers believe that African societies are inherently relational and communitarian. However, it is obvious from recent African history that building relationship among the ethnic groups and between different political and religious groups in Africa is proving an intractable challenge. "We cannot but highlight the fact that the nature of the relationship of Africans of different ethnic backgrounds living in their various nations, and of Christians of the same diverse ethnic groupings sharing one parish or Christian community in one part of their country in the continent is still characterized by recourse to primitive ethnicity at critical moments. Moreover, where the local populace do their best to live in harmony, love and respect; the other, the elite and often politicians would continue to evoke the divisive elements such as religion, tribe, etc., and exploit these to propagate their personal and political ambitions and interests."[4] Africa's ethnic diversity has been abused and exploited instead of being a rich interplay of positive values of diversity and complementary energies. The material resources in the continent have become sources of conflict and bitterness. For instance, the presence of diamonds in West and Central Africa has become a source of illegitimate business with arms dealers from Europe and the Middle East who sell arms to African rebel groups in exchange for illegal trade in diamonds. According to Douglas Farah, author of *Blood from Stones: The Secret Financial Network of Terror,* "One of the most alarming and shocking things in my dealing with the diamond trade in West and Central Africa was the willingness of Israelis and Arabs, who want to kill each other in their homelands, to do business with each other on the ground in Africa. I met Hezbollah diamond dealers who were selling to Israelis and Israelis who were selling to Hezbollah, knowing that Hezbollah was trying to kill Israelis in the Middle East, and Hezbollah knowing, that the Israelis wanted to kill their family members back there. I think it is one of the truly extraordinary demonstrations of the depth to which people will sink in their greed for diamonds."[5]

This could be said of the oil wealth of countries like Nigeria, Gabon, Equatorial Guinea, Libya, Chad, and Algeria. According to the 2004 corruption index of Transparency International, oil wealth is the breeding ground for corruption. In some of the oil-rich countries of Africa, public contracting, in the oil sector, is plagued by revenues vanishing into the pockets of Western oil executives, middlemen, and local officials.[6] Communities in the oil-producing countries of Africa continue to suffer from environmental destruction and ecological disasters from oil exploitation. Many Nigerians in the Niger Delta oil-producing area cannot forget easily, the full-scale destruction of Odi, a town of over 50,000 people between November 20-24, 1999, because the residents resisted the Western oil companies who were extracting oil in the area, without any regard to the environmental degradation that it brought to the people. There are legitimate fears about the fate of Chad since the discovery of oil in that country. Chad which formally became an oil exporting nation in 2003 is being 'helped' by the World Bank and a Western consortium, i.e.,

ExxonMobil, Petronas, and Chevron, to pump close to 200,000 barrels of oil a day. The mission of the consortium is to extract oil profitably, to share the proceeds in a transparent and equitable way, to protect the environment, and 'help' the Chadian government spend most of her percentage of oil earnings on reducing poverty in Chad (a country with a per capita income of $1,600, plagued by diseases, recovering from many years of civil war and national upheaval).

Judging from the experience of the Western oil companies in Nigeria and their Nigerian collaborators, Chad will soon witness the pain of oil exploitation, because like an African observed, the oil companies in Africa are giants and monsters that crush people.[7] This raises the questions: Why can't Africans manage their own resources? Why are African governments failing to prioritize educational goals to respond to the technical lack that is hampering industrialization and making their respective countries susceptible to Western exploitation? Why are the natural resources in Africa becoming sources of conflict and war (as we see in Nigeria, Congo-Kinshasa, Sudan, Cote d'Ivoire, Liberia and Sierra Leone) instead of means for improving the quality of life of the people?

The same could be said of cocoa, cereals, and cotton that are produced in many sub-Saharan African countries. In late 2004, the British High Commissioner in Kenya, Edward Clay, accused the Kenyan government of massive corruption, noting that the money lost through corruption is able to build half the number of schools needed in Kenya. Between 2002 and 2004, Kenya, a leading country in tourism and coffee trade, lost over $188 million through corruption. Kenya lost over $4 billion to corruption during the long regime of Daniel Arab Moi. Despite the promise of the Kibaki regime to stamp out corruption in Kenya, there are still many mountains to climb. In the 2005-2006 Kenyan federal budget, the government is reported by the *National Post of Canada* to have earmarked the sum of $6.5 million to buy a fleet of new vehicles for the Office of the President; a further $6.3 million has been set aside for the maintenance of his existing car-pool. This is happening in a country where there is over 60% unemployment rate. It does appear that President Kibaki of Kenya may be attempting to compete with President Obasanjo of Nigeria and Libya's Muammar Gaddafi on which African President has the longest motorcades in their entourage (some of these motorcades, comprising mainly of Mercedes cars, extend to over a kilometer).[8]

The roll call of African leaders with unenviable records of corruption is long and shameful: General Sani Abacha impoverished Nigeria of over $6 billion during the 5 years of his evil regime in that country. His predecessor, 'the smiling dictator,' General Babangida also left a shameful record in public accountability. All Nigeria's extra earnings from oil during the first Gulf War (totaling about $12.4 billion) were stolen during the regrettable regime of Babangida, who shamelessly calls himself 'the evil genius.' William Keeling, of the *Financial Times* who wanted to investigate how such a large amount disappeared from Nigeria's national vault, was forcibly deported from the country on June 30, 1991. That money alone could have given water and electricity to every Nigerian village (over 65% of Nigerians do not have access to water and power supply). The Economic and Financial Crimes Commission of Nigeria, estimates that over $500 billion of Nigeria's oil wealth has been embezzled by Nigerian dictators since the sad invasion of the military into Nigeria's politics in 1966. This amount represents approximately all Western aid to Africa in the last four decades.

Nigeria is evidently the most corrupt country in Africa according to Transparency International. What Nigeria has lost through corruption is more than half her GDP and would have been enough to give free education to every Nigerian living today. With 2,224,000 barrels of oil a day (8.2% of world's oil production) at the price of $61.68 a barrel as at January, 2006, Nigeria earns $137,176,320.00 from oil per day. Only 20% of this is actually used for the good of the people. While 40% of the oil wealth of Nigeria goes to multinational companies, the rest is often lost through corruption and mismanagement. The Nigerian Liquefied Gas Project (LGP), which brings in about $1 billion annually, has never been properly managed nor does anyone account for what has been done with the revenue realized from it. Most government-operated oil-based parastatals lack transparency and accountability and are cesspools of corruption.

Some of the notable African corrupt dictators include: Teodoro Obiong Nguema of Equatorial Guinea who runs the oil business of that country (which exports 300,000 barrels of oil per day) as his personal business; Mobutu Sese Seko of Democratic Republic of Congo was said to have siphoned his country's hard-earned wealth to the extent that what he stole from his fatherland far exceeded the $11 billion debt that the country owes to international lending agencies. Mobutu in the 1980s was said to have owned a personal fortune of over $5 billion. In 1976, when Mobutu's megalomania and kleptomania were beginning to manifest themselves in his misrule and corruption, when he was running his country's economy aground, perfecting his thieving mentality and strategies, and using his strong arm tactics and state-sponsored violence to silence and frighten his country men and women, the outspoken Catholic prelate of Lumumbashi, Archbishop Kabanga wrote a searing critique of his regime: "The thirst for money...transforms men into assassins. Many poor unemployed are condemned to misery along with their families because they are unable to pay off the person who hires. How many children and adults die without medical personnel who are supposed to care for them? Why are there no medical supplies in the hospitals, while they are found in the market place? How did they get there? Why is it that in our courts justice can only be obtained by fat bribes to the judge? Why are prisoners forgotten in jail? They have no one to pay off the judge who sits on the dossier. Why do our government offices force people to come back day after to day to obtain services to which they are entitled?"[9]

In the face of corrupt practices of all shades and colors in the governmental, the formal and informal sectors, all development projects or donor initiatives would come to naught in Africa. None of the African countries (except Botswana) have developed effective ways of optimizing their production or encouraging open and supervised private individual and community-based participation in the management of these resources. Corruption is endemic in the public and private sectors, because some African leaders have become the greatest enemies of their countries, and their predation on their national economies has been limitless, as they ravage and destroy the human and material resources of their respective countries. The situation is worsened by the absence of accountability, checks and balances, transparency amplified by a culture of secrecy and intimidation, the absence of rule of law and lack of due process.

The ordinary people are so disempowered that they cannot put pressure on corrupt politicians or hold them accountable and put an end to their unacceptable governments. Niall Ferguson rightly pointed out that, "Most poor countries stay poor because they lack the right institutions— not least the right institutions to encourage investment. Because they are not accountable to their subjects, autocratic regimes are more prone to corruption than those where the rule of law is well established. Corruption in turn inhibits economic development in a multitude of ways, diverting resources away from capital formation and the improvement of human capital through better health care and education. According to the African Union, the costs of corruption are equivalent to around one-quarter of African GDP."[10] The Good News is that Africans are becoming uncomfortable with self-serving leadership. This is particularly evident in Africans of my generation (those who are under 35) who have never known the good old days. There is a sense of urgency among the young people of Africa who want to put an end to the self-flagellations that are taking place in Africa. In their hearts burn a deep desire to put an end to corruption, to discover and use the rich resources of this potentially great continent.

Africans are hard working people. Only a resilient and hardworking people can survive the nightmares that many countries in Africa presently undergo. The feeling might be held in some Western quarters that Africans are lazy and backward people. My argument in this book is that stereotypes of this kind is what has blinded many non-Africans from seeing the true face of Africa, it is also the reason many Africans no longer believe in a better future for their country. A day in the life of a typical African is characterized by toils in the fields, long treks to the stream, engagement in community social, religious, and economic activities among others. Indolence is one of the greatest vices in the African community. One of the most famous commentaries on African work ethics and sense of duty was made in 1789, by an Igbo ex-slave, Olaudah Equiano, "We are habituated to labor from our earliest years. Everyone contributes something to the common stock, and as we are unacquainted with idleness we have no beggars. The benefits of such a mode of living are obvious. The West Indian planter prefers the slaves of Benin or Eboe (Igbo tribe) to those of any other part of Guinea for their hardiness, intelligence, integrity and zeal."[11]

Another gift of Africa to the world is the presence and growth of the Christian religion in Africa. I am convinced that if the Christian faith is well directed, that it promises to bring about the transformation of the African continent in a radical way. This will in turn have far-reaching consequences for global Christianity. One institution in Africa, which still has some legitimacy despite the structures of sin sustained by Christian religious leaders, is the Christian religion. It amazes me how Africans are so quick to forgive the misdemeanors of their priests and religious leaders. This has nothing to do with any dictatorship of the clergy, but it is rooted in the Africans' conviction that religious service is divine and that God in his mysterious ways can use an unworthy minister to carry out worthy works among his people.

Another reason is that many Christian religious leaders have played leading roles in the liberation movements in Africa and the process of democratization that took place in the 90s. Many clergy men and women have laid down their lives for the cause of truth and wellbeing of Africans. The Catholic Archbishop Christophe Munzihirwa, who was one of the most vocal critics of the misrule of Mobutu Sese Seko, was assassinated by Rwandan troops in Eastern Zaire and his corpse left on the streets for many days.[12] Archbishop Luwum was murdered on the orders of Idi Amin in 1977 because of his open condemnation of the malfeasance of the so-called 'butcher of Uganda.' In the same year, Catholic Cardinal Biayenda was murdered in the political strife in the two Congos; he was a defender of human rights and a culture of good governance and justice for the ordinary people. Catholic Archbishop Michael Francis of Liberia was given the 1999 Robert F. Kennedy Human Rights Award because of the role he played during the long-drawn crisis in Liberia. He was the only bishop who refused to leave Liberia during the heat of the Liberian Civil War. He refused to abandon the ordinary people of the land and opted to die with them. He condemned General Doe, Charles Taylor and Prince Johnson as men whose lust for power and greed turned Liberia into a river of human blood. He used the irrepressible *Radio Veritas* to inveigh against the human execration and destruction of Liberia. Several attempts were made on his life and even today he remains the leading moral light in Liberia. The same courage was brought to bear on Kenyan politics by David Makuba Gitari, former Anglican Primate of Kenya, who used the pulpit to bear prophetic witness to the need for a return to the path of good governance and accountability in Kenya. He suffered a lot of persecution from the ruling government of Arab Moi, who tried to muzzle him from carrying out his social crusade using the tools of the Gospel.

Many people the world over know Archbishop Desmond Tutu, who remains the moral leader of South Africa today. He gave his whole life to the liberation of the Blacks of South Africa and headed the Truth and Reconciliation Commission in that country that set the ground for the healing of memories and the establishment of a new South Africa on the foundations of equality, justice and freedom. He was however following in the footsteps of the great African religious clergy social activists like Bishop Ajayi Crowther of Nigeria and Bishop Abel Muzorewa all of whom in their different ways, pioneered a think home philosophy for Africans as a response to their homelessness. There are many Christian religious leaders in Africa who have been very active in the effort to build a better Africa and many others are doing their works silently in parishes, in social works, in the educational enterprise, in hospitals for orphans, HIV/AIDS patients, in social centers for widows, childless women, abandoned babies and rejected women and in agricultural projects. The Church in Africa is well positioned to be the leader in the development of Africa, but it has to first of all do a self-criticism so that Christians will respect the glorious tradition of liberation established by the pioneers and build on it to bring about a new Africa. The seeds of hope lie in the fact that the ordinary Christians will listen to the clergy if they showed them the way or after a long time, might sweep away the clergy and the establishment as happened in France during the French Revolution.

According to Philip Jenkins, by the middle of this century, two—thirds of active Christians will be living in Africa, Asia, or Latin America.

The question is what manner of Christianity is moving down South? How can it be defined and what does it represent? Global Christianity must hold African Christianity accountable for the fruits it is producing, just as African Christianity ought to hold global Christianity accountable for the fruits of their faith especially as it affects Africa. African Christians number about 380 million and in the Anglican Communion one third of her membership lives in Africa today. Today, African clerics are sustaining the Christian faith in the post-Christian era of Europe and North America. The impression is then given that all is well with the Christian religion in Africa, but this is far from the truth, as we have pointed out. What is important then for the Africans is to tap into the religious sentiments of the people and recover the ebbing sense of a better tomorrow. Religious groups should become the greatest agents for social change; they should be the basis for grassroots mobilization in the direction of good governance, creating a culture of hard work and accountability and a sense of purpose among the people, especially the restive jobless young people. They should help build loving, tolerant, and peaceful communities in those parts of Africa that have suffered from lack of political integration. They should help give life to the dead bones of Africa and resurrect a self-sacrificing love in the continent.

Life is only meaningful based on the love and concern we show to others. Mother Teresa was one of the greatest icons of love and sacrifice that the contemporary world has known. In her 1979 Nobel Prize lecture she said, "We are created to love and love must hurt, Jesus died for you and me so that we too must die for the other; we should see God in that man dying of hunger, in that naked person lying in the street of Calcutta, in the streets of Africa or New York." Love is the capacity to go beyond our own needs and to see the needs of the other; to love is to bring smiles and not sadness to the people we meet on the road of life. To love oneself alone is not the human thing to do, but to live for the other. This means to go beyond our own needs and wellbeing to see the needs of others and do something good for them. We love because we believe that there is something beautiful about every human person; that we all are bearers of dignity and respect. To love is to bring the good in us to bear on others so that their own good also would be realized. If one were to live for himself or herself alone he or she would only enjoy the happiness of the grave! In the capacity of the Africans to do the most natural thing in the world, which is to love, one could find hope. Love is still real and active in Africa in spite of wars and diseases, in spite of poverty and social dislocation.

The hope of Africa also lies in the growing sense of a common humanity, which is translating into concrete acts of solidarity towards Africa by men and women of goodwill the world over. The reason we have poverty in the world is because of the poverty of the human spirit. There is no deficiency in human resources but a defect in human goodwill. Rich individuals and nations sometimes are indifferent to the poverty and deprivation in their midst and around the world. The cats and dogs of the Western society can afford to eat on the same tables with their happy owners, but the men and women of most of Africa, especially those suffering from wars and famine, have neither tables nor food. The dogs of the Western world have cloths in abundance, while many of the children of Africa do not have cloths. The cats of Britain have beds, while the children of Africa have no houses; the dogs of London have special swimming pools, but the children of Africa have no water to drink; the dogs of Canada have nannies and pet hospitals, while the children of Africa in some places have no mothers and in many cases no access to healthcare. I obtained this information from a veterinary hospital in Peterborough, Ontario, Canada, on the estimate of the annual expenses for maintaining a dog (amounts in Canadian dollars):

Office visit	$45.00
1st shot after 9 weeks	$53.00
2nd Shot after 2 weeks	$36.00
Rabies shot after 16 weeks of birth	$54.00
Spay for females (kind of sterilization)	$210.00
X-ray	$35.00
Blood Work	$85.00
Thyroid Treatment	$93.00
Worm Check	$15.00
Cutting of Nails for the dog	$20.00
Lymphoma surgery	$5,000.00
Torsion (stomach twist) surgery	$2,000.00
Monthly feeding bill	$45.00
Kidney Dialysis	$25,000.00

Dogs are our best animal friends; however, any objective look at the expenses which many people in the West make for the pets, in a world where many people go hungry for days, would reveal a certain mistaken priority. In the United Kingdom, over £3.5 billion is spent annually on pets numbering about 13.6 million. Britons spent £1,500 on the health of their dogs annually and £600 on their cats per year.[13] In the United States, $40.6 billion is spent on dogs and $35.3 billion on cats annually. Some of these expenses, besides the pet food, are for changing the collar every six months to reflect the seasons, with names of both owners and dogs embroidered on the leash; they also cover the purchase of dogs' clothing, shoes and beds. In addition, pet toys, pet tooth brush, pet pictures, visits to a pet resort, chemotherapy, and hip replacement for sick dogs, and reservations for dogs on aircraft and at hotels for vacation, take a substantial amount of the annual budget for the pets.[14] Are the animals in the Western world more important than human beings in most developing countries? This could be applied also to wealthy Africans who have become 'Westernized' with regard to loving animals more than their fellow human beings.

The world of today must insist on certain ethics that set a high standard of generosity, especially towards the less privileged. My mother used to tell us that we have no right to waste any food, because there is someone out there who needs the food that we waste. She always reminded my siblings and I that we must respect our animals, and our family was never without a dog and a cat. However, I learned early in life, that the most important thing on earth is human life and that I should see myself in other people, and should try to put myself in other people's shoes. We human beings are the custodians of creation and should respect all creatures and nature as well. This should define a new global ethic of love and generosity. We can raise the question whether Westerners and their governments could forgive Africa's debt and commit a small percent of their expenses on pets to helping build up the African continent. Is the life of the dog more important than the life of the Africans? Or are we more connected to animals than to our brothers and sisters in Africa?

Everyone has a right to his or her luxury. I do have a beautiful dog staying with my parents in Nigeria, but he is not as important to me as the men and women I meet everyday on the road of life. We must care for our animals, but we must draw the line in our care for animals, because sometimes we wish to project ourselves into animals and find consolation and compensation through them as substitutes to failed or non-existent human relations. Dogs do not challenge us as much as human beings do, they do not complain, they do not make demands that make us come out of our comfort zones, they are always grateful and can always feed our fancy more than any human being can; however, they are not substitutes for human relationships. This applies to the abortion debate. I find it somewhat strange that a beached whale or baby dolphin will attract international attention in a massive rescue effort, but destroying millions of fetuses through abortion, embryonic stem cell research, cloning, etc., are justified by one strange logic or another. It is very curious that some people who are pro-abortionists are animal rights advocates and would go to any length to defend the right of an animal to live. I think both the life of the animal and the unborn baby should be defended and when a priority is to be made, the right to life for the human person is to be preferred. By the same token, no matter how much we love our animals, we cannot place their well-being above the condition of poor people around us and in other continents outside our own. Why can't people in the industrialized world care for Africans a little as they care for their pets?

Many people in Europe and North America do not know much about the condition of life in Africa, otherwise they would be moved to action. In most African countries, a child has only a one-in-three chance of completing primary school, the death of under-five-year-olds is two out of every five; and affirmative actions for the empowerment of women are still very low. Human capital is not developed and opportunities are not available for many. There is a clear absence of the basic social amenities of life like water, electricity, good roads, means of social communications, transportation, etc. This is the condition of life for the average African and it is unacceptable in this day and age. The international community has no excuse for abandoning Africa, the only continent within the last three decades where the standard of living and life expectancy have been going down at a rapid rate. The average life expectancy in the continent is between 45-55 years. The life of the typical African in today's world is extremely difficult as he or she struggles to survive on less than $1 a day. Can these lives be saved with the increasing tension and wars among nations?

The last century was the century of wars. It is estimated that over 187 million people perished by war, massacre, persecution, or policy-induced famine. It was the century in human history in which more people were killed by human agency than by natural disaster.[15] Even today, modern society has not yet solved the crisis of living together either as nations or as a global family. Billions of dollars are wasted stockpiling weapons of war that should have been used, for instance, in educating millions of people in developing countries. When I look at the defense budget of many countries like United States of America, Russia, Britain, Germany, Japan, China, etc., I wonder at our human folly. These weapons are external monuments of the evil passions of men and women; they are a symbol of our failure to rise to the bright heights of love and friendship.

The much needed capital input to Africa can be met if only some of these countries reduced their defense budget, removed poverty and injustice which are the main causes of war and committed a substantial percentage of it to international development. According to Pope Benedict XVI; "The true, and gravest, danger we face in the present moment is just this disequilibrium between technical capacities and moral energy. The security that we need as a basis for our freedom and dignity cannot, in the last analysis, come from technological systems of control, but can spring only from man's moral strength. Where this strength is lacking, or is only inadequately present, man's power will increasingly transform itself into a power of destruction."[16] A sharpened moral sensibility radicalizes our perception of the human condition and elicits a true sense of compassion and solidarity to those in need of our love.

How can humankind put an end to war and violence, to fear, terrorism, and hatred? Indeed, fighting is common to all animals, but the human person is the only animal for whom fighting is disruptive, as we see in the situation in Iraq, the forgotten wars in Africa (Congo-Kinshasa, Sudan, etc). We have seen also the evil effects of war in Auschwitz and Buchenwald during the Second World War. The world has seen the senseless destruction and disorder of war. However, the evils of the Holocaust are still unsurpassed and unspeakable. The 1992 crimes against humanity in Bosnia-Herzegovina, the genocide in Rwanda in 1994, the 1997 massacres in Zaire, and the human hemorrhage in Darfur are still fresh in our minds. The situation in the continent of Africa is very heart wrenching. It is unacceptable. A world that puts 80% of her wealth in the hands of 20% of her population is not a just world. It is a world that has not been converted from selfishness and fear—the primordial passion of our first ancestors. The man-made Tsunami in Africa is a permanent sore on the collective conscience of humanity. It should be the war that the world should be waging with greater intensity than any other.

4.2 Building a Civilization of Love in Africa[17]

The term *'civilization of love'* was first used by Pope Paul VI, in his concluding address during the Holy Year of 1975. Civilization in this context pertains to human culture. In the words of Pope John Paul II, "civilization belongs to human history because it answers man's spiritual and moral needs. Created in the image and likeness of God, man has received the world from the hands of the creator, together with the task of shaping it in his image and likeness. The fulfillment of this task gives rise to civilization, which in the final analysis is nothing else than the humanization of the world."[18] Civilization of love refers to a culture of love—that spurs human history to transcend its own limits and dark sides until reaching its final fulfillment in love. It is the attempt to reshape society through the dynamics of selflessness and not the limited perspective that begins and ends with the self. Civilization is central to the interpretation of the human person and actually shapes who we are. Hence, building a civilization of love would mean to shape men and women along the values of love—the only way to build peaceful and just societies.

One could argue that structures of sin are etched in human cultures. Social sins that we have identified in the religious and political institutions in Africa are the results of the subjective rejection of the will of God, which give rise to tension, rebellion, and conflict at the personal level, and then yield abundant negative fruits in communal life. It develops into concrete acts of injustice either as political systems, economic policy, and social norms that form the content of culture and thus shape human behavior and attitudes.

A culture of love, on the other hand, calls on humanity to understand that life is not an egoistic passion, but a gift to be accepted with gratitude; that our existence on earth is not a fortuitous and arbitrary game without any direction or moral guiding light. On the contrary, life is a project of love that is meaningful, and a vocation to be realized. Life is not a problem that is hard to resolve, but a mystery to be contemplated with humility and wonder.[19] The culture of love, which Christianity proposes, can penetrate all cultures, because all cultures are an effort to ponder the mystery of the world and in particular of the human person. It is a way of giving expression to the transcendental dimension of human life. The heart of every culture is its approach to the greater mystery: God and of the human person.[20]

Peoples and races have cultivated their relationship with nature, the human person, and God through culture, as a way of providing lenses of perception and cognition, providing motives for human behavior, providing criteria of evaluation, providing basis for identity, and offering an ethical system.[21] Every culture needs to be transformed, in the light of its ability to promote the quality of life of individuals, and to the extent to which it perfects the people in the dimension of integrated personalities. Any culture then that does not offer to the human person the joy of living and a healthy environment for the flourishing of the human spirit, is in need of healing. Unless cultures are imbued with a dynamic creativity, that is defined as love of life and nature, and the innate belief in the capacity of the human person to rise above evil, with the help of God's grace in order to build a new world, we would be endangering our collective destiny.[22]

Every culture has at its heart the longing of men and women for love and a good life. This longing is often the basis on which people want to live together and to work together in promoting the common good. The civilization of love is discoverable in the African sense of solidarity. The African traditional society has a deep sense of corporate personality, and of the supremacy of the community over the individual. The individual sees himself as a being-in–the-community.

This is the concept, which the *Nguni* African language calls *Ubuntu*, fraternity. This implies compassion and open-mindedness and is opposed to individualism or egotism. This concept is summarized by Desmond Tutu ; "A person is a person through other persons. It is not 'I think therefore I am.' It says, rather, 'I am human because I belong; I participate, I share.' A person with *Ubuntu* is open and available to others, affirming of others, does not feel threatened that others are able and good, for he or she has a proper self-assurance that comes from knowing that he or she belongs to a greater whole and is diminished when others are humiliated or diminished, when others are tortured or oppressed, or treated as if they were less than who they are."[23] *Ubuntu* also entails forgiveness because refusal to forgive is self- and group-debasing, and it disrupts the social harmony. Indeed, for Africans life is only meaningful if it is shared in solidarity and community. There is an ancient Bantu adage which says: *umuntu ngumuntu ngabantu,* which means "mutual inter-dependence," or more literally, "we are people through other people." There is another saying which the Africans use in moments of difficulty, in Hutu, which goes this way: *Ummera ummera-sha,* which means, "courage, find courage and let us use your courage."

Among the Igbo of Eastern Nigeria, this spirit is captured in the saying, *o nuru ube nwane agbakwala oso,* which means, "He who hears the cry of a neighbor should not turn the other way." *Ube* here signifies any human condition that cries for a remedy; it translates as *groans* but more of *a cry that anticipates a response.* It is framed in this saying to signify that the fact of a neighbor's cry presupposes that the nearest person will hear it and respond to the immediate need. This is a pointer to the fact of common implication in the pain of others, which is founded on the relational basis of African communal life. This saying is more appropriately translated: *'I cry knowing very well that I am not alone and someone in the neighborhood would come to my aid; I groan so that my fellow men and women would come to my aid. I do not need to cry if none would come, but I cry because I believe that I am not alone in my pain and that my fellow men and women cry with me and will help lift me up.'* It is this kind of cultural life that could reconcile the various groups fighting in African countries; it is the belief that should give Africans a sense of hope that together they will overcome present challenges.

In the early Medieval Age, St. Augustine had drawn the picture of the *civitas Dei* (city of God) and the *civitas terrena* (city of earth) where there is a dialectical tension between the values of the city of God incarnated in love, justice, happiness and peace, and the vices in the city of man carried in the vessels of secular culture characterized by greed, cruelty, war, avarice and the deadly sins. Augustine describes and anticipates a new civilization wherein the love and justice of God will reign in the hearts of all men and women: a love which he has revealed in his very nature and in the person of Jesus Christ. This analogy is comparable to the tension between the civilization of love and the culture of death, the structures of sin and the structures of love. In our times, there are palpable signs of the percolation in our society of negative values, which reflect a failed or misplaced value system. The civilization of love emphasizes the correct scale of values: the primacy of persons over things, of being over having; it also places emphasis on the personalist and communalist dimensions of human existence, rather than the utilitarian and individualist dimensions.

It is this often materialistic and individualistic culture prevalent in Western societies and which is gradually seeping into Africa that has given rise to what Pope John Paul II, referring to Acts 17, calls the 'Areopagi' of modern society.[24] That means the aspects of life in contemporary society that need to be healed in the higher light of a truly authentic religious value. The danger is that the values promoted in the Areopagi are human ends: structures of sin and of oppression that lead to exploitation, abuse of human freedom, ethical relativism, the barnyard of abortion, euthanasia, and other allied evils.

There is widespread loss of the transcendental dimension of human life, and confusion in the ethical sphere about fundamental values of life, family, sexual relations, and business ethics among others. The civilization of love is a summons to a new lifestyle that involves passing from indifference to human pain to compassion, concern, and an activist solidarity with others. Wars, hatred, corruption at all levels, violence and crime which sometimes draw the ugly calligraphy of the face of Africa, are the result of the disappearing African sense of community that sees people as brothers and sisters, and not rivals and enemies. Many Africans wonder why the communal spirit in Africa is being surrendered in the face of poverty and frustrating living conditions. What is happening in Africa today is totally alien to most traditional African societies and does not reflect any shared value or vision among various ethnic groups in Africa. It has no single strain that one can interpret and locate within any analytical cultural studies that have been done in Africa.

The civilization of love represents the whole ethical and social heritage, which Christianity offers for the liberation of any society from injustice, hatred, greed, poverty, and war, and for bringing authentic human development. It is based on the belief that Jesus Christ has offered all humanity the way to be human and the way to experience the divine. He was "a man-for-the-others" (Bonhoeffer) and even though he endured suffering, he was strong to confront evil and to triumph over it through love and sacrifice. "Christ fully discloses man to himself and unfolds his noble calling."[25] The human person is the only creature that God willed as his own; the human person is not a means to an end but an end. Human dignity consists in this call to live fully and realize the sublime nature of our vocation on earth.[26] God is the source of the civilization of love and the human person is its center. In the words of St. Gregory of Nyssa, "God is above all love and the fount of love." The great St. John says, "love is of God" and "God is love" (1 Jn. 4:7-8). The creator has impressed this character also on us. "By this all men will know that you are my disciples, if you have love for one another" (Jn. 13:35). Therefore, if this (love) is not present, the entire image becomes disfigured.[27]

Christ reveals the face of love and the Trinitarian Communion of love. This love has been poured into our hearts by the Holy Spirit (Rom. 5:5). Through his Incarnation in which he showed a generous solidarity with us, and by his Paschal Mystery in which the depth of God's mercy and breadth of his love were manifested to us, Christ has put in motion an intense dynamic of intimate communion between God and the whole of humanity. Communion means that we are called to live in a union of love that mirrors the communion of love in which the three persons of the Trinity love each other in the intimate mystery of the one divine life.[28] *The civilization of love is about how the reality of God's love, incarnated in Christ, and experienced by Christians and the whole of humanity can assume reality in the world, encompassing, seizing, and possessing it. It is also concerned with Christian praxis, that is, how the experience of salvation, liberation and love could lead to action, testimony, witness, mission, and dialogue, so as to make this salvation, liberation and divine love open to all, in its spiritual and temporal dimensions and thus lead to social transformation, peace, happiness for all men and women in all states of life. Love is the only way that our world can be transformed.* "Love must be present in and permeate every social relationship. This holds true especially for those who are responsible for the good of peoples. They 'must earnestly cherish in themselves, and try to rouse in others, charity, the mistress and the queen of virtues. For, the happy results we all long for must be chiefly brought about by the plenteous outpouring of charity; of that true Christian charity which is the fulfilling of the whole Gospel law, which is always ready to sacrifice itself for the sake of others, and is man's surest antidote against worldly pride and immoderate self love.' This love may be called 'social charity' or 'political charity' and must embrace the entire human race."[29]

The realization of a more humane society and just structures in Africa must begin with laying strong foundation for a civilization of love. This is predicated on the renewal of her cultural traditions and the insertion of this tradition into the various traditions that have taken root in Africa. In the stormy waters of ethical triumph, the nations of Africa must reach into their native genius to gain the primary energies for combating a world that aggressively wishes to ignore her, because "we are both the victims and agents of the negation of our fundamental cultural values, which are the resources we bring in our encounter with other groups of people and which may still constitute viable resources for transformation of the continent."[30] This path will open the land of Africa for a new kind of life that is full and worthy of the human person. There are five levels of the civilization of love, which I think Africans must embrace.

4.2.1 A Culture of Life and Love

It calls on all to respect and uphold the dignity and right of everybody to life, especially the unborn, the sick, and the aged. The senseless killing of innocent citizens in ethnic conflicts, by state agents or in wars within and between African countries, contradicts this principle of this new civilization. This also applies to any kind of human sacrifice or ritual killing or any destruction of human lives through violent take over of government. Life is being arbitrarily destroyed and many lives are lost through lack of healthcare services, carelessness by medical professionals, and senseless killings in road, boat, and air accidents. There is also the need for all religious traditions to fight for the abolition of the death penalty, which is opposed to African cultural tradition of punishment and retribution. The death penalty should be expunged from the penal codes of African countries and a more humane and African way (ostracizing the criminal from the community which in modern terms means life imprisonment) adopted for the rehabilitation and punishment of criminals. This aspect of this new civilization abhors all forms of discrimination and upholds the equality of all men and women. This applies to caste systems, which places a contagion on people because of ancient ties with deities or accidents of birth. It needs to be emphasized again and again that every life has a value and that a boy child is not more valuable than a girl child as is seen by most Africans. Indeed, everything contrary to the civilization of love is contrary to the whole truth about the human person and becomes a threat to personal fulfillment.

4.2.2 A Culture of Communion and Solidarity

Communion is tied to the theological category of solidarity. Beyond human and natural bonds, there is discerned in the light of faith a new model of the unity of the human race which inspires solidarity. God is love and truth in the fullness of the mutual gift of the Divine person and we should be constantly aware of our communion with Christ and with our brothers and sisters, which should propel us to the service of all in the community. This Trinitarian communion impels us not only to create a church of communion, but a new world where fellow-feeling and concern for the good of others stem from our appreciation of our common origin and destiny. Solidarity is thus the fruit of the communion, which is grounded in the mystery of the triune God, and in the Son of God who took flesh and died for all. It is expressed in Christian love which seeks the good of others, especially those most in need.[31] The principle of solidarity signifies a bond of mutual concern and obligation. It is a firm commitment to the common good. Through it the fraternity of men and women becomes concrete.[32]

According to Joseph Hoffner, the principle of solidarity follows from the personhood and sociality of the human person and implies mutual connection and obligation. Collectivism, which robs the human person of personal dignity and degrades him or her to a mere object of socio-economic process, as well as individualism which denies him or her of a social nature and sees in society only a utilitarian association for the mechanical balancing of individual interests, are therefore rejected as the principle of order. This principle is founded on the ontologically pre-given mutual connection and moral responsibility resulting from this mode of being (common liability).[33] The steps toward realizing solidarity in Africa are:

- recognition of each member of society as a person without discriminating against any person on the basis of ethnicity, sex, social class or religion;
- responsibility of the strong for those who are weak;
- responsibility of the weak for the weak through mutual cooperation;
- power of auto-transcendence on the part of the weak;
- greater sense of unity among African countries in regional groupings for mutual cooperation in transforming the face of Africa;
- global economic inter-dependence and mutual assistance;
- putting an end to all forms of exploitation of people and nations; and
- the religious dimension of total gratuity.[34]

Solidarity in African countries should not be a vague feeling of compassion and of pity for the poor by the rich, but a firm commitment to pull down the structures that make it possible for people to be poor. It demands a tireless infusion of values into our social structures; it means being conscious of the responsibility of each for all. Solidarity does not mean throwing money to crowds at political campaign rallies, organizing expensive parties on special occasions, giving hand-outs to political cronies, nor does it mean the unfortunate patron-client relations which sustain a prebendal framework between elected officials and their reference or support groups. It will also entail building support networks in families and communities; wealth-creation through the promotion of local initiatives for grassroots development projects and self-help projects and programs by small businesses and co-operative movements.

Solidarity must also entail subsidiarity, that is the effort to sustain development from below and the redesigning of society in such a way that individuals are empowered in a way that they can meaningfully engage in work and so actualize their potentials.

4.2.3 A Culture of Dialogue and Tolerance

Africa today is not at peace mainly because of structures of sin and injustice. These sins, undermine the possibility of abundant life for people, generate violence and disrupt harmony among African peoples. Indeed, injustice, selfishness, and poverty are always causes of violence. Many wars are fought today in Africa, because of the failure of individuals and groups to rise above their narrow interests to the greater good of society. Africans must embrace once more the wisdom of the village palaver, where people gather to discuss their problems and to find ways of solving them in an atmosphere of friendship and love. The situation where African ethnic groups are constantly fighting each other or where religious groups are hostile to each other, betrays a failure of dialogue.

The civilization of love opens religious groups to dialogue on these levels:

Dialogue among all Christians in Africa. This is the basis for the credibility and effectiveness of the Christians in the dialogue with the wider society. Pope Paul VI first posed this question: *"Ecclesia, quid dicis de teipsa?* (Church, what do you say of yourself?)"[35] Dialogue within the Christian faith entails reconciliation of divisions in the church in many African countries. There is the urgent need to dismantle the structures of sin in religious groups by greater commitment to accountability and through checks and balances on churches' leadership. Religious leadership should be motivated by pure altruism and service to God and humanity and not any egotistic end. The churches must listen to the signs of the Spirit in history and make the necessary adjustment and appropriate response to really become prophets of a tomorrow that lies before Africans. The church in Africa must be the moral standard bearer of society and address herself to the historical problems of structures of sin in Africa. Christian churches in Africa must unite to articulate an Afro-Christian vision for a better Africa and provide moral leadership for the ordinary people of Africa. However, if the problems of the wider society like dictatorship, marginalization, gratification, discrimination, unhealthy rivalry, and the unconscionable struggle for positions afflict the Christian communities in Africa, she loses the inner courage of truth, which she is called to bring to bear on the unjust structures of society.

Dialogue among all the religions. This involves ecumenical initiatives aimed at discovering a common ground among the various religious communities in Africa, in order to create a better understanding among the various religions, which will lead to sincere reconciliation. Some of the common elements among religious groups in Africa include: faith in One God, hope in the possibility of a different kind of world, and respect for the rights and dignity of the human person. The Christian groups can collaborate with the other religious communities in Africa in advancing the cause of justice, peace, and development; in fighting the scourge of HIV/AIDS and corruption in government and in civic education; and in the promotion of social services.

We need to remove the attitudes of prejudice, hostility, distrust, mutual condemnation and invectives, discrimination, and even wars and other acts of intolerance, which destroy common initiatives among Christians, Muslims, and practitioners of African Traditional Religion in Africa. Christians must come together with adherents of other religions to understand themselves better and articulate common insights. This is particularly important with regard to the practitioners of African Traditional Religions and Islam. The civilization of love offers the impulse for a new kind of religious experience that forges a harmony between faith and culture, the loosening of which is at the heart of the crisis of faith among many Africans. There is the need to bridge the gap between love of neighbor and the desire for justice, since the love of others demands not only a sharing in their suffering, but the real action for the reconstruction of the unjust structures of society that bring suffering to people.

4.2.4 A Culture of Forgiveness and Fraternity

There is today in Africa a stockpile of accumulated hatred and wounded memories. This is fuelled by prejudice, poverty, and lack of adequate education about others. African societies cannot progress in the midst of hatred and selective association founded on unjust structures and illegitimate stereotypes. The problems that confront men and women in our continent can be tackled through joint cooperation and collaboration among all. We can make Africa a better place when we no longer see ourselves as a hell (Sartre) from which we must escape. This is what the civilization of love reminds us: that the new name for religion is love and friendship and demands of us the creation of a community of friends in which there is a shared sense of a common destiny. All Africans must work together to build a family of God's kingdom in their neighborhoods (a) where all know and accept each other and feel at home, (b) where people pray and share the Word of God together, (c) where everybody is welcome to contribute his or her gifts and talents, (d) where one person's problems become every other person's problems, (e) where we are concerned with other ethnic groups as much as we are concerned with our own, and (f) where there is warmth in human relationships and a caring attitude.[36]

It is still possible to create in Africa an extended family of brothers and sisters, where there is a value shift from selfishness to selflessness, from religious intolerance to religious harmony, from political exclusion to political integration, and from fear of each to the love of all. This calls on all to extend a helping hand and a loving heart to those who are culturally rootless, politically voiceless, economically powerless and emotionally listless. In the words of Pope John Paul II, "There should be no more postponement of the time when the poor Lazarus can sit beside the rich man to share the same banquet and be forced no more to feed on the scraps that fall from the table."[37]

In Africa today, the greatest obstacle to the building of fraternity among men and women is prejudice and failure to forgive. Therein lies the need for the healing of memories of those who have for so long trudged the highway of suffering, and many battered by sad experiences of failed governments and those bearing the wounds of war, and religious and ethnic conflicts. The civilization of love is founded on the gratuitous mercy and love of God, which we see in Christ. All Africans are heirs of the emerging kingdom of peace and love in Africa. Every African is invited to become a herald of mercy with hearts open to universal friendship. We all must learn to forgive and to begin afresh a journey to the true future of African peoples that we must undertake together without excluding anyone. We must realize that if our religious expressions seek eternal peace and communion with God, but do not create conditions for peace and fraternity among men and women, our religions might be close to what Marx calls 'the heart of a *heartless world.*'

4.2.5 A Culture of Hope

The civilization of love invites all Africans to look up once more and not be bent in sorrow and tears of a terrible past and an uncertain future. God has a plan for the world in which Africans have a special place, because God chooses the weak and the poor to lift them up. Since God has a plan for the world (Jer.29:10-11; Gal.4:4), we are assured of the definitive coming of God's Kingdom, which has already begun. We should, therefore, prepare for this Kingdom by daily commitments founded on hope. This commitment should be extended, not only to individuals, but also to our communities, in particular social contexts and in world history. It is a hope founded on the promise of the Lord to remain with us even to the end of the world (Matt 28:20). We can, no doubt, break the iron cage of structures of sin that hold us down as a people. There is always the danger of despair when one looks at the magnitude of the problems that social sins have created in African society.

However, every African must seek the path of conversion to hopeful existence that looks beyond the shadows of the present moment. All religious men and women in Africa must become moral leaders through active prophetic witnessing. There is the need to build up African families by constructing a moral rampart around the children, so that a new generation of enlightened Africans will emerge to rebuild the fragments of our broken polities. Religious groups in Africa must also see it as their duty to infuse hope in the weary hearts of Africans by presenting the message of hope and action.

In the final analysis, the collapse of the structures of sin will begin with the collapse of the attitude of hopelessness and desperation in the hearts of many Africans, who are afraid of tomorrow thinking that African nations are on the certain and irremediable path of perdition. The social reconstruction, which we have proposed here, cannot come about unless the men and women of our continent gird the loins of hope and toe the path of interior transformation. No one is too insignificant in the reweaving of the contoured socio-political and economic geography of our wonderful continent. As Socrates warned the Greeks many years ago: The brilliant statesman had enriched and embellished the city; had created protective walls around it; had built ports and dockyards; had launched navies; had eternalized the glory of the city by the temples of undying grandeur and beauty; has multiplied in Attica the feasts of arts and reason; but he did not occupy himself with the problem of how to make Athenians better men and women. As a result his work has remained incomplete and his creation cadulous.

The Christians believe that Christ is alive. God is not dead but alive and active in a dynamic way. The celebration of the victory of Christ over death is what is marked at Easter. How can the reality of the Resurrection help to change the conditions of Africans who are carrying the cross of poverty and suffering? If Christ is alive for the Africans, how can they experience the liberation from the limit-situations that have kept this continent tottering on the edges of the valley of decay and death? I believe that the Easter event has significance for the world and Africa.

Easter opens a principle of hope in a radical way. Easter celebrates the possibility of a new beginning for all men and women of good will. This new beginning of life is the vitality of God which we all receive every day when we wake up. Life does not consist of the satisfaction of present needs only, but in the creative existence which springs from a purpose-driven longing that arises in the depths of a soul that is saved. Easter celebrates the triumph of Christ over the forces of evil and death; it also celebrates the possibility of our own triumph over the negative forces that weigh us down. Easter casts a long gaze beyond the shadows of present difficulties. It also opens the horizon of present transformation. By his Resurrection, Jesus has shown that he has power over the whole universe and its elements. There is nothing impossible for God; even the power of death could not defeat his Eternal Divine plan. If we see things through the eyes of God and in the light of the events in Christ's life, we can never lose hope in the possibility of the conquest of freedom and poverty among individuals and groups.

In the same way, for all believing Christians, and all men and women of good will throughout the world, there is the hope of victory against the *dead ends* of our lives as individuals and groups. The Resurrection of Jesus produced faith and hope in the disciples: men and women who were afraid to witness to Christ at his trial publicly stood up for Christ. Hope is borne of faith not in our abilities but in the power that we have received which precedes us and is above us. Easter celebrates the gift of liberation and salvation that God has granted to the world in Christ. Many people struggle with personal difficulties; others have health problems; and some are crippled by fear about the future. There are many who are caught in the intractable chain of poverty and frustration. These pains are felt in Africa at the personal and communal levels. There is hope for those who do not lose heart in the face of evil or wince against the structures of sin and those who sustain them.

The world today is gripped in the fear of terrorism. There are many people the world over who are condemned to a colorless life because of their personal histories or by unjust situations in society. We do not need to look too far to see that around us there are signs of hope; even in our inner self where our human fragility meets the power of God's grace. We hear of news of wars, sexual abuse especially against women and children, hate crimes, poverty, and natural disasters. Particularly, I think of the fate of *Mama Africa;* which appears to be in trouble. Africans and non-Africans have become weary of the bad news in and from Africa.

Africa has become the continent of tombs, but unlike the tomb of Jesus, the tombs of Africa are not empty. They are now filled with bleaching bones of the dead who have been killed in innumerable civil wars in the continent. These tombs are in a certain sense the tomb of the Risen Lord, who is the archetypical man whose face we see even in the most wrinkled or sad faces of the suffering sea of the least of our brethren. The tomb of Jesus is filled with the millions of Africans who are dying of HIV/AIDS and malaria. The tomb of Jesus has become the gathering place of many poor and hungry children of Africa who are orphaned, and the lost generations of Africa whose lives have become the tale of agony and sorrow. However, in the midst of these man-made difficulties, most of which are caused by bad government and the exploitation of the poor religious masses by many political and religious elites, there is still hope in the eyes of many young people. The Lord's victory is the sign that we too will overcome our own difficulties. Jesus has the power to change our human condition. *This liberation from the nets of sin, suffering, death, hatred, poverty, injustice, and the fear of what is to come and fear of each other is the meaning of Easter.* It offers strength for today and hope for tomorrow. Africans should dare to believe and to hope and act with fresh and renewed strength inspired by the presence and power of the God of hope in their personal and group history. Writing on God as the principle of hope, Jurgen Moltmann states: "The God of hope is the God of freedom. In him no boundaries are set nor does he set any. He breaks through defenses of anxiety and the walls of care. He breaks through boundaries which we ourselves have set in order to distinguish ourselves from other men and to affirm ourselves. He breaks into the boundary of our solitude in which we have hidden so that no one will come near us. He steps over the boundary of race, in which man loathes man, and the boundaries of class and strata in society. He despises difference between black and white, poor and rich, educated and uneducated; for he seeks men—poor, suffering, hating and ugly, cramped and stunted men—and accepts them as they are. That knowledge makes us free and is a source of support. We can hope in him-the God of freedom."[38]

4.3 The Gift of Africa to the World

What can Africa offer to the world of today? I see three gifts that Africa offers to the world (a) the gift of her human and material resources, (b) the gift of her cultural life, and (c) the gift of her thirst for higher truth that goes beyond the calculation of capital.

4.3.1 *The Gift of Africa's Human and Material Resources*

In the first place, Africans are a wonderful people: They are open to life; they are receptive to new ideas, and they do not discriminate against people of other races. One of the things that any visitor from Europe or North America discovers in Africa is the African sense of community and hospitality. They do not understand the language of exclusion or racial bar. There may be some animosity between the tribes, but it only occurs in the political and economic balancing game. The typical African is a person of the world. He or she is in love with newness and would love to meet people and make friends. In the villages, people know each other by name, they speak to each other, and they share in each other's pains and joys. The village life represents the African world in its fullness, richness, and diversity. It manifests the culture of hard work and solidarity and openness to sharing in the condition and spirit of the people. The cure for Africa's homelessness is the incarnation in modern African societies and in the hearts and attitudes of Africans, the spirit of the village life. Most Africans see their respective villages as true homes, where values are still upheld, where everyone is known by name and where all are implicated in a shared experience in the joys and sorrows of all. The African holds strongly to his traditional convictions, but he or she does not shut himself up in a box. The discovery by non-Africans of the real African personality would help to heal their racial prejudices against them. The African person is one who has a high regard for values; one who has a deep respect for life and the sacred and who sees life as governed by positive forces over the human world that could be turned into negative if our ethical preferences are not in tandem with the positive valences of the Creating One.

The Africans are also gifted in the arts and sciences, in creativity and sports. Discovering the hidden rationality of the Africans in their native science and technology is one of the challenges facing most educated

Africans. The wisdom of the Africans which gave birth to ancient civilization in many defunct African empires should be re-discovered, re-interpreted and adapted to the present African context. Many African writers have become best-selling authors like Chinua Achebe's *Things Fall Apart*, Mariama Ba's *So Long a Letter*, and Cheikh Anta Diop's *The African Origins of Civilization: Myth or Reality* among others. The African person when liberated from poverty and the bondage of mental enslavement can be the highest genius in the arts and sciences. Many Africans who study abroad are not easily released by their institutions, because they see that most of them are great individuals of high intellect whose conditions in Africa blighted their full blossoming.

The material resources of Africa are great sources of wealth to the world. Cote d'Ivoire, for instance, is the world's greatest producer of cocoa. It was a great source of pride for me when I visited the largest chocolate company in Italy, *Perugina*, and was acknowledged by the tour guide as "the goose that lays the golden egg," because my continent was their highest supplier of cocoa. It is sad, however, that Africans do not know how to use their raw materials and have to outsource the manufacturing of these resources to Western companies and pay a great deal to import the finished products. Whenever there is civil disturbance in the oil-producing delta region of Nigeria, the world oil prices go up. This is evidence of the influence that Nigeria and other oil producing countries command in the international oil market. Africa is home to the most beautiful wildlife sites in the world and the vegetation of the continent is a beauty to behold.

The high potential for agricultural production includes crops like maize, millet, groundnuts, yams, potatoes, pineapples, bananas, plantains, beans, rice, all kinds of vegetables, orange, mangoes, apples, grapes, and more. Africa is the third largest producer of cotton in the world. Cotton production in Benin, Burkina Faso, Chad, Mali, and Togo represents between 5-10% of GDP; more than a third of their annual income and over 60% of their agricultural production. There are numerous material resources in Africa like coal, diamonds, gold, copper, tin, lead, and uranium, to mention just a few that could enrich the world if they were properly developed in an enabling environment. Africa has everything in her land to make herself a rich continent and to provide for the good of Africans. The problem is that Africans appear not to value these gifts and many non-Africans do not realize how immensely gifted Africa is. Those non-Africans who discover the wealth in Africa exploit these resources and take the profit outside Africa.

If Africa was a poor continent why did Westerners go into it in the first place? Why are Westerners living in Africa and doing business against all odds in this continent especially in the oil industry? If Africa had nothing to offer the West and the rest of the world, many Westerners would not be doing business in Africa. They are in Africa because Africa has something to offer the world. The only unfortunate thing is that Africans are not getting any mutual benefit from their business contact with the West. A friend of mine sarcastically observed that Africans are like the man in the Christian Scripture who buried his talent instead of using it like the other servants (Matthew 25:14-30) and whose talents were taken away and given to the diligent servant (the West). I do not agree with that analogy, but sometimes I wonder why Africans are not realizing their potentials and why nothing is being done to inaugurate a new era of optimal development in Africa. What are Africans doing with the human and natural talents that God has blessed them with? Finding the response to this question is a necessary first step in the evolution of a new Africa.

4.3.2 *The Gift of Africa's Cultural Life*

Africa is a continent that is rich in cultural traditions. These traditions in themselves have undergone various degrees of metamorphoses, but they are customs and practices, which have stood the test of time, because they are basic to the survival of the African people. Some of them relate to respect for life, respect for family values, respect for elders, hospitality and friendliness to strangers and visitors, and respect for the sense of community.

There are many positive values enshrined in African traditional cultures, which Pope John Paul II observes, like the a sense of family, love and respect for life, veneration of ancestors, a sense of solidarity and community, respect for the chief and elders all of which could be framed into development initiatives and democratic ideals for Africa. As we have admitted in chapter three, every culture is always in need of salvation in the light of the true end of human life and the destiny of humanity and the universe. African culture has some dark spots that need to be purified, but the heart of African culture with regard to ultimate reality and the ordering of society must be integrated in any response to the African condition. The African culture continues to go through the process of finding the adequate compass to chart the turbulence of identity and relevance for the people of Africa. Some of these cultural practices against women and children and against the outcasts and slaves are being rejected in many ethnic groups. Some of them are proving to be hard nuts to crack, because cultural practices are not accidental realities, dropping them will sometimes radically mutate the ideational bases of a people's self-understanding and group-identity.

The African culture of life is one that offers the rest of the world something to think about. This is in relation to the African worldview on life and how life is lived in Africa today. Africans see life as a gift from God and a sacred good. Life is a super-value. There is nothing on earth as important as life both for the unborn as well as the elderly and the sick. There is no place in the African world for abortion, euthanasia, or suicide. These might occur in some cases, but they are not institutionalized or accepted as a way of life, but as evils that should be avoided. Where abortion or suicide takes place many rituals are carried out to expunge the evil from the root. "Africans have a profound religious sense, a sense of the sacred, of the existence of God the Creator and of a spiritual world. The reality of sin in its individual and social forms is very much present in the consciousness of these peoples, as is also the need for rites of purification and expiation."[39]

Many Africans, even those exposed to the Western way of life, still find it hard to deal with suicide or abortion in their family line. It is often seen as unmitigated evil that carries a bag-load of spiritual consequences. Life is sacred and no one should take his or her life or that of anyone else. Indeed, one of the greatest complexities of African societies today is that some of these values are being threatened by the social realities on the ground: war, ritual killings (of children, women, and the elderly), honor killings, ethnic cleansing, violence, coup d'etat, abortion, etc. These do not represent the face of Africa, but the dark sides of Africans who have lost their cultural bases and who in their homelessness have become swallowed up in greed, lust for power, selfishness, and godlessness.

4.3.3 *A Deeper Sense of the Meaning of Life and Happiness*

The kind of life that Africans lead today challenges the universal understanding of life. What is the meaning of life? What kind of definition do we give to the quality of life over bare existence? My faith as an African tells me that every life is priceless and invaluable; that every life is hidden in God as its source. At the same time, I feel a deep sadness when I look at the quality of life of some of my fellow Africans. How can we define the life of someone who has no water, road, education, food, house, and no future? How do you define the life of the Africans who are dying of HIV/AIDS and other preventable diseases? Many Africans live in abject poverty without anything to live for save the thin thread of hope buried in their hearts. I wonder how to define their kind of life and how much fulfillment they find in waking up and sleeping on a daily basis. There are many families in Africa that do not have anything to live for.

What meaning do we give to the life of the poor and wretched Africans of today? This is the very point where one should realize that the value of life may not after all be a matter of quality of life. The quality of life is no doubt important in Christian and African anthropology. Human dignity is insulted when human life is wasted or abused by poverty, inhumanities, and injustice. At the same time, human dignity shines through when people climb above their sufferings and pain and still remain human and happy.

When Nigeria was adjudged the happiest country in 2003, many people wondered whether happiness should not be found mainly in the richest countries of the world and not Nigeria. However, to some extent happiness relates more to *being* than to *having;* life is made not so much by *what we have*, as by *who we are*. At the same time, life could be more meaningful if people had the basic necessities, but these necessities of life are not in themselves absolutes. The question of the condition of life of Africans challenges the world to ask fundamental questions about the meaning and goal of life. It challenges the world about how people are treated and respected. Do we respect and treat people well, because they are useful to us? Do we judge the lives of people by the quality of the things they can produce? Do we see a human life as a gift in spite of the state of that life or as a gift because of the state and conditions of life? This is why a selfless love shown to a person dying of HIV/AIDS, to an elderly woman or man or to a stranger or a poor person without counting the cost is very heroic. The life of the African is a challenge to all the values that the world holds dear. It exposes the limits of the myopic conception of life in terms of productivity and excellence, which the world of the utilitarian calculus tends to create.

4.3.4 *Africans Value Marriage and Family Life*

The most important institution in Africa is the family. The family is everything. It is the window to society; it is the means through which one is integrated and identified in society. A man and a woman do not marry themselves; they are married into a family from two families. Marriage is not a private arrangement between two people who love and care for each other; it is a bond between two families and the wider community or tribal group. Marriage is not a union between two persons in Africa; it is more the community growing from within in the full blossoming of her children as they commit themselves to promote the life of the community through marriage. Two families are married when a man and a woman decide to join together in marriage. The question that is always asked in African societies when someone is successful or does something that is unacceptable is: "Whose son/daughter is he/she?" The question 'who are you?' is often answered by connecting the person's history to his family roots. Of Africans it could be said that 'like father like family, like daughter like family, etc.'

However, the most important aspect of family tradition in Africa is the role it plays in society and the bond between parents themselves and their children and the network of support and solidarity that arises from the extended family relation ties. It is the duty of the parents to teach and bring up their children and it is the duty and responsibility of the children to take care of their parents in their old age. A North American religious congregation, which specializes in ministry to the elderly in Nigeria, had to close down after few years of operation, because the Nigerian seniors did not want to live in the isolated walls of 'seniors residence', irrespective of the quality care they were provided with. Those seniors who went into these homes were constantly depressed and felt abandoned by their family members. Many of them had to return to their families. The care of the elderly is one of the most important advantages of the strong family ties in African families.

The extended family network provides an unlimited line of care and support for all members of the family, especially for the poor and the weak. It also helps in maintaining stability in the family line and in creating an environment of cultural identity and shared praxis of common ends. Many people have argued that this creates a chain of dependency, which hampers wealth creation and economic expansion, but I think this is a weak logic. The extended family represents the building up of a family through mutual support; it does not necessarily mean a chain of dependency. What happens in the family is that the wealthy members help the other members of the family to stand on their feet through mutual support, loans, advice, and even mentoring.

The extended family does not encourage idleness, but rather group-based initiative; it does not weaken individual growth, but enhances it through solidarity and encouragement. The extended family provides a home for orphans and destitute, and reorients children who are suffering emotionally as a result of the loss of either or both of their parents. The family tie in Africa is a great concept for evolving new forms of social organizations in the political and religious settings because it gives meaning to Africans and resonates at the very core of their being. Most African tribes can trace their origins to a primordial family. There is, as a result, a strong argument for African societies to seek a new way of seeing the tribes in Africa, as one large extended family that has various smaller family lines at various levels and to some larger or lesser degree. The image of the family is one that most Africans connect with, because it is the lens through which they see themselves and the world.

One major characteristic of African families is that they are life-affirming (liberating life from anything that threatens its full blossom), community-affirming (open to solidarity because of the intimate kinship spiritual tie that holds families together), and world-affirming (open to accept the stranger and offer him or her the intimate connection to the abundant life that flows from each family). The concept of family for the African is the image through which he or she sees the world. There is the need today to emphasize responsible parenting which entails that parents must only bring to earth children that they are able to bring up to reach their highest levels in life. At the same time, this should not be keyed into some Western-induced population control that has no respect for the family values of the Africans. African families are open to life and love. Indeed, the main reason for the existence of families is to generate new forms of love(human beings). The family is a center for the reception and transmission of tribal values; it is the birthplace of the new life for the tribe and for the creation of the 'new man.' Marriage is an institution, which is highly respected. Marriage preparations and rituals have so much symbolism in them that those who enter it see their new life as a covenant between themselves, their respective families, and their community. Marriage celebrations and childbirths are community events. The life of the community is inextricably tied to the life of new families and the life of new babies.

That is why most Africans are worried at the movement of Western societies with regard to children and families. This is more worrying when it has to do with the redefinition of marriage in order to accommodate same-sex relations. The issue of homosexual relations is one of those important questions which most religions have not properly addressed. More studies need to be done on same-sex orientation before drawing precipitate conclusions. Many so-called marginal groups are emerging from the 'closets' to assert their rights, because religious institutions have not carefully articulated them. This is also true of women and many poor people the world over. Institutions have a way of ignoring marginal groups, because their issues do not often have any tangential role in shaping the policies and programs of institutions.

However, any institution is to be judged not so much by what it claims as by what it does for the poor, the weak, and minorities. Any religious group or political establishment that promotes hatred towards homosexuals should examine its religious claims and is in need of conversion. At the same time, gay groups that are pushing for marriage as a right, need also to examine their understanding of human rights, marriage, and family life. Such advocacy goes beyond what reason and reality can validate. However, it is not enough to say that homosexuality is a condition, but exercising that condition is unacceptable as if to say that an egg is good as long as it does not hatch into a chick. Many non-homosexuals do not understand this orientation nor do they care to engage the issues in an open way. Africa will have to deal with this issue someday just as Africa has to deal with the condition and status of women, who to my mind, hold the key to Africa's future.

In order to assert their rights, many marginal groups have often gone overboard to push for what they know will be unacceptable to the wider society as they constitute a historico-cultural incubus. Change has to be gradual and systemic. Feminism as a movement is in a state of confusion today because of this kind of attitude. No one can actually give a clear position of what feminism is, because we now have different kinds of feminisms that hold mutually competing and contradictory positions. The same thing has happened to the issue of homosexual rights: there are a plethora of positions. One of the solutions to realizing equality of rights for the homosexual persons, which I think does not help the realization of a more open and accepting world for the homosexual person, is the idea of upgrading homosexual relations (which most Africans cannot imagine) to the level of marriage. I pastorally minister to homosexual persons here in Canada on a regular basis. I can testify that the conflict in the soul of some of our homosexual brothers and sisters is not helped by *imposing on some* of them 'a right' which they do not wish to exercise.

For an African, marriage and sexuality is all about life (physical and conjugal), community, and love. The idea of a marriage without children is a contradiction in term for Africans and so the idea of a homosexual marriage would be considered absurd and anti-life. The ordination of Gene Robinson, an openly gay man to the Anglican episcopate of New Hampshire in the United States, is threatening to tear the Anglican Communion apart. It is significant that it is the churches of the Global South who are trenchantly opposed to this, and threatening to pull out of the Anglican Communion entirely.[40]

It is the 'new Churches' in Africa and Asia that have been calling for renewal and revival of the Christian tradition, which is clearly threatened by contemporary cultural currents, especially in the Western world. The truth is that Christianity captures the imagination of the people of Africa.

African Christians find in Jesus Christ the message of salvation and Christianity remains a strong force of social and political change in Africa. At the same time, it has to enter into dialogue with Islam and African Traditional Religion for which values should shape society and govern the hearts and minds of the people. The original morality of the over 1,500 tribes in Africa, according to many African Traditional Religionists, is threatened by what they call the 'negative Western-Christian values' that have given rise to pornography, abortion, international prostitution (which flourishes in some Western 'Christian' countries), among other evils. The African Traditional Religionists also hold that Christian morality as practiced in the West and by African Christians is not superior to the African traditional ethos. Many of them do not see any reason to convert to Christianity.

4.3.5 Africans' Attitude to 'same-sex Marriage'

The key to understanding the African concept of morality with regard to sexual orientation is the basic communitarian concept of African societies. This communitarian spirit is based on family relationship. Building and strengthening of relationships in the community are predicated on the degree of stability in family lines with regard to procreation; child upbringing along the lines of the tribal mores; and the integration of children into the community by a gradual process of assimilation in and identification with the shared values of the community. In addition, sexual relation is only meaningful within the context of potentially life-generating marriage of man and woman. Any expression of sexual relation outside of this context is considered irresponsible living. This is the context within which sexual relation outside of marriage is considered. Marriage between a man and woman is the only way the African society perpetuates itself with regard to procreation, social stability, and a healthy moral life. The unmarried person without a family has no social identity. The African sense of family and sexual morality is different from the West. The question of gay rights or gay marriage has not become prominent in African religious and political discourse. Africans are fighting a battle for survival which takes precedence over every other thing in the continent. It is only when the Africans have food, water, electricity, healthcare, efficient and effective social services, education etc that they could address some other issues which have divided Western society. I do not however think these issues will be as divisive in Africa as they are in the West because of the absence of the liberal-conservative divide in Africa: a divide which tends to blur the perception of right and wrong in Western societies.

African society however must provide an adequate response to the problem of many unmarried professional women who are shunned by men in a male-dominated culture. These women do not find fulfillment in spite of their professional life because they are unmarried and have no children. There is also the problem of childless marriages, which are even seen in some parts of Africa as something close to a curse. To be a Catholic priest in Africa is particularly challenging, because an unmarried man in Africa is not a full man and is seen as 'lost,' because his generation ends with him. Some African theologians have called into question, this lifestyle, which within the African setting, makes a man incapable of being an ancestor, which analogously corresponds to the Christian idea of personal immortality.[41] Without a family, one cannot become an ancestor and without an ancestral connection one's life is considered wasted, because one did not write his autobiography in the concrete spiritual chain that connects one to life (children) and to eternity (ancestry). Chukwudum Okolo in this regard writes, "Clerical celibacy was part of the total package of Christian ideals imposed upon Africans by the early foreign missionaries. The traditional African priest enjoyed a totality of functions. He was a political leader, a respectable family man, an economist and even a lawyer. He had no qualms at all about associating himself with marriage, women and children. Celibacy in itself and as a distinct value was detestable. It was a waste of human value and worth as far as the African was concerned."[42]

However, it is interesting to note that some African clerics and lay members of Christ's faithful are often in the forefront in defense of the celibate life. Does this mean that priestly celibacy like Christianity is finding a new home in Africa? Does this mean an African cultural shift in the light of the new experience with Christianity and Catholicism? It is a complex situation and only time will tell where the pendulum swings. Interestingly, while Western churches have to deal sometimes with pedophile and homosexual priests, African churches wrestle sometimes with the very challenging situation that arise with regard to clerical sexual misdemeanors with the opposite sex. These are real challenges that demand objective response from the church and the clerics themselves, so that each person who offers his life totally to serve God and the church will find fulfillment through faithful and fruitful service.

There is no word for homosexuality in most African tribes. That does not mean that people with same-sex attractions are not found in African societies. However, traditional African societies have no place for homosexuals. Same-sex relations are seen as unnatural and objectionable in Africa, because they do not produce children (nature's gift to the world) nor do they, in the context of African communitarian spirit, help sustain the life of the community. "One is a human being only in the duality of man and woman, and this bipolarity generates the triad man-woman-child, which leads to full community. Against this background, a man-man or woman-woman relationship would not only be looked on as an egotistic isolationism which dares not take the step to full human existence; it also leads to a sexist discrimination against part of the human race that shows an unwillingness to accept the enrichment that comes from heterogeneity...even when there is no progeny...it is possible for the tripolarity to be supplied in another way..."[43]

In contemporary African societies, because of the high premium placed on children, some people who act out their same-sex orientation still marry the opposite sex to produce children, because sexuality in Africa has no meaning outside a life-orientation. Indeed, it would be right to conclude that the desire to produce children and perpetuate one's generation in African societies is so high that it 're-orients' the same-sex person to an end that goes beyond his/her sexual attraction: children through marriage to an opposite sex. Sexual orientation has not become an issue in Africa. This is because sexuality is expressed, properly speaking, within the context of marriage and in a family life of man, woman, and their children. Family life is the only way through which an African gains a true identity. Any other expression of sexuality outside of family life in Africa is considered a great moral evil and a threat to the communitarian life of society. In this context, African traditional morality agrees with Christian (Catholic) and Muslim morality.

4.3.6 *Africa's Respect for the Primacy of the Community*

Another gift that Africa offers to the world today is the primacy of community in the evolution of society. The human person is inherently social; we are co-made for each other. We live for each other and die for each other. The life of society is as important as the life of the individual, because the individual lives in time but the society is prior to the individual and outlives the individual. Thus, the idea of a person outside the life of society for Africans is unthinkable. This sense of community is a spiritual dynamic. The community is not the creation of anybody; it has a divine origin and carries the seed of survival over and above the choices of individuals. To wound the community spirit is to sin against God and to upset the temporal and spiritual equilibrium. Any evil acts like murder or dishonesty are interpreted as grave or minor to the extent that they wound the community spirit. In the sense of community, we find love and strength; we also see the supremacy of moral restraints to individual actions and choices: any action that any individual takes is predicated on how that action promotes or destroys the life of the community.

It is in this regard that many Africans wonder about the kind of cultural identity that African leaders manifest when they embezzle public funds; and when they deliberately destroy the common good for the sake of their selfish ambition and greed. The moral life of the African is opposed to relativism of any kind. We see our actions through the lenses of a higher truth, who is understood as God, and who rewards and punishes our actions according to how they promote or destroy creation. The authentic human person is the one who respects the values of the community and promotes the common good. Such a person is true to his or her God, upholds the spiritual and moral tradition of abundant life, which the ancestors lived and left behind for successive generations as basis for communal stability, growth and progress. He or she promotes the life of every member of the community, as well as the life of animals and the spiritual and cosmic world; he or she cares for and respects every member of the community and accommodates his or her neighbors' needs. This is a value, which the rest of the world could learn from Africa. This could save humanity from sinking into an era of limitless freedom characterized by the struggle over personal choices and the perception of freedom as the power to do whatever one wants without any moral restraints. A true sense of community radicalizes our settled prejudices and changes our perception of people and their good vis-à-vis our own.

AN APPEAL FOR AFRICA

Peace and prosperity, in fact, are goods which belong to the whole human race: it is not possible to enjoy them in a proper and lasting way if they are achieved and maintained at the cost of other peoples and nations, by violating their rights or excluding them from sources of well-being......It will be necessary to abandon a mentality in which the poor—as individuals and as peoples—are considered a burden, as irksome intruders trying to consume what others have produced. The poor ask for the right to share in enjoying material goods and to make good use of their capacity to work, thus creating a world that is more just and prosperous for all. The advancement of the poor constitutes a great opportunity for the moral, cultural and even economic growth for all humanity. - Pope John Paul II, ***Centesimus Annus***, 27, 28.

The present face of the world flashes diverging rays to many people. The world today longs for an organic synthesis. We live at a time of contradictions: we have so much knowledge but little wisdom about the meaning of love and life. We claim to have conquered nature, but we have not conquered the selfish instinct that has given rise to war, hatred, violence, and suppression of the weakest individuals and nations of the world. We live in the midst of great and immense wealth but we lack the riches of grace, generosity, and goodness. We live in a world of religious assertions of great proportions, but we see little fruits of religion in many of those who profess to know and worship God. We have enormous prosperity, but little happiness and peace in our hearts.

The world needs liberation from man-made evils. These evils have made it impossible for men and women to experience the finest qualities of the human person, the riches of nature and the world, and authentic human development. There is significant unease in many quarters of the world. The euphoria of a Golden Age, which was presaged by the New Millennium is becoming like a fleeting cloud that recedes as one approaches the margins of the horizon. Many positive and apocalyptic projections of a new world at the dawn of this Millennium are turning out to be mere human contrivances. We are gradually falling into the age-encrusted well of selfishness, nationalism, fundamentalism, and group profiling.

Many people today worry about their future and the direction of the world. This explains the present global fear brought about by the cumulus of terrorism that hangs over the global community since the September 11, 2001 attacks on the World Trade Center and the Pentagon. The pain and anguish suffered by the victims and those who were bereaved is unimaginable. It was by all calculation, the height of human wickedness and an uncontrolled capacity for evil. However, the twin towers represented the glories of the capitalist era, and the rising incense that fills the eerie altars of the new gods of technology and science that control our human world. They were also double signs of a dying world that subsisted on the shaky plains of materialism and exaggerated individualism.

After the fall of communism, many people, especially in the West, gloried in the ethical triumph and superiority of capitalism. The victory of capitalism does not, however, mean that it is a perfect system. Capitalism seeks to defeat communism on the level of pure materialism, by showing that a free market economy can help achieve greater happiness and liberty for humanity. However, like communism, capitalism excludes any spiritual values. "In reality, while on the one hand it is true that this social model shows the failure of Marxism to contribute to a humane and better society, on the other hand, insofar as it denies an autonomous existence and value to morality, law, culture, and religion, it agrees with Marxism, in the sense that it totally reduces the human person to the sphere of economics and the satisfaction of material needs."[1]

Capitalism, as it is practiced in most of the world, has no human face. It is the new idol that must be dismantled for the people of our day to live fully. According to Erich Fromm, modern capitalist societies suffer from a pervasive alienation or idolatry, which is expressed in consumerism. He argues that modern Western societies are driven by the desire to 'have more' than 'to be.' The human person can be a slave even without being in chains and one can be free even while being in chains. The difference is between one's fundamental orientations in life. The desires and thoughts for possession and consumption which modern society has imposed on people of our times, have removed external chains and put them inside and around the hearts of men and women. These imprison people more thoroughly by the forces of greed, irrational passion, rivalry, desire for fame, possessions, and control—idols that make it impossible for people to attain the great heights of love and compassion. "It is a striving that is rooted in the ambiguity of man's existence and that has the aim of finding answer to the uncertainty of life by transforming a person, an institution, an idea into an absolute, i.e., into an idol by the submission to which the illusion of certainty is created."[2]

Competition for profit and wealth creation for the strong nations and companies of the world, have become blind to the millions of people who have been permanently destroyed because of capitalism's insensitive bites. Protectionism has become a replacement for solidarity. Many poor countries of the world, as a result, will have to survive by eating the crumbs that fall from the tables of the rich. We need to pull down the idols of capitalism scattered all over the world. These idols make it possible for the lives of millions of people to be governed by a few companies and national interests. These, out of their greed inflict pain and suffering on millions of people around the world. According to the document, *There are Alternatives to Globalization*, prepared by the Justice, Peace and Creation Team of the World Council of Churches:

- The top three billionaires in the world hold asserts worth more than the combined GNP of all 48 least developed countries, with their population of some 600 million.
- The assets of the 200 richest people (over US$1 Trillion) are higher than the combined income of 41% of the world's people.
- The income gap between a fifth of the population in the world's richest countries and a fifth in the poorest is growing at an ever-increasing rate. It took 30 years for the ratio to double from 30 to 1 in 1960, to 60 to 1 in 1990, but it jumped up to 74 to 1 in 1997. The wealth gap is also widening in the rich countries too.
- About 1.5 billion people live in absolute poverty at the beginning of the new millennium. It would take just 55% of the wealth of the richest 225 people in the world to provide food, shelter, basic health care, and education to every one in the world who lacks access to these basic needs.
- Just 100 trans-national corporations based in the highly industrialized countries are the driving force for economic globalization. Of all trade 70% takes place within and between them. They generate 80% of foreign direct investment and own one fifth of all foreign-owned assets; however, they employ less than 3% of the world's labor force.

Capitalism is banishing God from Western society and reconfiguring the moral and religious plain along the lines of economics and exaggerated self-interest. What makes sense today is money; what is moral is what is economic. The truth is that money and wealth are only temporal things; they inherently have a limit, which is not easily seen or acknowledged in the advertisement and entertainment industries. The principles of capitalism are not founded on sound religious ethical principles that make provisions for the weak and the powerless, who cannot compete or who lose out in competition. Capitalism has assumed a life of its own in the world. It has also become a god that creates democracy, confers freedom on peoples and nations, relegates religion to private life, and divides nations according to how they have been lifted or lowered in the economic calculus of this merciless god.

The free market will not save the lives of millions who are dying of poverty and suffering in many parts of the world especially in Africa. The end result of the free market should constantly be scrutinized to see that it meets the requirements of the common good. Indeed, the international free market regime that has elevated private property and capital over the human person does not meet the requirements of natural law, social justice, and the universal common good. Africa is one continent that is being suffocated in the heat of capitalism. Her life and history within the last four centuries have been defined by the pain brought upon her by capitalism. This destruction is ongoing through privatization of public services, the contagion of globalization, the debt burden, and trade restrictions among others. This makes even fellow Africans allies in the conspiracy of destruction of the ordinary people and their national wealth. Many Africans believe that the traditional African sense of community has some elements of capitalism because it allows for competition. However, it has a deep sense of solidarity, communalism, social conscience, and morality that saves people from the blunt edges of capitalism. Capitalism is the mother of corruption in Africa and it is the father that sired the negative attitude of distancing on the part of the Western world to the plight of Africa. The truth is that helping Africa does not make sense in the capitalist calculation of the hawks and priests of the free market economic god in the industrialized world. This is because such help and generosity do not immediately translate into any financial profit.

It is a shame, for instance, that some Western companies supported by their national governments, will supply weapons of war to rebel groups in Africa and then cry out against the killings at the same time. How did the rebels in most African countries get their weapons and bombs, which are not made in Africa? The obnoxious trade in diamonds between Sierra Leone, Liberia, and some Western companies was the main stay for the weaponization of sub-Saharan rebel groups in places like Liberia and Sierra Leone. The people of Rwanda and Darfur would have been saved from self-destruction if they had oil like Iraq or if they were strategically positioned like Pakistan or Afghanistan.

Out of sheer economic interest, many Western countries would look the other way when corrupt African leaders siphon millions from their national treasury and invest them in Western banks. What sense does it make giving loans to African countries, which are deposited in banks outside Africa by corrupt African leaders? The money is given to the African countries, invested in foreign banks while the ordinary people in Africa suffer from all kinds of marginalization, because the debts are being repaid from loans that were never used to help the poor. How many Africans can explain when and why their countries are in odious debt today? When were these loans taken? What did the governments of Africa do with them?

The debt burden, which hangs over African nations, has remained one of the greatest obstacles to any meaningful economic development in Africa. Sub-Saharan Africa's debt represents 180% of exports; debt-servicing drains 12-13% of export receipts on average. The failure of most Western nations to forgive these debts is only a sign of the destructive nature of unbridled capitalism. These debts cannot bring any real boost to the economies of the Western countries if they were repaid—they would not make any tangential bearing on the GDP of Western countries—while servicing them alone is squeezing Africa of over 71% of her GDP! Africa's debt burden is unsustainable given the fact that it has grown from 30.7% of Africa's GNP in 1980 to 82.8% in 1994.[3] Most of the African countries are bankrupt and cannot kick start any kind of development initiatives without some major commitment of aid from international agencies and governments. Unfortunately, the official development assistance (ODA) from most of the G-8 countries to Africa averages a little above 0.30% of their GDP and has gone down in the 1990s from $28.6 billion to $16.4 billion a year. If capitalism, as it is conceived and practiced today, continues to set the tone for the process of world history, we risk destroying our species in the blaze of competition. Those most likely to suffer from brazen competition are the poor, vulnerable, powerless, and defenseless people all over the world, the majority of whom live in Africa. Most of them are dying everyday because their governments daily pay $100 million to Western creditors in a world where an elite of fewer than a billion people controls 80% of humanity's wealth.[4]

We already see signs of this emerging scenario in the gap between the rich and poor nations, in the chasm between the rich and the poor people in many industrialized countries, in broken homes and broken lives, and in growing alienation, depression, and other forms of mental sickness, and unease among the young people in industrialized capitalist societies. The human person is more than a mere possessor of wealth and purchaser of goods and services. We are all witnessing the failure of wealth to bring peace and reduce violence the world over. There is already a new breed of foot soldiers that are carrying out terrorist activities all over the world, because they hate capitalism and its ethical downside that has spread poverty and division around the world and within societies, built and sustained by economic and political differences, especially in the Muslim world.

One thing is sure, capitalism has no limit in its destructive spread, but the human person has a limit. This limit is set by an ultimate desire in each person's heart, which can never be fully satisfied by material goods alone. There is always the need for foundations to our actions, which confer creative meaning on our endeavors. We need to constantly ask the question about our origin and destiny: What are we doing here on earth? What is the reason for our being together on this planet? The true quest for a global family can only start with a new search for God and a renewed and sharpened ethical sense which will give us a sense of global responsibility, founded on our mutually shared beliefs, concerns, joys, and burdens.

The search for God is the search for our true home and our true human family, which has a divine origin and a transcendent destiny. Human homelessness can only be met by divine homeliness. It makes sense to see the world through the eyes of faith and not through the eyes of economics; both, however, are not mutually exclusive. Faith gives birth to a true sense of purpose and confers meaning on economics. It limits the rough edges of aggressive competition through an appeal to love and justice, which are more meaningful than the power of possession and domination. At the same time, faith and good works have the capacity of widening the hearts of people and nations, to see beyond the present difficulties the glories of a new future, made possible if only we are strong enough to overcome our prejudices and fears. Faith gives birth to hope and both stem from love: love for God, love for nature, and love for the whole of humanity.

Historically, neo-liberal capitalism arrived with the triumph of science, technology, industrialization, and the conquest of nature by a liberated human mind. The West continued to grow in the temporal sphere with the unconscious loss of the truth that humanity, like the human body, must breathe with the double lungs of the divine and the worldly—the fine marriage of which, in the Incarnation, stands for all time as a message to be adhered to and a mission to be undertaken.

The fall of the twin towers is a metaphor of the failure of the works of human hands to defend men and women. Our world stands and falls on the kind of values that we embody. Our values today are not enduring values. We live in a world presently built and sustained by historical and ongoing injustices. It is a world built on self-serving logic. It is a world where evil of all shades and colors are burgeoning in the name of institutional religions; where yesterday's evil has become tomorrow's ideals; where terrorist acts are being perpetrated in the name of God. In the past, peoples and nations fought wars because they did not understand each other and so had to destroy each other to know what each had in stock. Today, wars are waged and human lives destroyed in droves for economic purposes to serve the interest of a few developed nations. Many Iraqis would no doubt be wondering whether liberty has a human face; while the Blacks and the 'poorest poor of the land' in New Orleans and surrounding Gulf states of the United States of America will be wondering whether the American dream has been swept away by Hurricanes Katrina and Rita. We need some new lenses of perception to see reality in its full length and breadth. We need also to begin to adhere or rather inhere in the Truth which alone can save us collectively and salve the wounds in the hearts of our numerous brothers and sisters who suffer in both body and soul.

Many Africans are asking for world attention. They wonder why their continent has been ignored for so long. As a child, I often wondered why the Irish priest who wedded my parents and constantly visited our family looked so different and 'spoke with the nose.' I never understood any word that he spoke even when he tried to speak our native language. The question comes constantly to my mind, even today: Why are we so different and why can we not understand and encounter each other as brothers and sisters? Many of us were thrilled by the Irish priest's generosity; he always had some candies to give us whenever we came around to clean the rectory and to provide sundry services. That simple act of his shaped my mind that the world is a center of varieties, which are complementary and mutually sustaining. The positive exchanges between peoples, races, and nations can only bring about a better world. The problem is that we do not want to share; we lack the courage to believe in the inherent capacity of our humanity to recover again her lost sense of meaning and direction.

The world has enough for the needs of all, as Gandhi says, but not enough for our greed. Unfortunately, many Africans continue to wonder why the world is so silent about the condition of Africa and why greed should be preferred above human needs. Many Africans ask whether there are still men and women of good will in the world who believe in Africa. Africans are also asking what the leadership in Africa is doing to break the cycle of poverty and pain in the continent. I cannot forget one man who at a prayer meeting I held at Christmas (2003) in Eastern Nigeria addressed God as follows: *"God, we your people in this part of the world are living through the skin of our teeth; we scrape a living and we rise and wake without knowing the difference sometimes...Lord our night is too long and our day too dark..."* I cannot explain why the Africans are suffering so terribly. I do not find any religious ground for the suffering nor do I think that the God that we serve can bear to watch the unmitigated disaster and wretchedness of life in Africa. Many of the ordinary people in Africa constantly wonder whether God is dead in Africa or whether God is dead in the hearts of many people in the industrialized world that they have become insensitive to human pain.

There are real challenges facing Africa. However, they cannot be fully addressed by African countries alone because they affect the structures of African societies and, as we have pointed out, have much to do with external forces. I believe that human and cultural development is the most essential challenge facing Africa today. The human capital is low in Africa, because of the absence of integral education; hence, the immense material resources of the continent are being under-utilized. The real wealth of Africa can only be found when her human potential is discovered, enhanced, and optimized. The structures of African society have to be addressed, because as they stand today, they represent an unjust incubus that systematically destroys the people and nations of Africa.

The prospects of a failed African project, portends danger to the whole world. Until recently, many people in the West, felt that failed states in most parts of the world, were no problem to other people outside their region. However, in the emerging world of today, failed states are the greatest threats to world peace and security. Usama Bin Laden was able to find a nest in Afghanistan, because it was a failed state after the withdrawal of the Russians. African countries may be the next haven for terrorists, drug cartels, and other criminals who can only flourish in lawless societies. Africa needs well-functioning societies for the good of the Africans themselves and the world community. However, "behind every well-functioning democracy lie not just constitutions and institutions but a series of unwritten rules: that the army does not seize power, that the courts are politically neutral, that the losers in elections do no take to the hills, that certain levels of social justice will be preserved, that some balance among different communities will be preserved, that those in power will govern (up to a point) for the good of the country and will keep personal enrichment within bounds."[5] Africa's dream for a well-ordered society can be achieved, not through any ready-made democratic baggage

315

from the West, but through a mutually acceptable system of government, which the respective African countries have to fashion, based on their particular ethnic composition and historical challenges. Democracy has to be achieved by Africans, not given from outside Africa.

Africa is a permanent sore on the conscience of the world today. It questions any claim to a common humanity and points to a collapsing compassion platform in our world. I believe that the success of the African project will bring immense goodness and prosperity to the whole world. It would also restore the human face which the world once had, when the first man and woman emerged from the womb of the Eternal One. Beyond the shadows of the present gloom lies the true face of Africa. May this face shine once more with the splendor and beauty of goodness, happiness, fulfillment and peace for all God's children on this potentially great continent.

This is my hope, my desire and my prayer.

NOTES

INTRODUCTION

Ali Mazuri, *Africa's International Relations* (London: Heinemann Educational Books, 1977).

Anita Cheikh Diop, *The African Origin of Civilization*, (trans) Mercer Cook (ed), (Chicago, Illinois: Lawrence Hill Books, 1974).

Aylward Shorter, *African Culture: An Overview* (Nairobi: Paulines Publications Africa, 1998)

Eddy Maloka (ed), *Africa's Development Thinking Since Independence: A Reader* (Pretoria: Africa Institute of South Africa, 2004).

John S. Mbiti, *African Religions and Philosophy* (Nairobi: East African Educational Publishers, 1999).

Hans Kung (ed), *Yes to a Global Ethic* (New York: The Continuum Publishing Company, 1996).

Joseph Conrad, *Heart of Darkness* (London: Penguin Books, 2000).

Jared Diamond, *Guns, Germs, and Steel, The Fate of Human Societies* (New York: W. W. Norton and Company, 1999)

Martin Heidegger, *Basic Writings*, David Farrell Krell (ed), (New York: Harper Collins Publishers, 1993).

Michael Novak, *The Universal Hunger for Liberty, Why the Clash of Civilization is not Inevitable* (New York: Basic Books, 2004).

Claude Ake, *Is Africa Democratizing?* (Port Harcourt: Center for Advanced Social Sciences, 1996).

Francis Fukuyama, *The End of History and the Last Man* (New York: HarperCollins Publishers, 2002).

Samuel P. Huntington, *The Clash of Civilizations and the Remaking of World Order* (New York: Touchstone, 1997).

Frederick G. Weiss (ed), *Hegel: The Essential Writings* (New York: Harper Torchbooks, 1974).

George. W. F. Hegel, *The Philosophy of History*, (trans) J. Sibree (New York: Wiley Book Co., 1990).

Gustavo Gutierrez, *A Theology of Liberation* (New York: Orbis Books, 1973).

Frederick Buell, *From Apocalypse to Way of Life* (New York: Routledge, 2003).

Robert Kaplan, *The Coming Anarchy* (New York: Vintage Books, 2001).

Rubem A. Alves, *A Theology of Human Hope* (St. Meinrad, Indiana: Abbey Press, 1972).

317

Stephen Lewis, *Race Against Time* (Toronto: House of Anansi Press, Inc., 2005).

Teilhard de Chardin, *The Phenomenon of Man* (London: Fontana Books, 1969).

Unblurring the Vision, An Assessment of the New Partnership for Africa's Development by South African Churches, drafted by the Justice and Peace Department of the Southern African Catholic Bishops' Conference, 2002.

CHAPTER ONE: THE SHADOWS OF AFRICA

[1] See Michael Paul Gallagher, *Clashing Symbols, An Introduction to Faith and Culture* (London: Darton, Longman and Todd Ltd, 2003), 96. See also Rowan Williams, *Lost Icon: Reflections on Cultural Bereavement* (Edinburgh: T. & T. Clark. 2000).

[2] Samuel P. Huntington, *The Clash of Civilizations and the Remaking of World Order* (New York: Touchstone, 1997), 21.

[3] Roger Scruton, *An Intelligent Person's Guide to Modern Culture* (South Bend, Indiana: St. Augustine's Press, 2000),2.

[4] Michael Novak, *The Universal Hunger for Liberty Why the Clash of Civilizations is not Inevitable* (New York: Basic Books, 2004, XIII). Western commentators are divided on whether Islam is amenable to pluralism. However, a Muslim commentator Ziauddin Sardar has argued that modernization in Islam does not necessarily need to be Western. Commenting on the modernization of Islam in Turkey by Ataturk he argues, *"Ataturk presented secularism as a theology of salvation. Coming to terms with the 'European miracle' required embracing every component of Europe's ideology: being modern meant being exactly like Europeans. Imitation was duplicated in minute detail, up to and including how one dressed and behaved. He replaced Ottoman history based on religious community with a 'national history' he hoped would replicate the history of the West. In a real sense, Kemalism internalized how the West conventionally represented Islam: as the darker, degenerate opposite of the Christian and secular West. He represented Islam as 'the Orient' of the West suffused with all the ills conventionally ascribed to it, from being ignorant and stupid to inferior, ugly and fanatic."*(See *Desperately Seeking Paradise*, London: Granta Books, 2005, 261). Against this position, some Western commentators still believe that Islam has to be changed by Westerners or rather that the democratic tradition of the West is the only measuring rod that can be used to assess the presence of liberal civil rights in the Muslim world. Robin Wright, for instance, writes, *"As Islamist sentiment grows, policy makers in the West face two stark*

*alternatives: One is to use this important juncture–when interest in both democracy and Islam is expanding–to press Muslim-dominated countries on political pluralism, to encourage action that will include rather than exclude troubled populations, and then to accept the results of free and fair elections even if Islamist parties gain significant votes." (**Sacred Rage, The Wrath of Militant Islam,** New York: Touchstone, 2001), 288. Some others like Sam Harris will argue that, "It is clear that Muslims hate the West in the very terms of their faith and that the Koran mandates such hatred. It is widely claimed by 'moderate' Muslims that the Koran mandates nothing of the kind and that Islam is a 'religion of peace'. But one need only to read the Koran itself to see that this is untrue"* (see **The End of Faith, Religion, Terror and the Future of Reason,** New York: W.W. Norton & Company, 2004, 31). What is important is that Muslims themselves become the agent for the transformation of their religion to respond to the new challenges in the historical process. This is particularly important in Africa where there is a serious crisis of identity. However, given the fact that all the terrorist attacks in this new century have been traced to radical Muslim fundamentalists, Muslims must give the world the reason to see once again the true face of Islam.

[5] Georges Bernanos, **Le Chemin de la Croix des Ames** (Paris: Gallimard, 1948), 18.

[6] See Thomas E. Woods, **How the Catholic Church Built Western Civilization** (Washington, DC: Regnery Publishing Inc., 2005). His focus is on the contribution of the Catholic Church to Western civilization, but one could say that many other Christian denominations since the Reformation also made great contributions to the birth of Western civilization as we know it today. In page one of his book, Woods argues, *"The story of Catholicism, as far as they know, is one of ignorance, repression, and stagnation. That Western civilization stands indebted to the Church for the university system, charitable work, international law, the sciences, important legal principles, and much else besides has not exactly been impressed upon them with terrific zeal. Western civilization owes far more to the Catholic Church than most people-Catholics included-often realize. The Church, in fact, built Western civilization."*

[7] Christopher Dawson, "The Failure of Liberalism" in **The Wisdom of Catholicism,** Anton C. Pegis (ed), (New York: Random House, 1949), 862.

[8] Joseph Ratzinger, "Europe in the Crisis of Cultures" in **Communio International Catholic Quarterly,** Vol XXXII, no. 2, Summer 2005, 352-353.

[9] Lamin Sanneh, **Whose Religion is Christianity?** (Grand Rapids, Michigan: Wm. B. Eerdmans Publishing Co., 2003), 8-11.

[10] Henry Kissinger, *Years of Renewal* (New York: Simon & Schuster, 1999), 795.

[11] Michael Novak, *The Universal Hunger for Liberty, Why the Clash of Civilization is not Inevitable* (New York: Basic Gooks, 2004), 186.

[12] Matthew Hassan Kukah, *Democracy and Civil Society in Nigeria* (Ibadan: Spectrum Books Limited, 1999), 61-62.

[13] Robert Kaplan, *The Coming Anarchy* (New York: Vintage Books, 2000), 63-68.

[14] Cf. Gabriel Warburg, *Islam, Sectarianism and Politics in Sudan since the Mahdiyya* (Madison, Wisconsin: The University of Wisconsin Press, 2003), 224-225.

[15] Ibid., 66.

[16] Olufemi Taiwo, "Exorcising Hegel's Ghost: Africa's Challenge to Philosophy" in *African Studies Quarterly*, the Online Journal for African Studies, www.africa.ufl.edu/asq/vl/4/2.htm.

[17] Ibid.,

[18] Quoted in Ibid.,

[19] Jacqueline Kasun, *The War Against Population* (San Francisco: Ignatius Press, 1999).

[20] Ibid., 293-294.

[21] Romeo Dellaire, *Shake Hands with the Devil* (Toronto: Random House Canada, 2003), xvii.

[22] Quoted in Walter Rodney, *How Europe Underdeveloped Africa* (London: Bogle-L' Ouverture Publications, 1986), 28.

[23] William E. B. Dubois, *Dusk of Dawn* (New York: Harcourt, Bruce and World Inc., 1970), 129.

[24] Chinweizu, *The West and the Rest of Us* (Lagos: Nok Publications Ltd., 1998) and Walter Rodney, op cit.

[25] Basil Davidson, *The African Slave Trade* (Atlanta: Atlantic Little Brown Books, 1961), 13.

[26] See Assunta Tagliaferri, *Africa Needs Witnesses* (Verona: Unitary Missionary Centre UMC Foundations, 2004).

[27] Howard French, *A Continent for the Taking* (New York: Alfred A. Knopf, 2004), 24.

[28] Quoted in Augustine Nebechukwu, "Third World Theology and the Recovery of African Identity" in *Journal of Inculturation Theology*, Catholic Institute of West Africa, April 1995, Vol. 2, No. 1, 20.

[29] Bénézet Bujo, *The Ethical Dimension of Community*, (trans) Cecelia Namulondo Ngana (Nairobi: Paulines Publications Africa, 1998), 135.

[30] I have relied on this account of slavery in Africa on the well documented findings of Joseph. C. Anene. "Slavery and the Slave Trade" in *Africa in*

the Nineteenth and Twentieth Centuries, Joseph C. Anene & Godfrey N. Brown (eds), (Ibadan: Ibadan University Press, 1967).

[31] Aristotle, *The Politics*, (trans) F. A. Sinclair (London: Penguin Books, 1976), 36.

[32] Plato, *The Republic*, (trans) D. Lec (London: Penguin Books, 1979), 257.

[33] Anene & Brown, op cit, 97.

[34] See Giles Milton, *White Gold* (London: Hodder and Stoughton, 2005). I have not been able to critically review this book to find out the validity of its claims and sources of the information contained therein. Its attempt to mitigate the horrors of the Trans-Atlantic slave trade by claiming that North Africans also enslaved Europeans is very bold, but patently unconvincing. Parenthetically, we could be doing a merely historical recidivism by trying to justify one evil in a certain epoch with another evil in another. Evil can never be justified; it can only be condemned and extirpated as soon as it is discovered.

[35] Ali Mazrui, *The African Condition* (London: Cambridge University Press, 1980), 29-30.

[36] Basil Davidson, 156.

[37] Ibid., 101.

[38] Anene & Brown, 108-109.

[39] Daniel A. Offiong, *Imperialism and Dependency* (Enugu: Fourth Dimension, 1980), 87.

[40] Ottobah Cuguano, *Thoughts and Sentiments on the Evil of Slavery* (London: Davidson of Pall Hall, 1969), 91.

[41] Erich Fromm, *The Anatomy of Human Destructiveness* (New York: An Owl Book, 1992), 226, 334.

[42] Kevin Shillington, *History of Africa* (New York: St Martin's Press, 1995), 180.

[43] G. T. Stride & C. Ifeka, *Peoples and Empires of West Africa* (Lagos: Thomas and Nelson Nigeria Ltd, 1978), 213.

[44] Basil Davidson, 16.

[45] Shillington, 176.

[46] Obafemi Awolowo, *The Problems of Africa* (London: Macmillan Education Ltd, 1985), 21.

[47] Ali Mazrui, *The Africans, A Triple Heritage* (Toronto: Little, Brown and Company, 1986), 160.

[48] Walter Rodney, 104.

[49] The most important document from the Catholic Church against slavery was written by Pope Leo XIII on May 5, 1888. Titled, *In Plurimus, On the Abolition of Slavery*, was written after the abolition of slavery and

therefore was not directly influential in the abolition of the Trans-Atlantic Slave Trade. What is important in this document is that it presents a clear condemnation of the evil of slavery; a teaching which was not new but was always the teaching of Jesus, which should have been brought to bear on the evil act of the enslavement of Blacks for over four centuries. The document argues that slavery is not a natural condition (no one is made a slave by God but it is their fellow human beings who make them slaves), the division of people into slaves and masters is the result of human sin; the abolition of slavery is the necessary step to take in the continuing process of the redemption of the human race, which Jesus came to accomplish on earth. Pope Leo XIII writes, "From the first sin came all evils, and specially this perversity, that there were men who, forgetful of the original brotherhood of the race, instead of seeking, as they should naturally have done, to promote mutual kindness and mutual respect, following their evil desires began to think of other men as their inferiors and to hold them as cattle born for the yoke. In this way, through an absolute forgetfulness of our common nature, and of human dignity, and the likeness of God stamped upon us all, it came to pass that in the contentions and wars which then broke out, those were the stronger and reduced the conquered into slavery; so that mankind, though of the same race became divided into two sections, the conquered slaves and their victorious masters." Pope Leo XIII also quotes Pope St. Gregory the Great who condemned slavery in unmistakable terms when he wrote, "Since our Redeemer, the Author of all life, deigned to take human flesh, that by the power of his God hood the chains by which we were held in bondage being broken, He might restore us to our first state of liberty, it is most fitting that men by the concession of manumission should restore to the freedom in which they were born those whom nature sent free into the world, but who have been condemned to the yoke of slavery by the laws of nations." See Etienne Gilson (ed), *The Church Speaks to the Modern World, The Social Teachings of Leo XIII* (New York: Image Books, 1957), 291-295. Bénézet Bujo writes with regard to the visit of Pope John Paul II in February 1992 to the notorious slave island of Goree in order to beg Africa's forgiveness in the name of Christianity and humanity for the crime of slave trade. The Pope said during his visit, "The slave-trade is a tragedy of a civilization that called itself Christian. And deep causes of this human drama, of this tragedy, can be found in all of us, in our human nature, in sin. I have come here to pay homage to all the unknown victims of this crime, whose names and number can never be known." See Bénézet Bujo, *African Theology in its Social Context*, (New York: Orbis Books, 1992), 9.

[50] Jean Jacques Rosseau, *The Social Contract*, (trans) M. Granston (London: Penguin Books, 1982), 104.

[51] John Locke, "Second Treatise on Civil Government" in *Political and Social Philosophy*, J. Charles King and James A. Mcgilvray (eds), (New York: Mcgrow-Hill Books Co., 1973), 110.

[52] Quoted in Omafume Onoge, *The Democratic Imperative in Africa* (Jos: African Centre for Democratic Governance, 1998), 18.

[53] John E. Flint, "Chartered Companies and the Scramble for Africa" in *Africa in the Nineteenth and Twentieth Centuries*, Joseph C. Anene & Godfrey N. Brown (eds), (Ibadan University Press, 1970), 111.

[54] I have relied on John E. Flint's research and analysis of the scramble for Africa for this part of the work. His is perhaps the most penetrating I have found on the scramble and partition of Africa.

[55] Geoffery Hunt, "Antonio Labriola's Philosophy and Italian Colonialism in Africa" in *Philosophy in Africa*, P. O. Bodunrin (ed), (University of Ife Press, 1985), 132.

[56] Quoted in Adam Hochschild, *King Leopold's Ghost* (New York: Mariner Books edition, 1999), 78.

[57] Martin Meredith, *The Fate of Africa, From Hope of Freedom to the Heart of Despair* (New York: Public Affairs, 2005), 1.

[58] Cf. Stuart Mill, On Liberty in *Essays on Politics and Culture* (New York: Doubleday, 1962).

[59] Aimé Césaire, *Discourse on Colonialism*, (trans) John Pinkham (New York: Monthly Press Review, 2000), 39.

[60] Richard Onwuanibe, *A Critique of Revolutionary Humanism: Fanon* (Missouri: Warren H. Green Inc. 1983), 47.

[61] Walter Rodnery, 245-246.

[62] See Martin Meredith, *The Fate of Africa, From Hopes of Freedom to the Heart of Despair*, 3.

[63] John E. Flint, 112.

[64] Quoted in Ali Mazrui, *Cultural Forces in World Politics* (London: James Currey Ltd., 1990), 122.

[65] Aimé Césaire, 39.

[66] Olufemi A. Akinola, "The Colonial Heritage and Modern Constitutionalism in Africa" in *African Traditional Political Thought and Institutions*, John A. A. Ayoade and Adigun A. B. Agbaje (eds), (Lagos: Centre for Black and African Arts and Civilization, 1989), 264.

[67] Frantz Fanon, *The Wretched of the Earth* (London: Penguin Books, 1983), 32.

[68] Godwin Sogolo, *Foundations of African Philosophy* (Ibadan University Press, 1992), 198.

[69] Ibid., 266.

[70] Fredrick Lugard, *The Dual Mandate in British Tropical Africa* (London: William Blackwood & Sons, 1923), 917.

[71] Cf. Basil Davidson, *The Black Man's Burden* (Lagos: Spectrum Books Limited, 1993), 218.

[72] Ibid., 219.

[73] Andrew H. Foote, "Africa in the American Flag" in *Azikiwe and the African Revolution*, Olisa & Clark (eds), (Onitsha: Africana Fep Pub. Ltd, 1989), 54.

[74] K. B. C. Onwubiko, *School Certificate History of West Africa Book One*, (Onitsha: African Educational Pub., 1973), 259.

[75] Mokwugo Okoye, *The Growth of Nations* (Enugu: Fourth Dimension Publishers, 1978), 33.

[76] Quoted in Anya O. Anya, *Re-inventing Nigeria for the 21st Century* (Lagos: Obafemi Awolowo Foundation, 1996), 5.

[77] Paulo Freire, *Pedagogy of the Oppressed*, (trans) Myra Bergman Ramos (New York: The Seabury Press, 1968), 150-151.

[78] Basil Davidson, 47.

[79] Frantz Fanon, *Towards the African Revolution* (New York: Monthly Reviews Press, 1967), 33.

[80] K. B. C. Onwubiko, 274.

[81] Ali Mazrui, *Africa's International Relations* (London: Heinemann Educational Books, 1977), 89.

[82] Quoted in Walbert Buhlmann, *The Missions on Trial* (Slough: St Paul Publications, 1978), 45.

[83] Ibid., 27.

[84] Albert de Jong, "Church, Colonialism and Nationalism in Tanzania" in *Ethnicity: Blessing or Curse*, Albert de Jong (ed), (Nairobi: Paulines Publications Africa, 1999), 76-77.

[85] Chinweizu, 350.

[86] D. Offiong, 101.

[87] Frantz Fanon, 31.

[88] Author Nwankwo, *African Dictators* (Enugu: Fourth Dimension Publishers, 1990), 14.

[89] Richard Joseph, *Democracy and Prebendal Politics in Nigeria* (Ibadan: Spectrum Books Limited, 1999), 8.

[90] L. Adele Jinandu, *Fanon: In Search of the African Revolution* (Enugu: Fourth Dimension Publishers, 1980), 35.

[91] Quoted in Minoque & Molloy (eds), *African Aims and Attitude* (London: Cambridge University Press, 1974), 21.

[92] Cf. Claude Ake, *Democracy and Development in Africa* (Washington: The Brookings Institution, 1996), 2.

[93] Osita Eze, *Human Rights in Africa*, (Lagos: The Nigerian Institute of International Affairs, 1984), 108.

[94] R. W. Davenport, *The Dignity of Man*, (New York: Harper and Brothers, 1955,), 230.

[95] R. C. Onwuanibe, 46.

[96] Samuel Huntington, 310.

[97] *African Traditional Political Thought and Institutions*, 159-160.

[98] I have relied on some of the facts contained here in Max Hilaire's 1993 Obafemi Awolowo Memorial Lecture, *The Attitudes of African States Towards International Law in the Post Cold War Era* (Lagos: Obafemi Awolowo Foundation, 1996).

[99] René Lemarchand, "Patterns of State Collapse and Reconstruction in Central Africa: Reflections on The Crisis in the Great Lakes," in *African Studies Quarterly*, the Online Journal of African Studies, www.africa.ufl.edu/asp/vl/3/2.htm.

[100] Sadako Ogata, *The Turbulent Decade, Confronting the Refugee Crises of the 1990s* (New York: W. W. Norton & Company, 2005), 177.

[101] Claude Ake, 1.

[102] Odinga Odinaga, *Not Yet Uhuru* (London: Heinemann, 1967), 2-3.

[103] Nelson Mandela, *Long Walk to Freedom* (New York: Back Bay Books, 1995), 625.

[104] Desmond Tutu, *No Future Without Forgiveness* (New York: Doubleday, 2000), 273-274.

[105] Chukwudum Okolo, *Apartheid and the Blackman's Burden* (Obosi: Pacific College Press, 1985), 6.

[106] Patrick F. Wilmot, *Apartheid and African Liberation* (University of Ife Press, 1983), 139.

[107] Donald Wood, *Biko* (London: Penguin Books, 1978), 385.

[108] Quoted in *Apartheid and African Liberation*, 5.

[109] Adolf Hitler, *Mein Kampf* (London: Hutchinson and Co. Ltd., 1984), 258.

[110] Godwin Sogolo, 29-32.

[111] Teresa Okure, "The Place of Theology in Another Possible World," Panel Discussion at the World Forum on Theologies of Liberation, Porto Alegre, Brazil, January 21-25, 2005.

[112] Chukwudum Okolo, 49.

[113] Patrick F. Wilmot, XI.

[114] G. Novack (ed), *Existentialism Vs Marxism*, (New York: Nell Pub Co. Inc., 1966), 19.

[115] G. W. Sherpherd, *Anti-Apartheid* (London: Greenword Press, 1968), 3.

[116] R. Gibson, *African Liberation Movement*, (London: Oxford University Press, 1972), 20.

[117] R. Gibson, 327.

[118] R. Fack, *Human Rights and State Sovereignty*, (New York: Homes and Meier Publishers, 1981), 159.

[119] H. L. Smith, *Anatomy of Aparthied*, (Germiston, Khanya Publishers, 1979), 7.

[120] B. Lipman, *We Make Freedom*, (London: Pandora Press, 1986), 137.

[121] Allan Boesak, *If This is Treason, I am Guilty*, (Detroit: W. M. B. Eardams Publication, Co., 1987), 61.

[122] Frantz Fanon, *Black Skin White Masks*, (trans) Charles Lam Markmann (New York: Grove Press, 1967), 51.

[123] Ibid. 229-230.

[124] The Pontifical Council for Justice and Peace, *The Church and Racism*, 16, (Vatican: Vatican Press, 2001).

[125] Matthew Hassan Kukah, *The Fractured Microcosm: The African Condition and the Search for Moral Balance in the New World Order*, (Lagos: Lagos State University Press, 1998), 23.

[126] See *Africa Recovery*, Vol. 17, No. 2, July 2003.

[127] http://newsvote.bbc.co.uk/mpapps /pagetools/print/news.bbc.co.uk/36323.

[128] Antoinette Ntuli, "How Africa Develops Europe (and the rest of the Rich World): Real Development and Aid," in *African Voices on Development and Social Justice*, Firoze Manji and Patrick Burnett (eds), (Dar es Salaam, Tanzania: Mkuki na Nyota Publishers, 2005), 7.

[129] Jean Danielou, *The Lord of History*, (trans) Nigel Abercrombie (London: Longmans, 1960), 64-66.

[130] Quoted in Jean Danielou, 66.

[131] Pontifical Council for the Pastoral Care of Migrants and Itinerant People, *Instruction the Love of Christ Towards Migrants, Erga Migrantes Caritas Christi*, No.4. www.vatican.va/roman_curia/pontifical_councils/migrants/documents/rc_pc_migrants.

[132] Ibid.

[133] "The Dutch Transformation," in *Toronto Star*, Friday, October 1, 2004, A6.

[134] Ian Fisher and Richard Bernstein, "On Italian Isle, Migrant Debate" in *The New York Times*, Tuesday, October 4, 2004, pp 1, A6.

[135] Ibid.

[136] Diarmuid Martin, "The Work of the Holy See in Promoting Peace: Case Studies in Arms Control" in *Celebrating Christianity*, (Washington: FADICA, 2000), 13.

[137] Ibid.

[138] Luther's explanation of the Fifth Commandment in 'The Large Catechism,' *The Book of Concord*, Robert Kolb and Timothy J. Wengert (eds), (Minneapolis: Fortress Press, 200), 412.

[139] Martin Nkafu Nkemnkia, *African Vitology*, (Nairobi: Paulines Publications Africa, 1999), 8.

[140] Ellen Johnson Sirleaf, "Africa Must Develop its own Vision" in *Africa Recovery*, Vol. 9, No. 3, November, 1995, 3.

[141] Samuel Kobia, *The Courage to Hope, the Roots for a New Vision and the Calling of the Church in Africa* (Geneva: WCC Publications, 2003), 53.

[142] Cf. Mkadawire Thandika, "30 Years of African Independence: The Economic Experience" in *30 Years of Independence in Africa: The Lost Decades?* Peter Anyang Nyongo (ed), (Nairobi: African Association of Political Science and Academy Science Publishers, 1992).

[143] See UN Development Group, *Investing in Development: A Practical Plan to Achieve the Millennium Development Goals* (New York: Untied Nations Development Program, 2005), 147-157.

[144] Jeffrey D. Sachs, *The End of Poverty* (New York: Penguin Press, 2005), 191.

[145] *Investing in Development*, 147-148.

[146] Ibid.

[147] Claude Ake, *Is Africa Democratizing?* (Port Harcourt: Centre for Advanced Social Sciences, 1996), 5-6.

[148] Claude Ake, "Political Ethnicity and State Building in Nigeria" in *Global Convulsion: Race, Ethnicity, and Nationalism at the End of the Twentieth Century*, Winston Van Horne (ed), (Albany, New York: SUNY Press, 1997), 299.

[149] See Stephen Kareskezi, "Introduction" in *Capacity Building for a Reforming African Power Sector*, Mengistu Teferra and Stephen Karekezi (eds), (London: Zed Books Ltd, 2002), 1-2.

[150] Ernest Harsch, "Africa Beyond Famine" in *Africa Recovery*, Vol. 17, No. 1. May 2003, 10.

[151] *Investing in Development*, 155.

CHAPTER TWO: THE TWO FACES OF AFRICA

[1] Take Heart, AECAWA Bishops Speak, 1996, 5.

[2] Bénézet Bujo, *Foundations of an African Ethic*, (New York: The Crossroad Publishing Co., 2001), 112-113.

[3] Ibid.

[4] See the World Health Report 2001, http://www.who.int/whr2001/2001/main/en/chapter2/2002g.htm.

[5] Torild Skard, *Continent of Mothers, Continent of Hope* (London: Zen Books Ltd, 2003), 215.

[6] Francis Fukuyama, *The End of History and the Last Man* (New York: Perennial, 2002).

[7] "Impoverishment and Liberation: A Theological Approach for Africa and the Third World" in *Paths of African Theology*, (trans) Robert R. Barr, Rosino Gibellini (ed), (Maryknoll, NY: Orbis Books, 1994), 156.

[8] Gustavo Gutierrez, *A Theology of Hope* (New York: Orbis Books, 1973), 291-292.

[9] Kim Jim Youn, Joyce V. Millen, Alec Irwin & John Gershaman (eds), "Dying for Growth" in Samuel Kobia, *The Courage to Hope* (Geneva: WCC Publications, 2003), in 207.

[10] My exposition on the meaning of poverty will be based on that given by Jeffery Sachs in his influential work, *The End of Poverty*, 17-25.

[11] Martin Meredith, *The Fate of Africa From the Hopes of Freedom to the Heart of Despair* (New York: Publish Affairs, 2005), 682. See also *Investing in Development A Practical Plan to Achieve the Millennium Development Goals* (New York: UN Development Group, 2005), 15.

[12] "Human Development Report Documents Catastrophic Impact of AIDS in Africa, http://hdr.org/2004.

[13] Marcel Gabriel, *The Existentialist Background of Human Dignity*, (Massaccussets: Harvard University Press, 1963), 128.

[14] Pontifical Council for the Laity, *The Dignity of Older People and their Mission in the Church and in the World*, (Vatican City: Pontifical Council for the Laity, 1998), 25-26.

[15] http://new.bbc.co.uk/1/hi/world/Europe/3181941.stm. See also *Awake magazine*, October 8, 2004.

[16] UNAIDS in its *Epidemics Update, 2002*, page 18 notes that 90% of the African population are free of HIV/AIDS infections.

[17] Anya O. Anya, *Re-inventing Nigeria for the 21ˢᵗ Century*, (Lagos: Obafemi Awolowo Foundation, 1995), 4.

[18] Ibid., 5.

[19] Hugh McCullum, "Remembering the Nightmare of Biafra" in *Presbyterian Record*, September, 2004.

[20] Evelyn Leonard, "UN Envoy says Congo Leaders Consumed by Ambition" in *Reuters*, United Nations, 26 September, 1997.

[21] Robert Jay Lifton, *Super Power Syndrome*, (New York: Nations Books, 2004), 148-149.

[22] "What is the Lost Generation?" in http://ok.essortment.com/whatlostgenera_nkj.htm.

[23] Howard W. French, *A Continent for the Taking*, (New York: Alfred A. Knopf, 2004), 101.

[24] Father Carlos Rodrigues, "War in Acholi: What can be Done?" in *Abducted and Abused: Renewed Conflicts in Northern Uganda*, Human Rights Watch, July 2003, Vol. 15, No. 12 (A), 16.

[25] Report of the Secretary General of the Security Council, *The Causes of Conflict and the promotion of Durable Peace and Sustainable Development in Africa*, (New York: United Nations, 1998), 1.

[26] Claude Ake, *A Theory of Political Integration*, (Homewood: The Dorsey Press, 1967), 3-5.

[27] Claude Ake, *Democracy and Development in Africa*, (Washington: The Brookings Institution, 1996), 16.

[28] Ibid., 3.

[29] John F. Clark, "Transition and the Struggle to Consolidate" in *Political Reform in Francophone Africa*, John F. Clark and David E. Gardinier (eds), (Westview: Boulder, 1997), 78.

[30] Robert D. Kaplan, *The Coming Anarchy*, (New York: Vintage Books, 1997), 8-9.

[31] Ibid., 9.

[32] *Peacekeeping in West Africa: A Regional Report*, Refugees International, 2004, I.

[33] *A World Fit for Children*, UNICE, 2003, 37-38.

[34] Torild Skard, 21-24.

[35] Father Carlos Rodrigues, 17.

[36] *AIDS Epidemic Update*, December 2002, a UNAIDS publication, (Geneva: UNAIDS/WHO, 2002), 5.

[37] *African Recovery* Magazine, United Nations, New York, January 2001, 21.

[38] *African Recovery* Magazine, United Nations, New York, January 2004, 6.

[39] Executive Summary, *2004 Report on the Global AIDS Epidemic*, (Geneva: UNAIDS/WHO), 6.

[40] *AIDS Epidemic Update*, December 2003, a UNAIDS publication, (Geneva: UNAIDS/WHO, 2003), 7-8.

[41] "AIDS in Africa: Are pharmaceutical companies to Blame?" in *The Catholic World Report*, March 2004, 32-34.

[42] Skard, 31.

[43] *HIV/AIDS Human Resources and Sustainable Development*, UNAIDS Publications, (Geneva: UNAIDS, 2002) 5.

[44] African Recovery Magazine, United Nations, New York, January 2004, 6.

[45] AIDS Epidemic Update December 2002, 18.

[46] Quoted in *Africa's Orphaned Generations*, (New York: United Nations Children's Fund, 2003), 1.

[47] Ibid., 4.

[48] AIDS Epidemic Update, December 2002, 29.

[49] Ibid., 5.

[50] *Malaria a Major Cause of Child Deaths and Poverty in Africa*, (New York: UNICEF, 2004), 1.

[51] *AIDS Epidemic Update*, December 2002, 18.

[52] BBC website, http://news.bc.co.uk/hi/africa/3244564.stm.

[53] Kingsley Moghalu, "Africa's Condom Conundrum: Fighting HIV in Africa" in www.allAfrica.com/stories

[54] Reported in *Zenith* Daily Despatch, "Doubts About Condoms: Science Questioning their Efficacy in Halting HIV/AIDS," June 26, 2004.

[55] Ibid.

[56] Ibid.

[57] This was reported on BBC special documentary on Sunday, August 8, 2004 at 9.30 a.m.

[58] The issue of the use of condom is a moral argument and not one of effectiveness or lack of it. I do think that whether condom is effective for prevention should be left to the scientists to determine and this can be objectively established. The moral aspect of the question as to the effectiveness of condom is whether something that does not guarantee 100% protection should be proposed to people who want 100% protection. However, the message should not be that people should not use condom because it is unsafe, but rather that unmarried people should desist from indulging in casual and non-committed sexual relations which exposes them to HIV/AIDS and other sexually transmitted diseases. Those who preach that condom use is the answer to the spread of HIV/AIDS in Africa do not integrate the argument against its lack of 100% protection on one hand, and the fundamental moral question whether religious institutions should teach people the value of sexual morality or the better way to violate sexual ethics. It will be wrong for anyone to accuse the Catholic Church for its stand against the use of condom. This stand is based on a moral argument, which the opponents of the Church's position fail to address. This issue is not a closed question because within theological circle in global Christianity, there is an ongoing debate about the difference between the

contraceptive and the therapeutic value of condom with regard to the fight against HIV/AIDS. It is a debate which might lead to further insight on the question.

[59] I have relied on the impressive pastoral letter of Cardinal McCarrick in *Origin*, June 19, 2003, Vol. 33, No. 6, 83-84.

[60] "The Church in Africa in the Face of the HIV/AIDS Pandemic: Our Prayer is Always full of Hope," Message issued by SECAM, Dakar, 2003.

[61] This was reported in the *Catholic Herald* of London, January 2004.

[62] See Michael W. Higgins & Douglas R. Letson, *Power and Peril, The Catholic Church at the Crossroads* (Toronto: HarperCollins Publishers Ltd, 2002), 218-221.

[63] http://news.bbc.co.uk/go/pr/fr/-/2/hi/africa/3278619.stm.

[64] Statements of the plan of action developed by churches, ecumenical and church-related organizations in Africa, Europe and North America and World Council Churches at the Global Consultation on the Ecumenical Response to HIV/AIDS in Africa, Nairobi, Kenya, November 2001 in *What Religious Leaders can do About HIV/AIDS*, (Geneva: UNAIDS, 3003), 6.

[65] Zenith, January 29, 2004.

[66] Quoted in *Africa Recovery*, January 2004, 4.

[67] Ibid., 6.

[68] BBC

[69] *Africa Recovery*, January 2001, 22.

[70] *Origins*, August 2, 2001, 186ff.

[71] Quoted in Stan Chu Ilo, *Child Upbringing*, (Enugu: Snaap Press, 1994), 83.

[72] *Child Trafficking in West Africa Policy Response*, (Florence: UNICEF, Innocenti Research Center, 2002), 6.

[73] Ibid., 2.

[74] *End Child Exploitation*, UNICEF, February 4, 2003, No. 2.

CHAPTER THREE: THE CHALLENGES

[1] There is no clear-cut difference between the use of the term 'structures of sin' and 'social sins' in most theological and philosophical writings. For our purpose in this discussion, we shall define social sins as the fruits of the structures of sin, the former giving life to the latter. The structure of sin appears to be invisible, but when we use the term social sins we refer to actions discoverable in institutions, economic, political and social organizations and even in religious institutions, which concretely and

negatively affect the realization of the fullness of life of members of society and the end which they seek in these institutions.

[2] John Paul II, *Reconciliation and Penance*, 16.

[3] Ibid.

[4] *Catechism of the Catholic Church*, 1871

[5] A detailed discussion on the many-layered aspects of sin from a Catholic perspective could be seen in the document published by the Sacred Congregation on the Doctrine of Faith, *Instruction on Christian Freedom and Liberation.*

[6] John Paul II, *Solicitudo Rei Socialis*, 37.

[7] *Solicitudo Rei Socialis*, No. 36.

[8] Dulles A, *The Splendour of Faith*, (New York: Crossroads Publishing Co., 1999), 95.

[9] *Reconciliation and Penance*, No. 16.

[10] Cf. John Paul II, *Celebrate 2000*, (Ann Arbor: Servant Publication, 1996), 182.

[11] Cf Pastoral Constitution of the Church in the Modern World, *Gaudium et Spes*, 69.

[12] Musimbi R. A. Kanyoro, *Introducing Feminist Cultural Hermeneutics, An African Perspective*, (Cleveland, Ohio: The Pilgrim Press, 2002), 80.

[13] Takyiwaa Manuh, "Women in Africa's Development' in *Africa Recovery*, No. 11, April 1998, 4.

[14] Edith Stein, *Essays on Women, the Collected Works of Edith Stein Vol 11*, (Washington: ICS Publications, 1987), 177. See also Prudence Allen, 'Integral Sex Complementarity' in *Communio* International Catholic Quarterly, 17, Winter, 1990.

[15] John Paul II, *Letter to Women* (Nairobi: Paulines Publications, 1995), 7.

[16] Mercy Amba Oduyoye, *African Women's Theology*, (Cleveland, Ohio: The Pilgrim Press, 2001), 67.

[17] John Paul II, *Dignity and Vocation of Women*, (Kampala: St Paul Publications-Africa, 1989), 8.

[18] See Mercy Amba Oduyoye, *African Women's Theology*. This is a work of considerable scholarship in which the author traces the journey of the African women theology of liberation. She broaches the context of African women's theology and challenges the anthropological bases of the subordination of women in Africa. Based on an impressive Christological hermeneutics and ideology criticism, she proposes a new Christian interpretation of anthropology based on appropriate Christology and which is germane for inaugurating new structures for the full blossom of the personality, individuality, and dignity of African women.

[19] Takayiwaa Manuh, 5.

[20] Cf. Thomas Aquinas, *On the Truth of the Catholic Faith* Book 3, Part 2, (trans) Vernon J. Bourke, (New York: Image Books, 1996), 252.

[21] Robert J. Schreiter, *Constructing Local Theologies*, (New York: Orbis Books, 1985), 97.

[22] UN Statistical Division, World Bank, World Development Report for 1997, *UNICEF's State of World Children Report for 1998*.

[23] Rose Uchem, *Overcoming Women's Subordination*, (Enugu: Snaap Press, 2001), 23.

[24] According to Pope John Paul II, "Although the teaching that priestly ordination is to be reserved to men alone has been preserved by the constant and universal Tradition of the Church and firmly taught by the Magisterium in its more recent documents, at the present time in some places it is nonetheless considered still open to debate, or the Church's judgment that women are not be admitted to ordination is considered to have a merely disciplinary force. Wherefore, in order that all doubt may be removed regarding a matter of great importance, a matter which pertains to the Church's divine constitution itself, in virtue of my ministry of confirming the brethren (cf. Lk 22:32) I declare that the Church has no authority whatsoever to confer priestly ordination on women and that this judgment is to be definitively held by the Church's faithful." *On Preserving Priestly Ordination to Men Alone, Ordinatio Sacerdotalis* (Boston: Pauline Books and Media, 1994), 4.

[25] George Ehusani, *A Prophetic Church* (Ibadan, Nigeria: Society of St Paul's), 140.

[26] Chukwudum Okoro, *The Liberating Role of the Church in Africa Today* (Eldoret, Kenya: AMACEA Gaba Publications, 1991), 55.

[27] Elizabeth Amoah, 'Violence and Women's Bodies in African Perspectives' in *Women Resisting Violence*, Mary John Mananzan et al. (eds), (Eugene, Oregon: Wipf and Stock, 2004), 84-85.

[28] *Restoring the Dignity of the Nigerian Woman*, (Lagos: Catholic Secretariat of Nigeria, 2001), 8.

[29] Prudence Allen, *The Concept of Woman Vol. 11*, (Grand Rapids: Eerdmans, 2002), 1089.

[30] Jesse N. K. Mugambi, *The Church in Africa: Towards a Theology of Reconstruction* (Nairobi: AACC, 1991), 29, 32.

[31] See Kwame Bediako, *Christianity in Africa The Renewal of a Non-Western Religion* (New York: Orbis Books, 1997), 192-193.

[32] David B. Barrett & Todd M. Johnson, "Annual Statistical Table on Global Mission: 2004," in *International Bulletin of Missionary Research* 28 January 2004, 25. The *World Christian Encyclopedia* has a different

estimate, according to it of the 2 billion Christians alive today, 360 million are Africans. These estimates are not very accurate as there has never been a census of Christians in Africa, but they reflect to a large extent the burgeoning growth in African Christianity.

[33] Lamin Sanneh, "Introduction" in *The Changing Face of Christianity Africa, The West, and the World*, Lamin Sanneh & Joel A. Carpenter (eds), (Oxford: Oxford University Press, 2005), 4-5.

[34] Kwame Bediako, Theology and Identity (Oxford: Regnum Books, 1994), xv.

[35] Benezet Bujo, *Foundations of African Ethics, Beyond the Universal Claims of Western Morality* (NY: Crossroads, 2001), 74.

[36] Bolaji Idowu, *African Traditional Religion*, (London: SCM Press, Ltd, 1973), 104.

[37] John S. Mbiti, *African Religions and Philosophy*, (Nairobi: East African Educational Publishers Ltd., 1999), 2.

[38] http://newsvote.bbc.co.uk/mpapps/pagetools/print/news.bbc.co.uk/2/hi/africa/3756910.stm.

[39] Quoted in Iheanyi Enwerem, "Money Magic and Ritual Killing in Nigeria" in *Money Struggles and City Life*, Jane I. Guyer, LaRay Denzer &Adigun Agbaje (eds), (Portsmouth, NH: Heinemann, 2003), 194.

[40] Anthony A. Akinwale, "Religion as a Moral Virtue: Thomas Aquinas and a Recent Poll," CATHAN Presidential Address 2004, 8.

[41] Quoted in Nnamdi A. Odoemene, *The Fundamentals of African Traditional Religion*, (Enugu: Institute of Ecumenical Education, 1988), 46.

[42] Cf. Christopher J. Walsh, "Building a Civilization of Love: Recent Statements" in *Communio* International Catholic Review, Vol. XXIV, No. 4, Winter 1997, 792-793.

[43] Quoted in J. Russell Chandran, "A Methodological Approach to Third World Theology" in *Irruption of the Third World*, Virginia Fabella & Segio Torres (eds), (New York: Orbis Books, 1983), 82.

[44] Theophilus Okere, *Church, Theology and Society in Africa* (Enugu: Fourth Dimension Publishing Co. Ltd, 2005), 140.

[45] Chukwudum Okolo, *The African Synod: Hope for the Continent's Liberation* (Eldoret, Kenya: AMACEA: Gaba Publications Spearhead, Nos. 130-131, 1994), 24-25.

[46] Cf. Patrick Ryan, "The Shifting Context of Sin" in *Structures of Sin Seeds of Liberation*, 16.

[47] Pontifical Council for Justice and Peace, *Compendium of the Social Doctrine of the Church* (Rome: Libreria Editrice Vaticana, 2005), 165.

[48] The Pastoral Constitution of the Second Vatican Council on the Role of the Church in the Modern world, *Gaudium et Spes*, 75.

[49] Laurenti Magesa, "Theology of Integral Development in Africa" in *Church Contribution to Integral Development*, J. T. Agbasiere & B. Zabajungu (eds), (Eldoret, Kenya: AMACEA Gaba Publications, 1989), 121.

[50] *The Fate of Africa*, 687.

[51] This study could be found in www.csgr.org.

[52] Thomas L. Friedman, *The World is Flat, A Brief History of the Twenty-First Century* (NY: Farrar, Straus and Giroux, 2005), 460.

[53] Max L. Stackhuse, "The Fifth Social Gospel and the Global Mission of the Church" in *The Social Gospel Today*, Christopher H. Evans (ed), (Louisville: Westminster John Knox Press2001), 146-159.

[54] Jonathan Sacks, *The Dignity of Difference*, (London: Continuum, 2003), 25-26.

[55] Quoted in Samuel Kobia, *The Courage to Hope* (Geneva: WCC Publications, 2003), 207

[56] Taye Assefa, Severine M. Rugumamu, and Abdel Ghaffar M. Ahmed, "Introduction" in *Globalization, Democracy and Development in Africa*, Taye Assefa et al. (eds), (Addis Ababa: Organization for Social Science Research in Eastern and Southern Africa, 2001), vii.

[57] See Carol Collins, "Jubilee 2000 Debt Relief Campaign Targets G8 Leaders" in *African Recovery*, August 1998, 15.

[58] See Ken Wiwa, "Money for Nothing-and the Debt is for Free" in *Globe and Mail*, Saturday, May 22, 2004, A19. See also the online African social justice online news channel, www.pambazuka.org.

[59] Noreena Hertz, *The Debt Threat, how Debt is Destroying The Developing World* (Toronto: Harper Collins Publishers Ltd., 2004), 3.

[60] Max Stackhouse, 151.

[61] Richard Peet, *Unholy Trinity*, (London: Zed Books, 2003).

[62] Max L. Stackhouse, "Globalization, Public Theology and the New Means of Grace, 4, Santa Clara Lectures, Clara University, 2003. http://www.scu.edu/bannancenter/eventsandconferences/lecturs/archives/stackhouse.cfm.

[63] http://www.globalexchange.org/campigns/econ101/neoliberalism.html.pf.

[64] See Matthew Hassan Kukah, *The African Condition and the Search for Moral Balance in the New World Order*, (Lagos: Faculty of Social Sciences Lagos State University, 1998), 22.

[65] M. A. Mohamed Salih, "Globalization and Human Insecurity in Africa" in *Globalization, Democracy and Development in Africa: Challenges and Prospects*, Taye Assefa, Severine M. Rugumamu & Abdel Ghaffar M.

Ahmed (eds), (Addis Ababa: Organization for Social Science Research in Eastern and Southern Africa, 2001), 63-65.

[66] Ibid., 65.

[67] Ibid., 69.

[68] Quoted in *The Guardian*, Tuesday, September 6, 2005, 21.

[69] This point of view is strongly promoted in African countries that many African countries are denied loan facilities and are not allowed access to the so-called debt relief program of the Heavily Indebted Poor Country (HIPC) initiatives.

[70] *TransAfrica Forum Globalization Monitor*, Vol. 1, Issue 11, Summer 2003, 2.

[71] Jean—Marc Ela, *African Cry* (New York: Orbis Books, 1986), v.

[72] The Oversea Development Council (ODC) of the United Kingdom commissioned some African writers and foreigners who buy into this kind of thinking to produce series of publications that try to argue for a new African institutional configuration for development. See *Beyond Structural Adjustment The Institutional Context of African Development*, Nicolas Van De Walle, Nicole Ball & Vijaya Ramachandran (eds), (New York: Palmgrove Macmillan, 2003).

[73] See Ibrahim Elbadawi and Alan Geleb "Financing Africa's Development: Towards a Business Plan" in *Beyond Structural Adjustment*, 36

[74] Robert Kagan, *Of Paradise and Power, America and Europe in the New World Order* (New York: Vintage Books, 2004), 89.

[75] D. Fergin, "Birth of Buzzword" in *Newsweek Magazine*, Vol. CXXXIII, No. 7, February 15, 1999.

[76] Paul VI, *Populorum Pregressio*, 64, (Nairobi: Paulines Publications Africa, 1998).

[77] Claude Ake, *Democracy and Development in Africa* (Washington: The Brookings Institution, 1996), 31-41.

[78] *Newswatch* Magazine, Vol. 8, No. 9, August 29, 1988, 18.

[79] *TransAfrican Forum Globalization Monitor*, Vol. 1, Issue 11, Summer 2003, 2.

[80] Jane I. Guyer, LaRay Denzer and Adigun Agbaje (eds), *Money Struggles and City Life*, (Ibadan: Center for Social Science Research and Development, 2003), xix.

[81] John A. Tesha, "Reminiscences and Personal Reflections: Development Initiatives for Africa" in *Africa's Development Thinking Since Independence: A Reader*, Eddy Maloka (ed), (Pretoria, South Africa: Africa Institute of South Africa, 2002), 16

[82] See Anya O. Anya, *Re-inventing Nigeria for the 21st Century* (Lagos: Obafemi Awolowo Foundation, 1996), 20

[83] Thomas L. Friedman, 389.

[84] Ibid., 158-159.

[85] Mary Kerber, "Globalization: The Challenge for Africa" in *Structures of Sin, Seeds of Liberation*, Patrick Ryan (ed), (Nairobi: Paulines Publications Africa, 1998), 56-57.

[86] Bénézet Bujo, 160, 166,

[87] Pope John Paul II has called for a globalization of solidarity in *The Church in America*, (Boston: Pauline Books and Media, 1999), 55. See also Thomas Rourke, "Contemporary Globalization: An Ethical and Anthropological Evaluation." This article is found in the special edition of *Communio* International Catholic Quarterly, 27 (Fall 2000). This edition of the journal was dedicated to discussion of the theology of globalization taking from a broad horizon of discourses.

[88] See Susan George, *A Fate Worse than Debt* (London: Penguin Books, 1988); Susan George & Fabrizio Sabelli, *Faith and Credit: The World Bank's Secular Empire* (London: Penguin Books, 1994); Ulrich Duchrow, *Alternatives to Global Capitalism* (Heidelbert: Kairos Europe. 1995); Jonathan Sacks, *The Dignity of Difference* (London: Continuum, 2003); Robert Jay Lifton, *Super Power Syndrome* (New York: Thunder's Mouth Press, 2003).

[89] Thomas R. Rourke, "Contemporary Globalization: An Ethical and Anthropological Evaluation" in *Communio International Catholic Review*, (Fall 2000), 491-492.

[90] John Paul II, *The Church in America* (Boston: Pauline Books and Media, 1999), 55.

[91] Quoted in *Tell Magazine*, Nigeria, March 1, 1999, 50.

[92] I have relied for these statistics on Chares Abani, "Progress Towards Achieving EFA (Education For All) in Nigeria," a contribution to the *Monitoring Report*. This study is available as a policy watch publication at www.actionaidnigeria.org.

[93] Historically there were three conferences by African education ministers prior to Dakar Forum namely, the 1961 Addis Ababa Conference which tried to redefine the main thrust of education in post-independence Africa, the Nairobi conference of 1968 which appraised the status of the educational scheme in Africa in the light of the various recommendations of various international agencies especially UNESCO and emphasized the producing of skilled manpower for national development, and the 1976 conference in Lagos which was heavily influenced by the Nigerian National Policy on Education which was under revision within the time of that meeting and was later revised in 1977, 1981,1989 and 1999.

[94] See for instance the findings of Oxfam International, in Watkins, K. *Education Now-Break the Cycle of Poverty*, (London: Oxfam International Pub., 1999) 4. See also *AIDS Epidemic Update*, Joint United Nations Program on HIV/AIDS and World Health Organization, December 2003. This report notes that sub-Saharan Africa remains by far the region worst affected by the HIV/AIDS epidemic.

[95] See Karl Maier, *This House Has Fallen, Nigeria in Crisis* (Colorado: Westview Press, 2000), 298.

[96] A. Babs Fafunwa, *History of Education in Nigeria* (London: George Allen and Unwin Ltd., 1974), 20-48.

[97] I am grateful to the Maryvale Institute, Birmingham, UK for this useful insight on educational aims, which forms the guiding principle of this educational institution.

[98] Fafunwa, 17.

[99] Jacques Maritain, *Education at the Crossroads* (New Haven: Yale University Press, 1971), 15.

[100] Christopher Dawson has written extensively on the influence of Christianity on Western culture and how secularism threatens Christianity because it threatens Western culture. See *Religion and the Rise of Western Culture*, (New York: Image Books, 1958).

[101] Peter Gay has shown how the Enlightenment thinkers in their attempt to seek a viable alternative to Christian dogma and faith in which they had grown prove that Enlightenment is synonymous to a paganism that had little to do with religion and life. See Peter Gay, *The Enlightenment: An Interpretation, the rise of Modern Paganism* (Toronto: Random House Inc., 1967).

[102] Isaac Kramnick (ed), *The Portable Enlightenment Reader* (New York: Penguin Books, 1995), x. I have relied on this work for most of the presentation of the main philosophical trends that led to and rose from the Enlightenment, because of its condensed and profound insight on this significant epoch of human history.

[103] Ibid., 1

[104] Ibid., xxix.

[105] Ernst Cassirer, *The Philosophy of the Enlightenment*, (trans) Fritz C. A. Koelin & James P. Pettergrove (Princeton: Princeton University Press, 1951), 5.

[106] Jacques Barzun, *From Dawn to Decadence* (New York: HarperCollins Publishers, 2000), 413.

[107] See Colin Gunton, *Enlightenment and Alienation, especially Part Two on Thinking and Acting* (Grand Rapids: William Eerdmans Publishing Company, 1985).

[108] Quoted in *The Portable Enlightenment Reader*, xii.

[109] John Macquarrie groups Barth, Brunner, Cullman, Bonhoeffer etc., among the theologians of the Word who tried to recover the meaning of Christianity, by concentrating on the centrality of Christ in salvation history and the essentially revelational and transcendent nature of the Christian message and its hold on human life and reality in general. See *Twentieth Century Religious Thought* (Harrisburg: Trinity Press International, 2002), 318-338.

[110] Henry Denzinger, *The Sources of Catholic Dogma*, 1786, (trans) Roy J. Deferrari from the Enchridion Symbolorum (New Hampshire: Loreto Publications, 1954).

[111] See James Arthur, Hugh Walters & Simon Gaine (eds), *Earthen Vessels the Thomistic Tradition in Education* (Heredfordshire: Gracewing, 1999), 6.

[112] Ibid., 7.

[113] His theories of education as the reconstruction of experience and his pragmatic postulations which leaves the individual to the counter-veiling currents of a non-moral scientific regime is flawed in the search for integration and truth of being. His views has been proffered as adequate to Nigeria in D. I. Agwaranze "Pragmatic Philosophy: Basis for Educational Development in Nigeria, 252-260" in *Africa Philosophy and Public Affairs*, J. Obi Oguejiofor (ed), (Enugu, Delta Publications, 1998). I disagree with the position adduced in that paper and most prominent Nigerian educationists like Fafunwa, Ukeje, Ohuche, R. Onuche, and Festus Okafor are agreed that functional education for Nigeria is necessary but not sufficient ground for adopting pragmatic education.

[114] Raymond D. Boisvert, *John Dewey Rethinking our Time* (Albany: State University of New York Press, 1998), 93-97.

[115] I owe some of these ideas and facts to the insightful perspective developed by Christopher Dawson, *The Crisis of Western Education* (New York: Sheed and Ward, 1961), 129-144.

[116] John Paul II, *Fides et Ratio*, 5.

[117] James Davison Hunter has argued in his works on the need to restore the moral content of authentic education in the United States of America for instance. See *The Death of Character* (New York: Basic Books, 2000).

[118] Second Vatican Council's proclamation on Education, *Gravissimum Educationis*, 1

[119] Pius XI, *Divini Illius Magistri*, 29

[120] Thomas Groome, *Educating for Life* (New York: A Crossroad Book, 1998), 389.

[121] Bell Hooks, *Teaching Community: A Pedagogy of Hope* (New York: Routledge, 2003).

[122] *Gaudium et Spes*, No. 39.

[123] Halverson M and Cohen A., *A Handbook of Christian Theology* (London: Meridian Books, 1968), 200-201.

[124] Statement of the US Bishops, *Living the Gospel of Life: A Challenge to American Catholics* http://www.osjspm.org/cst/life.htm. p. 8.

CHAPTER FOUR: HOPES AND DREAMS

[1] Samuel Kobia, *The Courage to Hope* (Geneva: WCC Publications, 2003), 5.

[2] Kader Asmal, David Chidester & Wilmot James (eds), *Nelson Mandela in His own Words* (London: Abacus, 2004), 198.

[3] Adebayo Olukoshi, "Neo-Liberal Globalization and its Social Consequences" in *African Voices on Development and Social Justice*, Firoze Manji & Patrick Burnett (eds), (Dar es Salaam: Mkuki Na Nyota Publishers, 2004), 5.

[4] Francis Anekwe Oborji, *Towards A Christian Theology of African Religion* (Eldoret, Kenya: AMECEA Gaba Publications, 2005), 103.

[5] http://allafrica.com/stories/printable/200408050800.html.

[6] http://newsvote.bbc.co.uk/mpapps/pagetools/print/news.bbc.co.uk/2/hi/business/3758798.stm.

[7] Nick Kotch, "African Oil: Whose Bonanza?" in *National Geographic*, September 2005, 53-65.

[8] I have relied for these facts from the special edition of the *National Post*, Monday, July 4, 2005, which carried many facts about African leaders and how their corruption and self-enrichment have hampered donor initiatives in Africa. These facts may be true but interpreting them to be solely the cause of the sad face of Africa may be too minimalistic and a hasty generalization. Besides, not all African leaders are corrupt and vain nonetheless the grinding poverty that is sweeping through the continent like a merciless hurricane equally affects both the corrupt and non-corrupt states in Africa. There are thus many other factors for the present situation of Africa beyond the corruption theory. As Sebastian Mallaby has concluded, "After sixty years of development experiments, it is time for humility among donors. The prescriptions of northerners have often failed to reverse poverty, and the most startling development successes (communist China, notably) have come in countries that have taken donors' advice selectively. The factors that drive progress-strong institutions, stable societies, the presence of technocrats of Tumusiime's ilk—cannot be conjured up by aid donors; despite its portentous name, the

World Bank is not a proxy for world government." (Sebastian Mallaby, *The World's Banker, A Story of Failed States, Financial Crises and other Wealth and Poverty of Nations,* New York: The Penguin Press, 2004), 392.

[9] See Martin Meredith, *The Fate of Africa, From the Hopes of Freedom to the Heart of Despair* (New York: Public Affairs, 2005), 301-302. Meredith's book is a good presentation of the way and means through which African leaders have defeated the dreams and aspiration of Africans since Independence. He also writes of the involvement of Western leaders and companies in the destruction of the continent of Africa. Jeremy Pope, Founding Director of *Transparency International* has however warned that it will be wrong to blame African leaders alone for the corruption that is defeating the development policies of respective African countries. According to him, "When one focuses on corruption in Africa, the tendency is to think only in terms of Africa; but the international banks, the Western business men who bribe to get the contract, those who are in cahoots with all the millionaires, they are all up to their eyeballs in what is taking place. When it comes to moral standing, everybody belongs in the gutter together." (Quoted in *National Post,* July 4, 2005). Meredith's book did not bring out the full implication of this aspect of corruption which Pope has clearly underlined. He appears to have also some blinkers in his assessment of corruption in Africa. Africa is not in the 'heart of despair' as he put in the title of his book. It is important to clearly point out the dangers of self-inflicted problems in Africa like corruption and the exploitation of the masses by the political and religious elites, but it is more important to point the way forward more than just heaping blames on African leaders most of whom are now dead and have left present day Africans with the challenge of cleaning the mess and charting the path to a better future for the continent. It might help to remember for instance that the $25 billion loan which President Suharto of Indonesia took on behalf of his country from the World Bank went to the pockets of his cronies and his personal vaults. Indonesian economy was not badly affected by this because the country has a strong economy. Indonesia is today among the so-called G5 medium power (the rest being Mexico, South Africa, India and Brazil). There are more to Africa's poverty beyond corruption. The lending international agencies must re-evaluate their policies and programs and determine how to apply their aid to Africa. The failure of donor initiatives in Africa should be blamed both on the Africans and the donor agencies themselves who fail to understand Africa or are half-heatedly involved with African development.

[10] Niall Ferguson, *Colossus the Rise and Fall of the American Empire,* (New York: Penguin Books, 2005), 181.

[11] OLauda Equiano, *Equiano's Travels*, P. Edwards (ed), (London: Heinemann, 1967), 7.

[12] Philip Jenkins, *The Next Christendom* (Oxford: Oxford University Press, 2002), 147-150.

[13] http://news.bbc.co.uk/1/hi/uk2291815.stm.

[14] See Mindy Fetterman, "Dollars going to the dogs" in *USA Today*, No. 4182, Friday, February 11, 2005, 1-2.

[15] Cf. Martin Rees, *Our Final Hour* (New York: Basic Books, 2004), 23-24.

[16] Joseph Ratzinger, "Europe in the Crisis of Culture" in *Communio International Catholic Review*, Vol. XXXII, no. 2, Summer 2005, 346.

[17] I have elaborately discussed this theological concept which is the hermeneutical key to understanding the ethical permutation of the papacy of John Paul II in *Rejoice in the Lord: Jubilee 2000 Reflections*, (Lagos: Silver Rose United Pub., 2000), 44-56; and in "The Significance and Dimensions of Great Jubilee 2000" in *Bigard Theological Studies*, June 2000. I present here this teaching as it has developed especially after the Great Jubilee 2000 and specifically as it applies to the unsolved problem of African integral Renaissance.

[18] Pope John Paul II, *Letter to Families* (Vatican: Libreria Editrice Vaticana, 1994), 41.

[19] *Jesus Christ Word of the Father*, by the Theological-Historical Commission for the great Jubilee of the Year 2000 (Vatican: Vatican Press, 1997), 140.

[20] Pontifical Council for Culture, *Towards A Pastoral Approach to Culture* (Vatican: Editrice Vaticana, 1999), No. 1.

[21] Ali Mazrui, *Cultural Forces in World Politics* (Nairobi: Heinemann Kenya, 1990), 7-9.

[22] Sacred Congregation on Clergy, *General Directory on Catechesis* (Nairobi: Paulines Publications Africa, 1998), 211.

[23] Desmond Tutu, *No Future Without Forgiveness* (New York: Image book, 2000), 31.

[24] Sacred Congregation on Clergy, 211.

[25] *Gaudium et Spes* No. 21.

[26] Pope John Paul II, *Redemptor Hominis* (Nairobi: Paulines Publications Africa, 1989), 10.

[27] Cf. Gregory of Nyssa, *De Hom Op*. 5 PG 44, 137.

[28] John Paul II , *Dignity and Vocation of Women* (Kampala: St Paul Pub., 1989), 7.

[29] Pontifical Council for Justice and Peace, Compendium *of the Social Doctrine of the Church* (Vatican: Libreria Editrice Vaticana, 2005), 581.

[30] Eugene Uzukwu, E., *A Listening Church* (New York: Orbis Books, 1996), 6.

[31] John Paul II, *Ecclesia In America* (Boston: Pauline Books and Media 1999), 52.

[32] Peschke, R. H. *Christian Ethics* II (Bangalore: Theological Pub. In India, 1993), 223.

[33] Hoffner J., *Catholic Social Teaching* (Bratislava: Ordo Socialis, 1983), 43.

[34] See John Paul II, *Solicitudo Rei Socialis*, 38-40.

[35] See Dulles, A, "John Paul II Theologian," in *Communio International Catholic Review*, Vol. XXIV, No. 4, 717.

[36] AMECEA Pastoral Department, *The African Synod comes Home* (Nairobi: Paulines Publications Africa, 1997), 21-22. See also *Ecclesia in Africa*, No. 63, 88, 89, 104.

[37] Pope John Paul II, *Incarnationis Mysterium*, 12. See also *Tertio Millennio Adveniente*, 46-47.

[38] Jurgen Moltmann, *The Gospel of Liberation* (trans) H. Wayne Pipkin, (Waco, Texas: Word Books Publisher, 1973), 27.

[39] Pope John Paul II, *Ecclesia in Africa* (Nairobi: Paulines Publication Africa, 2000), 30.

[40] The crisis in the Anglican Church over the ordination of Gene Robinson and the threats of the Anglican Communion of the Global South to break up communion with the Episcopalian dioceses in the United States of America and other dioceses throughout the world that endorse the ordination of homosexual clerics, led to the setting up of the 2004 Lambert Commission on Communion. The committee's recommendations, *The Windsor Report*, which was considered by the House of Bishops made up of senior prelates of the worldwide Anglican Church, was inconclusive on what position to take with regard to the ordination of homosexual clerics. The report was ambivalent with regard to homosexual acts and the ordination of those who are active homosexuals when it says in article 43: *"We repeat that we have not been invited, and are not intending, to comment or make recommendations on the theological and ethical matters concerning the practice of same sex relations and the blessing or ordination or consecration of those who engage in them."* In article 61 it was inconclusive on the normativity of the scripture for Christian faith and morals when it says, "The current crisis thus constitutes a call to the whole Anglican Communion to re-evaluate the ways in which we have read, heard, studied and digested scripture. We can no longer be content to drop random texts into arguments, imagining that the point is thereby proved, or indeed to sweep away sections of the New Testament as irrelevant to today's world, imagining that problems

are thereby solved. We need mature study, wise and prayerful discussion, and a joint commitment to hearing and obeying God as he speaks in scripture, to discovering more of the Jesus Christ to whom all authority is committed, and to being open to the fresh wind of the Spirit who inspired scripture in the first place. If our present difficulties force us to read and learn together from scripture in new ways, they will not have been without profit." The *Windsor Report*, 2004 (London: The Anglican Communion Office, 2004).

[41] Bénézet Bujo, *Foundations of African Ethic* (New York: The Crossroad Publishing Co., 2001), 34-36.

[42] Chukwudum Okolo, *The African Synod: Hope for the Continent's Liberation* (Eldoret, Kenya: AMECEA Gaba Publications Spearhead, 1994), 33.

[43] Ibid., 6-7.

EPILOGUE: APPEAL FOR AFRICA

[1] John Paul II, *Centesimus Annus* (Vatican City: Liberia Editrice Vaticana, 1991), 19.

[2] Erich Fromm, *The Art of Being* (New York: The Continuum Publishing Co., 1997), 61.

[3] Facts from World Bank, World Debt Table, 1994-1995 in *African Recovery*, June 1995, 11.

[4] John Pilger, *The New Rulers of the World* (London: Verso, 2003), 2-3.

[5] Robert Cooper, *The Breaking of Nations* (Toronto: McCelland & Stewart Ltd., 2005), 178.

INDEX

S

Sadako Ogata 82, 325
Saddam Hussein 50
Saharawi Arab Democratic Republic
     146
Sahara Desert 53, 99
Sahel Region 116, 117, 259
Same sex marriage 304
Samuel Kobia 105, 268, 327, 328, 335,
     340
Sani Abacha 148, 274
SAP 227, 230, 235, 236
Sassou-Nguesso 141
Scotland 44
Scramble and partition 323
Sebastian Mallaby 340, 341
Second Slavery 92
Second Vatican Council 26, 251, 335,
     339
Secularism 11, 33, 34, 219, 245, 246,
     318, 338
Sekou Toure 4
Self-sustenance 23
Sense of responsibility 25, 101
Shaka the Zulu 67
Shakespeare 28
Shona 67
Sierra Leone 42, 46, 68, 78, 108, 128,
     132, 133, 149, 150, 151, 152,
     196, 197, 274, 311
slave trade. 51, 57, 59, 61, 63, 64, 69,
     230, 322
Social Justice 227, 234, 311, 315, 335
Social sins 210, 284
Solidarity xvii, xxvi, 3, 11, 16, 27, 28,
     39, 115, 122, 128, 177, 180, 184,
     187, 217, 260, 261, 263, 267,
     270, 271, 279, 283, 284, 285,
     286, 287, 289, 296, 298, 301,
     302, 310, 311, 337
Songhai 7
South Africa 6, 11, 39, 40, 44, 85, 86,
     87, 88, 89, 93, 105, 141, 146,
     153, 158, 159, 160, 185, 207,

237, 258, 278, 317, 336, 341
Soweto 87
Stan Chu Ilo v, vi, vii, xv, xxvii, 331
Stephen Lewis xviii, xix, 174, 318
Stochastic xxii
Structural Adjustment Programme
     xix, 22, 98, 113, 222, 227, 235,
     236, 336
Structures of Sin xxii, 24, 184, 185,
     187, 211, 213, 214, 220, 229,
     234, 239, 263, 265, 266, 272,
     277, 284, 286, 290, 291, 293,
     295, 331
Sudan 1, 6, 7, 23, 42, 46, 53, 65, 67,
     82, 108, 116, 143, 146, 232, 274,
     283, 320
Suez Canal 64
sugar plantations 56, 58
Suharto 341
Susan George 227, 337
Sustainable Development xxi, 18, 21,
     106, 109, 110, 115, 117, 147,
     159, 238, 257, 260
Sylvio Olympio 229

T

Taiwan 233
Tanzania 35, 40, 82, 114, 169, 185,
     206, 242, 255, 259, 324, 326
Taye Assefa 224, 335
Teilhard de Chardin 17, 24, 318
Teodoro Obiong Nguema 275
Teresa Okure 192, 325
Terrorism 15, 16, 17, 27, 36, 42, 50,
     60, 89, 96, 97, 135, 144, 185,
     245, 263, 283, 295, 309
Thabo Mbeki 159
theology of liberation. 332
Theophilus Okere 214, 334
The crisis reaction approach 18
The Face of Africa vi, xxiii, 13, 18, 20,
     22, 39, 123, 128, 134, 135, 164,
     204, 215, 220, 261, 286, 289,
     299

ABOUT THE AUTHOR

Stan Chu Ilo was born immediately after the Civil War in his native country, Nigeria. The sad tales of war told by few members of his family who survived the war, and the experience of growing up in a war-ravaged Igboland in Eastern Nigeria in the early 1970s, shaped his vision of life on the evils of war, poverty and injustice, and the need to build foundations of love and friendship for a better world. This vision is firmly rooted in his exposure to Christianity early in life and his rich formation on authentic African values of peace, love, community, hard work, integrity and support for the weak and poor. He was ordained a Catholic priest in 1998. Between 1992-1994, he taught summer courses on African Religious and Political Thought, and Ecumenism and Religious Tolerance at the Institute of Ecumenical Education, Enugu. He was appointed by the Catholic Bishops Conference of Nigeria in 1999 as the National Coordinator for Jubilee 2000. During this period, he gained national recognition through his regular appearances on Nigerian Television (NTA), Lagos; African Independent Television (AIT), and MINAJ Cable Network's program, *Celebrating Jesus*. His commentaries and homilies on social justice issues, good governance, human rights and religious tolerance have been broadcast on Nigeria's national radio network (Radio Nigeria), and published in more than 10 African newsmagazines, newspapers and online networks.

He received a *Millennium Plaque* in June 2000 from the Christian Association of Nigeria (CAN), Lagos Mainland for his contribution to Jubilee 2000. He was the Associate Editor of the official magazine of the Catholic Church in Nigeria, *CSN News* (1999-2001) and Editor of the Rome-based Journal of African Philosophy and Life, *The Encounter* (2001-2003). He has studied in universities in Africa, Europe and North America and has degrees in philosophy, theology, educational and pastoral studies and post-graduate diplomas in educational and human rights studies. He is one of the emerging young clerics from Africa, who are articulating alternative paths to Africa's future. His scholarly papers and articles have appeared in many national and international journals including *Bigard Theological Studies, Nacaths Journal of African Theology, Federation of Female Lawyers Nigeria news magazine* (Nigeria), *The Encounter* Journal of African Philosophy and Life (Rome), *Vulgata* Christian Journal (Canada), *Thisday Newspaper* (South Africa and Nigeria), *The Guardian Newspaper* (Nigeria), *World Igbo Times* (London), *National Catholic Reporter* (Kansas, USA), *Catholic Register* (Toronto), *Toronto Star, The Catholic Herald, Peterborough Examiner* (Ontario), among others. He edits the online journal of African life www.civilizationoflove.org. He has published three books in his country and co-edited a fourth, *Walking in the Light of Christ*. He is the founder and a director of the Peterborough based charitable organization, Canadian Samaritans for Africa, which is working in partnership with Engineers without Boarders USA to improve the water, sanitation and health needs of communities in Eastern Nigeria. He is both a member of the African Studies Association (ASA) and the American Academy of Religion (AAR). He ministers to God's people at St Peter-in-Chains Cathedral, Peterborough, Ontario, Canada.

Printed in the United States
117274LV00002B/1-75/A

9 781420 897050